Barcelona

written and researched by

Jules Brown

ROUGH
GUIDES

NEW YORK • LONDON • DELHI

www.roughguides.com

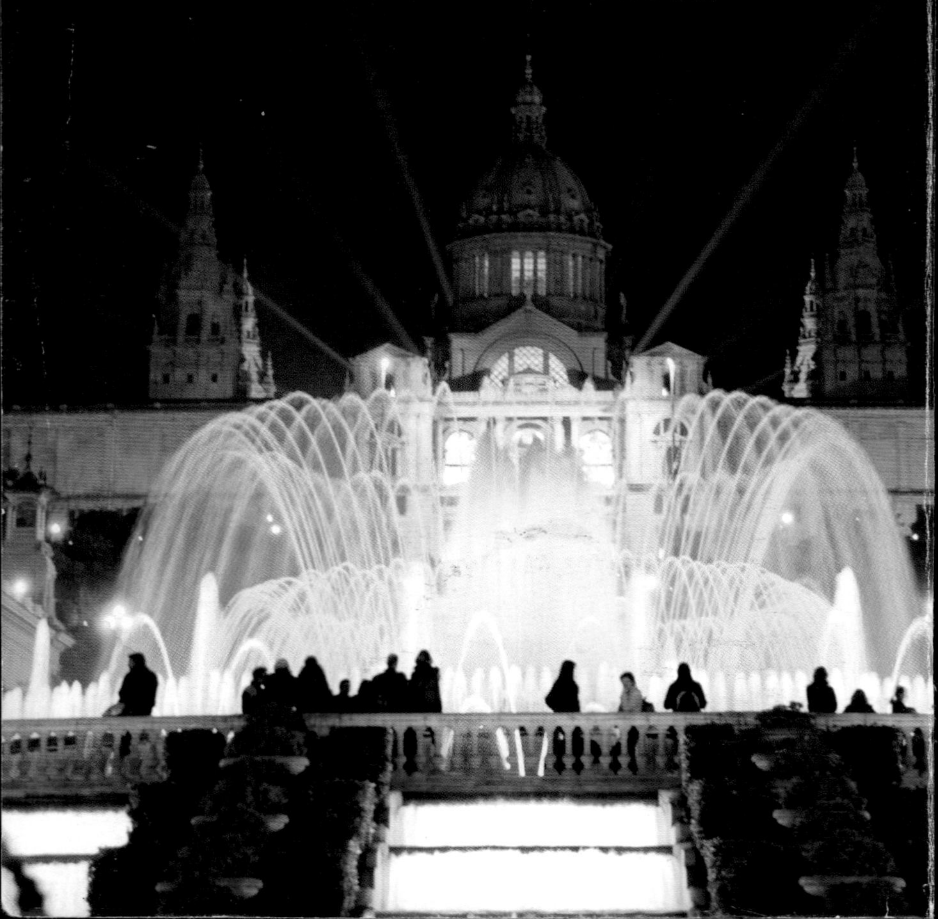

Contents

Antoni Gaudí and modernisme insert following p.112

Festive Barcelona insert following p.208

3

Introduction to

Barcelona

It's tempting to say that there's nowhere like Barcelona – there's certainly not another city in Spain to touch it for sheer style, looks or energy. The glossy mags and travel press dwell enthusiastically on its outrageous architecture, designer shopping, hip bars and vibrant cultural scene, but Barcelona is more than just this year's fad. It's a confident, progressive city, one that is tirelessly self-renewing while preserving all that's best about its past. As neighbourhoods are rebuilt with panache, and locals and visitors alike pursue the latest, most fashionable sensation, there's also an enduring embrace of the things

that make life worth living – the daily market visit, strolling down the famous Ramblas, a lazy harbourside lunch, frenetic festival nights, a Sunday by the beach or a ticket for FC Barcelona's next big game.

It's no accident that Barcelona is the least Spanish city in Spain. With the return to democracy following the death of Franco, the various regions were allowed to consolidate their cultural identities through varying degrees of political autonomy. **Catalunya** (Catalonia in English), of which Barcelona is the capital, has a historical identity going back as far as the ninth century, when the first independent County of Barcelona was established, and through the long period of domination by Castile, and even during the Franco dictatorship when a policy of cultural suppression was pursued, it proved impossible to stifle Catalan identity. Barcelona itself has long had the reputation of being at the forefront of Spanish political activism, and of radi-

4

cal design and architecture, but these cultural distinctions are rapidly becoming secondary to the city's position as one of the most dynamic commercial centres in the country.

Gaining the **1992 Olympics** was an important initial boost. Along with a construction programme that touched every corner of the city went the indisputable knowledge that these had been Barcelona's Games, and not Spain's – an important distinction to the Catalan people. Since then the economic and physical transformation of Barcelona in recent years has been extraordinary, with some remarkable new buildings and public spaces sharing the limelight with renovated historic quarters, revamped museums and a sparkling city beachfront.

If there's a pattern emerging in how Barcelona presents itself to the outside world, it's the emphasis on a remarkable fusion of economic energy and cultural expression. This is seen most perfectly in the glorious *modernista* (Art Nouveau) buildings that stud the city's streets and avenues. Antoni Gaudí is the most famous of those who have left their mark on Barcelona in this way: his Sagrada Família church is rightly revered, but just

Talking the talk

Catalan (Català) is a Romance language, stemming directly from Latin, and closely resembling Occitan. It's spoken by over ten million people in total, in Barcelona and Catalunya, part of Aragón, much of Valencia, the Balearic islands, Andorra, and parts of the French Pyrenees – and is thus much more widely spoken than Danish, Finnish and Norwegian. Other Spaniards tend to belittle it by saying that to get a Catalan word you just cut a Castilian one in half but, in fact, the grammar is more complicated and it has eight vowel sounds compared to Castilian's five. During Franco's time in power, Catalan was banned from the radio, TV, daily press and schools, which is why many older people cannot read or write it (even if they speak it all the time) – the region's best-selling Catalan-language newspaper sells far fewer copies than the most popular Castilian-language daily paper. Virtually every Catalan is bilingual, but most regard Catalan as their mother tongue and it's estimated that it is the dominant language in over half of Catalunya's households – a figure that's likely to grow given the amazing revival of the language in recent times.

Dragon lamp at Casa Amattler ▷

Much of what you'll want to see in the city centre – Gothic cathedral, Picasso museum, markets, Gaudí buildings, history museums and art galleries – can be reached on foot in under twenty minutes from the central Plaça de Catalunya.

as fascinating are the (literally) fantastic houses, apartment buildings and parks that he and his contemporaries designed. The city also boasts a stupendous artistic legacy, from national (ie Catalan) collections of Romanesque, Gothic and contemporary art to major galleries containing the life's work of the Catalan artists Joan Miró and Antoni Tàpies (not to mention a celebrated showcase of the work of Pablo Picasso). Add a medieval old town – full of pivotal buildings from an earlier age of expansion – a welter of churches and markets, and an encircling belt of parks and green spaces, and Barcelona demands as much time as you can spare.

For all its go-ahead feel, though, Barcelona does have its problems, not least a high petty crime rate. However, there's no need to be unduly paranoid and it would be a shame to stick solely to the main tourist sights, since you'll miss so much. Tapas bars hidden down alleys little changed for a century or two,

Finding an address

Addresses are written as: c/Picasso 2, 4° – which means Picasso street (*carrer*) number two, fourth floor. You may also see *esquerra*, meaning 'left-hand' (apartment or office); *dreta* is right; *centro* centre. C/Picasso s/n means the building has no number (*sense numero*). In the gridded streets of the Eixample, building numbers run from south to north (ie lower numbers at the Plaça de Catalunya end) and from west to east (lower numbers at Plaça d'Espanya).

The main address abbreviations used in Barcelona (and this book) are: Avgda. (for *Avinguda*, avenue); c/ (for *carrer*, street); Pg. (for *Passeig*, more a boulevard than a street); Bxda. (for *Baixada*, alley); Ptge. (for *Passatge*, passage); and Pl. (for *Plaça*, square).

designer boutiques in gentrified old town quarters, street opera singers belting out an aria, bargain lunches in workers' taverns, neighbourhood funicular rides, unmarked gourmet restaurants, craft outlets and workshops, *fin-de-siècle* cafés, restored medieval palaces, suburban walks and specialist galleries – all are just as much Barcelona as the Ramblas or Gaudí's Sagrada Família.

What to see

Barcelona is a surprisingly easy place to find your way around, despite a population of around three million people. Most things of historic interest are in the old town, with the modern city beyond a late nineteenth-century addition, part of a vast project conceived to link the small core of the old town with the villages around it. The greater city remains, in effect, a series of self-contained neighbourhoods stretching out from the harbour, flanked by a brace of parks and girdled by the wooded Collserola mountains. Much of what you'll want

to see in the city centre – Gothic cathedral, Picasso museum, markets, Gaudí buildings, history museums and art galleries – can be reached on foot in under twenty minutes from the central Plaça de Catalunya, while a fast metro system takes you directly to the more peripheral attractions and suburbs.

The **Ramblas** – a kilometre-long tree-lined avenue mostly given over to pedestrians, pavement cafés and performance artists – splits the **old town** (Chapter 1) in two. On the eastern side of the avenue is the **Barri Gòtic** (Gothic Quarter), the medieval nucleus of the city – around 500 square metres of twisting streets and historic buildings, including La Seu (the cathedral) and the palaces and museums around Plaça del Rei. Further east lies the equally venerable *barri* of **Sant Pere** and the fashionable boutique-and-bar neighbourhood of **La Ribera**, home to the Picasso museum; while over on the western side of the Ramblas is the edgier, artier neighbourhood of **El Raval**, containing both the flagship museum of contemporary art and the pick of the latest designer shops, bars and restaurants.

At the bottom of the Ramblas is **the waterfront** (Chapter 2), whose spruced-up harbour area is known as **Port Vell** (Old Port). Walking east from here takes you past the marina, through the old fishing and restaurant quarter of **Barceloneta**, past the **Parc de la Ciutadella** and out along the promenade to the cafés and restaurants of the **Port Olímpic**. There are city beaches right along the waterfront, from Barceloneta to **Diagonal Mar** – site of the 2004 Universal Forum expo – and it's here that Barcelona's inhabitants come to relax at weekends. Visitors, meanwhile, tend to gravitate at some point towards the fortress-topped hill of **Montjuïc** (Chapter 3) to the south-west, where the city's best museums and gardens, and the main Olympic stadium, are sited.

At the top of the Ramblas, **Plaça de Catalunya** marks the start of the gridded nineteenth-century extension of the city, the **Eixample** (Chapter 4), a symbol of the thrusting expansionism of Barcelona's early industrial age. No visit to Barcelona is complete without at least a day spent in the Eixample, as it's here that some of Europe's most extraordinary architecture – including Gaudí's **Sagrada Família** – is located. Beyond the Eixample lie the **northern suburbs** (Chapter 5), like **Gràcia**, with its small squares and lively bars, or the parks, museums and sights of **Horta**, **Sarrià** and **Pedralbes**. Gaudí left his mark in these areas, too, particularly in the hallucinatory **Parc Güell**, but also in a series of embellished buildings, private houses and unfinished chapels, which the enthusiast will find simple to track down. It's worth making for the hills, too, where you can join the crowds at Barcelona's famous **Tibidabo** amusement park – or escape them with a walk through the woods in the peaceful **Parc de Collserola**.

The good public transport links also make it easy to head further **out of the city** (Chapter 6). The mountain-top monastery of **Montserrat** is the most obvious day-trip to make, not least for the extraordinary ride up to the monastic eyrie by cable car or mountain railway. **Sitges** is the local beach town *par excellence*, while with more time you can follow various trails around the local **wine country**, head south to the Roman town of **Tarragona**, or north to medieval **Girona** or the Dalí museum in **Figueres**.

When to go

The best times to go to Barcelona are late **spring** and early **autumn**, when the weather is still comfortably warm (around 21–25°C) and walking the streets isn't a chore. In **summer**, the city can be unbearably hot and humid, with temperatures averaging 28°C (but often a lot more). August, especially, is a month to be avoided, since the climate is at its most unwelcoming and many shops, bars and restaurants close as local inhabitants head out of the city in droves. It's worth considering a **winter** break in the city, as long as you don't mind the prospect of occasional rain. It's generally still warm enough to sit out at a café, even in December, when the temperature hovers around 13°C.

Out of the city, the weather varies enormously from region to region. On the coast either side of Barcelona it's best – naturally enough – in summer, though from June to September tourist resorts like **Sitges** are packed. **Tarragona**, too, can be extremely hot and busy in summer, though it's worth knowing that **Girona** is considered to have a much more equable summer climate, and escaping from the coast for a few cool days is easy.

Temperature chart

Average maximum temperatures

	JAN	FEB	MAR	APR	MAY	JUNE	JULY	AUG	SEPT	OCT	NOV	DEC
degrees °C	13	14	16	18	21	25	28	28	25	21	16	13

things not to miss

It's not possible to see everything that Barcelona has to offer on a short trip – and we don't suggest you try. What follows is therefore a selective taste of the city's highlights, from modernista masterpieces and laid-back café life, to tranquil parks and great day-trip destinations around Catalunya – all arranged in five colour-coded categories to help you find the very best things to see, do and experience. All entries have a page reference to take you straight into the guide, where you can find out more.

01 **MACBA** Page **64** • Barcelona's luminous contemporary arts museum was designed to "create a dialogue" with its surrounding working-class neighbourhood.

02 **Museu Picasso** Page **70** • Trace the genesis of the artist's genius in the city that Picasso liked to call home.

04 **Las Ramblas** Page **48** • A stroll down Barcelona's famous thoroughfare is a must for both tourists and locals alike.

03 **Gran Teatre del Liceu** Page **52** • Take a tour or enjoy a night at the opera at the renowned Liceu opera house.

05 **Sagrada Família** Page **110** • The temple dedicated to the "Sacred Family" is the essential pilgrimage for Gaudí fans.

06 Museu Nacional d'Art de Catalunya (MNAC)

Page **91** • The National Museum of Art celebrates the grandeur of Romanesque and Gothic art, two periods in which Catalunya artists were pre-eminent in Spain.

07 Cross-harbour cable car

Page **84** • Wait for a clear day for a ride on the iconic cross-harbour cable car.

08 Monestir de Pedralbes

Page **127** • Half an hour from the centre lies the Pedralbes monastery, boasting the city's most harmonious cloister.

09 Camp Nou

Page **122** • Home of FC Barcelona, one of Europe's premier sides, with a cabinet full of trophies to prove it.

11 Fundació Joan Miró Page
97 • The adventurous Fundació
Joan Miró celebrates the work of one of the
greatest Catalan artists.

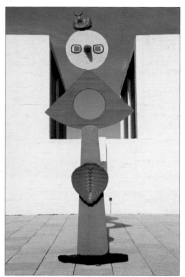

10 La Seu Page **59** • Built during the
thirteenth to fifteenth centuries on the
site of a Roman temple, La Seu is one of the
great Gothic cathedrals in Spain.

**12
Designer
shopping**
Page **232** •
Some of the
hottest European
designers display
their wares in the
city's funky shoe
shops and hip
boutiques.

**13
Monserrat**
Page **137** • For
centuries this
mountain and
monastery have
been a place
of pilgrimage
– and now make
a great day-trip
from the city.

15 Barri Gòtic Page **53** • The Barri Gòtic's evocative narrow streets were once the centre of Barcelona's medieval prosperity.

14 Parc de Collserola Page **130** • The wooded hills above Barcelona provide a welcome respite from the summer heat.

16

Barceloneta Page **83** • Busy neighbourhood which retains its village atmosphere amidst the best seafood restaurants in town.

17 Tibidabo Page **129** • Scale the heights of Mount Tibidabo for fantastic views and a wonderful amusement park.

Parc de la Ciutadella
Page **74** • Barcelona's favourite park and a Sunday afternoon rendezvous for families, friends and ducks.

19 **Sitges** Page **134** • Very popular "Barcelona-on-sea", Sitges is an easy day-trip from the city and frequented by families and gay visitors in equal numbers.

20 **Museu Frederic Marès** Page **61** • Don't miss Marès' extraordinary range of religious sculpture, household utensils, toys and ephemera, contained within a lovely old-town palace with a celebrated summer café.

21 Els Encants Page **113** • Haggle hard or pick up a bargain in the city's largest flea market

22 Bike tour Page **33** • Touring the city by bike is a great way to get out off the city's beaten track.

24 City beaches Page **84** • Barceloneta has 5km of sand-fringed ocean stretching from Barceloneta to Diagonal Mar.

23 La Boqueria Page **51** • The city's best-known market presents an extraordinary array of fresh produce.

25
Castell de Montjuïc
Page **98** • The ramparts of the hill-top Bourbon fortress offer an eagle eye view of the city.

Basics

Basics

Getting there

It's never been easier to reach Barcelona by air, with a variety of budget airlines from regional UK and European airports competing with the Spanish national carrier Iberia to get you directly to the city, quickly and cheaply. There's also a fair amount of choice from North America, though you may have to fly there via Madrid or another European city to get the best fare.

Air fares vary wildly, depending on how far in advance you book and on the season. To get the very cheapest fares advertised by the budget airlines you'll need to book weeks, if not months, in advance. Flights with Iberia and other major airlines tend to be more expensive and seasonal, with the highest fares from June to September, at Christmas, New Year and Easter, and at weekends all year.

Most airlines prefer you to book tickets online these days, and you can turn up some great deals, but always check the small print as most budget airline tickets are non-changeable and non-refundable. Many airline and **travel websites** now also offer online booking for accommodation, car rental, insurance and other travel-related services. Another option is to contact a general **flight or travel agent** – these have similar deals on flights and services, and some are particularly geared towards youth, student and independent travel. Other **specialist tour operators** can book you on to a variety of city breaks or themed tours in Barcelona and Catalunya.

Travelling to Barcelona from elsewhere in Europe by **train** or **bus** inevitably takes much longer than flying and usually works out more expensive given the travelling time involved. However, if Barcelona and Spain are part of a longer European trip it can be an interesting proposition. Driving to Barcelona is also something of an undertaking and, with motorway tolls in France and Spain, fuel costs, cross-Channel ferry and Eurotunnel fares, it's certainly not a cheap option.

Booking flights and services online

ⓦ**www.cheapflights.com**, ⓦ**www. cheapflights.com.au**, ⓦ**www.cheapflights.ca**

Price comparison on flights, short breaks, packages and other deals, with links to agents and other travel sites.

ⓦ**www.cheaptickets.com** Discount flight specialists, plus hotel and car bookings (US only).

ⓦ**www.ebookers.com** Efficient, easy-to-use flight finder with competitive fares.

ⓦ**www.expedia.com**, ⓦ**www.expedia.ca** Discount air fares, all-airline search engine, and daily deals on hotels, cars and packages.

ⓦ**www.hotwire.com** Cheap flights and accommodation from the US only.

ⓦ**www.lastminute.com**, ⓦ**www. us.lastminute.com**, ⓦ**www.au.lastminute. com** Good last-minute flights, holiday packages, hotel bookings and car rental deals.

ⓦ**www.travelocity.com**, ⓦ**www.travelocity. co.uk**, ⓦ**www.travelocity.ca** Destination guides, hot fares from North America on major airlines and good deals on car rental, rail passes and accommodation.

ⓦ**www.travelshop.com.au** Australian website offering discount flights, packages, accommodation and insurance.

ⓦ**www.travel.com.au/travel.co.nz** Comprehensive online travel company providing access to tours, packages, flights and car rental for Australians and New Zealanders.

ⓦ**www.travel.yahoo.com** Flights, accommodation and other deals, plus Rough Guide material in its destination coverage.

Flights and tours from the UK, Ireland and Europe

Flying time to Barcelona from the UK or Ireland is between two and two-and-a-half hours, depending on your departure airport.

A whole host of budget **no-frills airlines** compete on the Barcelona route from the UK and Ireland, notably easyJet (ⓦwww .easyjet.com), Monarch (ⓦwww.flymonarch .com), Jet2 (ⓦwww.jet2.com) and Aer Lingus (ⓦwww.aerlingus.com), with daily departures throughout the year from around a dozen regional airports, including all the London airports, plus Belfast, Bristol, Dublin, Liverpool, Manchester and Newcastle. The earlier you book, the cheaper your flight will be – and headline special offers can even mean the seats are free, or virtually free, with just the taxes to pay (from £15–20 each way). Even **Iberia** (ⓦwww.iberia.com) is forced to compete, with promotional fares as low as £30 (€50) return plus taxes – however, their more flexible tickets (allowing cancellation and/or date changes) are considerably more expensive and can rise to £200 (€300) return or more in peak season.

There's a second gateway to the city at **Girona**, 90km north of Barcelona, which is used almost exclusively by no-frills airline Ryanair (ⓦwww.ryanair.com), which flies there from around twenty British, Irish and European airports. The other regional airport is at **Reus,** 110km south of Barcelona, near Tarragona, served by Ryanair from Stansted and by Monarch summer charter flights from Gatwick and Dublin. You've over an hour's journey from either airport to the centre of Barcelona, but there are reliable connecting bus services.

Other **European budget airlines** fly into Barcelona airport from across the continent, including Air Berlin (ⓦwww.airberlin.com – from Germany), Spanair (ⓦwww.spanair.com – from Scandinavia, Germany and Spain), Vueling (ⓦwww.vueling.com – from Spain, the Balearics, Italy, Paris, Brussels and Amsterdam), Virgin Express (ⓦwww.virgin-express.com – from Brussels) and Transvia (ⓦwww.transvia.com – from Amsterdam).

Three-night **city breaks** to Barcelona start from as little as £200 (€300) per person flying from London, Manchester or Dublin. For this price, accommodation is most likely in a two-star hotel, and sometimes on a room-only basis. For three nights bed-and-breakfast in a three- or four-star hotel you can usually expect to pay more like £300–400. A few operators offer rather more **specialist holidays** in and around Barcelona, concentrating on things like art and architecture, cooking classes, wine tours or rural Catalunya – see below for details.

General flight and travel agents

North South Travel ☎01245/608 291, ⓦwww.northsouthtravel.co.uk. Competitive travel agency, offering discounted fares worldwide – profits are used to support projects in the developing world, especially the promotion of sustainable tourism.
STA Travel ☎08701/630 026, ⓦwww.statravel.co.uk. Worldwide specialists in low-cost flights and tours for students and under-26s, though other customers welcome.
usit NOW Republic of Ireland ☎01/602 1904, Northern Ireland ☎028/9032 7111, ⓦwww.usit.ie. Student, youth and independent travel specialists.

Specialist tour operators and agencies

Arblaster & Clarke ☎01730/893344, ⓦwww.arblasterandclarke.com. Annual four-night wine tours of Barcelona, and the Penedès and Priorato regions, with expert in tow plus tours, tastings and meals (£799, excluding flights).
Culinary Adventures Spain ☎915 214 170 or 934 170 715, ⓦwww.atasteofspain.com. Interesting food-based tours from a company with offices in Barcelona and Madrid – from one-day cooking-and-market excursions from Barcelona (€275) to a seven-day culinary Catalan tour (land-only, €3020).
Martin Randall Travel ☎0208/742 3355, ⓦwww.martinrandall.com. Experts lead small groups on annual, all-inclusive quality tours to Spain, concentrating on "Gastronomic Catalonia" (six nights, £1790) – though tours and themes change each year.
Mundi Color London ☎0207/828 6021, Manchester ☎0161/848 8680. Spanish specialists for flights, accommodation, tours and city breaks.
Ramblers Holidays ☎01707/331133, ⓦwww.ramblersholidays.co.uk. The walking specialists offer a one-week Barcelona holiday, with guided walks, sightseeing and trips out of the city; flights and most meals included, from £670.
Travellers' Way ☎0845/612 9001, ⓦwww.travellersway.co.uk. Tailor-made holidays and city breaks, perhaps combining Barcelona with Sitges or the Costa Brava.

Flights and tours from the USA and Canada

Most **direct scheduled services** to Spain from North America are to Madrid, and only Continental (ⓦwww.continental.com) and Delta (ⓦwww.delta.com) have year-round non-stop Barcelona services, daily from New York. European-based airlines (Air France, British Airways, Lufthansa, KLM and TAP) can also get you to Barcelona, though you'll be routed through their respective European hubs – Iberia (ⓦwww.iberia.com), the Spanish national airline, and Air Europa (ⓦwww.air-europa.com) tend to have the best connections through Madrid. Flying time from New York is around seven hours to Madrid, though with the onward connection it can take as much as eleven hours to reach Barcelona.

Return **fares** are as much as US$1000 in summer, though in low season you should be able to fly for under US$700. Special promotional deals can undercut these prices, while it might pay you to buy a cheap flight to the UK and travel on to Barcelona from there with a budget airline (see "Flights and tours from the UK, Ireland and Europe", p.19).

Tour companies tend to include a couple of days in Barcelona as part of a whirlwind escorted itinerary around Spain, costing from US$1500 to $2000 for a standard two-week tour, or up to $4000 for something more luxurious. However, for a more in-depth Barcelona experience, consider a **city break** – a typical three-night stay in a central Barcelona three-star hotel starts at around $1000, rising to around $2000 for a week, including flights, breakfast and transfers.

Specialist tour operators

Delta Vacations ☎1-800/654-6559, ⓦwww.deltavacations.com. City breaks with add-on options such as car rental and city tours.
Food & Wine Trails ☎1-800/367-5348, ⓦwww.foodandwinetrails.com. Their "Catalan Cuisine" tour spends two nights in Barcelona and four on the Costa Brava, visiting markets, taking cooking classes, touring and eating. From $3100.
Olé Spain ☎1-888/869-7156, ⓦwww.olespain.com. Eight-day cultural walking tours in Catalunya, beginning and ending in Barcelona, with time to explore the city. $3295.
Petrabax ☎1-800/634-1188, ⓦwww.epetrabax.com. City breaks, escorted Catalunya tours or self-drive Spanish holidays, plus independent travel services – such as accommodation bookings and car rental.
Saranjan Tours ☎1-800/858-9594, ⓦwww.saranjan.com. Upscale, fully guided, customized tours concentrating on unusual combinations, like Barcelona and its nearby wine country or a two-centre Barcelona and Bilbao holiday.

Flights from Australia and New Zealand

There are no direct flights to Spain from Australia or New Zealand. However, a number of airlines do fly to Barcelona with a stopover elsewhere in Europe or Asia (flights via Asia are generally the cheaper option). Another possibility is to fly to **Madrid**, from where you can pick up a connecting flight or train. It's best to discuss your route and preferences with a **flight** and **travel agent** like Flight Centre (ⓦwww.flightcentre.au/co.nz) or STA Travel (ⓦwww.statravel.com.au/co.nz), especially if your visit to Barcelona is part of a wider Spanish trip – in which case, you might be better off buying a **Round-The-World** (RTW) ticket. If you'd rather someone else made all the arrangements, talk to one of the special **tour operators** who can arrange an organized visit to Barcelona, sorting out your accommodation, guided tours and car rental.

Specialist tour operators

Explore Holidays Australia ☎1300/731 012, ⓦwww.exploreholidays.com.au. They arrange Barcelona stays, city tours, apartment and car rental.
Ibertours Australia ☎1800/500 016, New Zealand ☎0800/444 843, ⓦwww.ibertours.com.au. Spanish specialist offering two- or three-night Barcelona breaks, plus escorted tours and self-drive holidays.
Spanish Tourism Promotions Australia ☎1800/817 855, ⓦwww.spanishtourism.com.au. A good first stop for Spain information – tours, city breaks, hotel bookings, train trips, car rental and more.

By rail

Travelling by **train** to Barcelona can't compete in price with the cheapest budget-airlines fares – but it can be a real adventure. First stop should be ⓦ**www.seat61.com,** an amazingly useful website that provides route, ticket, timetable and contact information for all European train services.

The quickest and most straightforward option from the UK is to take the **Eurostar** service (☎08705/186 186, ⓦwww.eurostar.com; from £59 return) from London Waterloo International via the Channel Tunnel to Paris, and then the overnight **Paris–Barcelona**

Fly less – stay longer! Travel and climate change

Climate change is a serious threat to the ecosystems that humans rely upon, and air travel is among the fastest-growing contributors to the problem. Rough Guides regard travel, overall, as a global benefit, and feel strongly that the advantages to developing economies are important, as is the opportunity of greater contact and awareness among peoples. But we all have a responsibility to limit our personal impact on global warming, and that means giving thought to how often we fly, and what we can do to redress the harm that our trips create.

Flying and climate change
Pretty much every form of motorized travel generates CO_2 – the main cause of human-induced climate change – but planes also generate climate-warming contrails and cirrus clouds and emit oxides of nitrogen, which create ozone (another greenhouse gas) at flight levels. Furthermore, flying simply allows us to travel much further than we otherwise would do. The figures are frightening: one person taking a return flight between Europe and California produces the equivalent impact of 2.5 tonnes of CO_2 – similar to the yearly output of the average UK car.
Fuel-cell and other less harmful types of plane may emerge eventually. But until then, there are really just two options for concerned travellers: to reduce the amount we travel by air (take fewer trips – stay for longer!), and to make the trips we do take "climate neutral" via a carbon offset scheme.

Carbon offset schemes
Offset schemes run by climatecare.org, carbonneutral.com and others allow you to make up for some or all of the greenhouse gases that you are responsible for releasing. To do this, they provide "carbon calculators" for working out the global-warming contribution of a specific flight (or even your entire existence), and then let you contribute an appropriate amount of money to fund offsetting measures. These include rainforest reforestation and initiatives to reduce future energy demand – often run in conjunction with sustainable development schemes.
Rough Guides, together with Lonely Planet and other concerned partners in the travel industry, are supporting a **carbon offset scheme** run by climatecare.org. Please take the time to view our website and see how you can help to make your trip climate neutral.

Ⓦ www.roughguides.com/climatechange

"train-hotel", which arrives in Barcelona at around 8.30am (total journey time 15–17hr). This is a sleeper service (with restaurant and café), with various levels of comfort available – the cheapest ticket is in a four-berth compartment, from £89 return, depending on availability; you have to book well in advance to get the cheapest prices.

There are other alternatives, but they take longer (up to 27hr) and can be more complicated to arrange. For example, using the **cross-Channel ferries** and **Seacats** and the local trains to Paris could save you up to £50 on the Eurostar fare and instead of the "train-hotel" there are regular overnight **couchette sleeper** services with SNCF (French Railways) as far as the French border. Here you change onto the Spanish service, running down the Costa Brava to Barcelona.

You'll need to talk to a **rail agency** to sort out all the options. Rail Europe (℡0870/584 8848, Ⓦ www.raileurope.co.uk) can make through-bookings to Barcelona with the Eurostar option, as can the Spanish Rail Service (℡020/7224 0345, Ⓦ www .spanish-rail.co.uk) and French state railways, SNCF (Ⓦ www.voyages-sncf.com), which has a useful English-language version of its website. For the rail–sea–rail routes, talk to Ffestiniog Travel (℡01766/512400) or Railbookers (℡0870/458 9080, Ⓦ www .railbookers.com).

If you plan to travel extensively in Europe by train, a **rail pass** might prove a good investment. However, if you're just headed for Barcelona, InterRail (ⓦwww.raileurope.co.uk/inter-rail) and Eurail (ⓦwww.eurail.com) aren't a good deal, and even if you intend to travel around Catalunya by train, rail travel in that part of Spain is fairly limited (and quite cheap), so you may not get your money's worth.

By bus

Eurolines (ⓣ08705/808080, ⓦwww.nationalexpress.com) operates a year-round bus service to Barcelona from London which takes up to 27 hours. There are stops for around twenty minutes every four to five hours, and the routine is also broken by the cross-Channel ferry (included in the cost). It costs as little as £49 return if you book the forty-day advance fare, and there are other advance deals and special offers too – it's always cheapest to book online. Eurolines also sells Barcelona tickets and transport to London at all British National Express bus terminals.

Driving to Barcelona

It's about 1600km from London to Barcelona, which, with stops, takes almost two full days to drive. Motoring organizations (AA, ⓦwww.theaa.com; RAC, ⓦwww.rac.co.uk) provide useful route planners, including advice on how to avoid toll roads. For more details about documentations and driving conditions in the city, see "City transport: Driving and vehicle rental", p.32.

Many people use the conventional **cross-Channel** ferry links, principally Dover– Calais, though services from Portsmouth or Poole to Brittany or Normandy might be more convenient. However, the quickest way of crossing the Channel is to use the **Eurotunnel** service (ⓣ08705/353535, ⓦwww3.eurotunnel.com), which operates drive-on-drive-off shuttle trains between Folkestone and Calais/Coquelles. The twenty-four-hour service runs every twenty minutes throughout the day and, though you can just turn up, booking is advised, especially at weekends, or if you want the best deals (from £49 one way).

Alternatively, Brittany Ferries operates a car and passenger ferry from **Plymouth to Santander** (twice weekly; 24hr). From Santander, it's about nine hours' drive to Barcelona, via Bilbao and Zaragoza. Or there's the P&O service from **Portsmouth to Bilbao** (twice weekly; 35hr), east of Santander in the Basque country. Both services are very expensive, especially in summer, when return fares can cost as much as £800.

Any ferry company or travel agent can supply up-to-date schedules and ticket information, or you can consult the encyclopedic ⓦwww.directferries.com, which has details about, and links to, every European ferry service.

Red tape and visas

Citizens of EU countries, including the UK and Ireland, need only a valid national identity card or passport to enter Spain. Other Europeans, and citizens of the United States, Canada, Australia and New Zealand, require a passport but no visa and can stay as a tourist for up to ninety days. Other nationalities may need to get a visa from a Spanish embassy or consulate before departure. Visa requirements do change and it's always advisable to check the current situation before leaving home.

Most EU citizens who want to stay in Spain, rather than just visit as a tourist, are no longer required to apply for a residence permit. Instead, their **domestic passport or identity document** entitles EU citizens to reside as employees, self-employed or students.

23

However, there are benefits in acquiring a **permit** – it's better than carrying around your passport, for example, if you need to prove your identity. Meanwhile, retired EU citizens or those of "independent means" do still have to apply for a residence permit. US citizens can apply for one ninety-day extension, showing proof of funds, but this must be done from outside Spain. Other nationalities wishing to extend their stay will need to get a **special visa** from a Spanish embassy or consulate before departure (see below for addresses). Anyone planning to stay in Barcelona for more than just a few weeks will also need a *Numero de Identidade de Extranjeros* (NIE), an ID number that's essential if you're to open a bank account, sign a utilities, job or accommodation contract, or for many other financial transactions.

For details of the **offices in Barcelona** dealing with NIE applications and residence permits, see p.245. There's also a list of **foreign consulates in Barcelona** on p.243.

Spanish embassies and consulates abroad

Australia or New Zealand 15 Arkana St, Yarralumla, ACT 2600 ℡ 02/6273 3555, ⓦ www.embaspain.com; also consulates in Sydney and Melbourne, and honorary consulates in Wellington and Christchurch.
Canada 74 Stanley Ave, Ottawa, Ontario K1M 1P4 ℡ 613/747-2252, ⓦ www.embaspain.ca; also

consulate in Montreal.
Ireland 17a Merlyn Park, Ballsbridge, Dublin 4 ℡ 01/269 1640.
UK 20 Draycott Place, London SW3 2RZ ℡ 020/7589 8989, ⓦ www.conspalon.org; also consulates in Manchester and Edinburgh.
USA 2375 Pennsylvania Ave NW, Washington, DC 20037 ℡ 202/452-0100, ⓦ www.spainemb.org; also consulates in Boston, Chicago, Houston, Los Angeles, Miami, New York, and San Francisco.

Customs

EU travellers returning home from Spain do not have to make a declaration to Customs at their place of entry. In other words, you can bring almost as many Spanish cigarettes and as much wine or beer home as you can carry. The **guidance levels** are 3200 cigarettes, 10 litres of spirits, 90 litres of wine and 110 litres of beer – any more than this and you'll have to provide proof that it's for personal use only. If you're travelling back home to a non-EU country, you can still buy a limited amount of **duty-free goods** – the limits are posted at the airports – but this perk no longer exists within the EU.

Non-EU residents can also claim a **VAT (IVA) refund** on shopping purchases over the value of €90 – if there's a Tax-Free Shopping sticker displayed at the store, ask for the voucher and claim the refund at the airport before leaving.

Insurance

The European Health Insurance Card (which replaced the E111 form) gives EU citizens access to Spanish state public health services under reciprocal agreements. For application details consult ⓦ www.ehic.org.uk. While this will provide free or reduced-cost medical care in the event of minor injuries and emergencies, it won't cover every eventuality – and it only applies to EU citizens in possession of the card. For this reason, travellers of all nationalities should take out a comprehensive insurance policy before travelling.

Rough Guides travel insurance

In conjunction with Columbus Direct, Rough Guides provides tailor-made travel insurance. Readers can choose from policies that include a low-cost **backpacker** option for long stays; a short-break option for **city getaways**; a typical **holiday package** option; and many others. There are also annual **multi-trip** policies for those who travel regularly, with variable levels of cover available. Different sports and activities (such as trekking and skiing) can be included on most policies, if required.

Rough Guides travel insurance can be purchased by residents of 36 countries on our website, ⑩ www.roughguidesinsurance.com, which also has various language options. Alternatively, UK residents can call ⓣ 0800/083 9507; US citizens ⓣ 1-800/749-4922; and Australians ⓣ 1-300/669 999. All other nationalities should call ⓣ +44 870/890 2843.

A typical policy will provide cover for loss of baggage, tickets and – up to a certain limit – cash or travellers' cheques, as well as cancellation or curtailment of your journey. With **medical coverage** you should ascertain whether benefits will be paid as treatment proceeds or only after you return home, and whether there is a twenty-four-hour medical emergency number. When securing **baggage cover**, make sure that the per-article limit will cover your most valuable possession. Most policies exclude so-called **dangerous sports** unless an extra premium is paid: in Spain this can mean most water sports are excluded, though probably not things like hiking, mountain-biking or 4WD safaris.

If you need to make a claim, you should keep receipts for medicines and medical treatment, and in the event you have anything stolen you must obtain an official **statement from the police** – see p.244 for where to go in Barcelona to report a crime or loss.

Arrival

There are three main, adjacent terminals (A, B and C) at Barcelona's airport, with taxis and airport buses found immediately outside each terminal and the airport train station is a short distance away. The city's train stations – Barcelona Sants and Estació de França – and the Barcelona Nord bus station are all more central, with convenient metro stations for onward travel. In most cases, you can be off the plane, train or bus and in your hotel room within the hour. Driving into Barcelona is also reasonably straightforward, with traffic only slow in the morning and evening rush hours. Parking, however, is a different matter altogether – rarely easy and not cheap. If your trip is just to the city and its surroundings, our advice is not to bother with a car at all.

All transport contact telephone numbers and websites are listed in "Directory" (Chapter 17.

By air

Barcelona's **airport** is 12km southwest of the city at El Prat de Llobregat. EasyJet uses

Terminal A. British Airways and Iberia use Terminal B. There's a tourist office in each terminal, handling hotel bookings; there are also ATMs, exchange facilities and car-rental offices.

There's a **direct train service** from the airport train station to Barcelona Sants, though it was suspended during 2006 because of work on the high-speed AVE rail line. It should be running again by the time you read this – services were previously every 20 minutes, roughly 6am–midnight, journey time 18 minutes. If the direct service is still interrupted, it simply means a change of trains at El Prat de Llobregat station, from where there are frequent onward services to Barcelona Sants, Passeig de Gracia and Plaça de Catalunya (and metro connections at all of these). Eventually, there will also be a direct metro link between the airport and the new high-speed station at Sagrera, though this isn't expected until 2008.

Alternatively, you can use the **Aerobús** service (Mon–Fri 6am–midnight, Sat & Sun 6.30am–midnight; €3.60 one way, €5.90 return), which leaves every eleven minutes from outside the terminals, stopping in the city at Plaça d'Espanya, Gran Via de les Corts Catalanes (at c/Comte d'Urgell), Plaça Universitat, Plaça de Catalunya (in front of El Corte Inglés) and Passeig de Gràcia (at c/la Diputació). The bus takes around thirty minutes to reach Plaça de Catalunya, though allow longer in the rush hour.

A **taxi** from the airport to the city centre costs roughly €20–25, including the airport surcharge. The fares are metered, so as long as you take a taxi from the official rank outside (rather than anyone who may approach you), you'll have no problems. You will, however, be charged more after 10pm and at weekends, and there's a surcharge for any luggage that goes in the boot.

Ryanair arrivals at **Girona** airport, 90km north of Barcelona, can take the connecting Barcelona Bus service, which runs to Girona train station (for hourly trains to Barcelona Sants; 1hr 15–1hr 30) or direct to Barcelona Nord bus station (€11 one way, €19 return; 1hr 10) From **Reus** airport, 110km south of Barcelona (Ryanair and Monarch flights), there's a connecting bus service to Plaça de la Reina Maria Cristina and Barcelona Sants (€11 one way, €18 return; 1hr 20–1hr 30).

By train

The main station for national and international arrivals is **Barcelona Sants**, 3km west of the city centre. There is a tourist office here (with an accommodation booking service), as well as ATMs, an exchange office, car-rental outlets, a police station and left-luggage facilities. The **metro** station (accessed from inside Barcelona Sants) is called Sants Estació – line 3 from here runs direct to Liceu (for the Ramblas), Catalunya (for Plaça de Catalunya) and Passeig de Gràcia, while line 5 runs to Diagonal.

Some long-distance services stop at **Estació de França**, near Parc de la Ciutadella, 1km east of the Ramblas (Ⓜ Barceloneta), though many trains stop at both Sants and França. Other possible arrival points by train are **Plaça de Catalunya**, at the top of the Ramblas (for trains from coastal towns north of the city, from El Prat de Llobregat for the airport, and towns on the Puigcerdà–Vic line); **Plaça d'Espanya** (from Montserrat); and **Passeig de Gràcia** (from Lleida, Tarragona, Port Bou, Figueres and Girona).

The station at **La Sagrera** (under construction), east of the centre beyond Glòries, will be the terminal for the long-projected high-speed (AVE) rail line. When it's completed, direct AVE services from Madrid will stop here, and there will also be a direct metro link from the airport on the new line 9.

By bus

The main bus terminal, used by international, long-distance and provincial buses, is **Barcelona Nord** on Avinguda Vilanova (main entrance on c/Ali-Bei; Ⓜ Arc de Triomf), three blocks north of Parc de la Ciutadella. There's a bus information desk on the ground floor (daily 7am–9pm), plus an ATM, tourist office (Mon–Sat 9am–2pm), shops and luggage lockers, with the ticket offices above at street level. Some intercity and international services also make a stop at the bus terminal behind Barcelona Sants station on c/de Viriat (Ⓜ Sants Estació). Either way, you're only a short metro ride from the city centre.

By ferry

Ferries from the Balearics dock at the **Estació Marítima,** Moll de Barcelona, Port

Vell, located at the bottom of Avinguda Paral.
lel (ⓜDrassanes). There are ticket offices
inside the terminal, and taxis nearby, though
no other services, but you're only a short
walk from Drassanes metro station at the
bottom of the Ramblas. Ferries from Genoa
(Italy) dock at the **Moll de Sant Bertran,**
just along from the Moll de Barcelona, while
cruise ships tie up at several points in the
inner harbour – a shuttle-bus usually runs
cruise passengers to and from the Ramblas.

By car

Coming into Barcelona along any one of the
motorways (*autopistes*), head for the Ronda
Litoral, the southern half of the city's ring
road. Following signs for "Port Vell" will take
you towards the main exit for the old town,
though there are also exits for Gran Via de
les Corts Catalanes and Avinguda Diagonal
if uptown Barcelona is your destination.

There are many indoor **car parks** in the
city centre, linked to display boards that
indicate where there are free spaces. Central locations include Plaça de Catalunya,
Plaça Urquinaona, Arc de Triomf, Passeig
de Gràcia, Plaça dels Angels/MACBA and
Avinguda Paral.lel, and though parking in
one of these is convenient it's also fairly
expensive (60min from €1.60, 24hr up to
€20). There's a cheaper park-and-ride
facility called **Metropark** for day visitors at
Plaça de les Gloriés in the eastern Eixample
(junction of Avgda. Diagonal and Gran Via
de les Corts Catalanes; ⓜGloriés) the €5
fee includes a ticket for unlimited travel on
the city's public transport. **Street parking** is
permitted in most areas, but it can be tough
to find spaces, especially in the old town,
where it's nearly all either restricted access
or residents' parking only, and Gràcia. In the
Eixample the ubiquitous **meter-zones** are for
pay-and-display parking, usually with a two-
hour maximum stay. Don't be tempted to
double-park, leave your car in loading zones
or otherwise park illegally – the cost of being
towed can exceed €130, and no mercy is
shown to foreign-plated vehicles.

Information, websites and maps

**The Spanish National Tourist Office (SNTO) has international offices in
Europe and North America. Visits are by appointment only, but their various comprehensive websites are a useful resource for any traveller. Once
in the city, it is very easy to pick up leaflets and brochures, either at your
point of entry or from one of the city-centre information offices.**

SNTO offices abroad

Britain and Ireland ☎0207/486 8077, ⓦwww
.tourspain.co.uk.
Canada ☎416/961-3131, ⓦwww.tourspain
.toronto.on.ca.
USA New York ☎212/265-8822; Los Angeles
☎323/658-7188; Chicago ☎312/642-1992; Miami
33131 ☎305/358-1992; ⓦwww.okspain.org.

Information in Barcelona

Offices under the auspices of **Turisme de
Barcelona**, the city's tourist board, at the
airport, Barcelona Sants station, Plaça de
Catalunya and Plaça de Sant Jaume, are
most useful for information about the city.
You can also book accommodation, buy
discount cards (see box overleaf) and
reserve space on guided tours. There are
also staffed kiosks in main tourist areas,
such as outside the Sagrada Família and
on the Ramblas, which should be able to
point you in the right direction. For information about travelling in the wider province
of Catalunya, you need the Generalitat's
information centre (Centre d'Informació de
Catalunya) at **Palau Robert,** while events,
concerts, exhibitions, festivals and other
cultural diversions are covered in full at

the Institut de Cultura in the **Palau de la Virreina** on the Ramblas.

For anything else you might need to know, you can try the city's ☎**010 telephone enquiries service** (Mon–Sat 8am–10pm). They'll be able to help with questions about transport, public services and other matters, and there are English-speaking staff available. The city government's website (🌐**www .bcn.es**) is also a mine of information about every aspect of cultural, social and working life in Barcelona, such as sports centres and festival dates; it has an English-language version.

Information offices

Turisme de Barcelona ☎807 117 222 if calling from within Spain, ☎932 853 834 if calling from abroad, 🌐www.barcelonaturisme.com. Main office, Pl. de Catalunya 17, Ⓜ Catalunya (daily 9am–9pm); also at Pl. de Sant Jaume, entrance at c/Ciutat 2, Barri Gòtic, Ⓜ Jaume I (Mon–Fri 9am–8pm, Sat 10am–8pm, Sun & hols 10am–2pm); Airport Terminals A & B (daily 9am–9pm); and Barcelona Sants, Pl. dels Països Catalans, Ⓜ Sants Estació (Mon–Fri 8am–8pm, Sat, Sun & hols 8am–2pm; April–Sept daily 8am–8pm). The main Pl. de Catalunya office is down the steps in the southeast corner of the square. It's always busy and can be frustrating if you just want a quick answer to a question. There's also a money exchange service, separate accommodation desk, ticket sales and a gift shop.

Institut de Cultura Palau de la Virreina, Ramblas 99, Ⓜ Liceu ☎933 017 775, 🌐www.bcn. es/cultura (Mon–Sat 10am–8pm, Sun 11am–3pm). Cultural information office, with advance information on everything that's happening in the city; you can also buy tickets here.

Centre del Modernisme ☎902 076 621, 🌐www.rutadelmodernisme.com. Offices inside Turisme de Barcelona tourist office at Pl. de Catalunya (see above); Mon–Sat 10am–7pm, Sun & hols 10am–2pm); and Hospital de la Santa Creu i Sant Pau, c/Sant Antoni M. Claret 167, Eixample Ⓜ Hospital de Sant Pau (daily 10am–2pm). The staffed information desks provide details of visits to the city's *modernista* buildings and monuments, and sell the Ruta del Modernisme package (see box below).

Centre d'Informació de Catalunya Palau Robert, Pg. de Gràcia 107, Eixample, Ⓜ Diagonal ☎932 384 000, 🌐www.gencat.net/probert (Mon–Sat 10am–7pm, Sun & hols 10am–2.30pm). It has information about travel in Catalunya and provides maps, guides, details of how to get around and lists of places to stay.

Discount cards and packages

If you're going to do a lot of sightseeing, you can save yourself money by buying one of the available discount cards.

• **Barcelona Card** (full details on 🌐www.barcelonaturisme.com) gives reductions of up to fifty percent on entry into many museums and attractions, and between ten percent and thirty percent in some shops, theatres and restaurants. The card also permits free public transport and walking tours, and discounts on the Aeróbus, Tibibus to Tibidabo and Tomb Bus shopping service. It's valid for two days (€23), three days (€28), four days (€31) or five days (€34) – there's a €4 discount for children aged 4–12 years – and is available at tourist offices, El Corte Inglés stores, Casa Batlló, the Aquarium and Poble Espanyol.

• **Articket** (€20; valid for six months): provides free admission into seven major art centres and galleries (MNAC, MACBA, CCCB, Museu Picasso, Fundació Antoni Tàpies, Fundació Joan Miró, and Centre Cultural Caixa Catalunya at La Pedrera). You can buy the ticket at the participating centres and galleries, and at Plaça de Catalunya and Barcelona Sants tourist offices.

• **Ruta del Modernisme** (🌐www.rutadelmodernisme.com) is an excellent guidebook, map and discount-voucher package (€12, vouchers valid for one year) that covers 115 *modernista* buildings in Barcelona and other Catalan towns, offering discounts of up to fifty percent on admission fees, tours and gift shop purchases. All the major sights are included, and profits go towards conservation of the buildings. It's also packaged with *Let's Go Out*, a guide to *modernista* bars and restaurants (total package €18), with both available at the Centre del Modernisme desks listed under "Information in Barcelona" above.

Barcelona Informació (Oficina d'Atenció als Ciutadans) Pl. de Sant Miquel, Barri Gòtic, Ⓜ Jaume I ⓣ 010, ⓦ www.bcn.es (June–Sept Mon–Fri 8.15am–2.15pm, Sat 9am–2pm, Oct–May Mon–Fri 8.30am–6pm, Sat 9am–2pm). Citizens' information office, around the back of the Ajuntament in the new building. It's not really for tourists, but invariably helpful (though little English spoken).

Barcelona on the Internet

There's plenty of information available on the Web about Barcelona. The city **tourist office website** (ⓦ www.barcelonaturisme. com) is a good place to start and, along with those operated by the city hall (Ajuntament; ⓦ www.bcn.es) and local government (Generalitat; ⓦ www.gencat.es), has a full English-language version. From these three alone you'll be able to find out about museum opening hours, bus routes, local politics, all-night pharmacies, festivals, sports, theatres and much, much more. For **arts and events listings**, the websites of the local newspapers (see "The media", p.34) can be pretty useful, while the sites listed below offer either a less official view or more specialized information.

Art and architecture

ⓦ **www.bcn.fjmiro.es** The Joan Miró Foundation's official website is the main source for the artist – a complete biography, plus clickable art and a round-up of his works in the city and elsewhere, and exhibition news.

ⓦ **www.gaudiclub.com** The best first stop for Antoni Gaudí, his life and works, with plenty of links to other sites, plus Gaudí-related gifts, games, news, books and tours.

ⓦ **www.qdq.com** Every building in the city has been photographed – to view, click on "Callejero Fotografiico", then click on the map or type in the street name.

General

ⓦ **www.barcelona-on-line.es** Packed with information in English on Barcelona, with searchable listings, entertainment guide, accommodation-booking service, what's-on details and more.

ⓦ **www.catalanencyclopaedia.com.** English-language online encyclopaedia, for everything you ever wanted to know about Catalan people, history, buildings, economy, climate and geography. It also has

links to a Catalan dictionary and an Internet bookshop for Catalan books.

News and views

ⓦ **www.barcelonareporter.com** Barcelona Reporter offers daily updated news and views from the city in English, pulling in very useful reports from newspapers and other sources.

ⓦ **www.diaridebarcelona.com** Up-to-the-minute city news, comment, reviews, weather and listings (in Catalan), with links to all the other daily newspapers.

ⓦ **www.vilaweb.cat** Online newspaper, directory and portal, updated daily, with excellent links to Catalan sites, many in English. Also links to a huge variety of Barcelona webcams.

Miscellaneous

ⓦ **www.paginasamarillas.es** The Spanish Yellow Pages finds any business in Barcelona and has links to the Paginas Blancas (White Pages), to find a person, and to a Barcelona street-finder.

Maps

The city tourist offices charge a euro for their maps – you can pick up a good **free** one instead from the information desk on the ground floor of El Corte Inglés department store, right outside the main tourist office. With that, and the maps in this book, you'll easily be able to find your way around. You can also check the location of any building or address on the city council's extremely useful **interactive street plan** at ⓦ www. bcn.es (click on "BCN map" in the English-language version).

For an excellent **fold-out street plan** on durable waterproof paper, look no further than *Barcelona: The Rough Guide Map* (Penguin), which also includes practical information and dining, lodging and shopping listings. Map and travel shops in your home country should be able to supply a copy of this and, if you need one, a road map of Catalunya or northern Spain (by Michelin, Firestone or Rand McNally). Alternatively, try mail order from ⓦ www.amazon.co.uk/com or a world map specialist like ⓦ www.stanfords.co.uk or ⓦ www.randmcnally.com. In Barcelona, you'll find a good selection of maps in most bookshops (see p.232) and at street newspaper kiosks or petrol stations.

City transport

Barcelona's excellent integrated transport system comprises the metro, buses, trams and local trains, plus a network of funiculars and cable cars. Detailed transport information and timetables are available by telephone (☎010) and in English on the Internet (Ⓦwww.tmb.net), and there's an invaluable free public transport map available at the customer service centres (see box below) of *Transports Metropolitans de Barcelona* (TMB). The map and ticket information is also posted at major bus stops and all metro stations. Our public transport map is in the colour pages at the back of the book.

Tickets and travel passes

A transit plan divides the province into six zones, but as the entire metropolitan area of Barcelona falls within Zone 1, that's the only one you'll need to worry about on a day-to-day basis. On all the city's public transport (including night buses and funiculars) you can buy a **single ticket** every time you ride (€1.20), but even over only a couple of days it's much cheaper to buy a *targeta* – a **discount ticket strip** which you pass through the box on top of the metro or train barrier, or punch in the machine on the bus, tram or funicular. The *targetes* are available at metro, train and tram stations (at ticket windows or vending machines), but not on the buses.

The best general deal for most people is the **T-10** ("tay day-oo" in Catalan) *targeta* (€6.65), valid for ten separate journeys, with changes between methods of transport allowed within 75 minutes. The ticket can also be used by more than one person at a time – just make sure you punch it the same number of times as there are people travelling. It's also available at newsstands and tobacconists.

Other useful (single-person) *targetes* for Zone 1 include the **T-Dia** ("tay dee-ah"; one day's unlimited travel; €5), plus combinations up to the 5-Dies (five days; €20); the **T-50/30** (fifty trips within a thirty-day period; €27.55); or the **T-Mes** (one month; €42.75) – for the latter, the station ticket office will need to see some form of ID (driving licence or passport). The **Barcelona Card** (see p.28) also offers free city transport between two and five days.

Heading for the airport, Sitges, the northern coast, Montserrat and other out-of-town destinations, you'll need to buy a specific ticket or relevant zoned *targeta* as the Zone 1 *targetes* outlined above don't run that far. Anyone caught without a valid ticket anywhere on the system is liable to an on-the-spot fine of €40.

The metro

The quickest way of getting around Barcelona is by the efficient metro system, which currently runs on six lines; the new line 9 (under construction, expected to be completed by 2008) will open up hitherto poorly served suburban towns east and west of the city, but will also provide a direct metro link from the airport to the new Sagrera high-speed train station, with connections to the other metro lines.

Metro entrances are marked with a red diamond sign with an "M". Its **hours of operation** are Monday until Thursday, plus Sunday and public holidays 5am to midnight; Friday, Saturday and the day before a public holiday 5am to 2am. There's a colour **metro**

TMB customer service centres

Barcelona Sants station (RENFE Vestíbul) Mon–Fri 7am–9pm, Sat 9am–7pm, Sun 9am–2pm.
Ⓜ **Diagonal** Mon–Fri 8am–8pm.
Ⓜ **Sagrada Família** Mon–Fri 7am–9pm.
Ⓜ **Universitat** Mon–Fri 8am–8pm.

map at the back of this book, or you can pick up a little fold-out one at metro stations (ask for *una guia del metro*).

The system is perfectly safe, though many of the train carriages are heavily graffitied. Buskers and beggars are common, moving from one carriage to the next at stations.

Buses

Bus routes in the city are easy to master if you get hold of a copy of the public transport map and remember that the routes are colour-coded: **city-centre** buses are red and always stop at one of three central squares (Catalunya, Universitat or Urquinaona); cross-city buses are yellow; green buses run on all the **peripheral** routes outside the city centre; and **night buses** (*autobusos nocturns* or simply *Nitbus*) are blue (and always stop near or in Plaça de Catalunya). In addition, the route is marked at each bus stop, along with a timetable – useful bus routes are detailed in the text.

Most buses **operate daily**, roughly from 4am or 5am until 10.30pm, though some lines stop earlier and some run on until after midnight. The night buses fill in the gaps on all the main routes, with services every twenty to sixty minutes from around 10pm to 4am.

Useful Catalan words to look out for on timetables are *diari* (daily), *feiners* (Mon–Sat), and *diumenge* or *festius* (Sun & hols).

Trams

The tram system (☎902 193 275, ⓦwww.trambcn.com) runs on four lines, with departures every eight to twenty minutes throughout the day from 5am to midnight. **Lines T1, T2 and T3** depart from Plaça Francesc Macià and run along the uptown part of Avinguda Diagonal to suburban destinations in the northwest – useful tourist stops are at L'Illa shopping and the Maria Cristina and Palau Reial metro stations. Line **T4** operates from Ciutadella-Vila Olímpica (where there's also a metro station) and runs up past the zoo and TNC (the National Theatre) to Glòries before running down the lower part of Avinguda Diagonal to Diagonal Mar and the Fòrum site.

Trains

The city has a cheap and efficient commuter train line, the **Ferrocarrils de la Generalitat de Catalunya** (FGC; ☎932 051 515, ⓦwww.fgc.es), with its main stations at Plaça de Catalunya and Plaça d'Espanya. These go to Sarrià, Vallvidrera, Tibidabo, Sant Cugat, Terrassa and Montserrat, and details are given in the text where appropriate. The Zone 1 *targeta* is valid as far as the city limits, which in practice is everywhere you're likely to want to go except for Montserrat.

The national rail service, operated by **RENFE** (☎902 240 202, ⓦwww.renfe.es), runs all the other services out of Barcelona, with local lines – north to the Costa Maresme and south to Sitges – designated as Rodiales/Cercanías. The hub is Barcelona Sants station, with services also passing through Plaça de Catalunya (heading north) and Passeig de Gràcia (south). Arrive in plenty of time to buy a ticket, as queues are often horrendous, though for most regional destinations you can use the automatic vending machines instead.

Funiculars, cable cars, trams and trolleys

Other transport options in the city provide some fun ways of getting around. Details of hours of operation and prices are given in the relevant sections of the text.

Several **funicular railways** still operate in the city to Montjuïc, Tibidabo and Vallvidrera. Summer and weekend visits to Tibidabo also combine a funicular trip with a ride on the antique **tram,** the Tramvia Blau. There are two **cable car** (*telefèric*) rides: from Barceloneta across the harbour to Montjuïc, and then from the top station of the Montjuïc funicular right the way up to the castle. Both aerial rides are pretty good experiences, worth doing just for the views alone. Finally, a **train-trolley**, the Tren Turístic de Montjuïc, trundles around the Montjuïc area during the summer months.

Taxis

Black-and-yellow taxis (with a green roof-light on when available for hire) are inexpensive, plentiful and well worth using, especially late at night. There's a minimum charge of €1.45 (€1.55 after 10pm Sat, Sun & hols) and after that it's currently €0.78/1.00 per kilometre, with small surcharges for baggage and picking up from Barcelona Sants station and the airport, However, the taxis have meters so charges are transparent – if not, asking for a receipt (*rebut* in Catalan, *recibo* in Spanish) should ensure that the price is fair. Most short journeys across town (such as from Sants to the top of the Ramblas) run to around €6. There are **taxi ranks** outside major train and metro stations, in main squares, near large hotels and along the main avenues. To call a taxi in advance, see "Directory", p.245 for a list of cab companies (few of the operators speak English) – you'll be charged an extra €3–4 on top of the fare for calling a cab.

A fun way to get around the old town, port area and beaches is by **trixi** (ⓦ www.trixi.info), a kind of love-bug-style bicycle-rickshaw. They tout for business between noon and 8pm near the Columbus statue at the bottom of the Ramblas, and outside La Seu (cathedral) in the Barri Gòtic, though you can also flag them down if one cruises by. Fares are fixed (€6 for 15min, €10 for 30min, €18 for 60min) and the *trixistas* are an amiable, multilingual bunch for the most part.

Driving and vehicle rental

You don't need a car to get around Barcelona, but you may want to rent one if you plan to see anything else of the region. However, in summer the coastal roads in particular are a nightmare, so if all you aim to do is zip to the beach or wine region for the day, it's far better to stick to the local trains. Driving in the city itself is not for the faint-hearted either, with opinion divided on whether it's worse negotiating the impossibly narrow old-town streets, or the racetrack avenues of the Eixample. Moreover, fuel prices are only marginally lower than in Britain and almost double US prices, while you'll probably have to pay extra for parking (which is notoriously difficult in the city centre; see "Arrival: By car", p.27). **Vehicle crime** is rampant – never leave anything visible in the car.

Most foreign **driving licences** are honoured in Spain – including all EU, US and Canadian ones – or you can take an International Driver's Licence (available from recognized driving organizations). If you're bringing your own car, you must have a **green card** from your insurers. Carry your licence, vehicle registration and insurance documents with you at all times in the car; you should also have two warning triangles and a fluorescent vest, as well as spare bulbs of the correct wattage for your lights in case of breakdown.

Remember that you **drive on the right** in Spain, and away from main roads you yield to vehicles approaching from the right. Speed limits are posted – maximum on urban roads is 60kph, other roads 90kph, motorways 120kph. Wearing seatbelts is compulsory.

Vehicle rental

Car rental is usually cheaper arranged in advance from home through one of the large multinational chains (Avis, Budget, Hertz, Holiday Autos, National or Thrifty, for example). If you leave it until you arrive in Barcelona, you'll need to contact a city rental company (some are listed in "Directory" on p.243), which have inclusive rates from around €40 per day for an economy car (less by the week, and often with good rates for a three-day weekend rental, around €150). Drivers need to be at least 21 (23 with some companies) and to have been driving for at least a year.

Some of the Barcelona rental outlets (like Motissimo and Vanguard) have **mopeds** and **motorcycles** available, though given the traffic conditions (and the good public transport system) it's not really recommended as a means of getting around the city. Note that mopeds and motorcycles are often rented out with insurance that doesn't include theft – always check with the company first. You will generally be asked to produce a driving licence as a deposit.

City tours

Although you can find your way around the city easily enough with a map and a guidebook, taking a tour is a good way to orientate yourself on arrival. The highest profile belongs to the two tour-bus operators, whose board-at-will open-top services can drop you outside every attraction in the city. Otherwise, Barcelona has some particularly good walking tours, showing you parts of the old town you might not find otherwise, while guided bike tours and sightseeing boats offer a different view of the city.

Bike tours

Bike Tours Barcelona ☏ 932 682 105, ⊛ www.biketoursbarcelona.com. Find the red-T-shirted guides in Plaça de Sant Jaume in the Barri Gòtic, outside the tourist office (top of c/de la Ciutat) – tours last three hours (daily 11am, plus April–Sept Fri–Mon 4.30pm; €22) no reservations required.
Fat Tire Bike Tours ☏ 933 013 612, ⊛ www.fattirebiketoursbarcelona.com. Four-hour bike tours (€22) with genial guides to the old town, Sagrada Família, port area and beach – where there's time for a swim and a drink. Tours meet at the c/de Ferran side of Plaça de Sant Jaume, Barri Gòtic (three times daily mid-April to mid-Sept, once daily rest of the year; no tours mid-Dec to end of Feb). Reservations not required, but you can check details at the rental shop at c/Escudellers 48. No credit cards.

Bus and trolley tours

Barcelona Tours ⊛ www.barcelonatours.es. The orange-coloured rival to Bus Turístic; buses make twenty stops on a circular three-hour sweep through the city from Pl. de Catalunya (daily: 9am–8pm May–Sept 9am–9pm; departures every 10–20min). Tickets available on board: one-day €18, two-day €22 (under-14s €11/14 respectively). No credit cards.
Bus Turístic ⊛ www.tmb.net, ⊛ www.barcelonaturisme.com. Sightseeing service (departures every 6–20min) with over forty stops on three combined routes, linking all the main tourist sights. Northern and southern routes depart from Plaça de Catalunya (daily 9am–7pm, April–Sept 9am–8pm), and a full circuit on either route takes two hours. The Forùm route (daily April–Sept 9.30am–8pm) runs from Port Olímpic to the Forùm site at Diagonal Mar and back, via the beaches. Tickets (valid for all routes) cost €18 for one day,

€22 for two days (children aged 4–12 €11/14 respectively). The ticket also gives discounts at various sights, attractions, shops and restaurants. Buy on board the bus, at any tourist office, Sants station and TMB customer centres.
Tren Turístic de Montjuïc The train-trolley leaves from Pl. d'Espanya (mid-June to mid-Sept daily 10am–8.30pm; April–Oct Sat & Sun 10am–8.30pm; every 30min; €3.20) and runs to all the major sights on Montjuïc, including the castle. The round trip lasts about sixty minutes and your ticket allows you to complete the full circuit once, getting on and off where you like. No credit cards.

Walking and activity tours

Barcelona Walking Tours ☏ 932 853 832, ⊛ www.barcelonaturisme.com. Advance booking advised (at Pl. de Catalunya tourist office) for the popular 90min historical walking tour of the Barri Gòtic (daily 10am in English; €8.50). There are also 90min Picasso walking tours (Tues–Sun 10.30am in English; €10.50, includes entry to Picasso Museum), and a two-hour Modernisme tour (Sat & Sun 4pm in English; €8.50) and two-hour Gourmet and Cuisine tour (Fri 11am; €10.50, includes tastings).
My Favourite Things ☏ 637 265 405, ⊛ www.myft.net. Highly individual tours which reveal the city in a new light – whether it's bohemian Barcelona, where and what the locals eat, or the signature tour, My Favourite Fusion, which gives an insider's view of the city. Tours (in English) cost €26 per person and last around four hours, and there's always time for anecdotes, diversions, workshop visits and café visits. Tour numbers are limited to ten, and departures are flexible, so call or email for latest information or tailor-made requests.
Travel Bar c/Boqueria 27, Barri Gòtic ☏ 933 425 252, ⊛ www.travelbar.com; Ⓜ Liceu. The travellers' bar can sign you up on a variety of youth-oriented

knees-ups, including bar and tapas crawls, party nights, bike and activity tours and out-of-town excursions. Call at the bar for a current schedule. No credit cards.

Water tours

Catamaran Orsom ☎ 932 218 283, ⓦ www.barcelona-orsom.com. Afternoon catamaran trips around the port in season (Easter week & June–Sept daily, May & Oct daily except Tues & Thurs; €12) and summer evening jazz cruises (June–Sept;

€14.50). There's a ticket kiosk at the quayside opposite the Columbus statue, at the bottom of the Ramblas (Ⓜ Drassanes), but you should call in advance to be certain of departures.

Las Golondrinas ☎ 934 423 106, ⓦ www.lasgolondrinas.com. Daily sightseeing boats depart from Pl. Portal de la Pau, behind the Columbus monument (Ⓜ Drassanes) – trips are either around the port (35min €4; 60min €7.50), or port and coast including the Port Olímpic and Diagonal Mar (90min; €9.70). Departures are at least hourly June–Sept; less frequently Oct–May but still daily.

The media

You'll be able to keep up with the news while you're away since British, European and American newspapers are sold at street kiosks on the Ramblas and elsewhere (see "Directory", p.244 for locations). Many have special European editions, so they're on sale the same day from around 9am. The city also has some English-language publications, and useful listings magazines – for these, and a rundown of the local Spanish press, see below. The only local English-language radio programming is the talk-radio show on Radio Free Barcelona (Sat 9–11am, 107.7FM ⓦ www.radiofreebarcelona.com).

Newspapers and magazines

Of the Spanish newspapers the best is the Barcelona edition of the liberal **El País** (ⓦ www.elpais.es) – it's the only one with much serious analysis or foreign news coverage, plus it has a daily Catalunya supplement and is good on entertainment and the arts. The Barcelona paper **La Vanguardia** (ⓦ www.lavanguardia.es) is conservative; it also has a good arts and culture listings section on Friday. **El Periodico** (ⓦ www.elperiodico.com) is more tabloid in style, with big headlines and lots of photos; it also comes in a Catalan edition. **Avui** (ⓦ www.avui.cat) is the chief nationalist paper, printed in Catalan. You can also pick up two free daily papers outside metro stations on weekdays, **Metro** (ⓦ www.metrodirecto.com) and **20 Minutos** (ⓦ www.20minutos.es), both with useful local listings. For wall-to-wall coverage of sport (for which, in Barcelona, read FC Barcelona), buy the

specialist dailies **Mundo Deportivo** (ⓦ www.elmundodeportivo.es/fcbarcelona) or Sport (ⓦ www.sport.es). The most useful listings publication is the indispensable weekly **Guia del Ocio** (Thurs; ⓦ www.guiadelociobcn.es), a small paperback-book-sized magazine, available at kiosks all over the city. It's in Spanish but is easily deciphered.

English-language publications include **Catalonia Today** (ⓦ www.cataloniatoday.info), a weekly newspaper about the city and region. **Barcelona Metropolitan** (ⓦ www.barcelona-metropolitan.com) is a free monthly magazine for English-speakers living in Barcelona, available from hotels, bars and other outlets; or there's **b-guided** (ⓦ www.b-guided.com), a painfully cool quarterly style magazine on sale at newsagents. There's also the free monthly **Barcelona Connect** (ⓦ www.barcelonaconnect.com), containing an idiosyncratic mixture of news, views and classified ads.

Television

In Catalunya you can pick up **two national TV channels**, TVE1 and TVE2 (La 2), a couple of **Catalan-language channels**, TV3 and Canal 33, and the private Antena 3 and Tele 5 channels. In Barcelona you can also get the city-run **Barcelona TV** (Ⓦwww .barcelonatv.com), which is useful for information about local events, and news programmes on the otherwise subscriber-only Canal Plus channel. TVs in most pensions and small hotels tend to offer these stations, with cable and satellite channels available in higher-rated hotels.

The programming is a fairly entertaining mixture of grim game shows, tacky song- and-dance revues, news and sports. Soaps are a particular speciality, whether Catalan, Spanish or South American, while locally produced sitcoms and series compete with dubbed versions of North American favourites like *Will and Grace* and *Los Simpson*. Some foreign films and shows are broadcast in dual (simultaneously in the original and dubbed); undubbed films are marked "V.O. *(versión original)*" in listings (late-night only). Sports fans are well catered for, with regular live coverage of local and national basketball and football matches – in the football season, you can watch two or three live matches a week. The best local **weather** forecasting is on TV3.

Costs, money and banks

Although people still think of Spain as a budget destination, Barcelona is not a particularly cheap place to visit. Hotel prices have increased considerably over the last few years, while some major museums and attractions have steep admission charges. However, when balanced with the cost of visiting cities in countries such as Britain, France or Germany, Barcelona still rates as pretty good value, especially when it comes to dining out or getting around on public transport. Only if you do all your shopping in designer stores, and all your eating and drinking in gastronomic restaurants and style bars, can you expect to spend as much as you would at home, if not more.

Average costs

Your single biggest daily expense by far will be accommodation, with the very cheapest double rooms starting at around €40, though more realistically you'll be paying €60–80 a night for decent lodgings. Snacks and meals, on the other hand, are still extremely good value, with a three-course lunch anywhere in the city available for €8–10, while a one-day public transport pass gives you the freedom of the city for €5.

If you're prepared to stay in inexpensive pensions, stick to basic restaurants and bars, and pick and choose your sightseeing, you could get by on €50 a day.

Upgrade your accommodation, see all the museums, eat fancier meals and experience the Barcelona nightlife, and you'll need more like €100 a day – though, of course, if you're planning to stay in a four-star hotel this figure won't even cover your room. For more detailed accommodation costs, see Chapter 7.

Currency, cash, cards and cheques

Spain's **currency** is the euro (€), with notes issued in denominations of 5, 10, 20, 50, 100, 200 and 500 euros, and coins in denominations of 1, 2, 5, 10, 20 and 50

Budget Barcelona

Here's how to keep costs to a minimum in Barcelona.

• Eat your main meal of the day at lunchtime, when the *menú del dia* offers fantastic value (p.184).

• Buy a public transport travel pass (see p.30), which will save you around forty percent on every ride.

• Purchase one of the useful city discount cards or packages (p.28).

• Visit museums and galleries on the first Sunday of the month if you can, when admission is usually free.

• Drink and eat *inside* cafés – there's usually a surcharge for terrace service.

• Bring along any student, youth or senior citizen cards you're entitled to carry, as they often attract discounts on museum, gallery and attraction charges.

• Take advantage of the discount nights at the cinema (Mon & sometimes Wed), and at the theatre (Tues).

• Go to the Ramblas, La Seu, Santa María del Mar, Parc de la Ciutadella, Parc de la Collserola, Port Vell, Port Olímpic, city beaches, Els Encants flea market, Diagonal Mar/Fòrum, Olympic stadium, Caixa Forum and Parc Güell – all free.

cents, and 1 and 2 euros. The exchange rate currently fluctuates around €1.45 to £1 (€1 equals 70p) and €0.85 to US$1 (€1 equals $1.20).

By far the easiest way to get money in Barcelona is to use your bank debit card to withdraw cash from an **ATM** (cash machine). You'll find them all over the city, including the airport and major train stations, and you can usually withdraw up to €200 a day depending on the status of your account. Instructions are offered in English once you insert your card. The amounts withdrawn are not liable to interest payments, and the flat transaction fee is usually quite small – your bank will be able to advise on this. Make sure you have a personal identification number (PIN) that's designed to work overseas, and take a note of your bank's emergency contact number in case the machine swallows the card.

Credit cards are a handy backup source of funds, and can be used either in ATMs or over the counter. MasterCard, Visa and American Express are accepted just about everywhere. Remember that all cash advances on credit cards are treated as loans, with interest accruing daily from the date of withdrawal; there may be a transaction fee on top of this.

Travellers' cheques are no longer the cheapest nor most convenient option, although they do offer protection against loss or theft. Obviously, buying cheques in euros is the best option, since these can be cashed without incurring exchange service charges, though sterling and American dollars cheques will be accepted in all banks and exchange offices.

In an emergency, you might have to consider having money wired from home, though this is never a cheap way to access funds. **American Express** (see p.242 for Barcelona contact details) has a 24-hour money transfer service, while **Western Union** (Ⓦ www.westernunion. com) can transfer cash to and from various locations in the city, including most main post offices.

Banks and exchange offices

Spanish banks (*bancos*) and savings banks (*caixas*) have branches throughout Barcelona, with concentrations down the Ramblas and around Plaça de Catalunya. Normal **banking hours** in Barcelona are Monday to Friday from 8.30am to 2pm, although from October until May most institutions also open Thursday 4pm to 6.30pm (savings banks) or Saturday 9am to 1pm (banks). Outside these hours you can use *bureaux de change* or a foreign-exchange office (*canvi, cambio*), found along the Ramblas and elsewhere, often open well after midnight. Exchange offices don't always charge commission, though their rates aren't usually as good as the banks. Other exchange options are the **automatic currency exchange machines** (available at the airport, Barcelona Sants and outside some banks) or one of the larger hotels or travel agents, though again rates can be variable.

Taxes and tipping

Local sales tax, **IVA**, is seven percent in hotels and restaurants, and sixteen percent in shops. It's usually included in the price though not always, so some hotel or restaurant bills can come as a bit of a surprise – though quoted prices should always make it clear whether or not tax is included.

In most restaurants and bars service is considered to be included in the price of meals and drinks (hence the premium you pay for sitting at a terrace). **Tipping** is more a recognition that service was good or exceptional than an expected part of the server's wage. Locals actually tip very little, leaving a few cents or rounding up the change for a coffee or a drink, and a euro

To cancel **lost or stolen credit cards**, call the following 24 hour numbers (English spoken):
American Express ℡ 900 810 029
Diners Club ℡ 902 401 112
MasterCard ℡ 900 971 231
Visa ℡ 900 991 124

or two for most meals. Anything beyond is considered excessive, certainly the ten or fifteen percent that most visitors are used to at home. However, fancy restaurants may specifically indicate that service is not included, in which case you will be expected to leave ten to fifteen percent. Taxi drivers usually get around five percent, more if they have helped you with bags or been similarly useful, while hotel porters and toilet attendants should be tipped a euro or two for their assistance.

Mail, phones and email

You'll have no trouble keeping in touch whilst in Barcelona. Stamps are widely sold, public telephones and discount call centres are plentiful, and there is a glut of Internet cafés where you can check your email.

Post offices and mail

The main **post office** in Barcelona, near the harbour in the old town, is open daily, including Sunday, while other central branches have long weekday hours; see "Directory", p.245, for all the relevant details. However, if all you need are **stamps** it's usually quicker to visit a tobacconist (look for the brown-and-yellow tabac sign), found on virtually every street. These can also weigh letters and small parcels, advise about postal rates, and send express mail (*urgente).*Use the yellow **on-street post-boxes** and put your mail in the flap marked *províncies i estranger* or *altres destins*. Letters or cards take around three to four days

to European countries, five days to a week to North America.

Public phones and phone centres

Spanish **public telephones** have instructions in English. They accept coins, credit cards and phone cards, while dialling codes (Spanish provincial and overseas) and other information are displayed in the cabins. **Phone cards** with discounted rates for calls are available in tobacconists, newsagents and post offices, issued in various denominations either by Telefónica (the dominant operator) or one of its rivals. Credit cards are not recommended for local and national

37

Telephone information

Spanish regional prefixes are an integral part of the nine-digit telephone numbers. Thus, in Barcelona, the first two digits of all phone numbers are 93, and it is necessary to dial these digits even when calling from within the city. Spanish mobile numbers begin with a 6, freephone numbers begin 900, while other 90-plus- and 80-plus-digit numbers are nationwide standard-rate or special-rate services.

Useful numbers

Barcelona general information ☎010
National directory enquiries ☎11818
International operator (Europe) ☎1008
International operator (rest of the world) ☎1005
Weather forecast ☎932 211 600
Road conditions ☎938 892 211
The time ☎093
Alarm call ☎096

Phoning abroad from Barcelona

to Australia: dial ☎00, then 61 + area code minus first 0 + number
to Britain: dial ☎00, then 44 + area code minus first 0 + number
to Ireland: dial ☎00, then 353 + area code + number
to New Zealand: dial ☎00, then 64 + area code minus first 0 + number
to US and Canada: dial ☎00, then 1 + area code + number

Phoning Barcelona from abroad

from Australia: dial ☎0011 +34 + number
from Britain: dial ☎00 + 34 + number
from Ireland: dial ☎00 + 34 + number
from New Zealand: dial ☎00 + 34 + number
from US and Canada: dial ☎011 + 34 + number

calls, since most have a minimum charge which is far more than a normal call is likely to cost. The **ringing tone** is long; **engaged** is shorter and rapid; the standard Spanish response is ¿diga? (speak) or in Barcelona, a less linguistically committal ¿sí?.

You can also make calls from the old-style telephones in cafés and bars, though their rates are higher and you can't make anything except a simple coin call. If possible, avoid making any calls from your hotel room, as even local calls will be slapped with a heavy surcharge, and "no charge" calls to international operators may be charged as well.

For **international calls,** you can use any of the street cabins, paying with coins, phone card, credit card or **charge card** issued by your domestic telephone company. This way, all calls made from overseas will automatically be billed to your home account. Contact your home provider, which will provide you with a number that you can dial free from cabins and which will connect you directly with one of their operators in your home country. However, the cheapest way to make an international call is to go to one of the ubiquitous phone centres, or **locutorios**, which specialize in discounted overseas connections – you'll find them scattered through the old city, particularly in the Raval and Ribera. If the rates to the country that you want to call are not posted, just ask. You'll then be assigned a cabin to make your calls, and afterwards you pay in cash.

Mobile phones

Most European-subscribed **mobile phones** will work in Barcelona, though if you are planning to take your phone with you it's worth checking with your provider whether you need to get international access switched on and whether there are any extra charges involved. You may also have to ask your provider for a new access code if you want to retrieve messages from your voice-mail while in Barcelona.

Provided your own phone isn't blocked by your service provider, you can avoid international mobile charges by simply buying a new **SIM card** for your phone. Vodafone (ⓦwww.vodafone.es), Movistar (ⓦwww.movistar.es), Amena (ⓦwww.amena.es) and other provider's stores have SIM cards for around €25, which will include an intitial talk credit. Or if you plan to spend some time in the city it's almost certainly better to buy a **Spanish mobile.** The cheapest rechargeable prepaid phones cost around €60, which usually includes about €20 of free calls. Price plans vary, but charges of around €0.28 a minute for daytime use are standard. You can buy top-up cards, or have them recharged for you, in phone shops and post offices.

Email and Internet access

There are **Internet shops** and **cafés** all over Barcelona, while an increasing number of hotels, youth hostels and pensions provide cheap or free Internet access for their guests. Hotel business centres or hotel bedrooms wired for access tend to be far more expensive than going out on the street to get online, so always check charges carefully first. Wi-Fi access is increasingly common in bars, hotels and other public "hotspots", though if you take your own laptop make sure you've got insurance cover and all the relevant adaptors for recharging.

Admission to museums, galleries and churches

Most of the showpiece museums and galleries in Barcelona open all day, from 10am to 8pm, though some of the smaller collections and attractions close over lunchtime between 1 and 4pm. On Sundays most open in the morning only and on Mondays most are closed all day. On public holidays (see overleaf), most museums and galleries have Sunday opening hours, while everything is closed on Christmas and New Year's Day.

Museum opening hours tend to stay the same from year to year, perhaps varying by half an hour here and there. The current opening hours for all attractions are listed in the guide, and you can check any changes in the weekly *Guia del Ocio* listings magazine or on the websites of the museums and galleries themselves.

Admission charges for all attractions vary between €3 and €12, though most museums cost around €5 or €6. Many offer **free admission** on the first Sunday of every month, and most museums are free on the saints' days of February 12 and September 24. There's usually a reduction or free entrance if you show a student, youth or senior citizen card. Several **discount cards** are available (see p.28), that give heavily reduced admission to Barcelona's museums and galleries – worth considering if you're planning to see everything that the city has to offer.

Apart from the cathedral (La Seu) and the Sagrada Família – the two **churches** you're most likely to visit, which have tourist-friendly opening hours – other churches are usually kept locked, opening only for worship in the early morning (around 7–8am) and the evening (around 6–9pm). For all churches, "decorous" dress is required, with no shorts or bare shoulders.

Opening hours and public holidays

Basic working hours in Barcelona are Monday to Saturday 9.30 or 10am to 1.30pm and 4.30 to 8 or 9pm, though many offices and shops don't open on Saturday afternoons. However, local cafés, bars and markets open earlier, usually from around 7am, while shopping centres, major stores and large supermarkets tend to remain open all day from 10am to 9pm, with some even opening on Sunday.

In the lazy days of summer everything becomes a bit more relaxed, with offices working until around 3pm and many shops and restaurants closing for part or the whole of August. Conversely, while Barcelona seems semi-deserted, it can prove nearly impossible to find a free bed in the nearby coastal and mountain resorts in August; similarly, seats on planes, trains and buses should be booked well in advance.

Official **public holidays** can also disrupt your travel plans, though not all public and bank holidays in Spain are observed in Catalunya, and vice versa. On the days listed below, and during the many local festivals (see Chapter 12), you'll find most shops closed, though bars and restaurants tend to stay open.

Barcelona's public holidays

January 1 Cap d'Any, New Year's Day
January 6 Epifanía, Epiphany
Easter Good Friday & Easter Monday
May 1 Día del Treball, May Day/Labour Day
June 24 Día de Sant Joan, St John's Day
August 15 L'Assumpció, Assumption of the Virgin
September 11 Diada Nacional, Catalan National Day
September 24 Festa de la Mercè, Our Lady of Mercy, Barcelona's patron saint
October 12 Día de la Hispanidad, Spanish National Day
November 1 Tots Sants, All Saints' Day
December 6 Día de la Constitució, Constitution Day
December 8 La Imaculada, Immaculate Conception
December 25 Nadal, Christmas Day
December 26 Sant Esteve, St Stephen's Day

Crime and personal safety

Barcelona has a reputation as a city plagued by petty crime. However, you don't need to be unduly paranoid. Most of Barcelona is as safe as any other city you may be used to – and the potential for violent street crime is much lower than in Britain and the United States. But you should stay alert to possible threats and be on your guard on public transport and at tourist sites against pickpockets and bag-snatchers. While you can take many beggars at face value (deciding whether or not you give them money), you should beware of people directly accosting you or who in any other manner try to distract you.

Avoiding trouble

Almost all the problems tourists encounter

are to do with **petty crime** – pickpocketing and bag-snatching – rather than more serious physical confrontations. Sensible precautions include: carrying bags slung across your body, not off one shoulder; not carrying anything in zipped pockets which you can't keep an eye on; having photocopies of your passport and leaving the original and any tickets in the hotel safe; never leaving your wallet in your back pocket; and noting down travellers' cheque and credit card numbers.

The bottom end of the Ramblas and the medieval streets to either side are where you most need to be on your guard. Take the usual precautions at night: avoid unlit streets and dark alleys, don't go out brimming with valuables, and don't flash fancy cameras or look hopelessly lost in run-down areas. Other places to be especially wary are around the Sagrada Família and on the metro. Thieves often work in pairs, so watch out for people standing unusually close; keep a hand on your wallet or bag if it appears you're being distracted.

Some things to be aware of include:

• Being distracted by some very sophisticated operators, like the "helpful" person pointing out bird shit (shaving cream or something similar) on your jacket while someone relieves you of your money; the card or paper you're invited to read to distract your attention; the person trying to give you or sell you flowers, herbs, or small Catalan-flag stickers.

• In cafés and restaurants, never leave your bags unzipped or on a neighbouring chair – place them where you can see or feel them, and loop a chair leg through a shoulder strap.

• Don't leave anything in view in your car when you park it; take the radio with you. Vehicles are rarely stolen, but luggage and valuables left in cars do make a tempting target, and rental cars are easy to spot. When driving in the city, keep all car doors locked, as thieves can easily snatch a bag from a car's back seat and run off, leaving the driver stranded.

What to do if you're robbed

If you're robbed, you need to **go to the police** to report it, not least because your insurance company will require a police report. Don't expect a great deal of concern if your loss is relatively small – but do expect the process of completing forms and formalities to take ages.

In the unlikely event that you're **mugged**, or otherwise threatened, never resist; hand over what's wanted and run straight to the police, who will be more sympathetic on these occasions. For details of the main **police stations in Barcelona**, see p.244.

The police

There are four types of **police** – the Guàrdia Civil, the Policía Nacional, the municipal police known as the Guàrdia Urbana, and the Catalan Mossos d'Esquadra – all of them armed, and all of them under the authority of the Catalan government.

The **Guàrdia Civil** (ⓦ www.guardiacivil.org), in green uniforms and sometimes sporting black three-cornered hats, are a national police force and were formally a military organization but also investigate crime on a national (and, in some places, local) level. Traditionally associated with the oppressive Franco regime, their role in Catalunya has been gradually limited, though they can still be seen guarding some public buildings, and at airports and border crossings.

The **Policía Nacional** (ⓦ www.policia. es) wear uniforms resembling blue combat gear. In Barcelona they operate primarily as an anti-crime force, which includes street patrols, investigations, checking papers of suspected illegal immigrants, and crowd control. If you are mugged or robbed in Barcelona, it is the Policía Nacional who will take your statement.

More visible on the streets of Barcelona and generally more sympathetic are the **Guàrdia Urbana** (ⓦ www.bcn.es/ guardiaurbana), in blue shirts and navy jackets, who are responsible for controlling the traffic. They are likely to be the first to respond to calls for help. They also guard the Ajuntament installations.

Catalunya also has its own autonomous police force, the **Mossos d'Esquadra** (ⓦ www.mossos.net), in navy-blue uniforms with red trim. In Barcelona you'll see them guarding buildings that belong to the Generalitat, but in Catalunya in general they are gradually taking over duties from the Guàrdia Civil and Policía Nacional.

Sexual harassment

Sexual harassment is certainly a possibility in Barcelona but is no worse than in other European tourist destinations. In fact, Barcelona often seems a much safer place for women to walk the streets than London or New York, and there is little of the pestering that you have to contend with in the larger French or Italian cities. However, without a very clear understanding of Catalan or Spanish it can be hard to deal with situations that do arise and in which you'd cope quite routinely at home. Common sense should help you avoid getting into such difficulties in the first place, while using taxis to go home late at night (they are cheap and widely available) is always a good idea.

Offences

• In theory you're supposed to carry some kind of **identification** at all times, and the police can stop you in the street and demand to see it. In practice they're rarely bothered if you're clearly a tourist – and a photocopy of your passport, or photo-driving licence should suffice.

• While the **rules of the road** seem to be barely observed, to say the least, if you have an accident you can bet that, as a foreigner, it will be your fault. Try not to make a statement to anyone who doesn't speak fluent English.

• Possession and consumption of **drugs** in public is illegal. However, the police tend to be little worried about personal use of cannabis. Larger quantities (and any other drugs) are a very different matter, and if you're arrested or detained for a drugs offence, don't expect any sympathy or help from your consulate.

Travellers with disabilities

Travellers with disabilities will find it easier to get around Barcelona than most other Spanish cities, but that's not saying a great deal. However, there are plenty of accessible hotels in Barcelona, while ramps and other forms of access are gradually being added to museums, sites and sports facilities. By law, all new public buildings are required to be fully accessible.

Planning a holiday

Organizations like Holiday Care (☏0845/124 9971, from overseas 44-208/760 0072, ⓦwww.holidaycare.org.uk), or the US online resource Access-Able (ⓦwww.access-able. com), can put you in touch with **specialists for trips** specifically for people with disabilities. However, most Spanish holidays and tours tend to be to the costas.

As for pre-planning, read your travel insurance small print carefully to make sure that people with a pre-existing medical condition are not excluded. And use your **travel agent** to make your journey simpler: airline or bus companies can cope better if they are expecting you, with a wheelchair provided at airports and staff primed to help. A medical certificate of your fitness to travel, provided by your doctor, is also extremely useful; some airlines or insurance companies may insist on it. Make sure that you have extra supplies of any drugs you need – carried with you if you fly – and a prescription including the generic name in case of emergency. Carry spares of any clothing or equipment that might be hard to find.

In Barcelona

There's no better single resource for city information for disabled travellers than the **AccessibleBarcelona** website (ⓦwww. accessiblebarcelona.com). The city information line (☏010, English spoken) also has accessibility information for sights and services, while the Ajuntament information office in Plaça Sant Miquel (see p.29) can provide a map showing accessible routes for tourists.

Arriving in Barcelona is reasonably straightforward. Barcelona's **airport** is fully accessible to travellers in wheelchairs, with adapted toilets, lifts to the various levels, and special lifts for access to and from the planes. The Aerobús is also equipped to take wheelchairs, but it gets very busy and can be difficult if you have lots of luggage.

Getting around the city is more problematic since the **metro** system is perhaps the least wheelchair-friendly that can be imagined – though ongoing efforts are being made to improve access. At present only line 2 is fully accessible, with elevators at major stations (including Universitat, Paral.lel, Passeig de Gràcia and Sagrada Família) from the street to the platforms. At **Barcelona Sants** there are no access ramps for the trains themselves, and the steps and escalators are fairly steep, but there are access ramps at Estació de França and a lift to the platforms at Plaça de Catalunya's FGC station. Most **city buses** have been adapted for wheelchair use, with automatic ramps and steps and a designated wheelchair space inside; simply ring the bell on the bus door. All **night buses** are also wheelchair-accessible, as is the sightseeing Bus Turístic. The Transports Metropolitans de Barcelona (TMB) website (⊕ www.tmb.net, English version available) lets you view all adapted metro stations and bus routes (look under "Transport for everyone"). If you need a wheelchair-accessible **taxi** call Taxi Amic

(☎ 934 208 088, English rarely spoken).

Out on the streets, the number of acoustic traffic-light signals is slowly growing, while dropped kerbs are being put in place across the city. However, most old-town attractions, including the Museu Picasso, have steps, cobbles or other impediments to access. Fully accessible **sights and attractions** include MNAC, Fundació Antoni Tàpies, La Pedrera (though not the roof terrace), Caixa Forum, CosmoCaixa, Museu d'Història de Catalunya and the Palau de la Música.

Useful contacts

AccessibleBarcelona ☎ 934 462 303, © info @accessiblebarcelona.com, ⊕ www .accessiblebarcelona.com. An invaluable website that lists and reviews accessible city tourist sights, hotels, bars and restaurants. You can also book accommodation – all inspected for suitability – and arrange airport transfers and wheelchair-friendly guided tours (€70 for 4hr, including assistance by guide).

Institut Municipal de Persones amb Discapacitat Avgda. Diagonal 233, 1°, Eixample Ⓜ Glòries ☎ 934 132 775, ⊕ www.bcn.es/imd. Has information (in Catalan and Spanish) on most aspects of life and travel in the city for disabled residents and visitors.

Organización Nacional de Ciegos de España (ONCE) c/Calabria 66–76, Eixample Ⓜ Rocafort ☎ 933 259 200, ⊕ www.once.es. Sells a braille guidebook to Barcelona, and provides information about restaurants that have braille menus, and other services.

The City

The City

The Ramblas and the Old Town

t is a telling comment on Barcelona's character that one can recommend a single street – the **Ramblas** – as a highlight. No day in the city seems complete without a stroll down at least part of what, for Spanish poet Federico García Lorca, was "the only street in the world which I wish would never end". Lined with cafés, shops, restaurants and newspaper kiosks, and thronged by tourists, locals, buskers and performance artists, it's at the heart of Barcelona's life and self-image. There are important buildings and monuments along the way, but undoubtedly it's the street life which is the greatest attraction – and that you're a part of every time you set foot on Spain's most famous thoroughfare.

On either side of the Ramblas spreads Barcelona's **old town** (*ciutat vella*), bordered by Parc de la Ciutadella to the east and the slopes of Montjuïc to the west. Contained within this jumble of streets is a series of neighbourhoods – originally separate medieval parishes – that retain certain distinct characteristics today. By far the greatest concentration of interest is in the highly picturesque **Barri Gòtic**, east of the Ramblas, which curls out from around the cathedral. Here, the city's finest medieval buildings and churches are tucked into shaded squares and skinny alleys, alongside several fascinating museums and the surviving portions of walls and buildings dating back to Roman times. On the west side of the Ramblas is **El Raval**, less of an obvious draw for tourists since it's traditionally been known as the city's red-light area. The neighbourhood still has some very dingy streets and seedy corners, though it's changing rapidly, particularly in the "upper Raval" around Barcelona's notable contemporary art museum, from which ripple out cutting-edge galleries, see-and-be-seen restaurants and fashionable bars.

East of the Barri Gòtic across the broad Via Laietana lie the other two old-town neighbourhoods, split by c/de la Princesa. **Sant Pere**, to the north, is centred on its dramatic concert hall and restored market, while **La Ribera**, to the south, contains two of Barcelona's most popular sights – the graceful church of Santa María del Mar and the showpiece Museu Picasso. Even so, the neighbourhood is possibly even better known now for the hip galleries, workshops, bars and restaurants of the **Born** district at its heart. At the edge of La Ribera spreads **Parc de la Ciutadella**, the city's favourite park, loved by locals and tourists alike for its ornamental lake and gardens, palm-houses, museums and zoo. On lazy summer days here, the old town's historic intrigues and labyrinthine alleys seem a world away.

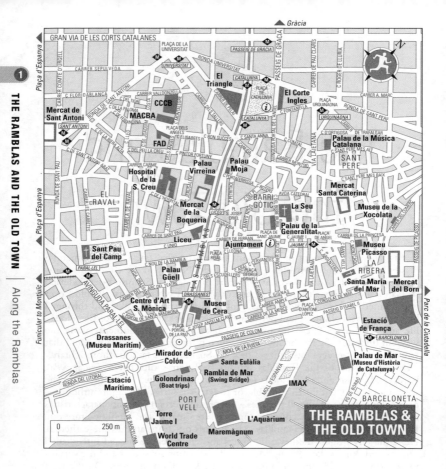

THE RAMBLAS &
THE OLD TOWN

Along the Ramblas

Everyone starts with the **Ramblas**, the city's most famous feature. The name, derived from the Arabic *ramla* (sand), refers to the bed of the seasonal stream that once flowed here. In the dry season, the channel was used as a road, and by the fourteenth century this had been paved over in recognition of its use as a link between the harbour and the old town. In the nineteenth century, benches and decorative trees were added, overlooked by stately balconied buildings, and today – in a city choked with traffic – this wide tree-lined swath is still given over to pedestrians, with cars forced up the narrow strips of road on either side. There are **metro stops** at Catalunya (top of the Ramblas), Liceu (middle) and Drassanes (bottom), or you can walk the entire length in about twenty minutes.

The Ramblas actually comprises five separate sections strung head to tail – from north to south, Rambla Canaletes, Estudis, Sant Josep, Caputxins and

Santa Mònica – though it's rare to hear them referred to as such. However, you will notice changes as you walk down the Ramblas, primarily that the streets on either side become a little less polished – seedier even – as you get closer to the harbour. The shops, meanwhile, reflect the mixed clientele, from patisseries to pizza takeaways, and stores selling handcrafted jewellery to shops full of sombreros, bullfight posters ("your name here"), Simpsons T-shirts and imitation Gaudí ashtrays. On the central avenue under the plane trees you'll find pet canaries, rabbits, tropical fish, flowers, plants, postcards and books. You can buy sunglasses from a blanket stretched out on the ground, cigarettes from itinerant salespeople, have your palm read and your portrait painted, or just listen to the buskers and watch the pavement artists. Human statues are much in evidence and will take any coins you can spare; card and dice sharps, operating from foldaway tables and cardboard boxes, will skin you for much more if you let them.

The show goes on at night, too, as people stroll arm in arm from newspaper stall to café before heading off for a meal or a drink. Later, in the small hours, there are still plenty of folk around, drinking in the late-opening bars or chatting on the street. Drag yourself home with the dawn, and you'll rub shoulders with the street cleaners, watchful policemen and bleary-eyed stallholders.

Plaça de Catalunya

The huge **Plaça de Catalunya** at the top of the Ramblas stands right at the heart of the city, with the old town and port below it, and the planned Eixample district above and beyond. It was laid out in its present form in the 1920s, centred on a formal arrangement of statues, circular fountains and trees, and is the focal point for local events and demonstrations – notably the mass gathering here on New Year's Eve. The most prominent monument is the towering angular slab and bust dedicated to **Francesc Macià**, leader of the Republican Left, parliamentary deputy for Barcelona and first president of the Generalitat, who died in office in 1933. It was commissioned from the pioneer of Catalan avant-garde sculpture, Josep María Subirachs, perhaps best known for his continuing work on the Sagrada Família.

For visitors, an initial orientation point is the massive white-faced **El Corte Inglés** department store on the eastern side of the square, whose ninth-floor cafeteria has some stupendous views. The main tourist office is just across from

The Ramblas statues

You can't move for human statues on the Ramblas, and there's no end either to the inventiveness of the protagonists or to the enthusiasm of the general public for this most inexplicable of art forms. As fads and fashions change, Greek statues and Charlie Chaplins have given way to recent movie or cartoon characters, standing immobile on their little home-made plinths, daring you to catch them out in a blink. Some join in the fun – "Mr Burns" and "Lisa Simpson" posing jauntily for photographs, "Matador" swirling a cape for the camera, "Orange Twirly Girl" windmilling her streamers as money is dropped in front of her. Many are actors (or at least waiters who say they're actors), and others make a claim to art – how else to begin to explain "Silver Cowboy", lounging on the railings at Liceu metro, or "Tree Sprite", clinging chameleon-like to one of the Ramblas plane trees. Then there's the plain weird, like "Lady Under Rock", crushed under a boulder, issuing plaintive shrieks at passersby, or the kennel-dwelling "Human Dog". They all put in long hours on the Ramblas, gratefully receiving small change, though tourists or no tourists, many of them would probably just turn up anyway, lock the bicycle, put down the battered suitcase and strike the pose. What else is a statue going to do?

here, while on the southwest side, over the road from the top of the Ramblas, **El Triangle** shopping centre makes another landmark. Incorporated in its ground floor is the **Café Zurich** a traditional Barcelona meeting place, whose ranks of outdoor tables – patrolled by supercilious waiters – are a day-long draw for beggars, buskers and pan-pipe bands.

Rambla Canaletes and Estudis

Heading down from Plaça de Catalunya, the first two stretches of the Ramblas are **Rambla Canaletes**, with its iron fountain (a drink from which supposedly means you'll never leave Barcelona), and **Rambla Estudis**, named after the university (L'Estudi General) that was sited here until the beginning of the eighteenth century. This part is also known locally as Rambla dels Ocells, as it contains a **bird market**, the little captives squawking away from a line of cages on either side of the street.

George Orwell in Barcelona

Barcelona is a town with a long history of street-fighting.

Homage to Catalonia, 1938

When he first arrived in Barcelona in December 1936, **George Orwell** was much taken with the egalitarian spirit he encountered, as loudspeakers on the Ramblas bellowed revolutionary songs, café waiters refused tips, brothels were collectivized and buildings draped in anarchist flags. After serving as a militiaman on the Aragonese front, Orwell returned on leave to Barcelona in April 1937 to find that everything had changed. Not only had the city lost its revolutionary zeal, but the various leftist parties fighting for the Republican cause had descended into a "miserable internecine scrap". From the **Hotel Continental** (Ramblas 138), where Orwell and his wife Eileen stayed, he observed the deteriorating situation with mounting despair, and when street-fighting broke out in May, Orwell was directly caught up in it. As a member of the Workers Party of Marxist Unification (POUM), Orwell became a target when pro-Communist Assault Guards seized the city telephone exchange near Plaça de Catalunya and began to try to break up the workers' militias. Orwell left the hotel for the **POUM headquarters** (Ramblas 128) just down the street, sited in the building that's now the *Rivoli Ramblas* hotel – a plaque here by the *Banco Popular* sign honours murdered POUM leader Andrés Nin ("victim of Stalinism"). With the trams on the Ramblas abandoned by their drivers as the shooting started, and Assault Guards occupying the adjacent **Café Moka** (Ramblas 126), Orwell holed up with a rifle for three days in the rotunda of the **Teatro Poliorama** (Ramblas 115) opposite, in order to defend the POUM HQ if necessary. Breakfasting sparsely on goat's cheese bought from the Boqueria market (its stalls largely empty), concerned about Eileen, and caught up in rumour and counter-rumour, Orwell considered it one of the most unbearable periods of his life.

When the fighting subsided, Orwell returned to the front, where he was shot through the throat by a fascist sniper. Yet that was only the start of his troubles. Recuperating in a sanatorium near Tibidabo, he learned that the POUM had been declared illegal, its members rounded up and imprisoned. He avoided arrest by sleeping out in gutted churches and derelict buildings and playing the part of a tourist by day, looking "as bourgeois as possible", while scrawling POUM graffiti in defiance on the walls of fancy restaurants. Eventually, with passports and papers arranged by the British consul, Orwell and Eileen escaped Barcelona by train – back to the "deep, deep sleep of England" and the writing of his passionate war memoir, *Homage to Catalonia*.

It seems hard to believe, but this part of the Ramblas became a combat zone during the Spanish Civil War as the city erupted into factionalism. George Orwell (see box opposite) was caught in the crossfire between the *Café Moka* – the current café of the same name is a modern replacement – and the Poliorama cinema, now the **Teatro Poliorama**. This was built in 1863 as the Royal Academy of Science and Arts, and restored as a theatre in 1985. Further down on the right, the **Església de Betlem** (daily 8am-6pm), built in 1681 in Baroque style for the Jesuits, was completely gutted during the Civil War as anarchists sacked the city's churches at will – an activity of which Orwell quietly approved. Consequently, the interior is plain in the extreme, though the main façade on c/del Carme sports a fine sculpted portal and relief.

Opposite the church, the arcaded **Palau Moja** at no. 188 dates from the late eighteenth century and still retains an exterior staircase and elegant great hall. The ground floor of the building is now a cultural bookshop, while the restored interior is open for art and other **exhibitions** relating to all things Catalan (Tues–Sat 11am–8pm, Sun 11am–3pm; usually free; ☎933 162 740) – the entrance is around the corner in c/Portaferrissa. Take a look, too, at the illustrated tiles above the **fountain** at the start of c/Portaferrissa, which show the medieval gate (the Porta Ferriça) and market that were once sited here. The streets to the west, towards Avinguda del Portal del Àngel, are good for shopping, especially for clothes.

Palau de la Virreina

The graceful eighteenth-century **Palau de la Virreina** stands at no. 99 (ⓂLiceu), on the corner of c/del Carme, set back slightly from the Ramblas. Commissioned by a Peruvian viceroy, Manuel Amat, and named after the wife who survived him, its five Ramblas-facing bays are adorned with pilasters and Rococo windows. Today the palace is used by the city council's culture department, with a ground-floor shop (Tues–Sat 10am–8.30pm) featuring locally produced *objets d'art* and souvenirs and a walk-in **information centre** and ticket office (see p.28) for cultural events. Two galleries are used for changing **exhibitions** of contemporary art and photography (Tues–Fri 11am–2pm & 4–8.30pm, Sat 11am–8.30pm, Sun 11am–3pm; admission usually charged; ☎933 017 775, ⓦwww.bcn.es/virreinaexposicions), while in the courtyard are usually displayed the city's two official **Carnival giants** (*gegants vells*), representing the celebrated thirteenth-century Catalan king, Jaume I, and his wife Violant. The origin of Catalunya's outsized (five-metre-high) Carnival figures is unclear, though they probably once formed part of the entertainment at medieval travelling fairs. The first record of specific city giants is in 1601 – they were later used to entertain the city's orphans but are now an integral part of Barcelona's festival parades.

La Boqueria and around

Beyond the Palau de la Virreina starts **Rambla Sant Josep**, the switch in names marked by the sudden profusion of flower stalls – it's sometimes known as Rambla de les Flors. The city's glorious main food market is over to the right, officially the Mercat Sant Josep though referred to locally as **La Boqueria** (Mon–Sat 8am–8pm; ☎933 182 584, ⓦwww.boqueria.info). Built on the site of a former convent between 1836 and 1840, the cavernous hall stretches back from the high wrought-iron entrance arch facing the Ramblas. It's a riot of noise and colour, as popular with locals who come here to shop daily as with snap-happy tourists. Everything radiates out from the central banks of fish and seafood stalls – great piles of fruit and vegetables, bunches of herbs and pots of spices, baskets of wild mushrooms, mounds of cheese and sausage, racks of bread, hanging hams, and meat counters dripping blood into the gutters below. If you're going to buy, do some browsing first, as the flagship fruit and veg stalls by the entrance tend to have higher prices than those further inside. There are also some excellent stand-up **snack bars** in here, open from dawn onwards for the traders – the *Pinotxo* (see p.182) is the most famous.

Past the market is the part of the Ramblas known as **Plaça de la Boqueria** marked by a large round **mosaic by Joan Miró** in the middle of the pavement. This is one of a number of public works in the city by the artist, who was born just a couple of minutes' walk away in the Barri Gòtic (there's a plaque to mark the building on Passatge del Credit, off c/de Ferran). Close by, at Ramblas 82, Josep Vilaseca's **Casa Bruno Quadros** – the lower floor is now the Caixa Sabadell – was built in the 1890s to house an umbrella store. Its unusual façade is decorated with a green dragon and Oriental designs, and scattered with parasols. On the other side of the Ramblas at no. 83 there are more *modernista* flourishes on the **Antiga Casa Figueras** (1902), which overdoses on stained glass and mosaics, and sports a corner relief of a female reaper. It's now a renowned bakery-café (see p.175).

Gran Teatre del Liceu

Facing the Ramblas at c/de Sant Pau is the restored **Gran Teatre del Liceu** (ⓂLiceu), Barcelona's celebrated opera house, which was founded as a private theatre in 1847. It was rebuilt after a fire in 1861 to become Spain's grandest theatre, regarded as a bastion of the city's late nineteenth-century commercial and intellectual classes – it still has no royal box in a nod to its bourgeois antecedents. The Liceu was devastated again in 1893, when an anarchist threw two bombs into the stalls during a production of *William Tell*. He was acting in revenge for the recent execution of a fellow anarchist assassin – twenty people died in the bombing. It then burned down for the third time in 1994, when a worker's blowtorch set fire to the scenery during last-minute alterations to an opera set.

The latest restoration of the lavishly decorated interior took five years, and the opera house opened again in 1999. **Tours** depart from the modern extension, the **Espai Liceu** (tours daily 10am, 11.30am, noon & 1pm; €4/6 ☎934 859 914, ⓦwww.liceubarcelona.com), which also houses a music and gift shop and café. You'll learn most on the more expensive 45-minute 10am guided tour; the other, cheaper tours are self-guided and last only twenty minutes. Highlights include the classically inspired Salon of Mirrors, unaffected by any of the fires and thus largely original in decor, and the impressive gilded auditorium containing almost 2300 seats – making it one of the world's largest opera houses. Offered as an option only on the 10am tour is the chance to visit the private rooms of the **Cercle del Liceu** (€3 extra), the opera house's members' club. The highly decorative rooms are certainly worth seeing, inlaid with burnished wood, and featuring tiled floors and painted ceilings, and culminating in an extraordinary *modernista* games room, illuminated by a celebrated series of paintings by Ramon Casas (see p.107) representing Catalan music and dance. For most of its 160-year history the Cercle membership was restricted to men, until challenged by **Montserrat Caballé**, who won a court battle to become one of the first women to join. They could hardly refuse. Caballé was born in Barcelona (1933), studied at the Liceu conservatory and made her Liceu debut in 1962, later becoming widely acknowledged as Spain's greatest soprano with a string of extraordinary performances in the 1960s and 1970s.

If you want to attend an opera or recital you should book well in advance – see p.210 for details. Meanwhile, the traditional meeting-place for post-performance refreshments for audience and performers alike is the famous **Café de l'Opera**, just across the Ramblas.

From the Liceu to the harbour

After the Liceu, attractions just off the Ramblas include the Palau Güell down c/Nou de la Rambla and, on the opposite side, the lovely Plaça Reial. Sticking with the Ramblas itself, the avenue widens out as it heads for the harbour, with the two final attractions sited on the last named stretch of the Ramblas, the **Rambla de Santa Mònica** (Ⓜ Drassanes). On the right, at no. 7, the Augustinian convent of Santa Mònica dates originally from 1626, making it the oldest building on the Ramblas. It was entirely remodelled in the 1980s and now houses the **Centre d'Art Santa Mònica** (Tues–Sat 11am–8pm, Sun 11am–3pm; free; ☏933 162 810, ⓦ www.cultura.gencat.net/casm), which displays temporary exhibitions of contemporary art – the current programme is detailed on the website. There's also a city events information office at the centre, and a café-bar upstairs. Pavement artists and palm readers set up stalls outside here on the Ramblas, augmented on weekend afternoons by a small street market selling jewellery and ornaments.

The city's wax museum, the **Museu de Cera** (July–Sept daily 10am–10pm; Oct–June Mon–Fri 10am–1.30pm & 4–7.30pm, Sat & Sun 11am–2pm & 4.30–8.30pm; €6.65; ☏933 172 649, ⓦ www.museocerabcn.com), is located on the opposite side of the Ramblas, at nos. 4–6, in an impressive nineteenth-century bank building; the entrance is along Ptge. de Banca. This presents an ever more ludicrous series of tableaux in the building's cavernous salons and gloomy corridors, depicting recitals, meetings and parlour gatherings attended by an anachronistic – not to say perverse – collection of personalities, film characters, public figures, heroes, villains, artists and musicians. Thus Yasser Arafat lectures Churchill, Hitler and Bill Clinton, while a concert by Catalan cellist Pau Casals numbers Princess Diana and Mother Theresa among the audience. Needless to say, it's extremely ropey and enormously amusing, culminating in cheesy underwater and space capsules and an unpleasant "Terror" room. You also won't want to miss the museum's extraordinary grotto-bar, the *Bosc de les Fades* (see p.201).

By now, you've almost reached the foot of the Ramblas, passing Drassanes metro station to be confronted by the column at the very bottom of the avenue that's topped by a statue of Columbus. For this, the neighbouring maritime museum and the rest of the harbour area, see the next chapter.

The Barri Gòtic

The **Barri Gòtic**, or Gothic Quarter (Ⓜ Jaume I), forms the very heart of the old town, spreading out from the east side of the Ramblas. Within lies a remarkable concentration of beautiful medieval buildings dating principally from the fourteenth and fifteenth centuries, when Barcelona reached the height of her commercial prosperity before being absorbed into the burgeoning kingdom

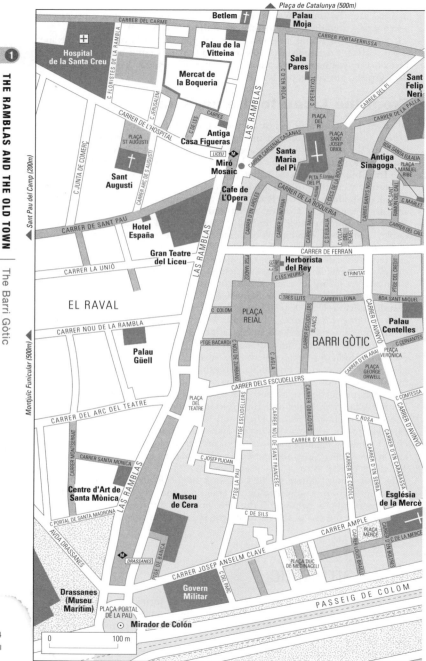

Plaça de Catalunya (500m)

Betlem

Palau Moja

CARRER DEL CARME

CARRER PORTAFERRISSA

Hospital de la Santa Creu

Palau de la Vitteina

Sala Pares

Sant Felip Neri

Mercat de la Boqueria

CARRER DE L'HOSPITAL

LAS RAMBLAS

CARRER DE LA PALLA

C. DE'N ROCA

C. PETRITXOL

CARRER DEL PI

C. FLORISTES DE LA RAMBLA

C. DE LES

C. JERUSALEM

PLAÇA ST AUGUSTI

CABRES

PLAÇA DEL PI

BDA SANTA EULALIA

Antiga Casa Figueras

Santa Maria del Pi

PLAÇA SANT JOSEP ORIOL

Antiga Sinagoga

PLAÇA MANUEL RIBE

CARRER CARDENAL CASANAS

LICEU

Miró Mosaic

Sant Augusti

CARRER ARC DE S. AGUSTI

PLTA DEL PI

C. LLEBRE

C. STA ANNA

C. CECS DE LA BOQUERIA

C. ARC SANT RAMON DEL CALL

Cafe de L'Opera

CARRER DE LA BOQUERIA

C. MARLET

C. JUNTA DE COMERÇ

CARRER DE FERRAN

CARRER DEL CALL

Hotel España

CARRER D'EN ARLES

CARRER QUINTANA

CARRER RAURIC

C. S. EULALIA

C. BANYS NOU

PTGE DEL CREDIT

CARRER DE SANT PAU

LAS RAMBLAS

C. VOLTA DEL REMEI

Gran Teatre del Liceu

Herborista del Rey

C. TRINITAT

CARRER LA UNIÓ

C. DEL VIDRE

C. DE LA LLUM

C. LES HEURES

C TRES LLITS

CARRER LLEONA

BDA SANT MIQUEL

EL RAVAL

C COLOM

PLAÇA REIAL

CARRER ESCUDELLERS BLANCS

Palau Centelles

CARRER NOU DE LA RAMBLA

BARRI GÒTIC

C. CERVANTES

PTGE BACARDI

CARRER D'AVINYÓ

PLAÇA VERÓNICA

Palau Güell

C AGLA

C. REIAL OVITRAL

PLAÇA GEORGE ORWELL

CARRER D'EN ARAI

CARRER DEL ARC DEL TEATRE

CARRER DELS ESCUDELLERS

C COMTESSA

PLAÇA DEL TEATRE

PTGE ESCUDELLERS

CARRER OBRADORS

C. ROSA

CARRER D'AVINYÓ

CARRER MONTSERRAT

CARRER D'ENRULL

CARRER D'EN CARRABASSA

CARRER SANTA MONICA

C JOSEP PIJOAN

CARRER NOU DE SANT FRANCESC

CARRER D'EN SERRA

Esglèsia de la Mercè

Centre d'Art de Santa Mònica

PTGE LA PAU

CARRER DE CODOLS

Museu de Cera

C DE SILS

CARRER AMPLE

CARRER LLUIS BRAILE

LAS RAMBLAS

C. PORTAL DE SANTA MADRONA

PLAÇA MERCÈ

C DE LA MERCÈ

C DE BOLTRES

AVDA DRASSANES

DRASSANES

PTGE DE BANCA

CARRER JOSEP ANSELM CLAVE

C DEL PARC

PLAÇA DUC DE MEDINACELI

PASSEIG DE COLOM

Drassanes (Museu Marítim)

Govern Militar

PLAÇA PORTAL DE LA PAU

Mirador de Colón

0   100 m

Sant Pau del Camp (200m)

Montjuïc Funicular (500m)

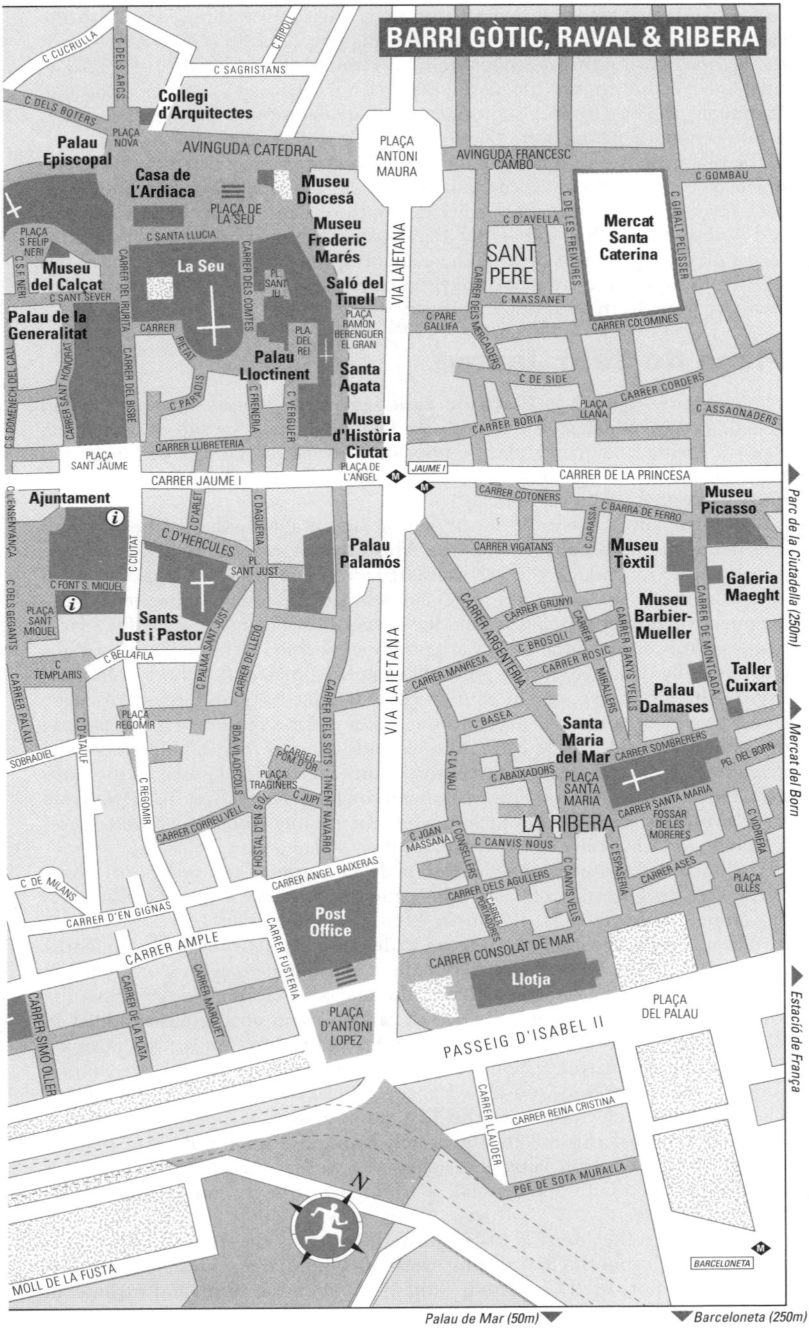
BARRI GÒTIC, RAVAL & RIBERA
C CUCRULLA
C DELS ARCS
C RIPOLL
C SAGRISTANS
Collegi d'Arquitectes
C DELS BOTERS
PLAÇA NOVA
Palau Episcopal
AVINGUDA CATEDRAL
PLAÇA ANTONI MAURA
AVINGUDA FRANCESC CAMBO
C GOMBAU
Casa de L'Ardiaca
Museu Diocesá
PLAÇA DE LA SEU
PLAÇA S.FELIP NERI
C SANTA LLUCIA
Museu Frederic Marés
VIA LAIETANA
C D'AVELLA
C DE LES FREIXURES
Mercat Santa Caterina
C GIRALT PELISSER
C S.F. NERI
Museu del Calçat
C SANT SEVER
La Seu
CARRER DEL IRURITA
CARRER DELS COMTES
PL. SANT IU
Saló del Tinell
SANT PERE
CARRER DELS MERCADERS
C MASSANET
Palau de la Generalitat
CARRER
PIETAT
PLAÇA RAMON BERENGUER EL GRAN
PL. DEL REI
C PARE GALLIFA
CARRER COLOMINES
Palau Lloctinent
Santa Agata
C DE SIDE
CARRER CORDERS
C S. DOMENECH DEL CALL
CARRER SANT HONORAT
CARRER DEL BISBE
C PARADIS
C FRENERIA
C VERGUER
PLAÇA LLANA
C ASSAONADERS
Museu d'Història Ciutat
CARRER BORIA
CARRER LLIBRETERIA
PLAÇA SANT JAUME
PLAÇA DE L'ANGEL
JAUME I
CARRER JAUME I
CARRER DE LA PRINCESA
CARRER COTONERS
C BARRA DE FERRO
Museu Picasso
C L'ENSENYANÇA
Ajuntament
C D'ARLET
C DAGUERIA
C CARASSA
C D'HERCULES
C CIUTAT
PL. SANT JUST
Palau Palamós
CARRER VIGATANS
Museu Tèxtil
Galeria Maeght
C FONT S. MIQUEL
CARRER GRUNYI
CARRER ARGENTERIA
Museu Barbier-Mueller
C DELS GEGANTS
PLAÇA SANT MIQUEL
Sants Just i Pastor
C PALMA SANT JUST
CARRER DE LLEDÓ
C BROSOLI
CARRER
CARRER ROSIC
CARRER BANYS VELLS
CARRER DE MONTCADA
C BELLAFILA
C TEMPLARIS
CARRER MANRESA
MIRALLERS
Taller Cuixart
Palau Dalmases
CARRER PALAU
C D'ATAULF
PLAÇA REGOMIR
CARRER DELS SOTS - TINENT NAVARRO
C BASEA
Santa Maria del Mar
CARRER SOMBRERERS
SOBRADIEL
CARRER POM D'OR
C LA NAU
PG. DEL BORN
C REGOMIR
BDA VILADECOLS
PLAÇA TRAGINERS
C JUPI
C ABAIXADORS
PLAÇA SANTA MARIA
CARRER SANTA MARIA
C VIDRIERA
CARRER CORREU VELL
C HOSTAL D'EN SOL
LA RIBERA
FOSSAR DE LES MORERES
C JOAN MASSANA
C CONSELLERS
C CANVIS NOUS
C ESPASERIA
C DE MILANS
CARRER ANGEL BAIXERAS
CARRER ASES
PLAÇA OLLES
C CANVIS VELLS
CARRER DELS AGULLERS
CARRER PORTADORES
CARRER D'EN GIGNAS
Post Office
CARRER AMPLE
CARRER FUSTERIA
CARRER CONSOLAT DE MAR
Llotja
CARRER SIMÓ OLLER
CARRER DE LA PLATA
CARRER MARQUET
PLAÇA D'ANTONI LOPEZ
PLAÇA DEL PALAU
PASSEIG D'ISABEL II
CARRER LLAUDER
CARRER REINA CRISTINA
PGE DE SOTA MURALLA
N
MOLL DE LA FUSTA
BARCELONETA
Parc de la Ciutadella (250m)
Mercat del Born
Estació de França
Palau de Mar (50m)
Barceloneta (250m)

of Castile. It will take the best part of a day to see everything here, with the cathedral – La Seu – a particular highlight, and you certainly won't want to miss the archeological remains at the Museu d'Història de la Ciutat or the unclassifiable collections of the Museu Frederic Marès. That said, sauntering through the medieval alleys or simply sitting at a café table in one of the lovely squares is just as much an attraction.

The picture-postcard images of the Barri Gòtic are largely based on the streets north of c/de Ferran and c/de Jaume I, where tourists throng the boutiques, bars, restaurants, museums and galleries. South of here – from Plaça Reial and c/d'Avinyo to the harbour – the Barri Gòtic is rather more traditional (or sometimes just plain run-down). There are no specific sights or museums in this section, though there are plenty of great cafés, tapas bars and restaurants – just take care at night in the poorly lit streets.

Plaça de Sant Jaume

The quarter is centred on **Plaça de Sant Jaume**, a spacious square at the end of c/de Ferran, which runs east from the Ramblas. Once the site of Barcelona's Roman forum and marketplace – the foundations of Roman buildings and houses lie under the square - it's now the traditional point of call for demonstrations, gatherings and local festivals.

The square contains two of the city's most significant buildings. On the south side stands the restored town hall, the **Ajuntament**, parts of which date from as early as 1373, though the Neoclassical façade is nineteenth-century, added when the square was laid out. You get a much better idea of the grandeur of the original structure by nipping around the corner, down c/de la Ciutat, for a view of the former main entrance. It's a typically exuberant Catalan-Gothic facade, but was badly damaged during renovations in the nineteenth century. On Sundays (10am–2pm; free; entrance on c/Font de Sant Miquel; English-language leaflet provided) you're allowed into the building for a self-guided tour around the rather splendid marble halls, galleries and staircases. The highlights are the magnificent restored fourteenth-century council chamber, known as the **Saló de Cent**, and the dramatic historical murals by Josep Maria Sert in the **Saló de les Cròniques** (Hall of Chronicles), while the ground-floor courtyard features sculpted works by some of the most famous Catalan artists.

Right across the square rises the **Palau de la Generalitat**, traditional home of the Catalan government, from where the short-lived Catalan Republic was proclaimed in April 1931. Begun in 1418, this presents its best – or at least its oldest – aspect around the side on c/del Bisbe, where the early fifteenth-century facade by Marc Safont contains a spirited medallion portraying St George and the Dragon. (Incidentally, the enclosed Gothic bridge across the narrow street – the so-called Bridge of Sighs – is an anachronism, added in 1928, though it's at one with its surroundings and features on many a postcard of the "Gothic" quarter. It connects the Generalitat with the former canons' houses across c/del Bispe, now used as the official residence of the president.) There's a beautiful cloister on the first floor with superb coffered ceilings, while opening off this are the intricately worked chapel and salon of Sant Jordi (St George, patron saint of Catalunya as well as England), and an upper courtyard planted with orange trees, overhung by gargoyles and peppered with presidential busts.

You can visit the interior on a **guided tour** on the second and fourth Sunday of each month (10am–2pm, every 30–60min; free; entrance on c/Sant Honorat, passport or ID required) – these last about an hour, and include an introductory video about the Catalan state and its history, though only one or two of the tours each day are conducted in English. The Generalitat is also open to the public on the **Dia de Sant Jordi**, or Saint George's Day (April 23; expect a two-hour wait), which has been conflated with a Catalan version of St Valentine's Day – it's traditional to exchange books and roses, available from stalls on Plaça de Sant Jaume and the Ramblas.

Plaça de Sant Just

Behind the Ajuntament, off c/de la Ciutat, **Plaça de Sant Just** is a medieval gem, sporting a restored fourteenth-century fountain and flanked by unassuming palaces. Highlight here is the **Església dels Sants Just i Pastor** (open for Mass Mon–Sat 7.30pm, Sun at noon, and occasional other times), whose very plain stone facade belies the rich stained glass and elaborate chapel decoration inside (enter from the back, at c/de la Ciutat; the main doors on Pl. de Sant Just are open less often). The name commemorates the city's earliest Christian martyrs, and it's claimed (though there's no real evidence) that this is the oldest parish church site in Barcelona, held to have first supported a foundation at the beginning of the ninth century; the restored interior, though, dates from the mid-fourteenth century. In the late Middle Ages it was the only place where Jews could swear legal oaths in deals with Christians, and even today a last will and testament declared verbally here has the full force of a written document.

Plaça Reial and around

Southwest of Plaça de Sant Jaume, many people's first old-town halt is the elegant nineteenth-century **Plaça Reial** – it's hidden behind an archway, off the Ramblas (to the left, walking down; ⓂLiceu) and is surprisingly easy to miss. Laid out in around 1850 by Francesc Daniel Molina, the Italianate square is studded with tall palm trees and decorated iron lamps (by the young Gaudí), bordered by high, pastel-coloured arcaded buildings, and centred on a fountain depicting the Three Graces. Taking in the sun at one of the benches puts you in strange company – punks, bikers, buskers, Catalan eccentrics, tramps and bemused tourists taking a coffee at one of the pavement cafés. It used to be a bit dodgy in Plaça Reial, but most of the really unsavoury characters have been driven off over the years as tourists have staked an increasing claim to the square. There's an almost permanent police presence, and the surrounding bars, clubs and restaurants are becoming increasingly more upmarket – a social indicator is the office of MBM Arquitectes (Pl. Reial 18, next to *Tarantos*), the designers of many of the contemporary city's flagship development projects. If you pass through Plaça Reial on a Sunday morning, look in on the **coin and stamp market** (10am–2pm).

The arcaded passageways connecting the square with the surrounding streets throw up a few interesting sights. Tucked away on the north side on c/del Vidre is the quirky **Herborista del Rey**, an early nineteenth-century herbalist's shop, while if you walk down the opposing alley on the south side of the square you'll emerge on c/dels Escudellers, right opposite the turning spits of **Los Caracoles** restaurant, whose ranks of grilled chickens make a good photograph. **Carrer dels Escudellers** itself was once a thriving red-light street but it has gradually hauled itself up by its bootlaces and teeters on the edge of respectability. Bars and restaurants around here attract a youthful clientele, nowhere more so than those flanking **Plaça George Orwell**, at the eastern end of c/dels Escudellers. The wedge-shaped square was created by levelling an old-town block – a

△ Plaça Reial

favoured tactic in Barcelona to let in a bit of light – and it has quickly become a hangout for the grunge crowd.

Carrer d'Avinyo and La Mercè

Carrer d'Avinyo, running south from c/de Ferran towards the harbour, cuts through the most atmospheric part of the southern Barri Gòtic. Again, it used to be a red-light district of some renown, littered with brothels and bars, and frequented by the young Picasso, whose family moved into the area in 1895 (see box on p.71). It still looks the part – a narrow thoroughfare lined with dark overhanging buildings – but the fashionable cafés and boutiques tell the story of its recent gentrification. The locals aren't overly enamoured of the influx of bar-crawling fun-seekers – banners and notices along the length of this and neighbouring streets plead with visitors to keep the noise down.

Carrer d'Avinyo ends at the junction with **Carrer Ample** (Wide Street), the latter an aristocratic address in the eighteenth century. Here, in the neighbourhood known as **La Mercè**, lived nobles and merchants enriched by Barcelona's maritime trade, though most fashionable families took the opportunity to move north to the Eixample later in the nineteenth century. The streets of La Mercè – just a block from the harbour – took on an earthier hue, and for years this has been a place to come and frequent the characteristic old-style **taverns** known as *tascas* or *bodegas*. Carrers Ample, Mercè and d'en Gignas sport a fine array of these (see pp.181–182 for reviews of the best), most of them defiantly unfashionable, though even here are signs of encroaching regeneration in the shape of new bars and boutiques.

At Plaça de la Mercè, the eighteenth-century **Església de la Mercè** is the focus of the city's biggest annual celebrations, the Festa de la Mercè every September, dedicated to the co-patroness of Barcelona. The church was burned in 1936 but the gilt side-chapels, stained-glass medallions and apse murals have been authentically restored. The square outside was remodelled in the twentieth century around its statue of Neptune, though the more pleasing local square is the older **Plaça Duc de Medinaceli**, a block to the west, with its palms and commemorative cast-iron column saluting a Catalan admiral.

La Seu

North of Plaça de Sant Jaume, Barcelona's cathedral, **La Seu** (daily 8am–12.45pm & 5.15–7.30pm, cathedral and cloister free; otherwise 1–5pm, €4, includes entrance to all sections; ⊛www.catedralbcn.org), is one of the great Gothic buildings of Spain. Located on a site previously occupied by a Roman temple and then an early Christian basilica, it was begun in 1298 and finished in 1448, with one notable exception commented on by Richard Ford in 1845: "The principal façade is unfinished, with a bold front poorly painted in stucco, although the rich chapter have for three centuries received a fee on every marriage for this very purpose of completing it." Perhaps goaded into action, the authorities set to and completed the facade within a ten-year period in the 1880s. Some critics complain that this delay cost the cathedral its architectural harmony, though the facade is Gothic enough for most tastes – and is seen to startling effect at night when it's floodlit.

The cathedral is dedicated to the city's second patroness, **Santa Eulàlia** (known as Laia in Barcelona), a young girl brutally martyred by the Romans in 304 AD for daring to prefer Christianity. Her remains were first placed in the original portside church of Santa María del Mar in La Ribera, which explains why she's also patron saint of local sailors and seafarers. In 874 Laia was re-interred in the cathedral and her ornate alabaster tomb rests in a crypt beneath the high altar. Among the finest of the carved and painted tombs of the 29 **side-chapels** are those reputedly belonging to Ramon Berenguer I (Count of Barcelona from 1035 to 1076) and his wife Almodis, but which actually hold the remains of an earlier count and Petronila, the Aragonese princess whose betrothal to Ramon Berenguer IV united Aragon and Barcelona.

The most renowned part of the cathedral is its magnificent fourteenth-century **cloister** (Mon–Sat 8.30am–12.30pm & 5.15–7pm, Sun 9am–1pm & 5.15–7pm), which looks over a lush tropical garden complete with soaring palm trees and – more unusually – a gaggle of honking geese. If they disturb the tranquillity of the scene, they do so for a purpose: white geese have been kept here for over five hundred years, either (depending on which story you believe) to reflect the virginity of Santa Eulàlia, or as a reminder of the erstwhile Roman splendour of Barcelona (geese having been kept on the Capitoline Hill in Rome). Finally, don't leave the cathedral without ascending to the **roof** (Mon–Fri 10.30am–12.30pm & 5.15–6.30pm, Sat 10.30am–12.30pm; €2) – the lift (*ascensor als terrats*) is just to the left of the crypt steps – which provides intimate views of the cathedral towers and surrounding Gothic buildings and spires. It's by no means the highest view in town, but nowhere else do you feel so at the heart of medieval Barcelona.

Plaça de la Seu and Plaça Nova

Outside the cathedral, across Plaça de la Seu, is the **Museu Diocesà** (Tues–Sat 10am–2pm & 5–8pm, Sun 11am–2pm; €5; ☎933 152 213), which occupies the soaring spaces of a hexagonal fourth-century Roman tower that later formed part of the cathedral almshouse (La Pia Almoina). It's been beautifully adapted, with exhibition space spread across four floors, and with views over the cathedral square from the top. The impressive permanent collection is of religious art, artefacts and church treasures from around Barcelona, notably a series of frescoes of the Apocalypse (1122 AD) from Sant Salvador in Polinyà and a series of graphic retables, including one of St Bartholomew being skinned alive.

Plaça de la Seu itself is a regular Sunday venue for the dancing of the *sardana*, the Catalan national dance (see p.211), while in front of here, the wide, pedestrianized Avinguda de la Catedral hosts an **antiques market** every Thursday, and a **Christmas craft fair** every December.

Flanking the cathedral, on the west side of Plaça de la Seu, are two fifteenth-century buildings closely associated with it. The **Casa de l'Ardiaca** (once the archdeacon's residence, now the city archives) encloses a tiny cloistered and tiled courtyard with a small fountain. To the right of the badly worn Renaissance gateway on c/de Santa Llúcia look for the curious carved swallow-and-tortoise postbox. The **Palau Episcopal**, just beyond at the western end of c/de Santa Llúcia, was the bishop's palace and built on a grander scale altogether. Though you're not allowed inside, you can go as far as the courtyard to see the fine outdoor stairway; there's a patio at the top with Romanesque wall paintings. Next to the Palau Episcopal, some of the city's remaining **Roman walls** are clearly visible – they once entirely enclosed the Barri Gòtic, though were largely pulled down in the nineteenth century.

The large **Plaça Nova**, facing the cathedral, marks one of the medieval entrances to the old town – north of it, you're fast entering the wider streets and more regular contours of the modern city. Even if you're sticking with the Barri Gòtic for now, walk over to study the frieze surmounting the modern College of Architects, the **Collegi d'Arquitectes** on the other side of the square. Designed in 1960 from sketches supplied by Picasso, it has a crude, almost graffiti-like quality, at odds with the more stately buildings to the side. Picasso himself refused to come to Spain to oversee the work, unwilling to return to his home country while Franco was still in power.

Plaça del Rei and around

The most concentrated batch of historic monuments in the Barri Gòtic is the grouping around the neat **Plaça del Rei**, behind the cathedral apse. The square was once the courtyard of the palace of the counts of Barcelona, and across it stairs climb to the great fourteenth-century **Saló del Tinell**, the palace's main hall. It was on the steps leading from the Saló del Tinell into the Plaça del Rei that Ferdinand and Isabella stood to receive Columbus on his triumphant return from his famous voyage of 1492. With the old town streets packed, Columbus advanced in procession with the monarchs to the palace, where he presented the queen with booty from the trip – exotic birds, sweet potatoes and six Indians (actually Haitians, taken on board on Columbus' return). The hall itself is a fine example of secular Gothic architecture, with interior arches spanning 17m. At one time the Spanish Inquisition met here, taking full advantage of the popular belief that the walls would move if a lie was spoken. Nowadays it hosts temporary exhibitions, while concerts are occasionally held in the hall or outside in the square. The palace buildings also include the beautiful fourteenth-century **Capella de Santa Àgata**, with its tall single nave and fine Gothic retable, and the romantic Renaissance **Torre del Rei Martí,** which rises above one corner of the square. There's currently no public access to the tower, but the interiors of the hall and chapel can be seen during a visit to the Museu d'Història de la Ciutat (see opposite).

The mid-sixteenth-century **Palau del Lloctinent**, the former viceroy's palace, has a facade facing the Plaça del Rei and another fine courtyard with staircase and coffered ceiling (enter on c/dels Comtes). Around the corner from here, down c/Paradís at no. 10, the little interior courtyard of the Centre Excursionista de Catalunya conceals some original Corinthian columns from the city's **Temple Romà d'Agusti** (usually open Tues–Sat 10am–2pm & 4–8pm, Sun 10am–3pm, though may vary; free). To see the best-preserved sections of Barcelona's **Roman city walls**, walk around to Plaça Ramon Berenguer el Gran, at Via Laietana. Some of the fourth-century walls and towers here are over 13m high, and back onto the chapel of Santa Agata on Plaça del Rei.

Museu d'Història de la Ciutat

The building that closes off the rest of Plaça del Rei houses the splendid **Museu d'Història de la Ciutat** (June–Sept Tues–Sat 10am–8pm, Sun & hols 10am–3pm; Oct–May Tues–Sat 10am–2pm & 4–8pm, Sun & hols 10am–3pm; €5, first Sat of the month free; ☎933 151 111, @www.museuhistoria.bcn.es). The museum's crucial draw is its underground archeological section – nothing less than the extensive remains of the Roman city of Barcino. Descending in the lift (the floor indicator shows "12 BC"), you are deposited onto walkways that run along the 4000 square metres excavated thus far, stretching under Plaça del Rei and the surrounding streets as far as the cathedral. The remains date from the first century BC to the sixth century AD and reflect the transition from Roman to Visigothic rule – at the end of the sixth century, a church was erected on top of the old Roman salt-fish factory, the foundations of which are preserved down here almost in its entirety. Not much survives above chest height, but explanatory diagrams show the extent of the streets, walls and buildings – from lookout towers to laundries – while models, mosaics, murals and displays of excavated goods help flesh out the reality of daily life in Barcino.

Museu Frederic Marès

Another extraordinary display greets visitors in the **Museu Frederic Marès** (Tues–Sat 10am–7pm, Sun 10am–3pm; €3, Wed afternoon & first Sun of month free; ☎933 105 800, @www.museumares.bcn.es), which occupies a further wing of the old royal palace, behind Plaça del Rei; the entrance is through Plaça de Sant Iu, off c/dels Comtes. The large arcaded courtyard, studded with orange trees, is one of the most romantic in the old town, and the **summer café** here (*Café d'Estiu*, open April–Oct; Tues–Sun) makes a perfect place to take a break from sightseeing.

Frederic Marès (1893–1991) was a sculptor, painter and restorer who more or less single-handedly restored, often not entirely accurately, Catalunya's decaying medieval treasures in the early twentieth century. The **ground** and **basement floors** of the museum consist of his personal collection of medieval sculpture – an important body of work that includes a comprehensive collection of wooden crucifixes showing the stylistic development of this form from the twelfth to the fifteenth century. There are also antiquities, from Roman busts to Hellenistic terracotta lamps, while the craftsmanship of medieval masons is displayed in a series of rooms focusing on carved doorways, cloister fragments, sculpted capitals and alabaster tombs. However, it's the **upper two floors**, housing Marès' personal collectibles, that tend to make jaws drop. These present an incredible retrospective jumble gathered during fifty years of travel, with entire rooms devoted to keys and locks, pipes, cigarette cards and snuffboxes, fans, gloves and brooches, playing cards, draughtsmen's tools, walking sticks, dolls' houses, toy theatres, old gramophones and archaic bicycles, to list just a sample of what's on show. In the artist's library on the second floor, some of Marès' own reclining nudes, penitent saints and bridling stags give an insight into his more orthodox work.

Església de Santa María del Pi and around

With the cathedral area and Plaça del Rei sucking in every visitor at some point during the day, the third focus of attraction is to the west, around the church of Santa María del Pi – five minutes' walk from the cathedral or just two minutes from the Ramblas (ⓜLiceu).

The fourteenth-century **Església de Santa María del Pi** (daily 9.30am–1 or 2pm & 5–8.30pm, ⓦwww.parroquiadelpi.com) stands at the heart of three delightful little squares. Burned out in 1936, and restored in the 1960s, the church boasts a Romanesque door but is mainly Catalan-Gothic in style, with just a single nave with chapels between the buttresses. The rather plain interior only serves to set off some marvellous stained glass, the most impressive of which is contained within a ten-metre-wide rose window, often claimed (rather boldly) as the largest in the world. The church flanks **Plaça Sant Josep Oriol**, the prettiest of the three adjacent squares, an ideal place to take an outdoor coffee, listen to the buskers or browse the weekend **artists' market** (Sat 11am–8pm, Sun 11am–2pm). The statue here is of Àngel Guimerà, nineteenth-century Catalan playwright and poet, who had a house on the square.

The church is named – like the squares on either side, Plaça del Pi and Placeta del Pi – after the pine trees that once stood here (there's a solitary example still in Plaça del Pi). A **farmers' market** spills across Plaça del Pi on the first and third Friday and Saturday of the month, selling honey, cheese, cakes and other produce, while **Carrer de Petritxol** (off Plaça del Pi) is the place to come for a hot chocolate in one of the traditional cafés that still thrive here. One of the city's most famous galleries is at c/de Petritxol 5, where the **Sala Pares** (see p.216) was already well established when Picasso and Miró were young.

Head east from Plaça Sant Josep Oriol, back towards the cathedral, and behind the Palau Episcopal you'll stumble upon **Plaça Sant Felip Neri**, scarred by a bomb dropped during the Civil War and now used as a playground by the children at the square's school. Antoni Gaudí walked here every evening after work at the Sagrada Família to hear Mass at the eighteenth-century church of Sant Felip Neri. Many of the other buildings that now hedge in the small square come from other points in the city and have been reassembled here over the last fifty years. One of these, the former headquarters of the city's shoemakers' guild (founded in 1202), houses a one-room footwear museum, the **Museu del Calçat** (Tues–Sun 11am–2pm; €2.50; ☎933 014 533), whose collection of reproductions (models dating back as far as the first century), originals (from as early as the 1600s) and oddities is of some interest, not least the world's biggest shoe, made for the Columbus statue.

Antiga Sinagoga

South of Plaça Sant Felip Neri, down c/Sant Domènec del Call, you enter what was once the medieval Jewish quarter of Barcelona (see box opposite). Historical research has located the site of the main synagogue, the **Antiga Sinagoga** (daily 11am–3pm, sometimes closed Sat for services, possible longer hours May–Sept; ☎933 170 790, ⓦwww.calldebarcelona.org; €2) – it's at c/Marlet 5, on the corner with c/Sant Domènec del Call. A small synagogue existed here, on the edge of the Roman forum, from the third century AD until the pogrom of 1391, but even after that date the building survived in various guises – the sunken dye vats from a family business of fifteenth-century New Christian

Jewish Barcelona

Barcelona's **medieval Jewish quarter**, El Call, was centred on c/Sant Domènec del Call (*Call* is the Catalan word for a narrow passage). As elsewhere in Spain, Barcelona's Jewish quarter lay nestled in the shadow of the cathedral – under the Church's careful scrutiny. In the thirteenth and early fourteenth centuries some of the realm's greatest and most powerful administrators hailed from here, but reactionary trends sparked pogroms and led to the closing off of the community in these narrow, dark alleys. Nevertheless a prosperous settlement persisted until the pogrom and forced conversion of 1391 and exile of 1492. Today little, except the street name and the rediscovered synagogue, survives as a reminder of the Jewish presence – after their expulsion, most of the buildings used by the Jews were torn down and used for construction elsewhere in the city. A fact that the Catalan government does not eagerly publicize is that the Generalitat itself was constructed on the ruins of expropriated Jewish houses. With the demise of the Franco regime, a small community was again established in Barcelona, and in recent years there has been a revival in interest in the Call. As well as the synagogue, the sites of the butchers', bakers', fishmongers' and Jewish baths have all been identified, while over on the eastern side of Montjuïc (Jewish Mountain) was the Jewish cemetery – the castle at Montjuïc displays around thirty tombstones recovered from the cemetery in the early twentieth century.

(forcibly converted Jews) dyers are still visible, alongside some original Roman walling. Most other local Jewish buildings were destroyed, though a plaque further down c/Marlet (junction with c/Arc Sant Ramon del Call) marks the site of the former rabbi's house. Not many people stop by the synagogue – if you do, you'll get a personalized tour of the small room by a member of the local Jewish community.

North towards Plaça de Catalunya

Across c/de Portaferrissa, the landscaped **Plaça Vila de Madrid** retains a line of sunken Roman tombs, flanking both sides of what was the Roman road that led to the northern gate of Barcino. Further north still, off the shopping street of c/de Santa Anna, the **Església de Santa Anna** is one of the oldest religious foundations in the city. A monastery was established here as early as the twelfth century and a fine fifteenth-century cloister survived the turmoil of the Civil War.

Cross busy, pedestrianized Avinguda del Portal de l'Angel from here to find c/Montsió and **Els Quatre Gats** (The Four Cats), on your left at no. 3, the tavern opened by Pere Romeu and other *modernista* artists in 1897 as a gathering place for their contemporaries. The building itself is gloriously decorated inside and out – it was the architect Josep Puig i Cadafalch's first commission – and *Els Quatre Gats* soon thrived as the birthplace of *modernista* magazines, the scene of poetry readings and shadow-puppet theatre and, in 1901, the setting for Picasso's first public exhibition. It was a short-lived venture – the tavern closed down by 1903 – but a modern restoration displays something of its former glory, with today's restaurant (see p.187) overseen by a copy of Ramon Casas' famous wall-painting of himself and Pere Romeu on a tandem bicycle (the original is in MNAC).

El Raval

The old-town area west of the Ramblas is known as **El Raval** (from the Arabic word for "suburb"). Standing outside the medieval city walls, this has always formed a world apart from the power and nobility of the Barri Gòtic. In medieval times it was the site of hospitals, churches and monasteries and, later, of noxious trades and industries that had no place in the Gothic quarter. Many of the street names still tell the story, like c/de l'Hospital or c/dels Tallers (named for the district's slaughterhouses). By the twentieth century the area south of c/de l'Hospital had acquired a reputation as the city's main red-light area, known to all (for obscure reasons) as the Barrio Chino, or Barri Xinès in Catalan – China Town. According to the Barcelona chronicler Manuel Vázquez Montalbán, in the days when Jean Genet crawled its streets – an experience he recounted in his *Thief's Journal* – the district housed "theatrical homosexuals and anarcho-syndicalist, revolutionary meeting places; women's prisons . . . condom shops and brothels which smelled of liquor and groins". George Orwell later related how, after the 1936 Workers' Uprising, "in the streets were coloured posters appealing to prostitutes to stop being prostitutes". Even today in the backstreets around c/de Sant Pau and c/Nou de la Rambla there are pockets of sleaze, while a handful of old bars – the *Bar Pastis*, *London Bar*, *Marsella* and *Almirall* – trade on their former reputations as bohemian hangouts.

However, El Raval is changing rapidly. The 1992 Olympics and then European Union funding achieved what Franco never could, and cleaned up large parts of the neighbourhood almost overnight. North of c/de l'Hospital the main engine of change was the building of the contemporary art museum, MACBA, around which entire city blocks were demolished, open spaces created and old buildings cleaned up. To the south, between c/de l'Hospital and c/de Sant Pau, a new boulevard – the Rambla de Raval – has been gouged through the former tenements and alleys, providing a huge new pedestrianized area. The local character of the neighbourhood is changing perceptibly, too. The new, young, more affluent and arty residents rub shoulders with the area's older, more traditional population, though this in turn is being supplanted by a growing influx of immigrants from the Indian subcontinent and North Africa. Alongside the surviving spit-and-sawdust bars you'll find new restaurants, galleries and boutiques, not to mention a burgeoning number of specialist grocery stores, curry houses, *halal* butchers and hole-in-the-wall telephone offices advertising cheap international calls.

You'd hesitate to call El Raval gentrified, as it clearly still has its rough edges. You needn't be unduly concerned during the day as you make your way around, but it's as well to keep your wits about you at night, particularly in the southernmost streets.

Museu d'Art Contemporani de Barcelona and around

Reached along c/del Bonsuccés and c/d'Elisabets from the Ramblas, and anchoring the northern reaches of the Raval, is the **Museu d'Art Contemporani de Barcelona**, or **MACBA**, in Plaça dels Angels (mid-June to mid-Sept Mon & Wed–Fri 11am–8pm, Sat 10am–8pm, Sun 10am–3pm; July & Aug also Thurs 8pm–midnight; rest of the year closes weekdays at 7.30pm; admission €4/5.50/7, depending on exhibitions visited, Wed €3; ☎934 120 810, ⑩www.macba.es; ⓂCatalunya/Universitat), which opened in 1995. The contrast between the huge, white, almost luminous, structure of the museum and the buildings around it couldn't be more stark. The aim of the architect, American Richard Meier, was to make as much use of natural light as possible and to "create a dialogue" between the museum and its surroundings; this is reflected in the front side of the building, which is entirely of glass. Once inside, you go from the ground to the fourth floor up a series of swooping ramps which afford continuous views of the square below – usually full of careering skateboarders – and the sixteenth-century Convent dels Àngels.

The **collection** represents the main movements in contemporary art since 1945, mainly in Catalunya and Spain but with a smattering of foreign artists as well. The pieces are not shown together in a permanent space but in smaller rotating exhibitions, so, depending on when you visit, you may catch works by major names such as Joan Miró, Antoni Tàpies, Eduardo Chillida, Alexander Calder, Robert Rauschenberg or Paul Klee. Joan Brossa, leading light of the Catalan Dau al Set group of the 1950s, has work here too, as do Catalan conceptual artists like the Grup de Treball, Muntadas and Francesc Torres. There's also a broad collection of abstract and kinetic sculpture, and cutting-edge work by Spanish and Catalan artists using audiovisual techniques and other new technologies. Probably the best way to acquaint yourself with the collection is to take the free **guided tour** (usually Wed & Sat 6pm, Sun & public hols noon). There's also a good museum shop selling everything from designer espresso cups to art books, and a café-bar around the back that's part of the CCCB.

Across the square, part of the former Convent dels Àngels now houses the headquarters of the **Foment de les Artes Décoratives** (**FAD**; Tues–Fri 11am–8pm, Sun 11am–4pm; free; ☏934 437 520, ⊛www.fadweb.com), a decorative art and design organization founded in 1903. Their exhibition spaces (including the former convent chapel) are dedicated to industrial and graphic design, arts, crafts, architecture, contemporary jewellery and fashion. Drop by to see the latest temporary exhibitions, or call in for the spiffy bar and restaurant. While you're in the vicinity, it's worth looking around the other small private galleries or having a drink or meal in one of the new bars and restaurants that have sprung up in the wake of MACBA, especially on c/del Pintor Fortuny, c/de Ferlandina, c/dels Angels and c/del Dr Joaquim Dou. For a sit-down in one of Barcelona's nicest traffic-free squares, head back along c/d'Elisabets to the arcaded **Plaça de Vicenç Martorell**, where *Kasparo*'s tables overlook a popular children's playground.

Centre de Cultura Contemporània de Barcelona

Adjoining the MACBA building, up c/Montalegre, is the **Centre de Cultura Contemporània de Barcelona**, or **CCCB** (Tues, Thurs & Fri 11am–2pm & 4–8pm, Wed & Sat 11am–8pm, Sun 11am–7pm; €4.40 or 6 depending on exhibitions visited; ☏933 064 100, ⊛www.cccb.org; Ⓜ Catalunya or Universitat), which hosts temporary art and city-related exhibitions as well as supporting a cinema and a varied concert programme. The building is a prime example of the juxtaposition of old and new; built as the Casa de la Caritat in 1714 on the site of a fourteenth-century Augustine convent, and added to in the late eighteenth and nineteenth centuries, it was for hundreds of years an infamous workhouse and lunatic asylum. In the entrance to the centre, in what is now called the Plaça de les Dones, you can see the old tile panels and facade in a patio presided over by a small statue of Sant Jordi (patron saint of Catalunya)

– the glass side of the square gives views of the patio as you go up the escalators to the exhibition spaces inside the new part of the building. At the back of the building, the *C3* **café–bar** has a sunny *terrassa* on the modern square joining the CCCB to the MACBA. Further up on c/Montalegre is another eighteenth-century patio, the arcaded and tiled **Pati Manning**, used for occasional open-air concerts.

Hospital de la Santa Creu and around

The district's most substantial historic relic is the **Hospital de la Santa Creu** (ⓂLiceu), which occupies a large site between c/del Carme and c/de l'Hospital. The attractive complex of Gothic buildings was founded as the city's main hospital in 1402, a role that it assumed for over 500 years – Antoni Gaudí, knocked down by a tram in 1926, was brought here for treatment but died three days later. The hospital shifted site to Domènech i Montaner's new creation in the Eixample in 1930 and the spacious fifteenth-century hospital wards were subsequently converted for cultural and educational use, and now hold the Academy of Medicine, an artisanal school and two libraries, including the Catalan national library, the Biblioteca de Catalunya. Visitors can wander freely through the pleasant medieval cloistered **garden** (daily 10am–dusk; access from either street), with its orange trees and makeshift café. From c/de l'Hospital you get the best views of the building's façade, while just inside the c/del Carme entrance (on the right) are some superb seventeenth-century *azulejos* of various religious scenes and a tiled Renaissance courtyard. The hospital's former chapel, **La Capella de l'Antic Hospital**, entered separately from c/l'Hospital, is now an exhibition space (see p.219).

Walking west along c/de l'Hospital, it's 100m or so to the bottom of **c/de la Riera Baixa**, a narrow street that's at the centre of the city's secondhand and vintage clothing scene. Walking the other way down c/de l'Hospital, back towards the Ramblas, one of the Raval's prettiest squares reveals itself: **Plaça de Sant Agusti**, backed by the Catalan Baroque bulk of the Església de Sant Agusti, an Augustinian foundation from 1728. Turning north, up c/de Jerusalem, you soon find yourself at the back of the Boqueria market, another area in which hip bars have proliferated recently. A couple overlook the **Jardins Dr Fleming**, a children's playground tucked into an exterior corner of the Hospital de la Santa Creu on c/del Carme.

Rambla de Raval and around

Opening off the western end of c/de l'Hospital is the **Rambla de Raval**, the latest urban boulevard to be driven through the old town. In many ways it's still finding its feet – a large gap in the buildings halfway down is the ongoing construction site of a proposed new luxury hotel, offices and social housing, while the juvenile trees are yet to throw much shade on the *rambla*'s benches. But the local inhabitants – many of Asian origin – have been quick to appreciate the space, while an increasing number of fashionable bars are interspersed amongst the video stores, kebab shops, phone offices and cafés. A Saturday street market adds a bit more character, while children find it hard to resist a clamber on the massive bulbous cat sculpture.

The two extremes of the *rambla* offer a snapshot of the changing neighbourhood. At the bottom end, off **c/de Sant Pau**, the *barri*'s remaining prostitutes accost passers-by as they head back towards the Liceu and the Ramblas. The top end, meanwhile, leads you straight into the streets of the upper Raval, flush with

△ Street entertainers on Las Ramblas

boutiques, bars and galleries. Pause at least in **Plaça del Pedro** (junction of c/ del Carme and c/de l'Hospital), where a cherished statue of Santa Eulàlia (co-patronress of the city) stands on the site of her supposed crucifixion, facing the surviving apse of a Romanesque chapel. Carrer de Botella, just off the square, is unremarkable, save for the plaque at no. 11 which records the **birthplace of Manuel Vasquez Montalban** (see p.274), probably the city's most famous writer, whose likes and prejudices found expression in his favourite character, detective Pepe Carvalho.

Hotel España

Modernista buildings are fairly rare in the Raval and save for the Palau Güell (see below), the best known is probably the **Hotel España** at c/Sant Pau 9–11, just off the Ramblas at the back of the Liceu. Some of the most influential names in Catalan architecture and design came together at the beginning of the twentieth century to transform the dowdy *España* hotel (originally built in 1860) into one of the city's most lavish addresses. With a tiled dining room designed by Lluis Domènech i Montaner, a bar with an amazing marble fireplace by Eusebi Arnau, and a ballroom whose marine murals were executed by Ramon Casas, the hotel was the fashionable sensation of its day. Many of the features have been well preserved and you can have a good look around for the price of lunch in the restaurant.

Palau Güell

El Raval's outstanding building is the **Palau Güell**, at c/Nou de la Rambla 3 (☎933 173 974, Ⓜ Drassanes/Liceu), an extraordinary townhouse designed by the young Antoni Gaudí for wealthy shipowner and industrialist Eusebi Güell i Bacigalupi. It was commissioned in 1885 as an extension of the Güell family's house located on the Ramblas, and was subsequently the first modern building to be declared a World Heritage Site by UNESCO.

At a time when architects sought to conceal the iron supports within buildings, Gaudí turned them to his advantage, displaying them as decorative features in the grand rooms on the main floor, which are lined with dark marble hewn from the Güell family quarries. Columns, arches and ceilings are all shaped, carved and twisted in an elaborate style that was to become the hallmark of Gaudí's later works. Even the underground stables bear Gaudí's distinct touch, a forest of brick capitals and arches that with a touch of imagination become mushrooms and palms. Meanwhile the roof terrace culminates in a fantastical series of chimneys decorated with swirling patterns made from fragments of glazed tile, glass and earthenware. The family rarely ventured up here – it was the servants instead who were exposed to the fullest flight of Gaudí's fantasy as they hung the washing out on lines hung from chimney to chimney.

The building has been under longterm restoration, but is expected to open again in mid-2007. In previous years access has been via mandatory guided tour, so you can expect to have to queue or be given a specific time-slot, as visitor numbers at any one time tend to be limited. Tourist offices will have up-to-the-minute details.

Església de Sant Pau del Camp

Carrer de Sant Pau cuts west through the Raval to the church of **Sant Pau del Camp** (St Paul of the Field; ⓂParal.lel), its name a graphic reminder that it once stood in open fields beyond the city walls. The oldest and one of the most interesting churches in Barcelona, Sant Pau was a Benedictine foundation of the tenth century, built after its predecessor was destroyed in a Muslim raid of 985 AD and constructed on a Greek cross plan. It was renovated again at the end of the thirteenth century; above the main entrance are curious, primitive carvings from that period of fish, birds and faces, while other animal forms adorn the twin capitals of the charming twelfth-century cloister. Inside, the church is dark and rather plain, enlivened only by tiny arrow-slit windows and small stained-glass circles high up in the central dome. The church was under restoration at the time of writing, but it's worth the walk down the street anyway to peek through the railings, if only for the jarring contrast between medieval church and adjacent sports centre.

Mercat de Sant Antoni to Paral.lel

The Raval's western edge is defined by the Ronda de Sant Pau and the Ronda de Sant Antoni, and where the two meet stands the handsome **Mercat de Sant Antoni** (Mon–Thurs & Sat 7am–2.30pm & 5.30–8.30pm, Fri 7am–8.30pm; ⓂSant Antoni), the neighbourhood's major produce market, dating from 1876. It makes a pointed contrast to the Boqueria – there are not nearly so many tourists, for a start – and unlike the other city markets, it's surrounded by enclosed aisles packed with stalls selling cheap shoes, underwear, T-shirts, children's clothes, bed linen, towels and other household goods. Come on Sunday and there's a **book and coin market** (8am–2pm) here instead. There are plans to remodel the market completely between 2007 and 2010, though its external character should be retained – a temporary market will be installed while works continue. The traditional breakfast, lunch and drinks spot is **Els Tres Tombs**, the café across the road on the corner of Ronda de Sant Antoni, open from 6am until late for a good-natured mix of market traders, locals, students and tourists.

Three blocks west of the market, lies **Avinguda Paral.lel**, one of Barcelona's major thoroughfares, which runs from the port to Plaça d'Espanya. The street was once the hub of Barcelona nightlife, famed for its cabarets, theatres and dance halls, only a few of which have survived the city's changing taste in entertainment. On the other side of the avenue lies the working-class district of Poble Sec, while if you walk down Paral.lel towards the harbour you'll pass the **funicular station** for Montjuïc (access is through ⓂParal.lel) and then skirt the surviving **medieval walls** of the former shipyards (now the Museu Maritim; see p.80).

Sant Pere

The Barri Gòtic is bordered on its eastern side by Via Laietana, which was cut through the old town at the beginning of the twentieth century. Across it to the east stretches the quiet neighbourhood of **Sant Pere**, named after its medieval monastic church, Sant Pere de les Puelles. Visits to the *barri* tend to concentrate on its one remarkable building, the Palau de la Música Catalana, just off the northern end of Via Laietana, but the neighbourhood rewards a slow stroll through on your way to the richer tourist area of La Ribera. This also gives you the opportunity to swing by the restored market, as well as one of Barcelona's more esoteric museums, devoted entirely to chocolate.

Mercat Santa Caterina and around

The very centre of the neighbourhood is dominated by the **Mercat Santa Caterina** (Mon 7.30am-2pm, Tues, Wed & Sat 7.30am-3.30pm, Thurs & Fri 7.30am-8.30pm; ☎933 195 740, ⓦwww.mercatsantacaterina.net; ⓂJaume I), approached from Via Laietana by the broad Avinguda Francesc Cambó. The splendid restoration has retained its nineteenth-century balustraded walls and added slatted wooden doors and windows and a dramatic wave roof. The discovery of the foundations of a major medieval convent held up its renovation for a while (parts of the medieval walls are visible behind glass at the rear), but it's in full swing again now and there's an excellent bar-restaurant attached (see p.187) where you can soak up the atmosphere.

To the north, three old streets, carrers de Sant Pere Més Baix (lower), Mitja (middle) and Alt (upper), contain the bulk of the district's finest medieval buildings and the nicest shops, and they converge to the east at **Plaça de Sant Pere**, site of the much-restored church, one of the oldest in the city, founded in 945. It's been destroyed and burned too many times to retain any interior interest, and the high-walled facade – although it looks medieval – is a twentieth-century renovation. The square is pretty, though, a little paved triangle with a cast-iron drinking fountain, while just to the south **Plaça de Sant Agusti Vell** makes a great target for lunch, with *Restaurant L'Economic* (see p.187) offering a particularly good deal.

Palau de la Música Catalana

Lluis Domènech i Montaner's stupendous **Palau de la Música Catalana** (for concert details, see p.210; ⓂUrquinaona) doesn't seem to have enough breathing space in the tiny c/Sant Pere Més Alt. Built in 1908 for the Orfeo Català choral group, its bare brick structure is smothered in tiles and mosaics, the highly elaborate facade resting on three great columns, like elephant's legs; the corner sculpture, by Miquel Blay, represents Catalan popular song, its allegorical figures protected by a strident Sant Jordi. The dramatic tiled lobby provides a taster of the stunning interior, which incorporates a bulbous stained-glass skylight capping the second-storey auditorium – which contemporary critics claimed to be an engineering impossibility.

Fifty-minute-long **guided tours** of the interior (daily 10am–3.30pm, plus July–Sept 10am–7pm, in English on the hour; €8; ☎902 442 882, ⓦwww.palaumusica.org) are offered, but as visitor numbers are limited you'll almost certainly have to book in advance, which you can do in person or by phone at the box office or at the nearby gift shop, **Les Muses del Palau**, c/Sant Pere Mes Alt 1 (daily 9.30–3pm; no tel).

Museu de la Xocolata

Barcelona's **Museu de la Xocolata** (Mon & Wed–Sat 10am–7pm, Sun 10am–3pm; €3.80; ☎932 687 878, ⓦwww.patisseria.com; ⓜJaume I), on the eastern edge of Sant Pere, at c/del Comerç 36, is housed in the former Convent de Sant Agustí. The thirteenth-century cloister, rediscovered when the building was renovated, can still be viewed through the building's main doors. Audio-visual displays in the museum recount the history of chocolate, from its origins as a sacred and medicinal product of prehistoric Central America through to its introduction to Europe as a confection in the sixteenth century. It's a topic with some local relevance – in that the Bourbon army, which was once quartered in this building, demanded the provision of chocolate for its sweet-toothed troops. However, whether you go in or not depends on how keen you are to see models of Gaudí buildings or religious icons sculpted from chocolate. The admission money is probably better spent at the museum café (open to all) and *choccie* counter, while at the adjacent Escola de Pastisseria, glass windows allow you to look onto the students learning their craft in the kitchens. There are chocolate workshops and tastings organized on a regular basis – enquire at the museum.

La Ribera and the Born

La Ribera – bordered by Via Laietana to the west, c/de la Princesa to the north and Parc de la Ciutadella to the east – is one of the most visited old-town neighbourhoods, by virtue of the presence of the **Museu Picasso**, Barcelona's biggest single tourist attraction. This lies on **Carrer de Montcada**, a handsome street of medieval mansions, which runs down to the church of **Santa María del Mar**, the city's most perfect expression of the Catalan-Gothic style. The sheer number of tourists in this neighbourhood rivals the busiest streets of the Barri Gòtic, and this has had a knock-on effect in terms of the bars, shops and restaurants found here. The *barri* is at its most hip, and most enjoyable, in the area around the **Passeig del Born**, the pleasant elongated boulevard leading from Santa María church to the old Born market.

Museu Picasso

The **Museu Picasso**, at c/Montcada 15–23 (Tues–Sun & hols 10am–8pm; €6, exhibitions €5, museum and exhibitions €8.50, first Sun of month free; ☎933 196 310, ⓦwww.museupicasso.bcn.es; ⓜJaume I), occupies five adjoining

Picasso in Barcelona

Although born in Málaga, **Pablo Picasso** (1881–1973) spent much of his youth – from the age of 14 to 23 – in Barcelona. He maintained close links with Barcelona and his Catalan friends even when he left for Paris in 1904, and is said to have always thought of himself as Catalan rather than *andaluz*. The time Picasso spent in Barcelona encompassed the whole of his Blue Period (1901–04) and provided many of the formative influences on his art.

Apart from the Museu Picasso, there are echoes of the great artist at various sites throughout the old town. Not too far from the museum, you can still see many of the buildings in which Picasso lived and worked, notably the **Escola de Belles Arts de Llotja** (c/Consolat del Mar, near Estació de França), where his father taught drawing and where Picasso himself absorbed an academic training. The **apartments** where the family lived when they first arrived in Barcelona – Pg. d'Isabel II 4 and c/Reina Cristina 3, both near the Escola – can also be seen, though only from the outside, while Picasso's first real **studio** (in 1896) was located over on c/de la Plata at no. 4. A few years later, many of his Blue Period works were finished at a studio at c/del Comerç 28. His first **public exhibition** was in 1901 at *Els Quatre Gats* tavern (c/Montsió 3, Barri Gòtic); you can still have a meal there today. Less tangible traces line **c/Avinyó** in the Barri Gòtic, which cuts south from c/Ferran to c/Ample. Large houses along here were converted into brothels at the end of the nineteenth century, and Picasso used to haunt the street sketching what he saw. Some accounts of his life – based on Picasso's own testimony, it has to be said – claim that he had his first sexual experience here at the age of 14, but certainly the women at one of the brothels inspired his seminal Cubist work, *Les Demoiselles d'Avignon*.

medieval palaces converted specifically to house the artist's works. It's one of the most important collections of Picasso's work in the world, but even so some visitors are disappointed: the museum isn't thoroughly representative, it contains none of his best-known works, and few in the Cubist style. But what is here provides a unique opportunity to trace Picasso's development from his early paintings as a young boy to the major works of later years. It's always thronged with visitors, though arriving when it opens is a good way to beat the worst of the crowds. A **café** with a *terrassa* in one of the palace courtyards offers refreshments, and there is of course a **shop**, stuffed full of Picasso-related gifts.

The collection

The museum opened in 1963 with a collection based largely on the donations of Jaime Sabartes, longtime friend and former secretary to the artist. On Sabartes' death in 1968, Picasso himself added a large number of works – above all the works of the Meninas series – and in 1970 he donated a further vast number of watercolours, drawings and paintings.

The works on show are extremely well laid out, following the artist's development chronologically, with the early periods the best represented. The **early drawings**, particularly, are fascinating, in which Picasso – still signing with his full name, Pablo Ruiz Picasso – attempted to copy the nature paintings in which his father specialized. Paintings from his art-school days in **Barcelona** (1895–97) show tantalizing glimpses of the city that the young Picasso was beginning to know well – the Gothic old town, the cloisters of Sant Paul del Camp, Barceloneta beach – and even at the ages of 15 and 16 he was producing serious works, including knowing self-portraits and a closely observed study of his mother from 1896. Works in the style of Toulouse-Lautrec, like the menu Picasso did for *Els Quatre Gats* tavern in 1900, reflect his burgeoning interest in Parisian art at the turn of the century, while other sketches, drawings and illustrations (many undertaken for competitions and magazines) clearly show Picasso's development of his own unique personal style. His paintings from the famous **Blue Period** (1901–04) burst upon you – whether its moody Barcelona rooftops or the cold face of *La Dona Morta* – and subsequent galleries trace the Pink Period (1905–06), though with the barest nod to his Cubist (1907–20) and Neoclassical (1920–25) stages.

The large gaps in the main collection (for example, nothing from 1905 until the celebrated *Harlequin* of 1917) only underline Picasso's extraordinary changes of style and mood. This is best illustrated by the large jump to 1957, a year represented by his 44 interpretations of Velázquez's masterpiece, **Las Meninas**, completed in just four months between August and December. In these, Picasso brilliantly deconstructed the individual portraits and compositions that make up Velázquez's work; in addition, and neatly juxtaposed, are displayed nine more donated works by Picasso, gorgeous light-filled Mediterranean scenes inspired by the pigeons and dovecotes of his Cannes studio.

The museum ends with Picasso the **ceramist**, highlighting the vibrantly decorated dishes and jugs given to the museum by his wife, Jacqueline. There are various portraits of Jacqueline here, too, though it's the deep friendship Picasso shared with Jaime Sabartes for almost seventy years that provokes the clearest expression of endearment, in a separate room of mature portraits, character studies and jokey sketches by one friend of another.

Along Carrer de Montcada

The street on which the Museu Picasso stands – **Carrer de Montcada** – is one of the best-looking in the city. It was laid out in the fourteenth century and, until the Eixample was planned almost five hundred years later, was home to most of the city's leading citizens. They occupied spacious mansions built around central courtyards, from which external staircases climbed to the living rooms on the first floor; the facades facing the street were all endowed with huge gated doors that could be swung open to allow coaches access to the interior.

Almost opposite the Museu Picasso, at no. 12, the fourteenth-century Palau de Llió and its next-door neighbour contain the extensive collections of the **Museu Textil i d'Indumentaria** (Tues–Sat 10am–6pm, Sun 10am–3pm; €3.50, first Sun of month free; ☎933 197 603, ◉www.museutextil.bcn.es). Selected items, from late Roman fabrics to 1930s cocktail dresses, all beautifully presented, demonstrate the art and technique behind cloth-making, embroidery, lace and tapestry work. The upper floor concentrates on Spanish and Catalan designers of the 1970s to 1990s, with a room devoted to Pedro Rodríguez (1895-1990), the first *haute couture* designer to establish a studio in Barcelona. Special exhibitions at the museum are well regarded (for which there's usually a separate charge), while the courtyard *Textil Café* (see p.179) is one of the nicest in the old town. In the associated shop, funky jewellery, silk ties, candles, kitchen aprons, bags and other design-led gifts and trinkets abound. A joint ticket system also allows you entry to the ceramics and decorative arts museum at Pedralbes (see p.126).

The adjacent **Museu Barbier-Mueller,** c/de Montcada 14 (Tues–Fri 11am–7pm, Sat 10am–7pm, Sun 10am–3pm; first Sun of month free; ☎933 104 516) is a terrific collection of pre-Columbian art housed in the renovated sixteenth-century Palau Nadal. Temporary exhibitions – all beautifully presented – highlight wide-ranging themes, and draw on a peerless collection of sculpture, pottery, jewellery, textiles and everyday items, with some pieces dating back as far as the third century BC. Depending on the exhibition, you're as likely to see decorated Mongolian belt-buckles as carved African furniture – there's nothing restrictive about the term "pre-Columbian" – and, again, the shop is worth a browse, with a wide range of ethnic artefacts for sale.

Further down, at no. 20, the **Palau Dalmases** is a handsome Baroque building of the seventeenth century, remodelled from its fifteenth-century roots. This is open in the evenings as a grand Baroque bar, *Espai Barroc* (see p.204 for details). At the end of the street, in the little Placeta Montcada, **Taller Cuixart BCN** (Tues–Sat 11am–3pm & 5–8pm, Sun 11am–3pm; €3, free on Tues; ☎933 191 947, ⓦwww.cuixart.org) is a collection of the works of Catalan artist Modest Cuixart, co-creator of the influential magazine and art movement Dau al Set. Four rooms trace the development of his work, from early Surrealism in the 1940s and 1950s to the sober, abstract landscapes of the 1990s.

At the bottom of c/de Montcada, the graceful lines of Santa María church impose themselves, but before you move on, and for a change of tack from palaces and art, drop into the lavishly tiled **El Xampanyet** bar at c/de Montcada 22 (see p.183), serving champagne, cider and tapas.

Església de Santa María del Mar

The church of **Santa María del Mar** (daily 9am–1.30pm & 4.30–8pm; Sun choral Mass at 1pm; ⓜJaume I/Barceloneta) was begun on the order of King Jaume II in 1324, and finished in only five years. Built on what was the seashore in the fourteenth century, the church was at the heart of the medieval city's maritime and trading district (c/Argentería, named after the silversmiths who worked there, still runs from the church square to the city walls of the Barri Gòtic), and it came to embody supremacy of the Crown of Aragon (of which Barcelona was capital) in Mediterranean commerce. Built quickly, and therefore consistent in style, it's an exquisite example of Catalan-Gothic architecture, with a wide nave and high, narrow aisles, and for all its restrained exterior decoration is still much dearer to the heart of the average local than the cathedral, the only other church in the city with which it compares. The Baroque trappings were destroyed during the Civil War, which is probably all to the good, since the long-term restoration work has concentrated on showing off the simple spaces of the interior; the stained glass, especially, is beautiful.

Behind the church is the square known as **Fossar de les Moreres**, which was formally opened in 1989 to mark the spot where, following the defeat of Barcelona on September 11, 1714, Catalan martyrs fighting for independence against the king of Spain, Felipe V, were executed. A red steel scimitar with an eternal flame commemorates the fallen.

Passeig del Born

Fronting the church of Santa María is the fashionable **Passeig del Born**, once the site of medieval fairs and tournaments and now lined with a parade of plane trees shading a host of classy bars and shops. Cafés at the eastern end put out tables in front of the old **Mercat del Born** (June–Sept Sat 10am–8pm, Sun 10am–3pm; Oct–May Sat & Sun 10am–3pm; free), which was built in 1876 and served as the city's main wholesale fruit and veg market until 1971. It was due to be demolished but was saved by local protests, with the idea of turning it into a library. However, during initial works it became apparent that the market stood directly on top of the remains of part of the eighteenth-century city, dating from before the huge works associated with the building of the Ciutadella fortress and the Barceloneta district (see below). The massive rectangular cast-iron frame of the market is still in place, now protecting the surviving metre-high walls of eighteenth-century shops, factories, houses and taverns, with the paved streets between clearly visible. It's quite a remarkable sight, viewed from a platform down c/de la Ribeira; the current plan is to retain the extensive archeological remains within a cultural and interpretation centre.

Back along the *passeig*, boutiques and **craft workshops** (see p.231) hide in the narrow vaulted medieval alleys on either side – carrers Flassaders and Vidreria in particular are noted for clothes, shoes, jewellery and design galleries. At night the Born becomes one of Barcelona's biggest bar zones as spirited locals frequent a panoply of drinking haunts, from old-style cocktail lounges to thumping music bars. The streets all around this area also harbour some excellent restaurants, while the finest place to sit outside for a drink or lunch, other than the Born itself, is pretty little **Plaça de les Olles**, just to the south.

△ Passeig del Born

Parc de la Ciutadella and around

The Bourbons took no chances after the War of the Spanish Succession. Barcelona had put up a spirited resistance, and to quell any further dissent Felipe V ordered the building of a star-shaped citadel close to the water, on the edge of the old town. A great part of La Ribera was destroyed, and a garrison, parade ground and defensive walls were constructed over a twenty-year period in the mid-eighteenth century. This Bourbon symbol of authority survived uneasily until 1869, when the military moved base. Many of the buildings were subsequently demolished and the surrounding area made into a park, the **Parc de la Ciutadella**. In 1888, the park was chosen as the site of the **Universal Exhibition** and the city's *modernista* architects, including the young Gaudí, left their mark here in a series of eye-catching buildings and monuments.

The Parc de la Ciutadella is still the largest green space in the city centre, home to a splendid fountain, large lake, plant houses, two museums and the city zoo. It's a very popular place for a stroll, and Sundays especially see couples and families taking time out here, while a younger crowd assembles for a bit of vigorous didgeridooing or bongo-work. The only surviving portion of the citadel, the much-altered Arsenal in the southeastern reaches of the park, has since 1980 housed Catalunya's legislative assembly, the **Parlament** (no public access – see Contexts, p.263, for more on the institution). Near the park, within short walking distance, are a couple of other attractions, including one of the city's most peculiar museums, devoted to funeral carriages.

The park's **main gates** are on Passeig de Picasso (ⓂBarceloneta), and there's also an entrance on Passeig de Pujades (ⓂArc de Triomf); only use ⓂCiutadella-Vila Olímpica if you're going directly to the zoo, as there's no access to the park itself from that side.

Inside the park

Perhaps the most notable of the park's sights is the **Cascada**, the monumental fountain in the northeast corner. Designed by Josep Fontseré i Mestrès, the architect chosen to oversee the conversion of the former citadel grounds into a park, this was the first of the major projects undertaken here. Fontseré's assistant in the work was the young Antoni Gaudí, then a student: the Baroque extravagance of the Cascada is suggestive of the flamboyant decoration that was later to become Gaudí's trademark. The best place to contemplate the fountain's tiers and swirls is from the small **open-air café** just to the south. Here you'll also find a lake, where for a few euros you can **rent a rowboat** and paddle about among the ducks. Gaudí is also thought to have had a hand in the design of the Ciutadella's iron park gates.

Just inside the northern entrance of the park, Domènech i Montaner designed a castle-like building intended for use as the exhibition's café-restaurant. Dubbed the *Castell dels Tres Dragons*, it became a centre for *modernista* arts and crafts, and many of Domènech's contemporaries spent time here experimenting with new materials and refining their techniques. It's now the **Museu de Zoologia** (Tues, Wed & Fri–Sun 10am–2.30pm, Thurs 10am–6.30pm; €3, first Sun of month free; ☎933 196 912, ⊛www.bcn.es/museuciencies), whose decorated red-brick exterior knocks spots off the rather dry displays of stuffed birds, insects and animals on the first floor. Special popular-science exhibitions (€3.50) on the ground floor tend to be of more interest. The sister museum is the nearby **Museu de Geologia** (same hours, price and contact number as Museu de Zoologia; combined ticket €4), which opened in 1882, the first public museum in the city. Based on the geological bequest of Francesc Martorell i Peña, who gave his name to the original museum, it's another restored period piece, with nineteenth-century cases of exhibits housed in a classical, pedimented building. There are rocks and minerals on one side, and fossils on the other, with many of the exhibits found in Catalunya, from fluorescent rocks to mammoth bones.

The two unsung glories of Ciutadella are its plant houses, arranged either side of the Geological Museum. The imposing **Umbracle** (palmhouse) is a handsome structure with a barreled wood-slat roof supported by cast-iron pillars, which allows shafts of light to play across the palms and ferns. Both materials and concept are echoed in the larger **Hivernacle** (conservatory), whose enclosed greenhouses are separated by a soaring glass-roofed terrace. A refined café-bar at the Hivernacle (see p.204) is the best stop in the park for drinks or a meal.

Parc Zoològic

Ciutadella's most popular attraction by far is the city's zoo, the **Parc Zoològic** (daily: June–Sept 10am–7pm; March–May & Oct 10am–6pm; Jan, Feb, Nov & Dec 10am–5pm; €15; ☎932 256 780, ◉www.zoobarcelona.com), taking up most of the southeastern part of the park. The main entrance is on c/Wellington, and is signposted from Ⓜ Ciutadella-Vila Olímpica, or tram T4 stops outside. It boasts 7000 animals from 400 different species – which is simply too many for a zoo that is still essentially nineteenth-century in character, confined to the formal grounds of a public park and devoted to entertainment rather than education. Brown bears beg for food, dolphins perform antics daily, while elephants, giraffes and tigers pace their minimal concrete enclosures, and although there's a nod to conservation issues it's difficult to see beyond the unimaginative presentation, fast-food concessions, picnic areas and mini-train rides.

However, the zoo's days here in its current form are numbered – the powers that be perhaps having finally appreciated the irony of its juxtaposition next to the Parlament, and grown weary of explaining to visiting dignitaries the source of the strong smell pervading the area. There are advanced plans to move the marine animals at least to a new coastal zoo and wetlands area (possibly by 2008) at Diagonal Mar.

Arc de Triomf and around

From the northern entrance of the Parc de la Ciutadella, the wide Passeig Lluís Companys runs up to the giant brick **Arc de Triomf** (Ⓜ Arc de Triomf). Roman in scale, yet reinterpretetd by its *modernista* architect, Josep Vilaseca i Casanoves, as a bold statement of Catalan intent, it's studded with ceramic figures and motifs, and topped by two pairs of bulbous domes. The reliefs on the main facade show the city of Barcelona welcoming visitors to the 1888 Universal Exhibition.

To the east lies the **Barcelona Nord** bus station, behind which stretches the undistinguished **Parc de l'Estacío del Nord**, which cuts across several city blocks as far as Avinguda Meridiana, ten minutes from the arch. The only reason to walk or ride out this way would be to present yourself at the front desk of the Serveis Funeraris (funerary services) de Barcelona, a few metres along c/Sancho de Ávila from the avenue (by the blue "Banc Sabadell" sign). You'll be escorted into the bowels of the building and the lights will be thrown on in the **Museu de Carrosses Fúnebres** (Mon–Fri 10am–1pm & 4–6pm, Sat & Sun 10am–1pm; free; Ⓜ Marina; ☎934 871 710) to reveal a staggering set of twenty-two funerary carriages, each parked on its own cobbled stage, complete with ghostly attendants, horses and riders suspended in frozen animation. Used for city funeral processions from the end of the nineteenth century onwards, most of the carriages and hearses are extravagantly decorated in gilt, black or white – the service was mechanized in the 1950s, when the silver Buick, also on display, came into use. Old photographs show some of the carriages in use in the city's streets, while showcases highlight antique uniforms, mourning wear and formal riding gear.

2

The waterfront: from Port Vell to Diagonal Mar

P erhaps the greatest recent transformation in the city has been along the **waterfront**, where harbour and Mediterranean have once again been placed at the heart of Barcelona. Dramatic changes here over the last two decades have shifted the cargo and container trade away to the south, opened up the old docksides as promenades and entertainment areas, and landscaped the city's beaches to the north – it's as if a theatre curtain has been lifted to reveal that, all along, Barcelona had an urban waterfront of which it could be proud.

Reaching the bottom of the Ramblas puts you within strolling distance of some heavyweight tourist attractions, including the **Mirador de Colón** (Columbus statue), **Museu Marítim,** the sightseeing harbour **boat trips**, and the boardwalks and promenades of the inner harbour, known as **Port Vell**. The old wharves and warehouses have been replaced by an entertainment zone that encompasses the **Maremàgnum** shopping and nightlife centre, the city's high-profile aquarium and IMAX screens and, across the marina, the impressive **Museu d'Història de Catalunya.** The wedge of land backing the marina is **Barceloneta**, an eighteenth-century fishing quarter that's the most popular place to come and sample the fish and seafood dishes of which Barcelona is most proud.

From Barceloneta six interlinked **beaches** stretch up the coast, backed by an attractive promenade. The city's inhabitants have taken to these in a big way, strolling, jogging and skating their length and descending in force at the weekend for a leisurely lunch at a nearby restaurant. The main development is around the **Port Olímpic**, filled with places to eat, drink and shop, and although fewer tourists keep on as far as the old working-class neighbourhood of **Poble Nou**, its beaches, historic cemetery and pretty *rambla* make for an interesting diversion. The coastal redevelopment extends as far as **Diagonal Mar**, where the Avinguda Diagonal meets the sea. This new conference and exhibition district expands upon the buildings and infrastructure of the Universal Forum of Cultures, the diversity and sustainability exposition held here in 2004.

You can reach all the areas covered below by **metro**, though there's a fair amount of walking required between neighbourhoods – from the bottom of the Ramblas to Poble Nou, for example, would take an hour. In addition, **buses** #17 (from Pl. de Catalunya) and #64 (from Avgda. Paral.lel and Pg. de Colom) run to Barceloneta's Passeig Joan de Borbó (the restaurant strip) and on to the Sant Sebastià cable-car station. The #45 (from Via Laietana) and #59 (from the

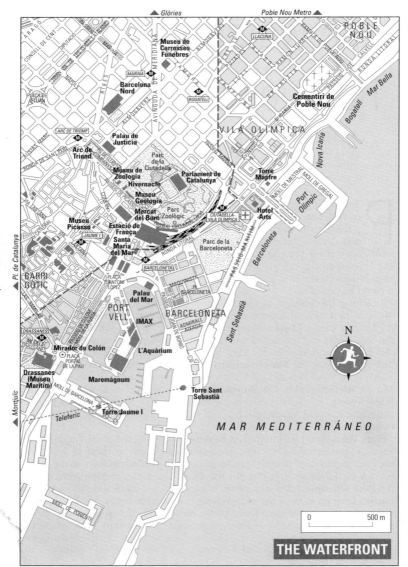

Ramblas) run through Barceloneta and out to the Port Olímpic. The #71 connects Passeig Marítim to Poble Nou metro.

Plaça Portal de la Pau and around

The Ramblas ends at **Plaça Portal de la Pau** (Ⓜ Drassanes), coming up hard against the teeming traffic that runs along the harbourside road. The maritime museum is over to the right, and the Columbus monument is straight ahead in the middle of the traffic circle, with the quayside square beyond flanked by the rather pompous **Port de Barcelona** (Port Authority) and **Duana** (Customs House) buildings. Away to the south (right) is the Moll de Barcelona, a landscaped wharf leading to the Torre de Jaume I **cable-car station** (see feature on p.84) and the **Estació Marítima,** where ferries leave for the Balearics. The large, bulbous building perched in the centre of the wharf is the city's **World Trade Centre**, where a luxury hotel complements the complex of offices, convention halls, shops and restaurants.

From the quayside just beyond the foot of the Columbus monument, **Las Golondrinas** sightseeing boats and the **Catamaran Orsom** depart on regular trips throughout the year around the inner harbour – all the details are on p.34.

The Mirador de Colón

Inaugurated just before the Universal Exhibition of 1888, the **Mirador de Colón** (June–Sept daily 9am–8.30pm; Oct–May daily 10am–6.30pm; €2.50, combined ticket with Torre de Collserola €5.25) commemorates the visit made by Christopher Columbus to Barcelona in June 1493. The Italian-born navigator was received in style by the Catholic monarchs Ferdinand and Isabella, who had supported his voyage of exploration a year earlier, when Columbus had set out to chart a passage west to the Orient. Famously, he failed in this, as he failed also to reach the North American mainland (instead "discovering" the Bahamas, Cuba and Haiti), but Columbus did enough to enhance his reputation and made three more exploratory voyages by 1504. Later, nineteenth-century Catalan nationalists took the navigator to their hearts – if he wasn't exactly Catalan, he was the closest they had to a local Vasco da Gama, and so they put him on the pedestal that they thought he deserved. Awkwardly for the locals, the statue is actually pointing in the general direction of Libya, not North America, but, as historian Robert Hughes puts it, at least "the sea is Catalan".

Columbus himself tops a grandiose, iron column, 52m high, guarded by lions at the base, around which unfold reliefs telling the story of his life and travels – here, if nowhere else, the old mercenary is still the "discoverer of America". On the harbour side of the column, steps lead down to a ticket office and lift, which you ride up to the enclosed *mirador* at Columbus' feet. The 360-degree views are terrific but the narrow viewing platform, which tilts perceptibly outwards and downwards, is emphatically not for anyone without a head for heights.

The Drassanes and the Museu Marítim

Opposite Columbus, set back from the avenue, are the **Drassanes**, unique medieval shipyards dating from the thirteenth century. Originally used as a dry dock to fit and arm Catalunya's war fleet in the days when the Catalan-Aragonese crown was vying with Venice and Genoa for control of the Mediterranean, the shipyards were in continuous use until well into the eighteenth century. The basic structure – long parallel halls facing the sea – has changed little; its singular size and position couldn't be bettered, whether the shipbuilders were fitting out medieval warships or eighteenth-century trading vessels destined for South America.

The huge, stone-vaulted buildings make a fitting home for the **Museu Marítim** (daily 10am–8pm; €6, free afternoon of 1st Sat of month; ⓦwww.museumaritimbarcelona.org; ⓜDrassanes), whose centrepiece is a copy of the sixteenth-century *Royal Galley* (*Galera Reial*), a soaring red-and-gold barge which was originally constructed here and was present at the great naval victory

△ Sunbathing at Port Vell

over the Ottoman Turks at Lepanto in 1571. This aside, it's really the building that's the main attraction, since the rest of the exhibits - fishing skiffs, sailing boats, figureheads, old maps and charts, ship portraits, navigation instruments – fail to spark much casual interest. You'll get most out of a visit if you pick up the audio-guide (included in the entrance fee) and hone in on some of the more illuminating digressions, for example on steam navigation, fishing methods, life at sea or the growth of the port of Barcelona. Combination tickets available at the desk are more worthwhile, offering trips on the harbour sightseeing boats (from €8.50), while **children's activities** at weekends and school holidays are well regarded. There's also a good restaurant at the museum, and the café puts out tables in the pleasant courtyard.

Moored over on the Moll de la Fusta (beyond the harbour's swing bridge), the **Santa Eulàlia** (May–Oct Tues–Fri noon–7.30pm, Sat & Sun 10am–7pm; rest of the year closes 5/5.30pm, €2.40, free with Museu Marítim ticket) is another of the museum's showpiece exhibits. Dating from 1908, and previously named the *Carmen Flores*, the three-masted ocean-going schooner once made the run between Barcelona and Cuba. It's been fully restored since being acquired by the museum, and a short tour lets you walk the deck and view the interior.

Port Vell

Barcelona's inner harbour has been rebranded as **Port Vell** (Old Port; ⓂDrassanes/Barceloneta), an area that encompasses the Moll d'Espanya wharf, the adjacent marina and the Palau de Mar development at the northwestern head of the Barceloneta district. It has its local critics – it's undoubtedly tourist-oriented, showy and expensive – but there's no denying the improvement made to what was formerly a largely neglected, decaying port area. The city's old timber wharf was among the first to be prettified. Backed by sedate nine-teenth-century buildings along the Passeig de Colom, the **Moll de la Fusta** is a landscaped promenade with a note of humour injected by the addition of a giant fibreglass crayfish by Catalan designer Xavier Mariscal and, further on, the Roy Lichtenstein totem-pole sculpture known as "Barcelona Head". From the Columbus statue end of the wharf, the wooden **Rambla de Mar** swing bridge strides across the harbour to the **Moll d'Espanya**, whose main features are the leisure complex known as **Maremàgnum** – jammed with fast-food joints, shops, restaurants and bars – plus the aquarium and IMAX cinema. The eastern arm of the Moll d'Espanya connects back to the Moll de la Fusta, providing pedestrian access to the **Palau de Mar** at the northern end of Barceloneta's Passeig Joan de Borbó. This old warehouse has been beautifully restored, with a series of **restaurants** in the lower arcade overlooking the marina and the **regional history museum** occupying the upper floors.

Maremàgnum and the Moll d'Espanya

Maremàgnum (daily 11am–11pm; ⓦwww.maremagnum.es; ⓂDrassanes) is a typically bold piece of Catalan design, the soaring glass lines of the complex tempered by the surrounding undulating wooden walkways. Inside are two floors of gift shops and boutiques, plus a range of bars and restaurants with harbourside seating and high prices. It's a fun place to come at night, though no self-respecting local would rate the food as anything but ordinary. Outside, benches and park areas provide fantastic views back across the harbour to the city.

Anchoring Moll d'Espanya, **L'Aquàrium** (daily: July & Aug 9.30am–11pm; Sept–June 9.30am–9pm, until 9.30pm at weekends; €15; ☏932 217 474, ⊛www.aquariumbcn.com; ⓜDrassanes) drags in families and school parties throughout the year to see "a magical world, full of mystery". Or, to be more precise, to see fish and sea creatures in 21 themed tanks representing underwater caves, tidal areas, tropical reefs and the planet's oceans. It's vastly overpriced and despite the claims of excellence it offers few new experiences, save perhaps the eighty-metre-long walk-through underwater tunnel which brings you face to face with gliding rays and cruising sharks. Some

Monturiol and the Catalan submarine

Narcís Monturiol i Estarriol (1819–1885) was born in Figueres in northeastern Catalunya but studied in Barcelona, soon falling in with radicals and revolutionaries. Although a law graduate, he never practised, turning his energetic talents instead to writing and publishing, setting up his first publishing company in 1846 (the year he married Emilia; they later had eight children). A series of journals and pamphlets followed, all espousing Monturiol's radical beliefs – in feminism, pacifism and utopian communism – and it was no surprise when one of his publications was suppressed by the government in the heady revolutionary days of 1848. Monturiol was forced briefly into exile and on his return to Barcelona, with the government now curtailing his publishing activities, he turned his hand instead to self-taught science and engineering.

It was a period in which scientific progress and social justice appeared as two sides of the same coin to utopians like Monturiol – indeed, his friend, the civil engineer Ildefons Cerdà, would later mastermind the building of Barcelona's Eixample on socially useful grounds. Monturiol's mind turned to more immediately practical matters and, inspired by the harsh conditions in which the coral fishermen of Cadaques worked, he conceived the idea of a man-powered submarine. It would improve their lot, he had no doubt, though Monturiol's grander vision was of an underwater machine to explore the oceans and expand human knowledge.

The **Ictineo** – the "fish-boat" – made its maiden voyage in Barcelona harbour on June 28, 1859. At 7m long, it could carry four or five men, and eventually made more than fifty dives at depths of up to 20m. An improved design was started in 1862 – Ictineo II – a seventeen-metre-long vessel designed to be propelled by up to sixteen men. Trials in 1865 soon showed that human power wasn't sufficient for the job, so Monturiol installed a steam engine near the stern. This, the world's first steam-powered submarine, was launched on October 22, 1867 and dived to depths of up to 30m on thirteen separate runs (the longest lasting for over seven hours). However, Monturiol's financial backers had finally run out of patience with a machine that, though technically brilliant, couldn't yet pay its way. They withdrew their support and the submarine was seized by creditors and sold for scrap – the engine ended up in a paper mill.

Monturiol spent the rest of his life in a variety of jobs, but continued to come up with new inventions. With the Ictineo, he had pioneered the use of the double hull, a technique still used today, while Monturiol also claimed advances in the manufacture of glues and gums, copying documents, commercial cigarette production and steam engine efficiency. He died in relative obscurity in 1885 and was buried in Barcelona, though his remains were later transferred to his home town. There's a memorial there, while others to Monturiol's pioneering invention, the Ictineo, are scattered throughout Barcelona. Monturiol himself is remembered in the city by a simple plaque at the Cementiri de Poble Nou.

child-centred displays and activities, and a nod towards ecology and conservation matters, pad out the attractions before you're tipped out in the aquarium shop so they can part you from even more of your money.

IMAX Port Vell (☏932 251 111, ⊛www.imaxportvell.com) stands next to the aquarium, with three screens showing films hourly from 11am in 3D or in giant screen format. The themes are familiar – the mysteries of the human body, forces of nature, alien adventure etc – and tickets are fairly reasonably priced (€7 or €10, depending on the film), but you'll find that the films are in Spanish or Catalan only. Instead, you might saunter down to the sloping lawn nearby, where there's usually a school party examining the replica of the strange fish-shaped submarine, the **Ictineo**, a genuine Catalan curiosity (see box, opposite). From here, it's only a ten-minute walk down the *moll*, past the towering Roy Lichtenstein sculpture, and around the marina to the Palau de Mar and Barceloneta.

Palau de Mar and the Museu d'Història de Catalunya

The only surviving warehouse on the Port Vell harbourside is known as the **Palau de Mar**, home to the **Museu d'Història de Catalunya** (Tues & Thurs–Sat 10am–7pm, Wed 10am–8pm, Sun 10am–2.30pm; €3, first Sun of month & public holidays free; ☏932 254 700, ⊛www.mhcat.net; ⓜBarceloneta), which traces the history of Catalunya from the Stone Age to the twentieth century. It's a spacious exhibition area wrapped around a wide atrium, with temporary shows on the **ground floor** and a lift to take you to the permanent displays on the upper floors: **second floor** for year dot to the Industrial Revolution, and **third** for periods and events up to 1980 (though later coverage is planned). You can pick up full English notes at the desk, and there's plenty to get your teeth into, whether it's poking around the interior of a Roman grain ship or comparing the rival nineteenth-century architectural plans for the Eixample. There's a dramatic Civil War section, while other fascinating asides shed light on matters as diverse as housing in the 1960s or the origins of the design of the Catalan flag. On the **fourth floor**, *La Miranda* boasts a glorious view from its huge terrace of the harbour, Tibidabo, Montjuïc and the city skyline – you don't need a museum ticket to visit this and it's open as a café during museum hours, with a set lunch, plus *à la carte* dinners.

The fish and seafood **restaurants** in the Palau de Mar arcade are some of the most popular in the city, especially at weekends. Here you overlook the packed **marina**, where Catalans park their yachts like they park their cars – impossibly tightly – fronted in summer by hawkers spreading blankets on the ground to sell jewellery and sunglasses. A boat near the Palau de Mar in the marina has been converted into a floating bar, the *Luz de Gas* (see p.204).

Barceloneta

Barceloneta (ⓜBarceloneta) was laid out in 1755 – a classic eighteenth-century grid of streets where previously there had been mud flats – to replace part of La Ribera that was destroyed to make way for the Ciutadella fortress to the north. Bound by the harbour on one side and the Mediterranean on the other, the long, narrow streets are still very much as they were planned, bro-

The cross-harbour cable car

The most thrilling ride in the city centre is across the inner harbour on the cable car, the **Trasbordador Aeri** (☎932 252 718), which sweeps right across the water from the **Torre de Sant Sebastiá**, at the foot of Barceloneta, to Montjuïc, with a stop in the middle at **Torre de Jaume I**, in front of the World Trade Centre on the Moll de Barcelona. The views are stunning, and you can pick out with ease the familiar towers of the cathedral and Sagrada Família, while the trees lining the Ramblas look like the forked tongue of a serpent.

Departures are every fifteen minutes (daily 10.45am–7pm), though in summer and at weekends you may have to wait for a while at the top of the towers for a ride as the cars only carry about twenty people at a time. **Tickets** cost €7.50 one way or €9 return for the whole journey, or €7.50 one way/return if you join at the middle station, Torre de Jaume I.

ken at intervals by small squares and lined with abundantly windowed houses designed to give the sailors and fishing folk who originally lived here plenty of sun and fresh air. These days, it's the neighbourhood's many fish and seafood **restaurants** that are its *raison d'être*, found scattered right across the tight grid of streets but most characteristically lined along the harbourside **Passeig Joan de Borbó**. The best are reviewed on p.192.

Modern apartment building has scarred the neighbourhood's eighteenth-century proportions, but there are still a few reminders of the old days. Some original houses venture a decorative flourish, a sculpted balcony or a carved lintel, while in the central Plaça de la Barceloneta is an eighteenth-century fountain and the Neoclassical church of **Sant Miquel del Port**. The *Can Ganassa* café here puts out tables in the summer and, though you're just a couple of blocks from the tourist-filled restaurants of the *passeig*, the atmosphere remains resolutely local – people filling water-bottles or simply passing the time of day, kids riding bikes and playing ball. The adjacent Plaça de la Font holds the neighbourhoods **Mercat de la Barceloneta** (Mon–Sat 7am–3pm, plus Fri (except Aug) 4.30–8.30pm) currently housed in a temporary building while the square and market building are remodelled (by 2007).

On the seaward side of Barceloneta, what was once a scrappy fishermen's strand is now furnished with boardwalks, showers, benches, climbing frames, water fountains and public art. **Platja de Sant Sebastià** is the first in a series of landscaped beaches that stretches north from here along the coast to the River Besòs. A double row of palms backs the **Passeig Marítim**, a sweeping stone esplanade that runs as far as the Port Olímpic, a fifteen-minute walk away. On the way, just before the hospital and port, you'll pass the **Parc de la Barceloneta**, a rather plain expanse enlivened only by its whimsical *modernista* water tower (1905), rising like a minaret above the palms.

Vila Olímpica and the Port Olímpic

From any point along the Passeig Marítim, the soaring twin towers of the Olympic village and port impose themselves upon the skyline, while a shimmering golden mirage above the promenade slowly reveals itself to be a **huge copper fish** (courtesy of North American Frank Gehry, architect of the Bilbao

Guggenheim). These are the showpiece manifestations of the huge seafront development constructed for the 1992 Olympics. The **Vila Olímpica** (Olympic Village) housed the 15,000 competitors and support staff, with the apartment buildings and residential complexes converted into permanent housing after the Games. It was a controversial plan, not least because the local population from the old industrial neighbourhood of Poble Nou – part of which was destroyed in the process – were excluded as property prices here later soared. Generally agreed to have been more beneficial is the **Port Olímpic**, site of the Olympic marina and many of the watersports events. Backed by the city's two tallest buildings – the **Torre Mapfre** and the steel-framed **Hotel Arts Barcelona**, both 154m high – the port area has filled up with restaurants, bars, shops and nightspots, and is a major target for visitors and city dwellers at weekends and on summer nights. Two wharves contain the bulk of the action: the **Moll de Mestral** has a lower deck by the marina lined with cafés, bars and *terrassas*, while the **Moll de Gregal** sports a double-decker tier of seafood restaurants. Beyond here, on the far side of the port, **Nova Icària** and **Bogatell** beaches – each with a beachside café, play facilities, showers and loungers – stretch up to the Poble Nou neighbourhood.

It's another fifteen minutes' walk from the port to the end of Bogatell beach and Poble Nou. Heading back into the city, the entrance to Ⓜ Ciutadella-Vila Olímpica lies over the main Ronda del Litoral, behind the port.

Poble Nou

The next neighbourhood along from the Port Olímpic is **Poble Nou** (New Village), a largely nineteenth-century industrial area that has long been slated for redevelopment. Since the early 1990s its gradual transformation has formed part of the overall scheme that envisions turning the 5km of shoreline from Barceloneta to the River Besòs into a hi-tech business, leisure and residential corridor. As with the Vila Olímpica before it, the redevelopment has its critics amongst the locals, who feel they're being pushed out as the money floods in – "Poble Nou is not for sale" reads the ubiquitous graffiti, though it's an increasingly forlorn cry. The authorities have given the regeneration area a suitably contemporary epithet, **22@**, and are currently overseeing the transformation of almost 120 city blocks.

The redevelopment of old factories and the like has already had a significant effect, as some of the city's hottest clubs, galleries and art spaces are now found in Poble Nou. Meanwhile, the few local attractions are easily seen by anyone with a couple of hours to spare. The spruced-up **beaches** – Bogatell, Mar Bella and Nova Mar Bella – are reached along the promenade from the Port Olímpic, while crossing the main highway backing Bogatell beach puts you at the bottom of the pretty, traffic-free, tree-lined **Rambla Poble Nou**. This runs inland through the most attractive part of nineteenth-century Poble Nou and is entirely local in character – no cardsharps or human statues here. Stop off for an *orxata* or a crushed lemon drink at *El Tío Ché* (see p.179), or lunch at one of the local restaurants (p.194) – Ⓜ Poble Nou (yellow line 4) is at the top of the *rambla* and a block over to the right, and will take you back to Ciutadella, Barceloneta or the city centre.

Back near the beach, it's also worth taking the time to walk around the long walls to the entrance of the **Cementiri de Poble Nou** (daily 8am–6pm), at the northern end of Avinguda d'Icaria. This vast nineteenth-century mausoleum has its tombs set in walls 7m high, tended by families who have to climb great stepladders to reach the uppermost tiers. With traffic noise muted by the high walls, and birdsong accompanying a stroll around the flower-lined pavements, quiet courtyards, sculpted angels and tiny chapels, this village of the dead is a rare haven in contemporary Barcelona.

Diagonal Mar

The waterfront north of Poble Nou has seen the latest city transformation, in the wake of the works associated with the Universal Forum of Cultures Expo, held here in 2004. The extension of Avinguda Diagonal to the sea provided the necessary rebranding, and it's as **Diagonal Mar** that the area is promoted, anchored by the huge Diagonal Mar **shopping mall** at the foot of the avenue (ⓜEl Maresme Fòrum, or tram T4), and with several new five-star hotels, convention centres and exhibition halls grouped nearby. The **Edifici Fòrum** itself, a giant blue biscuit tin hovering – seemingly unsupported – above the ground, is the work of Jacques Herzog, architect of London's Tate Modern. Everything here is on a grand scale: the main convention centre is the biggest in southern Europe, while the boast about the main open space – the **Plaza** – is that it's the second largest square in the world (150,000 square metres) after Beijing's Tiananmen Square. This immense, undulating expanse spreads towards the sea, culminating in a giant solar-panelled canopy that overlooks the new marina, landscaped beach, park areas and leisure zones. It's all still a bit soulless at present – hot as Hades in summer, buffeted by biting winter winds - but it's worth the metro ride if you're interested in heroic-scale public projects. The new tram system comes down here too, so you could always glide there or back via Avinguda Diagonal and Glòries to see more of Barcelona in transformation.

Montjuïc

You'll need to reserve at least a day to see **Montjuïc**, the steep hill and park rising over the city to the southwest. It takes its name from the Jewish community that once settled on its slopes, and there's been a castle on the heights since the mid-seventeenth century, which says much about the hill's obvious historical defensive role. But it's as a cultural leisure park that contemporary Montjuïc is positioned, anchored around the heavyweight art collections in the **Museu Nacional d'Art de Catalunya** (**MNAC**). This unsurpassed national collection of Catalan art is supplemented by works in two other superb galleries, namely international contemporary art in the **Caixa Forum** and that of the famous Catalan artist Joan Miró in the **Fundació Joan Miró**. In addition, there are separate archeological, ethnological, military and theatrical **museums**, quite apart from the buildings and stadiums associated with the 1992 **Olympics**, which was centred on the heights of Montjuïc.

As late as the 1890s, the hill was nothing more than a collection of private farms and woodland on the edge of the old town, though some landscaping had already taken place by the time Montjuïc was chosen as the site of the **International Exhibition** of 1929. The slopes were then laid with gardens, terraces and fountains, while monumental Neoclassical buildings were added to the north side, many of them later adapted as museums. The famous **Poble Espanyol** (Spanish Village) – a hybrid park of collected Spanish buildings – is the most extraordinary relic of the Exhibition, while the various lush **gardens** still provide enjoyment and respite from the crowds. Above all, perhaps, there are the **views** to savour from this most favoured of Barcelona's hills: from the steps in front of the Museu Nacional, from the castle ramparts, from the Olympic terraces, or from the cable cars that zigzag up the steepest slopes of Montjuïc.

The hill covers a wide area, so it's vital to plan your visit carefully around the various opening times. If you're intent on covering everything, it might be better to see Montjuïc in two separate visits – MNAC, Poble Espanyol and Olympic area on one day, and Fundació Joan Miró, cable car and castle on the other. There are several approaches to Montjuïc, depending on where you want to start, and various means of **transport** around the hill: the box on p.89 has all the details. The **Barcelona Card and Articket** (see p.28), and **Bus Turístic pass** (p.33), provide discounted entry into Montjuïc's museums, galleries and attractions. Places to eat are thin on the ground, though there are good **cafés** in Caixa Forum and the Fundació Joan Miró, outdoor snack bars at the castle and on the slopes below MNAC, and a **restaurant** with outdoor terrace at the Font del Gat in the Jardins Laribal, below the Fundació Joan Miró. There are also plenty of decent restaurants in the neighbouring *barri* of Poble Sec (see p.191).

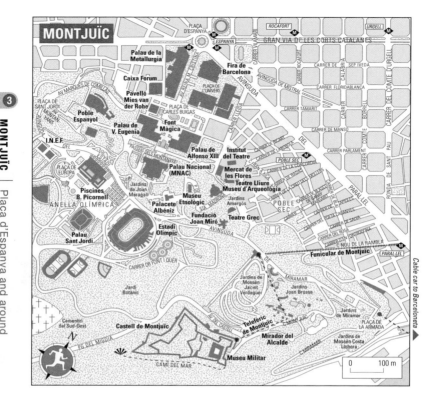

Plaça d'Espanya and around

Gateway to the 1929 International Exhibition was the vast **Plaça d'Espanya**, based on plans by noted architect Josep Puig i Cadalfach. Arranged around a huge Neoclassical fountain, and offset by the old Les Arenes bullring on the northern side, the square is unlike any other in Barcelona, a radical departure from the *modernisme* so in vogue elsewhere in the contemporary city. Striking twin towers, 47m high, stand at the foot of the imposing **Avinguda de la Reina Maria Cristina**, which heads up towards Montjuïc, the avenue lined by huge exhibition halls used for trade fairs. At the end of the avenue is Plaça de Carles Buïgas, from where monumental steps (and modern escalators) ascend the hill to the Palau Nacional, past water cascades and under the flanking walls, busts and roofline "kiosks" of two grand Viennese-style pavilions. It's an overtly showy approach to Montjuïc, with little whimsy in evidence, save for the **Font Màgica**, at the foot of the steps, which, on selected evenings (May–Sept Thurs–Sun 8pm–midnight, music starts 9.30pm; Oct–April Fri & Sat only at 7pm, 7.30pm, 8pm & 8.30pm; free), becomes the centrepiece of an impressive if slightly kitsch sound-and-light show – the brightly coloured water appears to dance to the strains of Holst and Abba.

Montjuïc transport

Getting there

• **Metro** ⓂEspanya deposits you at the foot of Avinguda de la Reina Maria Cristina, for easy access to Caixa Forum, Poble Espanyol and the Museu Nacional d'Art (MNAC). The Olympic area can then be reached by escalators behind MNAC.

• **Funicular** The Funicular de Montjuïc (daily 9am–10pm every 10min; normal city transport tickets and passes apply) departs from inside the station at ⓂParal.lel and takes a couple of minutes to ascend the hill. At the upper station on Avinguda de Miramar you can switch to the Montjuïc cable car (see "Getting around" below), or you're only a few minutes' walk from the Fundació Joan Miró.

• **Cable-car** The Trasbordador Aeri, or cross-harbour cable car (see p.84), from Barceloneta drops you outside the Jardins de Miramar, on the far southeastern slopes. From here, it's a ten-minute walk to the Montjuïc cable-car and funicular stations and another five to the Fundació Joan Miró.

Getting around

• **Walking** It takes a good hour to walk on the road around the hill from Avinguda de la Reina Maria Cristina, past the Poble Espanyol, Olympic area and Fundació Joan Miró to the cross-harbour cable-car station at the far end of Montjuïc – and it's steep and shadeless in parts. Escalators up the hill between MNAC and the Olympic area cut out the worst of the slog. Walking up the steep hill all the way to the castle is not advised in hot weather (though there are steps through the gardens and between the roads) – use the cable car.

• **Buses** From Plaça d'Espanya (Avgda. de la Reina Maria Cristina) take: bus #13 for Caixa Forum and the Poble Espanyol; #50 for Caixa Forum, Poble Espanyol, Olympic area, botanical gardens, funicular and cable-car stations; or bus #PM (Parc de Montjuïc; weekends only) for the same route plus the castle. The Bus Turístic also stops at the main Montjuïc attractions.

• **Tren Turístic de Montjuïc** The train-trolley leaves from Plaça d'Espanya (every 30min 10am–8.30pm: mid-June to mid-Sept daily; April to mid-June & mid-Sept–Oct Sat & Sun; €3.20; ☎934 156 020) and runs to all the major sights on Montjuïc, including the castle. The return trip lasts about an hour and your ticket allows you to complete the full circuit once, getting on and off where you like.

• **Telefèric de Montjuïc** The Montjuïc cable car (renovated for 2006; ticket and time-table info ☎934 430 859, ⓦwww.tmb.net), from Avinguda de Miramar, whisks you up to the castle and back in automated eight-seater gondolas.

Caixa Forum

To the right of the fountain (before climbing the steps/escalators), and hidden from view until you turn the corner around Avinguda del Marquès de Comillas, is **Caixa Forum** (Tues–Sun 10am–8pm; free; ☎934 768 600, ⓦwww.fundacio. lacaixa.es), an arts and cultural centre set within the old Casamarona textile factory. Constructed in 1911 in the finest modernist style of Josep Puig i Cadafalch, the factory shut down in 1920 and lay abandoned until pressed into service as a police building after the Civil War. The subsequent renovation and expansion under the auspices of the Fundacío La Caixa has produced a remarkable building, entered beneath twin iron-and-glass canopies representing spreading trees. You descend into a palatial white marble foyer, where a vibrant Sol LeWitt mural splashes across one wall. Beyond here are found the exhibition halls, fashioned within the former factory buildings, whose external structure has been left untouched – original girders, pillars and stanchions, factory brickwork and crenellated walls appear at every turn. The Casamarona tower, etched in blue and yellow tiling, rises high above the walls, as readily recognizable as the huge Miró starfish logos emblazoned across the building.

The centre houses the foundation's celebrated **contemporary art collection**, focusing on the period from the 1980s to the present, with hundreds of artists represented, from Antoni Abad to Rachel Whiteread. Works are shown in partial rotation, along with touring exhibitions. There's also a library and resource centre, the Mediateca multimedia space, regular children's activities, and a 400-seat auditorium with a full programme of music, art, poetry and literary events. The **café** is worth knowing about, too – an airy converted space within the old factory walls, serving breakfast, sandwiches, snacks and lunch.

Pavelló Mies van der Rohe

Immediately across Avinguda del Marquès de Comillas from Caixa Forum, set back from the road, is the 1986 reconstruction by Catalan architects of the **Pavelló Mies van der Rohe** (daily 10am–8pm; guided visits Wed & Fri 5–7pm; €3.50; ☎934 234 016, ⊚www.miesbcn.com), which recalls part of the German contribution to the 1929 Exhibition. Originally designed by Mies van der Rohe, and used as a reception room during the Exhibition, it's considered a major example of modern rationalist architecture. The pavilion has a startlingly beautiful conjunction of hard straight lines with watery surfaces, its dark-green polished onyx alternating with shining glass. It's open to visitors but unless there's an exhibition in place (a fairly regular occurrence) there is nothing to see inside save Mies van der Rohe's iconic tubular steel *Barcelona Chair*, though you can buy postcards and books from the small shop and debate quite how much you want a Mies mousepad or a "Less is More" T-shirt.

Poble Espanyol

A five-minute walk up Avinguda del Marquès de Comillas brings you to the **Poble Espanyol**, or Spanish Village (Mon 9am–8pm, Tues–Thurs 9am–2am, Fri & Sat 9am–4am, Sun 9am–midnight; €7.50, combined ticket with MNAC €12; ☎935 086 300, ⊚www.poble-espanyol.com). This was an inspired concept for the International Exhibition – a complete village consisting of streets and squares with reconstructions of famous or characteristic buildings from all over Spain, such as the fairy-tale medieval walls of Ávila through which you enter. "Get to know Spain in one hour" is what's promised and it's nowhere near as cheesy as you might think. It works well as a crash-course introduction to Spanish architecture – everything is well labelled and at least reasonably accurate. The echoing main square is lined with cafés, while the surrounding streets, alleys and buildings contain around forty workshops, where you can see engraving, weaving, pottery and other crafts. Inevitably, it's all one huge shopping experience – castanets to Lladró porcelain, religious icons to Barcelona soccer shirts – and prices are inflated, but children will love it (and you can let them run free as there's no traffic). Your ticket also gets you entry to the **Fran Daurel Col. lecció d'Art Contemporani** so you might as well drop in to see the minor Tàpies and Miró lithographs and the series of Picasso ceramics.

Get to the village as it opens if you want to enjoy it in relatively crowd-free circumstances – once the tour groups arrive, it becomes a bit of a scrum. You could, of course, always come at the end of the day, when the village transforms into a vibrant centre of Barcelona nightlife. Two of Barcelona's hippest designers, Alfredo Arribas and Xavier Mariscal, installed a club in the Ávila gate in the early 1990s (the *Torres de Avila*, now the *Real Club Danzatoria*). Other fashionable venues followed and, this being Barcelona, the whole complex now stays open until the small hours.

Museu Nacional d'Art de Catalunya

The towering, domed **Palau Nacional**, set back on Montjuïc at the top of the long flight of steps from the fountains, was the flagship building of Barcelona's 1929 International Exhibition. Partly the work of Pere Domènech i Roura (son of the more famous Lluís Domènech i Montaner), its massive frescoed oval hall hosted the opening ceremony of the Exhibition, providing a fittingly grandiose backdrop for the city's biggest show since the Universal Exhibition of 1888. The palace was due to be demolished once the exhibition was over, but gained a reprieve and ultimately became home to one of Spain's great museums.

After a major refit lasting several years, the **Museu Nacional d'Art de Catalunya** (**MNAC**; Tues–Sat 10am–7pm, Sun & hols 10am–2.30pm; €8.50, ticket valid 48hr, first Thurs of the month free; ☏936 220 376, ◍www.mnac. es) is now the city's most renowned art experience, showcasing a thousand years of Catalan art in stupendous surroundings. For first-time visitors, it can be difficult to know where to start, but if time is limited it's recommended that you concentrate on the medieval collection, which is split into two main sections, one dedicated to Romanesque art and the other to Gothic – periods in which Catalunya's artists were pre-eminent in Spain. The collection of Romanesque frescoes in particular is the museum's pride and joy, and is perhaps the best collection of its kind in the world. MNAC also has impressive holdings of European Renaissance and Baroque art, as well as an unsurpassed collection of "modern" (ie nineteenth- and twentieth-century) Catalan art up until the 1940s – everything from the 1950s and later is covered by MACBA (see p.64). In addition there are collections of Catalan photography, drawings and engravings, and a numismatic section, items from which are either displayed as part of the general collection or sometimes appear in **temporary exhibitions** (separate admission charge, varies), which change every two to four months. Finally, there's a **café-bar**, gift shop and art **bookshop** in the gloriously restored oval hall, and a museum **restaurant** on the upper floor with views over the city.

The Romanesque collection

Great numbers of Romanesque churches were built in the Catalan Pyrenees as the Christian conquest spread, though there are far fewer further south, where Christianity arrived later. Medieval Catalan studios concentrated on decorating the churches with frescoes depicting biblical events, and even the most remote Pyrenean valleys could boast lavish masterpieces of great skill. However, by the nineteenth century many of these churches and their decorative frescoes had either been ruined by later renovations or lay abandoned, prone to theft and damage. Not until 1919 was a concerted effort made to remove the frescoes to the museum, where they could be better preserved and displayed.

Six remarkable sections present the **frescoes** in a reconstruction of their original setting, so you can see their size and where they would have been placed in the church buildings. Full explanatory notes (in English) cover the artistic techniques, interpretation and iconography of the paintings, which for the most part have a vibrant, raw quality, best exemplified by those taken from churches in the Boí valley in the Catalan Pyrenees. In the apse of the early twelfth-century church of Sant Climent in Taüll, the so-called **Master of Taüll** painted an extraordinarily powerful *Christ in Majesty*, combining a Byzantine hierarchical composition with the imposing colours and strong outlines of contemporary manuscript illuminators. Look out for details such as the leper, to the left of the Sant Climent altar, patiently allowing a dog to lick his sores. Frescoes from other churches explore a variety of themes, from heaven to hell, with the displays complemented by sculptures, altar panels, woodcarvings, religious objects and furniture retrieved from the mouldering churches themselves.

The Gothic collection

The Gothic collection is extensive, ranging over the whole of Spain and particularly good on Catalunya, Valencia and Aragón. There's a well-written commentary in each section, explaining the development of artistic movements from the thirteenth to the fifteenth century and the influence of other European styles on Catalan art. The evolution from the Romanesque to the Gothic period was marked by a move from mural painting to painting on wood, and by the depiction of more naturalistic figures in scenes showing the lives of the saints, and later in portraits of kings and patrons of the arts. In the early part of the period, the Catalan and Valencian schools particularly were influenced by contemporary Italian styles, and you'll see some outstanding altarpieces, tombs and church decoration. Later began the International Gothic or "1400" style in which the influences became more widespread; the important figures of this movement were the fifteenth-century artists **Jaume Huguet** and **Lluís Dalmau**. Works from the end of this period show the strong influence of contemporary Flemish painting, in the use of denser colours, the depiction of crowd scenes and a concern for perspective. The last Catalan artist of note here is the so-called **Master of La Seu d'Urgell**, represented by a number of works, including a fine series of six paintings (Christ, the Virgin Mary, SS Peter, Paul and Sebastian, and Mary Magdalene) that once formed the covers of the organ in La Seu's cathedral. The section concludes with examples of funerary art – tombs, sarcophagi and sepulchres of the fourteenth and fifteenth centuries – and cases of religious gold and silverware.

The Renaissance and Baroque collections

Many of the **Renaissance** and **Baroque** works on display have come from private collections bequeathed to the museum, notably by conservative politician Francesc Cambó and Madrid's Thyssen-Bornemisza (the latter collection formerly displayed at Barcelona's Pedralbes monastery). Selections from these bequests rate their own rooms in the Renaissance and Baroque galleries, while other rooms here trace artistic development from the early sixteenth to the eighteenth century. Major European artists displayed include Peter Paul Rubens, Giovanni Battista Tiepolo, Jean Honoré Fragonard, Francisco de Goya, El Greco, Francisco de Zurbarán and Diego Velázquez, though the museum is of course keen to play up Catalan works of the period, which largely absorbed the prevailing European influences – thus Barcelona artist **Antoni Viladomat**

(1678–1755), whose twenty paintings of St Francis, executed for a monastery, are shown here in their entirety. However, more familiar to most will be the masterpieces of the Spanish Golden Age, notably Velázquez's *Saint Paul* and Zurbarán's *Immaculate Conception*.

The modern art collection

MNAC ends on a high note with its important **nineteenth- and twentieth-century Catalan art** collection, which is particularly good on *modernista* and *noucentista* painting and sculpture, the two dominant schools of the period. Rooms highlight individual artists and genres, shedding light on the development of art in an exciting period of Catalunya's history, while there are fascinating diversions into *modernista* interior design (with some pieces by Gaudí), avant-garde sculpture and historical photography.

Although he died young, in 1874, **Marià Fortuny i Marsal** is often regarded as the earliest *modernista* artist; he was certainly the first Catalan painter known widely abroad, having exhibited to great acclaim in Paris and Rome. He specialized in minutely detailed pictures, often of exotic subjects – his set-piece *Battle of Tetuan* was based on a visit to Morocco in 1859 to observe the war there. Closer to home are the intricate street and market scenes of the Born, the work of the main name in Catalan Realism, Ramon Martí i Alsina, while the master of nineteenth-century Catalan landscape painting was Joaquim Veyreda i Vila, founder of the Olot School (Olot being a town in northern Catalunya), whose members were influenced both by the work of the early Impressionists and by the distinctive volcanic scenery of the Olot region. However, it wasn't until the later emergence of **Ramon Casas i Carbó** (whose famous picture of himself and Pere Romeu on a tandem once hung on the walls of *Els Quatre Gats*) and **Santiago Rusiñol i Prats** that Catalan art acquired a progressive sheen, taking its cue from the very latest in European styles, whether the symbolism of Whistler or the vibrant social observation of Toulouse-Lautrec. Hot on their heels came a new generation of *modernista* artists – Josep Maria Sert, Marià Pidelaserra i Brias, Ricard Canals i Llambí and others – who were strongly influenced by the scene in contemporary Paris. The two brightest stars of the period, though, were **Joaquim Mir i Trinxet**, whose highly charged landscapes tended towards the abstract, and **Isidre Nonell i Monturiol**, who from 1902 until his early death in 1911 painted sombre naturalistic studies of impoverished gypsy communities.

Noucentisme was a style at once more classical and less consciously flamboyant than *modernisme* – witness the portraits and landscapes of Joaquim Sunyer i Miró, perhaps the best known *noucentista* artist, and the work of sculptors like Pau Gargallo i Catalán. This was also a period when the Barcelona art world flourished under the patronage of private galleries like the Galeries Dalmau, whose important shows in the city after World War I promoted Cubism and avant-garde works to a wider audience.

La Ciutat del Teatre and around

Downhill from MNAC, just to the east, steps descend the hillside to the theatre area known as **La Ciutat del Teatre,** which occupies a corner at the back of the old working-class neighbourhood of **Poble Sec.** A road, the Passeig de

Santa Madrona, snakes down this way too, passing the **museums of ethnology and archeology** – the also-rans of Montjuïc really, though both are decent wet-weather targets – and the **Teatre Grec**, a reproduction of a Greek theatre cut into the hillside. This was built for the 1929 Exhibition and is now used during Barcelona's summer theatre and music festival.

Museu Etnològic

The **Museu Etnològic** (June–Sept Tues–Sat 11am–8pm, Sun 11am–3pm; Oct–May Tues & Thurs 10am–7pm, Wed & Fri–Sun 10am–2pm; €3; ☎934 246 807, ⊛www.museuetnologic.bcn.es) boasts extensive cultural collections from across the globe, particularly the Amazon region, Papua New Guinea, pre-Hispanic America, Australia, Morocco and Ethiopia. There are simply too many pieces to show at any one time, so the museum has rotating exhibitions, which usually last for a year or two and concentrates on a particular subject or geographical area. Refreshingly, Spain and its regions aren't neglected, which means that there's usually also a focus on the minutiae of rural Spanish life or an examination of subjects like medieval carving or early industrialization. For these exhibits, the museum draws on the work of Spanish ethnographers such as Ramon Violant who spent much of the 1940s recording the daily routine of inhabitants in the Pyrenees. In addition, the museum has opened up the **reserved rooms** in its basement to the general public, where the conservers and staff have traditionally worked, and it's a real treat to walk past the storage cabinets, piled high with anything from African masks to Spanish fans.

Museu d'Arqueològia de Catalunya

Just down the hill from the city's ethnological museum is the impressive **Museu d'Arqueològia de Catalunya** (Tues–Sat 9.30am–7pm, Sun & hols 10am–2.30pm; €2.40; ☎934 246 577, ⊛www.mac.es), whose array of relics spans the centuries from the Stone Age to the time of the Visigoths, with the Roman and Greek periods particularly well represented. The sections dealing with prehistoric, Stone and Bronze Age periods are the most disappointing, with any interest well hidden by the old-fashioned case-by-case presentation – though to be fair some exhibits are gradually being updated. However, there's no such reservation about the displays in the central rotunda, which concentrate on sixth-and-seventh-century-BC finds from the Greek site at Empúries on the Costa Brava, some beautiful figures from the Carthaginian settlements in Ibiza, and ceramics from the Iberian era, including tablets bearing inscriptions in an indecipherable script. The highlights are many and varied, including a notable marble statue of Asclepius, Greek god of medicine, which dominates the hall. The Second Punic War (218–201 BC) saw the Carthaginians expelled from Iberia by the Romans, who made their provincial capital at Tarragona (Tarraco), with a secondary outpost at Barcelona (Barcino). There's some fine Roman glassware and mosaic work on display, while an upper floor interprets life in **Barcino** itself through a collection of tombstones, statues, inscriptions and friezes found all over the city. Some of the stonework is remarkably vivid, depicting the faces of some of Barcino's inhabitants as clearly as the day they were carved.

La Ciutat del Teatre

The theatre buildings that make up La Ciutat del Teatre sit in a tight huddle off c/de Lleida, with the Mercat de les Flores theatre (see p.210) – once a flower market – and progressive Teatre Lliure (p.214) occupying the spaghetti-western-style Palau de l'Agricultura premises built for the 1929 Exhibition. Walk through the terracotta arch from c/de Lleida, and off to the left is the far sleeker Institut del Teatre (p.214), with its sheer walls contrasting markedly with the neighbourhood's cheap housing, whose laundry is strung just metres away from the gleaming Theatre City. The institute brings together the city's major drama and dance schools, and various conservatories, libraries and study centres.

Poble Sec

The streets to the south and east make up the neighbourhood of **Poble Sec** (ⓂPoble Sec), or "dry village", so called because it had no water supply until the nineteenth century. Confined by the hill of Montjuïc on one side and the busy Avinguda del Paral.lel on the other, it's a complete contrast to the landscaped slopes behind it – a grid of contoured narrow streets, down-to-earth grocery stores, bakeries, old-fashioned bars and good-value restaurants (see p.000 for these). There's nothing much to see, though you might walk through on your way back to the Raval and Barcelona's old-town areas, in which case it's worth negotiating the precipitous c/Nou de la Rambla for a drink in the *Bar Primavera* (closed Mon). It's an old cottage at the very top of the street, with partial views from its tables set on a vine-clad terrace. The **funicular** (from ⓂParal.lel to the cable-car station for the castle) departs from right at the other end of this street.

The Olympic area

From Poble Espanyol, the main road through Montjuïc climbs around the hill and up to the city's principal **Olympic area**, sometimes known as the Anella Olímpica (Olympic Ring). The 1992 Olympics were the second planned for Montjuïc. The first, in 1936 – the "People's Olympics" – were organized as an alternative to the Nazis' infamous Berlin games of that year, but the day before the official opening Franco's army revolt triggered the Civil War and scuppered the Barcelona games. Some of the 25,000 athletes and spectators who had turned up stayed on to join the Republican forces.

Avinguda del Estadi leads you right past some of Barcelona's most celebrated sporting edifices – like Ricardo Bofill's Institut Nacional d'Educació Física de Catalunya (**INEF**; a sort of sports university), the **Piscines Bernat Picornell** (swimming pools and sports complex) and the Japanese-designed, steel-and-glass **Palau Sant Jordi**. Opened in 1990 with Luciano Pavarotti in attendance, this sports and concert hall seats 17,000 people and is overshadowed only by the Olympic stadium itself, the **Estadi Olímpic**, which comfortably holds 65,000. Built originally for the 1929 Exhibition, and completely refitted to accommodate the 1992 opening and closing ceremonies, it's a marvellously spacious stadium, its original Neoclassical facade left untouched by the Catalan architects in charge of the project. There's usually a gate open if you just want a glimpse of the pitch, while inside the stadium the **Galeria Olímpica** (April–Sept Mon–Fri 10am–2pm & 4–7pm; Oct–March Mon–Fri 10am–1pm & 4–6pm; €2.70; ☎934 260 660, Ⓦwww.fundaciobarcelonaolimpica.es) exhibits assorted items from the opening and closing ceremonies, and shows videos of the Games themselves. Between the stadium and the Palau Sant Jordi, a vast *terrassa* provides one of the

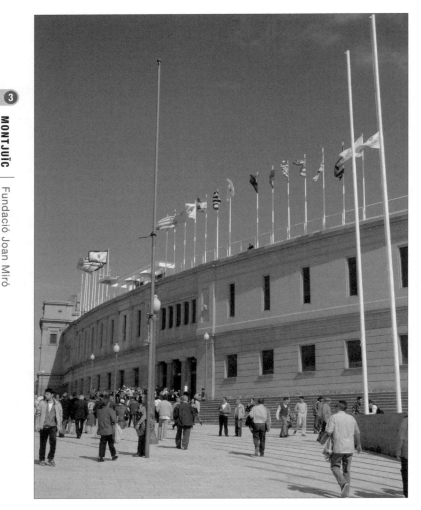

△ Estadi Olímpic

finest vantage points in the city. Long water-fed troughs break the concrete and marble expanse, while the confident, space-age curve of Santiago Calatrava's **communications tower** dominates the skyline.

Fundació Joan Miró

Montjuïc's highlight for many is the **Fundació Joan Miró** (Tues, Wed, Fri & Sat 10am–7pm, July–Sept until 8pm, Thurs 10am–9.30pm, Sun & hols

10am–2.30pm; €7.50, exhibitions €4, price includes audioguide; ☎934 439 470, ⊕www.bcn.fjmiro.es), possibly Barcelona's most adventurous art museum and certainly its most attractive. The impressive white structure is set in lovely gardens overlooking the city, and it lies just a few minutes' walk from either the Olympic stadium or the Montjuïc funicular and cable-car stations.

Joan Miró (1893–1983) was one of the greatest of Catalan artists, establishing an international reputation while retaining links with his homeland. He had his first exhibition in 1918 and after that spent his summers in Catalunya and the rest of the time in France, before moving to Mallorca in 1956, where he died. His friend, the architect Josep-Luis Sert, designed the beautiful building that now houses the museum, which comprises a permanent collection of paintings, graphics, tapestries and sculptures donated by Miró himself and covering the period from 1914 to 1978. With good English notes available, and a layout that uses natural light and space to good effect, it's a museum that's a positive pleasure to negotiate.

Miró, meanwhile, has a grip on the city that's hard to ignore, whether it's T-shirts for tourists or branding for businesses. You'll notice his sculptures and designs littering the city: the starfish logo which he designed for the Caixa de Pensions; the España logo on Spanish National Tourist Board publications; his sculpture in the Parc Joan Miró; and the mosaic on the Ramblas.

The Fundació sponsors excellent temporary exhibitions, film shows, lectures and children's theatre: check the website or listings magazines, or consult the notices on display. There's also a **library**, with books and periodicals on contemporary art, a **bookshop** selling posters and a **bar-restaurant** (lunch 1.30–3pm, otherwise drinks, pastries and sandwiches) with outdoor tables on a pleasant patio – you don't have to pay to get into the museum to use this.

The collection

The **paintings and drawings** are instantly recognizable, among the chief links between Surrealism and abstract art. Miró showed a childlike delight in colours and shapes and developed a free, highly decorative style – one of his favourite early techniques was to spill paint on the canvas and move his brush around in it. Much of the collection is, in fact, of his later works, since the museum was only proposed – and works specifically set aside – in the 1960s, when Miró had already been painting for almost fifty years. But there are early Realist works from before the mid-1920s, like the effervescent *Portrait of a Young Girl* (1919), while other gaps are filled by a collection later donated by Miró's widow, Pilar Juncosa, which demonstrates Miró's preoccupations in the 1930s and 1940s. It's this period when he began his *Constellations* series, in which first appeared the colours, themes and symbols that later came to define his work – reds and blues, women, birds and tears, the sun, moon and stars, all eventually pared down to the minimalist basics. The same period also saw the fifty black-and-white lithographs of the *Barcelona Series* (1939–44), executed in the immediate aftermath of the Civil War. They are a dark reflection of the turmoil of the period; snarling faces and great black shapes and shadows dominate. For a rapid appraisal of Miró's entire *oeuvre* look in on the museum's **Sala K**, whose 23 works are on long-term loan from a Japanese collector. Here, in a kind of potted retrospective, you can trace Miró's development as an artist, from his early Impressionist landscapes (1914) to the minimal renderings of the 1970s.

Perhaps the most innovative room of all is one full of work by other artists in homage to Miró, including fine pieces by Henri Matisse, Henry Moore, Max Ernst, Richard Serra, Robert Motherwell and Eduardo Chillida. The single most compelling exhibit, however, has to be Alexander Calder's **Mercury Fountain**, which he built for the Republican pavilion at the Paris Universal Exhibition of 1936–37 – the same exhibition for which Picasso painted *Guernica*. Like *Guernica*, it's a tribute to a town, this time the mercury-mining town of Almáden – its name spelled out in dangling metal letters above the fountain – which saw saturation bombing during the Civil War.

Other exhibits include Miró's enormous bright **tapestries** (he donated nine to the museum), pencil drawings (particularly of misshapen women and gawky ballerinas), and **sculpture** outside in the gardens. All these started life in the form of **sketches and notes**, and the museum has retained five thousand separate examples, of which it usually displays a selection. From a doodle on a scrap of old newspaper or on the back of a postcard, it's possible to trace the development of shapes and themes that later evolved into full-blown works of art.

Castell de Montjuïc and around

The Telefèric de Montjuïc tacks up the hillside, offering magnificent views on the way, before depositing you within the walls of the eighteenth-century **Castell de Montjuïc**. Built on seventeenth-century ruins, the fort's outer defences are constructed as a series of angular concentric perimeters, designed for artillery deflection, but the inner part is startlingly medieval in appearance, with its straight walls and square shape. The fort served as a military base and prison for many years, and it was here that the last president of the pre-war Generalitat, **Lluís Companys i Jover**, was executed on Franco's orders on October 15, 1940 – he had been in exile in Paris after the Civil War, but was handed over to Franco by the Germans upon their capture of the French capital. He's buried in the nearby Cementiri del Sud-Oest (see opposite).

You can walk along the ramparts, taking photographs from the various viewpoints, and there's a little outdoor **café** within the walls. Leave by the drawbridge and you can skirt the outer walls of the bastion as well, where the locals come at weekends to practise archery in the moat. You have to pay to go inside the inner **fortress** (Tues–Sun: mid-March to mid-Nov 9.30am–8pm; mid-Nov to mid-March 9.30am–5pm), where there's another café, expansive parade ground and *mirador* (viewpoint); this costs €1 or it's €2.50 if you also want to visit the **Museu Militar** (☎933 298 613), which presents endless swords, guns, medals, uniforms, armour, model castles, maps and portraits in a series of rooms around the parade ground and down on the lower level of the bastion. The fortress is army (and therefore state) property and its museum has long been considered an anachronism by the city – there was an equestrian statue of Franco here for many years, and even now there's barely a hint in the museum displays (other than some Republican uniforms and weaponry) that Barcelona was rent by Civil War. However, the Spanish government recently decided to hand the fortress over to the city and it will eventually be converted into a Peace Museum.

Below the castle walls, a panoramic pathway – the **Camí del Mar** – has been cut from the cliff edge, providing magnificent views, first across to Port Olímpic and the northern beaches, and then southwest as the path swings around the castle. This is an unfamiliar view of the city, of the sprawling docks and container yards, and cruise ships and tankers are usually visible negotiating the busy sea lanes. The path is just over 1km long and ends at the back of the castle battlements near the **Mirador del Migdia**, where there's an open-air café (weekends from 10am) and a place that rents out bikes (weekends only) for use on the surrounding wooded trails. It's worth strolling through the trees to the *mirador* itself, a balcony with extensive views over the Baixa Llobregat industrial area. You can see across to the Olympic stadium from here, while in the immediate foreground is the extraordinary **Cementiri del Sud-Oest**, stretching along the ridge below, whose tombs are stacked like apartment blocks on great conifer-lined avenues.

The gardens of Montjuïc

Montjuïc's main gardens are scattered across the southern and eastern reaches of the hill, below the castle. Principal among them is the **Jardí Botànic de Barcelona** (July & Aug daily 10am–8pm; April–June & Sept Mon–Fri 10am–5pm, Sat & Sun 10am–8pm; Oct–March daily 10am–5pm; €3, free last Sun of the month; ☎934 264 935; ⊛www.jardibotanic.bcn.es), on c/Dr Font i Quer, on the slopes behind the Olympic stadium – you can get here directly on buses #50 or #PM from Plaça d'Espanya. It's a beautifully kept contemporary garden, where easy-to-follow paths wind through landscaped zones representing the flora of the Mediterranean, Canary Islands, California, Chile, South Africa and Australia. There are **tours** every weekend (except Aug) on the half-hour between 10.30am and 1pm.

Signposted off Avinguda de Miramar, west of (and below) the Fundació Joan Miró, the terraces, clipped hedges and grottoes of the **Jardins Laribal** (daily 10am–dusk; free) date from 1918. They surround the spring of **Font del Gat**, which has been a picnic site since the nineteenth century. Josep Puig i Cadafalch built a restaurant here of the same name for the 1929 International Exhibition, and it's open now for lunch (1–4pm; closed Mon), with wonderful views from its terrace.

East of here, the Montjuïc cable car passes over the **Jardins de Mossèn Jacint Verdaguer** and adjacent **Jardins Joan Brossa** (both daily 10am–dusk; free), which tack up the hillside to the castle. Walking down through the gardens from the castle is a pleasant way to return to the lower slopes of Montjuïc, through what used to be the site of the old Montjuïc amusement park, though it's now fully landscaped, with childrens' play areas – halfway, there are sweeping city views from the **Mirador de l'Alcalde**.

Finally, outside the upper cross-harbour cable-car station, the formal **Jardins de Miramar** are still undergoing restoration as part of the works associated with the revamped *Gran Hotel Miramar*. However, there are more fine views from the cable-car station café-*terrassa*, while steps lead down from a point close to the cable-car station into the precipitous cactus gardens of the **Jardins de Mossèn Costa i Llobera** (daily 10am–dusk; free), which look out over the port. The flourishing stands of Central and South American, Indian and African cacti, some over 6m high, make a dramatic scene, little experienced by most visitors to Montjuïc, though the people lounging on the steps and in the shade of the bigger specimens suggest it's something of an open secret among the locals.

The Eixample

The **Eixample** – the gridded, nineteenth-century new-town area north of Plaça de Catalunya – is the city's main shopping and business district. It covers a vast expanse spreading north to the outlying hills and suburbs, though most of what there is to see lies within a few blocks of the two central, parallel thoroughfares, Passeig de Gràcia and Rambla de Catalunya. To visitors, the district's regular blocks and seemingly endless streets can appear offputting, while many locals experience only a fraction of the district on a daily basis. Indeed, the Eixample can't really be said to be a neighbourhood at all – at least not in the same way that the old-town *barris* distinguish themselves – though its genesis lay in the increasingly crowded streets and alleys of the Ciutat Vella.

As Barcelona grew more industrialized throughout the nineteenth century, the old town became overcrowded and unsanitary. Conditions were such that in 1851 permission was given by the Spanish state to knock down the encircling walls so that the city could expand beyond its medieval limits, across the plain to the hills beyond the old town. The Barcelona authorities championed a fan-shaped plan by popular municipal architect **Antoni Rovira i Trias**, whose elegant if conventional design radiated out from the existing shape of the old town. However, much to local chagrin, this was passed over by the Spanish government in favour of a revolutionary blueprint drawn up by utopian engineer and urban planner **Ildefons Cerdà i Sunyer**. This envisaged a grid-shaped new town marching off to the north, intersected by broad avenues cut on the diagonal. Districts would be divided into mathematically defined groups of blocks, with buildings limited in height, and central gardens, schools, markets, hospitals and other services provided for the inhabitants. Work started in 1859 on what became known as the Ensanche in Castilian, and Eixample in Catalan – the "Extension" or "Widening". Space and light were part of the very fabric of the design, with Cerdà's characteristic wide streets and shaved corners of the blocks surviving today. However, he saw most of his more radical social proposals ignored, as the Eixample rapidly became a fashionable area in which to live. Speculators developed buildings on the proposed open spaces as the moneyed classes sought to move from their cramped quarters by the port in the old town to spacious new apartments and business addresses. As the money in the city moved north, so did a new class of **modernista architects**, who began to pepper the Eixample with ever-more-striking examples of their work, which were eagerly commissioned by status-conscious merchants and businessmen.

These extraordinary buildings – most notably the work of Antoni Gaudí i Cornet, Lluís Domènech i Montaner and Josep Puig i Cadafalch (see colour section) – provide the main attraction for the visitor in the Eixample, turning it into a sort of open-air urban museum. The best-known examples are those in the famous block known as the Mansana de la Discòrdia, as well as Gaudí's La Pedrera apartment building, all found on the attractive central spine of **Passeig de Gràcia**. Almost everything else you're likely to want to see is found to the east of here in the area known as **Dreta de l'Eixample** (the right-hand side), including Gaudí's extraordinary **Sagrada Família** church – the one building in the city to which a visit is virtually obligatory. Other attractions in the Dreta include museums concentrating on Egyptian antiquities, Catalan art and ceramics, and perfume, with a special draw provided by the gallery devoted to the works of Catalan artist Antoni Tàpies. A few blocks south of the Sagrada Família, Barcelona's major avenues all meet at the swirling roundabout of **Glòries**, where a further set of cultural and architectural attractions await.

There's less to get excited about on the western, or left-hand side – the so-called **Esquerra de l'Eixample** – which houses many of the public buildings contained within Cerdà's nineteenth-century plan. Nevertheless, certain areas provide an interesting contrast with the *modernista* flourishes over the way, particularly the urban park projects close to Barcelona Sants train station.

As the Eixample covers a very large area, you're unlikely to be able to see everything described below as part of a single outing. You'll need to take **public transport** where you can to individual sites and then walk around the surrounding area; all the relevant details are given in the text. For a map and guide showing all the city's *modernista* sights, and for other benefits, the **Ruta del Modernisme** package might be of interest, while the Barcelona Card or the Articket also offer useful discounts (see p.28 for details of all). You'll find plenty of reasonable places to stop for lunch, while many of the city's designer bars and restaurants are found here too – the relevant chapters have useful listings.

Along Passeig de Gràcia

The wide **Passeig de Gràcia** runs northwest from Plaça de Catalunya as far as the southern reaches of Gràcia. Laid out in its present form in 1827, it's a splendid, showy avenue, bisected by the other two main city boulevards, the Gran Via de les Corts Catalanes and Avinguda Diagonal. If you walk its length as far as the Diagonal (a 25min stroll) you'll get a view of some of the best of the city's architecture, flaunted in a series of remarkable buildings on and just off the avenue. At intervals you can rest at the elaborate benches and lamps designed in 1900 by the city's municipal architect, Pere Falqués.

Mansana de la Discòrdia

The most famous grouping of buildings, the so-called **Mansana de la Discòrdia**, or "Block of Discord" (ⓂPasseig de Gràcia), is just four blocks up from Plaça de Catalunya. It gets its name because the adjacent buildings – built within a decade of each other by three different architects – show off wildly varying manifestations of the *modernista* style and spirit.

Casa Lleó Morera and the Museu del Perfum

On the corner with c/Consell de Cent, at Pg. de Gràcia 35, the six-storey **Casa Lleó Morera** is by Lluís Domènech i Montaner, completed in

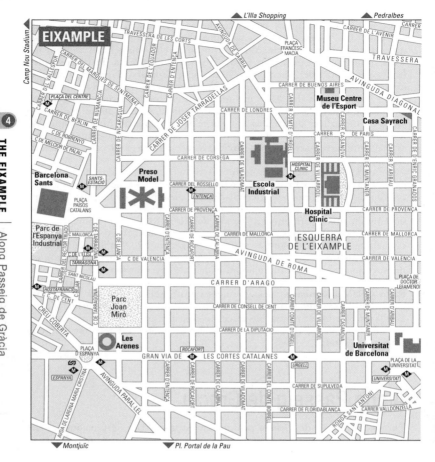

1906. It's the least appealing of the buildings in the block (in that it has the least extravagant exterior), and has suffered more than the others from "improvements" wrought by subsequent owners, which included removing the ground-floor arches and sculptures. A Loewe leather clothes and goods store occupies the whole of the ground floor, while the main entrance to the building is resolutely guarded to prevent more than a peek inside. This is a pity, because it has a rich Art Nouveau interior, flush with ceramics and wood, as well as exquisite stained glass, while its semicircular jutting balconies are quite distinctive.

An oddity a couple of doors up is the **Museu del Perfum** (Mon–Fri 10.30am–2pm & 4.30–8pm, Sat 11am–2pm; €5; ☎932 160 121, ⓦwww .museodelperfume.com), in the back of the Regia perfume store at Pg. de Gràcia 39. They may have to turn the lights on for you, but there's no missing the exhibits as a rather cloying pong exudes from the room. It's a private collection of over five thousand perfume and essence bottles from Egyptian times onwards, and there are some exquisite pieces displayed, including Turkish filigree-and-

crystal ware and bronze and silver Indian elephant flasks. More modern times are represented by scents made for Brigitte Bardot, Grace Kelly and Elizabeth Taylor, and if you're diligent enough to scan all the shelves you might be able to track down the perfume bottle designed by Salvador Dalí.

Casa Amatller

Josep Puig i Cadafalch's striking **Casa Amatller** is at Pg. de Gràcia 41, an apartment building from 1900 created largely from the bones of an existing building and paid for by Antoni Amatller, a Catalan chocolate manufacturer. The facade rises in steps to a point, studded with coloured ceramic decoration and with heraldic sculptures over the doors and windows. Inside the hallway, the ceramic tiles continue along the walls, while twisted stone columns are interspersed by dragon lamps, all of which are further illuminated by fine stained-glass doors and an interior glass roof. The ground floor displays temporary exhibitions under the auspices of the **Fundació Amatller** (usually Tues–Sat 10am–8pm, Sun 10am–3pm; free; ☎934 877 217, ⓦwww.amatller.org). Antoni Amatller was also an art collector, photographer and traveller – and the shop here sells Amatller chocolates, plus *modernista*-related postcards and books.

Casa Batlló

Perhaps the most extraordinary creation on the Block of Discord is at Pg. de Gràcia 43, where Antoni Gaudí's **Casa Batlló** (daily 9am–8pm, access occasionally restricted; main floor or attic and chimneys €10 each, complete visit €16; ☎932 160 306, ⌨www.casabatllo.es) – designed for the industrialist Josep Batlló and finished in 1907 – was similarly wrought from an apartment building already in place but considered dull by contemporaries. Gaudí was hired to give it a face-lift and contrived to create an undulating facade that Dalí later compared to "the tranquil waters of a lake". There's an animal aspect at work here, too: the stone facade hangs in folds, like skin, and from below, the twisted balcony railings resemble malevolent eyes. The higher part of the facade is less abstruse and more decorative, pockmarked with circular ceramic buttons laid on a bright mosaic background and finished with a little tower topped with a three-dimensional cross. The sinuous interior, meanwhile, resembles the insides of some great organism, complete with snakeskin-patterned walls and window frames, fireplaces, doorways and staircases that display not a straight line between them.

Self-guided audio tours show you the main floor (including the salon overlooking Passeig de Gràcia), the patio and rear facade, the ribbed attic and the celebrated mosaic roof-top chimneys. It's best to reserve a ticket in advance (by phone with Tel-Entrada on ☎902 101 212 or in person) as this is a very popular attraction – the scrum of aimless visitors, audio-stick glued to their ears, can be a frustrating business at peak times.

Fundació Antoni Tàpies

Lluís Domènech i Montaner's first important building, the **Casa Montaner i Simon**, c/Aragó 255, was finished in 1880. This was one of the earliest of all *modernista* projects in Barcelona: like Gaudí after him, the architect incorporated Moorish-style flourishes into his iron-framed work, which consists of two floors, supported by cast-iron columns and with no dividing walls. The building originally served the publishing firm of Montaner i Simon, but, as the enormous aluminium tubular structure on the roof announces, it was converted in 1990 to house the **Fundació Antoni Tàpies** (Tues–Sun 10am–8pm; €4.20; ☎934 870 315, ⌨www.fundaciotapies.org; ⓂPasseig de Gràcia).

Born in the city in 1923 (on c/de la Canuda in the Barri Gòtic), Antoni Tàpies i Puig left school to study law at the University of Barcelona in 1944, though he left before completing his degree. Drawn to art from an early age, and largely self-taught (though he studied briefly at Barcelona's Academia Valls), he was a founding member (1948) of the influential Dau al Set ("Die at Seven"), a grouping of seven artists producing a monthly avant-garde magazine of the same name which ran until 1956. His first major paintings date from as early as 1945, at which time he was interested in collage (using newspaper, cardboard, silver wrapping, string and wire) and engraving techniques. In the Dau al Set period, after coming into contact with Miró, among others, he underwent a brief Surrealist phase. However, after a stay in Paris he found his feet with an abstract style that matured in the Fifties, during which time he held his first major exhibitions, including shows in New York and Europe. His large works – many on show in the main gallery – are deceptively simple, though underlying messages and themes are signalled by the inclusion of everyday objects and symbols on the canvas. Tàpies has also continually experimented with unusual materials, like oil paint mixed with crushed marble, or employing sand, clay, cloth or straw in his collages. His work became increasingly political during the Sixties and Seventies. *A la memòria de Salvador Puig Antich* (*In Memory of Salvador Puig Antich*, 1974) commemorates a Catalan anarchist executed by Franco's regime, while slogans splashed across other works, or the frequent use of the red bars of the Catalan flag, leave no doubt about his affiliations. His most recent works are more sombre still, featuring recurring images of earth, shrouds and bodies, as echoes of civil war and conflict.

Temporary exhibitions focus on selections of Tàpies' work from all these periods, while three or four exhibitions a year on the basement level highlight works and installations by other contemporary artists. The foundation also includes a peerless archive on Tàpies' work held in the gorgeous **library** on the upper floor fashioned from the original shelves of the publisher's warehouse. In his later years Tàpies himself has concentrated on public art and sculpture; important **outdoor works in Barcelona** include *Homenatge a Picasso* (*Homage to Picasso*; 1983), on Passeig de Picasso, outside the gates of the Parc de la Ciutadella, while the foundation building is capped by *Núvol i Cadira* (*Cloud and Chair*; 1990), a tangle of glass, wire and metal.

Museu Egipci de Barcelona

Half a block east of Passeig de Gràcia, the **Museu Egipci de Barcelona**, at c/de València 284 (Mon–Sat 10am–8pm, Sun 10am–2pm; €6; ☎934 880 188, ⓦwww.fundclos.com; ⓂPasseig de Gràcia), is an exceptional private collection of artefacts from ancient Egypt, ranging from the earliest kingdoms to the era of Cleopatra. It was founded by hotelier Jordi Clos – whose *Hotel Claris*, a block away, still has its own private museum for guests – and displays a remarkable gathering of over six hundred objects, amulets to sarcophagi. The emphasis is on the shape and character of Egyptian society, and visitors are given a hugely detailed English-language guidebook, which enables you to nail down specific periods and descriptions, case by case, if you so wish. But the real pleasure here is a serendipitous wander, turning up items like a wood-and-leather bed of the First and Second Dynasties (2920–2649 BC), some examples of cat mummies of the Late Period (715–332 BC) or a rare figurine of a spoonbill (ibis) representing an Egyptian god (though archeologists aren't yet sure which). If you'd like to know more, an egyptologist leads **guided tours** every Friday at 5pm in English, included in the entry price. There are temporary exhibitions, a library and a good book and gift shop on the lower floor, and a terrace café upstairs. The museum also hosts a full programme of study sessions, children's activities and themed evening events – the reception desk or website can provide details.

Fundacío Francisco Godia

The building next door to the Egyptian museum on c/de València houses the private art collection of the **Fundacío Francisco Godia** (Mon & Wed–Sat 10am–2pm & 4–7pm, Sun 10am–2pm; €4.50, joint admission with Museu Egipci €9; ⓦwww.fundacionfgodia.org; ⓂPasseig de Gràcia). Harnessing medieval art, ceramics and modern Catalan art, in many ways it serves as a taster for the huge collections at Montjuïc in MNAC, while its small size makes it immediately more accessible. The pieces here – displayed in hushed rooms where the only sound is the hum of the air-conditioning – were collected by aesthete and 1950s racing driver Francisco Godia, whose medals and cups are the first things you encounter. Beyond lie selected Romanesque carvings and Gothic paintings, notably work by fifteenth-century artist Jaume Huguet, and then there's a jump to the *modernista* and *noucentista* paintings of Isidre Nonell, Santiago Rusiñol and Ramon Casas, among others. There's a varied selection of ceramics on show, too, from most of the historically important production centres in Spain. From fifteenth-century Valencia originate the *socarrats*, decorated terracotta panels used to stud ceilings. Not all of the collection can be shown at any one time, so pieces are rotated and added on occasion, while special exhibitions also run in tandem, for which there's usually no extra charge. For a guided tour of the exhibits, visit on Saturday or Sunday at noon.

La Pedrera

Gaudí's weird apartment building at Pg. de Gràcia 92 (Ⓜ Diagonal) is simply not to be missed – though you can expect queues whenever you visit. Constructed as the Casa Milà between 1905 and 1911, and popularly known as **La Pedrera** – "The Stone Quarry", it was declared a UNESCO World Heritage Site in 1984. Its hulking, rippled facade, curving around the street corner in one smooth sweep, is said to have been inspired by the mountain of Montserrat, while the apartments themselves, whose balconies of tangled metal drip over the facade, resemble eroded cave dwellings. Indeed, there's not a straight line to be seen – hence the contemporary joke that the new tenants would only be able to keep snakes as pets. The building, which Gaudí himself described as "more luminous than light", was his last secular commission – and one of his best – but even here he was injecting religious motifs and sculptures into the building until told to remove them. A sculpture of the Virgin Mary was planned to complete the roof, but the building's owners demurred, having been alarmed by the anti-religious fervour of the "Tragic Week" in Barcelona in 1909, when anarchist-sponsored rioting destroyed churches and religious foundations. Gaudí, by now working full-time on the Sagrada Família, was appalled, and determined in future to use his skills only for religious purposes.

The **self-guided visit** (entrance on c/Provença, daily 10am–8pm; ☎902 400 973, ⓦ www.fundaciocaixacatalunya.org; €8) includes a trip up to the extraordinary *terrat* (roof terrace) to see at close quarters the enigmatic chimneys, as well as an informative exhibition about Gaudí's work installed under the 270 curved brick arches of the attic. El Pis ("the apartment") on the building's fourth floor re-creates the design and style of a *modernista*-era bourgeois apartment in a series of extraordinarily light rooms that flow seamlessly from one to another. The apartment is filled with period furniture and effects, while the moulded door and window frames, and even the brass door handles, all follow Gaudí's sinuous building design. Perhaps the best experience of all, however, is **La Pedrera de Nit**, when you can enjoy the rooftop and night-time cityscape with a complimentary *cava* and music (June–Aug Fri & Sat 9.30pm; €11; ticket sales from Tel-Entrada on ☎902 101 212 or from Caixa Catalunya banks) – advance booking is essential, either from Caixa Caluya banks or on the day in person at the ticket office.

Casa Milà is still split into private apartments and is administered by the Fundació Caixa de Catalunya. Through the grand main entrance of the building you can access the Fundació's first-floor **exhibition hall** (daily 10am–8pm; free; also free guided visits Mon–Fri 6pm), which hosts temporary shows by major international artists.

△ The rooftop at La Pedrera

Casa Ramon Casas: Vinçon

Right next to La Pedrera, in the same block on Passeig de Gràcia, the **Casa Ramon Casas** (1899) was built for the wealthy Barcelona artist Ramon Casas i Carbó (1866-1932). He had found early success in Paris with friends Santiago Rusiñol and Miquel Utrillo, and the three of them were later involved in *Els Quatre Gats* tavern, which Casas largely financed. In 1941, the **Vinçon** store (Mon–Sat 10am–8.30pm; ☎932 156 050, ⊛www.vincon.com) was established in the building, which emerged in the Sixties as the country's pre-eminent purveyor of furniture and design, a reputation today's department store still maintains. There are several entrances – at Pg. de Gràcia 96, c/Provença 273 and c/Pau Claris 175 – and apart from checking out the extraordinary furniture floor, which gives access to a terrace with views of the interior of La Pedrera, you should try and make time for **La Sala Vinçon** (open same hours as the store). This is Vinçon's exhibition hall and art gallery, located in Casas' original studio, and it puts on excellent shows of graphic and industrial design and contemporary furniture.

Dreta de l'Eixample

The right-hand side of the Eixample – the so-called **Dreta de l'Eixample** – sports a series of extraordinary buildings, mostly contained within the triangle east of Passeig de Gràcia formed by the *passeig*, **Avinguda Diagonal** and the Gran Via de les Corts Catalanes. Several are by the two hardest-working architects in the Eixample, Domènech i Montaner and Puig i Cadafalch, while Gaudí's first apartment building, the **Casa Calvet**, is also here, along with a great neighbourhood market and several interesting restored public spaces. Apart from the Casa Calvet, all the buildings are within a few blocks of each other, or you could pass most of them on a long walk further east to the Sagrada Família, Antoni Gaudí's most celebrated monument. There's more detail of this district on the colour map at the back of the book.

Along Avinguda Diagonal

At the top of Passeig de Gràcia you'll find the **Palau Robert**, Pg. de Grà-cia 107 (Mon–Sat 10am–7pm, Sun 10am–2.30pm; ☎932 388 091, ⓦwww.gencat.net/probert; free; ⓂDiagonal), the information centre for the region of Catalunya, which hosts changing exhibitions on all matters Catalan; the pretty gardens around the back are a popular meeting point for the local nannies and their charges. Cross Avinguda Diagonal here and over to the right stands **Casa Comalat** (1909), Avgda. Diagonal 442, at the junction with c/de Corsega. It's a tricky corner plot, handled with aplomb by the architect Salvador Valeri i Pupurull, who gave it two very different *modernista* facades. On the other side of the avenue, at no. 373, Puig i Cadaflach's almost Gothic **Palau Quadras** from 1904 is typically intricate, with sculpted figures and emblems by Eusebi Arnau and a top row of windows that resemble miniature Swiss chalets. Further down Diagonal, on the left at nos. 416–420, is Puig i Cadafalch's largest work, the soaring Casa Terrades, more usually known as the **Casa de les Punxes** (House of Spikes) because of its red-tiled turrets and steep gables. Built in 1903 for three sisters, and converted from three separate houses spreading around an entire corner of a block, the crenellated structure is almost northern European in style.

Keep to the avenue and you'll pass a sculpture of the **Ictineo** (Diagonal at c/de Provença), the world's earliest powered submarine, courtesy of the Catalans (see p.82), before turning up Passeig de Sant Joan to see Puig i Cadafalch's palatial **Casa Macaya** (ⓂVerdaguer). Dating from 1898–1900, it's a superbly ornamental building with a Gothic-inspired courtyard and canopied staircase from which griffins spring. You might be able to poke your head inside for a look, since the house has been used in the past as a gallery run by the Fundació La Caixa, but even from the outside it's worth pausing to view the unusual exterior carvings by craftsman Eusebi Arnau – like the angel with a box brownie or the sculptor himself on his way to work by bike. You're only four blocks west of the Sagrada Família at this point, but you might as well stay with the Diagonal until you reach Josep Maria Jujol i Gilbert's **Casa Planells** at Avgda. Diagonal 332. Jujol was one of Gaudí's early collaborators, responsible for La Pedrera's undulating balconies and much of the mosaic work in the Parc Güell. Built in 1923–24, this apartment block – a sinuous solution to an acute-corner building – simplifies many of the themes that Gaudí exaggerated in his own work.

South of Avinguda Diagonal

The area around the junction of c/de Mallorca and c/Roger de Llúria (ⓂPasseig de Gràcia) boasts two contrasting Domènech i Montaner buildings, dating from the mid-1890s. The ground floor of the neo-Gothic **Casa Thomas** at c/de Mallorca 291, with its understated pale ceramic tiles, is given over to BD Ediciones de Diseño, a furniture-design showroom. A little way along, set back from the crossroads in a small garden, the **Palau Ramon de Montaner** (c/de Mallorca 278) was built in 1896 for a member of the Montaner i Simon publishing family, and is now the seat of the Madrid government's delegation to Catalunya. Beyond the severe facade is an exquisitely decorated interior of rich mosaic pictures, glass and woodwork, and a monumental staircase, which you can see on **guided tours** (Sat 10.30am in English, plus 11.30am & 12.30pm and Sun at 10.30am, 11.30am & 12.30pm in Spanish/Catalan; €5).

Two blocks south, on c/Roger de Llúria, a doorway gives onto the quiet cloister of the church of **La Concepció** (daily 8am–1pm & 5–9pm; free). It's a surprising haven of slender columns and orange trees, part of a fifteenth-century Gothic convent that once stood in the old town. Abandoned in the early nineteenth century, the convent church and cloister were transferred here brick by brick in the 1870s, along with the Romanesque belfry from another old town church. The neighbouring **Mercat de la Concepció** (Mon 8am–3pm, Tues–Fri 8am–8pm, Sat 8am–4pm; July & Aug closes 3pm; ℗www.laconcepcio.com) was inaugurated in 1888, its iron-and-glass tram-shed structure reminiscent of others in the city. Flowers, shrubs, trees and plants spill out of the entrance on c/de Valencia; inside, there are a couple of good snack bars and a few simple restaurants outside.

A couple of restored corners showing something of the spirit of the original Eixample plan are found just to the south, by walking down c/Roger de Llúria. At no. 56, between carrers Consell de Cent and Diputació, a herringbone-brick tunnel leads into the **Jardins de les Torres de les Aigües** (daily 10am–dusk; free), an enclosed square centred on a Moorish-style water tower. Cerdà's plan was for the city's nineteenth-century inhabitants all to have access to such gardens and public spaces, though this is one of the few human-scale elements to survive and has been handsomely restored by the city council. Another example of what might have been lies directly opposite, across c/Roger de Llúria, where the cobbled **Passatge del Permanyer** cuts across an Eixample block, lined by candy-coloured single-storey townhouses.

Casa Calvet

Gaudí fans will want to finish an Eixample tour by crossing the Gran Via de les Corts Catalanes to tick off the great man's earliest commissioned townhouse building, erected for a prominent local textile family. **Casa Calvet**, at c/de Casp 48 (Ⓜ Urquinaona/Catalunya), dates from 1899 and, though fairly conventional in style, the Baroque inspiration on display in the sculpted facade and church-like lobby was to surface again in his later, more elaborate buildings on Passeig de Gràcia. If you want a closer look inside, you'll have to book a table in the restaurant (see p.196) that now occupies the premises.

Sagrada Família and Glòries

The easternmost reaches of the Dreta de l'Eixample are dominated by the one building that is an essential stop on any visit to Barcelona – Antoni Gaudí's great church of the **Sagrada Família**. Most visitors make a special journey out by metro to see the church and then head back into the centre, but it's worth diverting the few blocks south to the area known as **Glòries** where you can visit the city's biggest flea market, the flagship national theatre building and the sole surviving bullring in Barcelona. This is an area destined for dramatic redevelopment over the next few years, as part of the city council's ongoing attempt to breathe new life into peripheral urban areas.

Sagrada Família

However diverting, and occasionally provocative, the pockets of architectural interest throughout the Eixample, nothing prepares you for the impact of the **Temple Expiatori de la Sagrada Família** (daily: April–Sept 9am–8pm; Oct–March 9am–6pm; €8, €11.50 including guided tour, audio guide €3.50; ☏932 073 031, ⓦwww.sagradafamilia.org; ⓂSagrada Familia), which occupies an entire block between c/de Mallorca and c/de Provença, north of the Diagonal.

In many ways the church of the "Sacred Family" has become a kind of symbol for the city, and was one of the few churches (along with the cathedral, La Seu) left untouched by the orgy of church-burning which accompanied both the 1909 "Tragic Week" rioting and the 1936 revolution. More than any building in the Barri Gòtic, it speaks volumes about the Catalan urge to glorify uniqueness and endeavour. It is the most fantastic of the modern architectural creations in which Barcelona excels – even the coldest hearts will find the Sagrada Família inspirational in form and spirit.

Some history

Begun in 1882 by public subscription, the Sagrada Família was originally intended by its progenitor, the Catalan publisher Josep Bocabella, to be an expiatory building that would atone for the city's increasingly revolutionary ideas. Bocabella appointed the architect Francesc de Paula Villar to the work, and his plan was for a modest church in an orthodox neo-Gothic style. Two years later, after arguments between the two men, Gaudí – only 31 years of age – took charge and changed the direction and scale of the project almost immediately, seeing in the Sagrada Família an opportunity to reflect his own deepening spiritual and nationalist feelings. He spent most of the rest of his life working on the church. Indeed, after he finished the Parc Güell in 1911, Gaudí vowed never to work again on secular art, but to devote himself solely to the Sagrada Família (where, eventually, he lived in a workshop on site), and he was adapting the plans ceaselessly right up to his untimely death. Run over by a tram on the Gran Via on June 7, 1926, he died in hospital three days later – initially unrecognized, for he had become a virtual recluse, rarely leaving his small studio. His death was treated as a Catalan national disaster, and all of Barcelona turned out for his funeral procession. Following papal dispensation, he was buried in the Sagrada Família crypt.

Work on the church was slow, even in Gaudí's day, mainly due to a persistent lack of funds. It took four years to finish the crypt (1901) and the first full plan of the building wasn't published until 1917. The first tower was erected the following year, but by the time of Gaudí's death only one façade was complete. Although the church building survived the Civil War, Gaudí's plans and models were destroyed in 1936 by the anarchists, who regarded Gaudí and his church as conservative religious relics that the new Barcelona could do without: George Orwell – whose sympathies were very much with the anarchists during the Civil War – remarked that the Sagrada Família had been spared because of its supposed artistic value, but added that it was "one of the most hideous buildings in the world" and that the anarchists "showed bad taste in not blowing it up when they had the chance".

Work restarted in the late 1950s amid great controversy, and has continued ever since – as have the arguments. Some maintain that the Sagrada Família should be left incomplete as a memorial to Gaudí, others that the architect intended it to be the work of several generations, each continuing in its own style. The current work has attracted criticism for infringing Gaudí's original spirit, not least the work on the Passion facade, by sculptor Josep María Subirachs. Certainly, contemporary methods and materials are being used – including computer-aided design and hi-tech construction techniques – but on balance it's probably safe enough to assume that Gaudí saw the struggle to finish the building as at least as important as the method and style. As the project draws inexorably towards realization (current projections predict a completion date of around 2017), a fresh set of arguments has arisen as to how to wrap the whole thing up – whether to continue with the design, which calls for an even taller central dome and tower, or to go for a quicker but more modest alternative.

The building

The size alone is startling – Gaudí's original plan was to build a church capable of seating over 10,000 people. In particular, eight **spires** rise to over 100m. They have been likened to everything from perforated cigars to celestial billiard cues, but for Gaudí they were symbolic of the twelve apostles; he planned to build four more and to add a 170-metre central dome and tower topped with a lamb (representing Jesus) over the transept.

A precise symbolism also pervades the façades, each of which is divided into three porches devoted to Faith, Hope and Charity, and each uniquely sculpted. Gaudí made extensive use of human, plant and animal models (posing them in his workshop), as well as taking casts and photographs, in order to produce exactly the likenesses he sought for the sculptural groups. The eastern **Nativity facade** (facing c/de la Marina) was the first to be completed and is alive with fecund detail, its very columns resting on the backs of giant tortoises. Contrast this with the Cubist austerity of Subirach's work on the western **Passion facade** (c/de Sardenya), where the brutal story of the Crucifixion is played out across the harsh mountain stone. Gaudí meant the so-far unfinished south facade, the **Gloria**, to be the culmination of the Temple – designed (he said), to show "the religious realities of present and future life . . . man's origin, his end". Everything from the Creation to Heaven and Hell, in short, is to be included in one magnificent ensemble.

The reality is that the place is a giant building site, with scaffolding, pallets, dressed stone, cranes, tarpaulins and fencing scattered about, and contractors hard at work. However, construction of the vaults over the side-aisles began in 1995 and for the first time a recognizable church interior is starting to take shape. In 2001 the vaults of the central nave were finished, and the whole church is due to be roofed in due course. Extraordinary columns branch towards the spreading stone leaves of the roof, a favourite Gaudí motif inspired by the city's plane trees – he envisaged the temple interior as a forest from very early days.

Once inside the structure, all considerations except the building itself soon fall away. An **lift** (open same hours as the church; €2) runs up the towers of the Passion facade, or you can make the long, steep climb up the towers of the Nativity facade (a twisting 400 steps and 75m). Either way, you'll be rewarded by partial views of the city through an extraordinary jumble of latticed stone-work, ceramic decoration, carved buttresses and sculpture.

Your entrance ticket also gives you access to the **crypt**, where a **museum** (times as for the church) traces the career of the architect and the history of the church. Models, sketches and photographs help to make some sense of the work going on around you, and you can see sculptors and model-makers at work in the plaster workshop. There's a film show about Gaudí's career, too (hourly in English), which is likely to set you on the trail of his earlier projects, all of which, astonishingly, date from before 1911.

Hospital de la Santa Creu i de Sant Pau

While you're in the neighbourhood, it would be a shame not to stroll from the Sagrada Família to Lluis Domènech i Montaner's innovative **Hospital de la Santa Creu i de Sant Pau** (Ⓜ Hospital de Sant Pau), possibly the one building that can rival the church for size and invention. The hospital has its own metro stop, but it's far better to walk up the four-block-long Avinguda de Gaudí, which gives terrific views back over the spires of the Sagrada Família.

Work started on the hospital in 1902, the brief being to replace the medieval hospital buildings in the Raval (see p.66) with a modern series of departments and wards. Domènech i Montaner spent ten years working on the building and left his trademarks everywhere: cocking a snook at Cerdà, the buildings are aligned diagonally to the Eixample, surrounded by gardens; and everywhere, turrets and towers sport bright ceramic tiles and little domes. Domènech retired in 1912, once funds had run out, and the building wasn't fully completed until 1930, seven years after his death, though the latter stages were overseen by Domènech's son Pere, ensuring a certain continuity of style.

You are free to walk into the sloping landscaped **grounds**, past the whimsical **pavilions** that make up the hospital interior. Craftsmen adorned every inch with sculpture, mosaics, stained glass and ironwork, while much of the actual business of running a hospital was hidden away in a series of underground corridors that connects the buildings together. It's a stunning, harmonious achievement – that it's a hospital seems almost incidental, which is doubtless the effect that the architect intended. Naturally, given the demands now made upon them, the *modernista* hospital buildings are deemed to have served their purpose; behind them spreads the hi-tech central block of the new hospital. The pavilions have been turned over to educational and cultural use (a Museum of Medicine is mooted), with a **Centre del Modernisme** installed in the Pavelló de Santa Apol.lònia (daily 10am–2pm; ☎902 076 621, ⊛www.rutadelmodernisme.com). This is one of the places you can find out about and buy the city's **Ruta del Modernisme guide** (see p.28), and it also coordinates **guided tours** of the hospital complex (daily at 10.15am & 12.15pm in English, plus others in Spanish/Catalan; €5), which can tell you more about the six-hundred-year history of the hospital.

Plaça de les Glòries Catalanes and around

Barcelona's major arterial routes all meet at the **Plaça de les Glòries Catalanes** (Ⓜ Glòries), named for and dedicated to the "Catalan glories", from architecture to literature. Although now stuck out at the eastern edge of the city centre, Glòries was conceived by nineteenth-century designer Ildefons Cerdà as the nucleus of his Eixample blueprint. This never materialized and for years it's been no more than a swirling traffic roundabout, though current plans put Glòries at the heart of the city's latest wave of regeneration. By 2012, the roundabout traffic is to be tunnelled underground, thus opening up a grand pedestrianized park which will contain a cultural centre to house the city's municipal museum collections (see the colour section for more) Glòries is already positioned as a gateway to the new Diagonal Mar district (p.86), with trams running down Avinguda Diagonal to the Diagonal Mar shopping centre and Fòrum site. Meanwhile, the signature building on the roundabout is Jean Nouvel's cigar-shaped **Torre Agbar** (142m), the headquarters of the local water company, which is a highly distinctive aluminium-and-glass tower with no less than 4000 windows, its shape inspired by the rocky protuberances

Antoni Gaudí

and
modernisme

Antoni Gaudí i Cornet is the most famous proponent of Barcelona's modernisme (Art Nouveau style) and, together with his contemporaries Lluís Domènech i Montaner and Josep Puig i Cadafalch, created the weird and wonderful buildings that are a major draw for visitors to Barcelona today. The Catalan offshoot of Art Nouveau was the expression of a renewed upsurge in Catalan nationalism. The early nineteenth-century economic recovery in Catalunya had provided the initial impetus, and the subsequent cultural renaissance – the Renaixença – led to the fresh stirrings of a new Catalan awareness and identity.

Gaudí's work and style

Born in Reus, near Tarragona, to a family of artisans, the work of **Antoni Gaudí i Cornet** (1852–1926) was never strictly *modernista* in style (it was never strictly anything in style), but the imaginative impetus he provided was incalculable. His buildings are the most daring creations of all Art Nouveau, yet whether apartment building (La Pedrera), private housing estate (Parc Güell), or church (Sagrada Família), Gaudí's apparently lunatic flights of fantasy are always rooted in functionality. Spiritual symbolism

Parc Güell

and Catalan pride are evident in every building too – by inclination, Gaudí was a fervent Catholic and nationalist – while his architectural influences were Moorish and Gothic, embellished with elements from the natural world. Gaudí rarely wrote a word about the theory of his art, preferring the buildings to demand reaction – and still today, no one stands mute in front of an Antoni Gaudí masterpiece.

The other *modernistas*

With Gaudí in a class (and world) of his own, it was **Lluís Domènech i Montaner** (1850–1923) who was perhaps the greatest pure *modernista* architect. Drawing on the rich

Gargoyles on Casa Macaya

Catalan Romanesque and Gothic traditions, his work combined traditional craft methods with experiments in modern technology, seen to triumphant effect in both the Hospital de la Santa Creu i de Sant Pau and the Palau de la Música Catalana, respectively the city hospital and concert hall. This exciting marriage of techniques first inspired the young **Josep Puig i Cadafalch** (1867–1957) to become an architect, and his work too bears the hallmark stamp of *modernisme* in the wildly inventive use of ceramic tiles, ironwork, stained glass and decorative stone carving. His first commission, the

Gaudí: 6 of the best

Casa Batlló The extraordinary townhouse anchors the Mansa de la Discòrdia (Block of Discord), comprising a trio of elaborate mansions built for wealthy industrialists. See p.104.
Colònia Güell A utopian industrial town with an uplifting chapel whose design foreshadowed that of the Sagrada Família. See p.141

Palau Güell Gaudí's longtime patron, industrialist Eusebi Güell, ordered an extension to the family home just off the Ramblas. The result: a bravura expression of individuality and style. See p.67.

La Pedrera at night

Pavellons Güell The Güell family summer-house and stables, with Gaudí's celebrated dragon-gate warding off unwelcome visitors. See p.126.
La Pedrera Taking the folds and gullies of the mountain of Montserrat as his starting point, the architect concocted a sinuous apartment building that caused a sensation in its day. See p.106.
Sagrada Família The most famous church in the world is a work in progress, but Gaudí's original themes, plans and designs inform the continuing construction. See p.109.

Sagrada Família under construction

flamboyant Casa Martí, housed the *Quatre Gats* tavern for the city's *modernista* artists and avant-garde hangers-on, while in mansions like Casa Macaya and Casa de les Punxes Puig i Cadafalch brought to bear distinct Gothic and medieval influences.

Crafts and collaborators

Modernisme was a collaborative effort between the architects and the craftsmen, designers and artisans who helped bring the projects to fruition. Domènech i Montaner in particular recognized the importance of ensemble working, establishing a craft workshop in the

Eat, drink, sleep, shop – the modernista way

Almirall The city's oldest bar is also a fine example of period decor, notably the main entrance, marble counter and display cabinet. See p.203.

Antiga Casa Figueras Bakeries and confectioners' often got the *modernista* treatment – this Ramblas pastry shop is a famous example. See p.175.

Casa Calvet A private townhouse built by Gaudí is the setting for an upscale Catalan restaurant. See p.196.

Casa Fuster This hugely stylish hotel takes a landmark *modernista* building and adds state-of-the-art comforts. See p.170.

Casa Thomas Browse designer furniture and household goods in a building by Domènech i Montaner. See p.108.

Hotel Espanya Have lunch in one of the city's most splendidly decorated dining rooms. See p.67.

El Indio You're in town for the weekend, you need some linen or a new pillowcase? There's only one place to go. See p.235.

London Bar There's live music here most nights in a bar that's been open since 1910. See p.203.

Muy Buenas Behind the *modernista* facade is one of the Raval's best bars. See p.203.

Els Quatre Gats Mingle with the ghost of the young Picasso in Barcelona's original style bar. See p.63.

Palau Guell

building he designed initially as a restaurant for Barcelona's Universal Exhibition of 1888 (now the Museu de Zoologia). Gaudí's longtime collaborator was **Josep Maria Jujol i Gilbert**, a master of mosaic decoration, responsible for most of the startling ceramic work in Parc Güell, while sculptor **Eusebi Arnau** provided meticulous carvings for all the main *modernista* architects – much loved are his quirky figures adorning Puig i Cadafalch's Casa Macaya. Some projects brought together the cream of *modernista* craft talent, so at Domènech i Montaner's Palau de la Música Catalana, for example, the glorious stained glass by **Antoni Rigalt** and facade sculpture by **Miquel Blay** are an integral, indivisible part of the whole.

of Montserrat. Across the Gran Via from here, the park and play areas of **Parc del Clot** show what can be done in an urban setting within the remains of a razed factory site.

On the north side of Glòries, on c/Dos de Maig, the open-air **Els Encants** (Mon, Wed, Fri & Sat 9am–6pm, plus Dec 1–Jan 5 Sun 9am–3pm; ⓂEncants/ Glòries) is an aboslute must for flea-market addicts. It takes up the entire block below c/Consell de Cent, and you name it, you can buy it: old sewing machines, cheese graters, photograph albums, cutlery, lawnmowers, clothes, shoes, CDs, antiques, furniture and out-and-out junk. Go in the morning to see it at its best – haggling is *de rigeur*, but you're up against experts.

Off to the southwest of Glòries lie the twin cultural pillars of the **Teatre Nacional de Catalunya** and **L'Auditori** contemporary city concert hall. The national theatre, designed by Ricardo Bofill, makes a particularly dramatic statement - a glass box encased within the frame of a soaring Greek temple. There are guided building and backstage **tours** for anyone interested in learning more (reservations required; see p.214 for contact details).

The city's only surviving bullring, the **Plaza de Toros Monumental**, stands three blocks west of Glòries, at Gran Via de les Corts Catalanes 749 (ⓂMonumental). Its brick facade and Moorish domes provide a taste of Andalucia in a city where the bullfight doesn't have much of a following – tellingly, the ring is one part of Barcelona where not a word of Catalan is seen. Matador costumes, photographs, posters and the stuffed heads of vanquished bulls occupy the small **Museo Taurino** (Mon–Sat 10.30am–2pm & 4–7pm, Sun 11am–1pm; €4; ☎932 455 804) – enter at the corner with c/de la Marina – while an overhead walkway provides a view into the bull pens.

Esquerra de l'Eixample

The long streets west of Rambla de Catalunya as far as Barcelona Sants train station – making up the **Esquerra de l'Eixample** – are perhaps the least visited on any city sightseeing trip. With all the major architectural highlights found on the Eixample's eastern (or right-hand) side, the Esquerra (left-hand side) was intended by its nineteenth-century planners for public buildings, institutions and industrial concerns, many of which still stand. However, the Esquerra does have its pockets of interest, including the city university, some fine *modernista* houses and a small sports museum, while Barcelona Sants train station is the starting-point of a short walk through the public spaces created in the style known as *nou urbanisme* – typified by a wish to transform former industrial sites into urban parks accessible to local people.

Universitat de Barcelona and around

Built in the 1860s, the grand Neoclassical main building of the **Universitat de Barcelona**, at Plaça de la Universitat (ⓂUniversitat), is now mainly used for ceremonies and administration purposes, but no one minds if you stroll through the doors. There's usually an exhibition in the echoing main hall, while beyond lie two fine arcaded courtyards and extensive gardens, providing a welcome escape from the traffic. Students eat at the self-service café and bar in the basement, though the traditional meeting point is the *Bar Estudiantil*, outside in Plaça Universitat, where you can usually grab a pavement table.

In the streets behind the university – particularly around carrers Muntaner, Casanova and Consell de Cent – Barcelona has its own gay district, known as the **Gaixample**. Gay-friendly bars, clubs, restaurants and businesses have mushroomed here over the last decade (the best are reviewed in chapter 12), though if you're

Contemporary architecture

It's easy to get sidetracked by the *modernista* architecture of the Eixample, and to forget that Barcelona also boasts plenty of contemporary wonders. Following the death of Franco, there was a feeling among architects that Barcelona had a lot of catching up to do, but the last three decades have seen the city take centre stage in the matter of urban design and renewal. Now the world looks to Barcelona for inspiration.

Even in the Franco years exciting work had taken place, particularly among the Rationalist school of architects working from the 1950s to the 1970s. José Antonio Coderch produced such marvels as the dark curved-glass Trade Towers at Gran Vía de Carles III 86–94. Less dramatic but still very pleasing are his blocks of Mediterranean-style apartments at c/Raset 21–31 and those adorned with adjustable blinds and screens at c/Johann Sebastian Bach 7. From the latter part of this period, too, dates the earliest work by the Catalan architects – among them **Oriol Bohigas**, **Carlos Buxadé**, **Joan Margarit**, **Ricardo Bofill** and **Frederic Correa** – later to transform the very look and feel of the city. You can see Bohigas' Habitatges Treballadors Metal·lurgics, for example, at c/Pallars 301–319; Correa's Atalaia de Barcelona at Avgda. Sarrià 71; and Bofill's Bloc Residencial at c/Nicaragua 99.

The impetus for change on a substantial level came from hosting the **1992 Olympics**. Nothing less than the redesign of whole city neighbourhoods would do, with decaying industrial areas either swept away or transformed. While Correa, Margarit and Buxadé worked on the refit of the Estadi Olímpic, Bofill was in charge of INEF (the Sports University) and had a hand in the airport refit. Down at the harbour Bohigas and others were responsible for creating the visionary **Vila Olímpica** development, carving residential, commercial and leisure facilities out of abandoned industrial blackspots.

Attention later turned to other neglected areas, with signature buildings announcing a planned transformation of the local environment: Richard Meier's contemporary art museum, **MACBA**, in the Raval, and Helio Piñon and Alberto Viaplana's **Maremàgnum** complex at Port Vell, anchor those neighbourhoods' respective revivals. Meanwhile, the city acquired new landmarks, like Norman Foster's **Torre de Collserola** at Tibidabo, the twin towers of the *Hotel Arts* and Torre Mapfre at the Port Olímpic, and Bofill's Greek-temple-style **Teatre Nacional de Catalunya** (TNC) at Plaça de les Glòries. The latter was subsequently joined by the even more eye-catching 142-metre-high **Torre Agbar**, a giant glowing cigar of a building by Jean Nouvel. **Plaça de les Glòries** itself is currently undergoing radical restructuring as a public plaza, with plans advanced for a new transport interchange, plus a Cultural Centre del Disseny (Design Museum) by Oriol Bohigas that will bring together the collections currently held at the city's various applied art museums. Zaha Hadid has a "Cinema City" in the pipeline at nearby Plaça de les Arts, while to the northeast at **La Sagrera** work is under way on the city's new AVE (high-speed train) station, with a dramatic 34-storey Frank Gehry office building to follow.

At the foot of Avinguda Diagonal, down on the shoreline, the former industrial area of Poble Nou was transformed by the works associated with the Universal Forum of Cultures held in 2004. At **Diagonal Mar**, as the area is now known, Jacques Herzog (architect of London's Tate Modern) provided the centrepiece **Edifici Fòrum**, which sits at the heart of a new business and commercial district linking Barcelona with the once-desolate environs of the River Besòs. Meanwhile, on the other side of the city, it's been left to Richard Rogers to revitalize the city's neglected bullring, **Les Arenes** at Plaça d'Espanya, intended as a gateway landmark, incorporating a domed garden, viewing platform and leisure centre.

expecting the overt street scene of a San Francisco or even London's Soho, you'll be disappointed.

Along Avinguda Diagonal

The most interest lies in the buildings on and off the upper reaches of Avinguda Diagonal (Ⓜ Diagonal). At the top of Rambla de Catalunya, Puig i Cadafalch's pseudo-medieval **Casa Serra** (1903) has been much altered, though it retains its original tiles, canopies and jaunty tower. A bronze statue of Sant Jordi, patron saint of Catalunya, guards the Diagonal side of the building, now used as offices. Further up the Diagonal, also on the left, at no. 423 at the junction with c/Enric Granados, **Casa Sayrach** (1918) flows around its corner site, a vision of pink granite and marble, with a central tower topped by a cupola and a Pedrera-style roof.

Three blocks west you'll find the quirky **Museu i Centre d'Estudis de l'Esport** (Mon–Fri 10am–2pm & 3–7pm; free; ☎ 934 192 232; Ⓜ Hospital Clinic), at c/de Buenos Aires 56–58. Built as the Casa Companys in 1911 by Puig i Cadafalch, the little cream-coloured house contains probably the most unassuming sporting hall of fame found anywhere in the world. In a couple of quiet, wood-panelled rooms photographs of 1920s Catalan rally drivers and footballers are displayed alongside a motley collection of memorabilia, from a signed water polo ball used in the 1992 Olympics to Everest mountaineer Carles Vàlles' ice pick.

Beyond here Avinguda Diagonal flows on to **Plaça Francesc Macià** and the uptown shopping and business district – you can catch a tram from the *plaça* along the avenue up to L'Illa shopping centre (see p.235), or just walk the short distance north up Avinguda Pau Casals to **Turó Parc** (daily 10am–dusk), a good place to rest weary feet, with a small lake and a café kiosk.

Avinguda Diagonal to Barcelona Sants

South of the Diagonal stand several much larger examples of the *modernista* and Neoclassical spirit which infused public buildings of the nineteenth century. The Batlló textile mill on the corner of c/del Comte d'Urgell and c/del Rossello underwent major refurbishment in 1908 to emerge as the **Escola Industrial** (Ⓜ Hospital Clinic). It occupies four entire Eixample blocks, with later academic buildings added in the 1920s, including a chapel by Joan Rubió i Bellvér, who worked with Antoni Gaudí. Students usually fill the courtyards, and no one minds if you take a stroll through. A block to the east is the massive **Hospital Clinic** (1904), with its fine pedimented portico, while the neighbourhood **Mercat del Ninot** (Mon 7am–2pm, Tues–Thurs 7am–2pm & 5.30–8.30pm, Fri 7am–8pm, Sat 7am–3pm) takes up a large area to the south, between carrers Villaroel and Casanova. This is almost entirely tourist-free, with produce, meat and fish inside and rows of shops around the block outside selling clothes, jewellery, accessories and homeware.

Barcelona Sants to Plaça d'Espanya

Basque architect Luis Peña Ganchegui's **Parc de l'Espanya Industrial** (Ⓜ Sants Estació) lies two minutes' walk away around the southern side of Barcelona Sants station. Built on the site of an old textile factory, it has a line of red-and-yellow-striped lighthouses at the top of glaring white steps, with an incongruously classical Neptune in the water below. Altogether, six sculptors are represented here and, along with the boating lake, café kiosk, playground and sports facilities provided, the park takes a decent stab at reconciling local interests with the mundane nature of the surroundings.

To the south, down c/de Tarragona, **Parc Joan Miró** (ⓂTarragona) was laid out on the site of the nineteenth-century municipal slaughterhouse. It features a raised piazza whose main feature is Joan Miró's gigantic mosaic sculpture *Dona i Ocell* (*Woman and Bird*), towering above a shallow reflecting pool. It's a familiar symbol if you've studied Miró's other works, but the sculpture is known locally by several other names – all of them easy to guess when you consider its erect, helmeted shape. The rear of the park is given over to games areas and landscaped sections of palms and firs, with a kiosk café and some outdoor tables found in amongst the trees. The children's playground here is one of the best in the city, with a climbing frame and aerial runway as well as swings and slides.

The former **Les Arenes** bullring (ⓂEspanya) backing Parc Joan Miró is undergoing a massive Richard Rogers–inspired refit, to convert it into a leisure and retail complex with enormous roof terrace, while retaining the circular Moorish facade of 1900. Also spared the wrecker's ball is the six-storey *modernista* **Casa Papallona** (1912), on the eastern side of Les Arenes on c/de Llança. It's one of the city's favourite house facades, crowned by a huge ceramic butterfly.

5

The northern suburbs

U ntil the Eixample stretched out across the plain to meet them, a string of small towns and villages ringed the city to the north. Today, they're firmly entrenched as suburbs of Barcelona, but most still retain an individual identity worth investigating even on a short visit to the city. Some of the sights will figure on most people's tours of the city, while others are more specialized, but taken together they do help to counter the notion that Barcelona begins and ends in the Barri Gòtic.

Gràcia – the closest neighbourhood to the Eixample – is still very much the liberal, almost bohemian stronghold it was in the nineteenth century. Visits tend to revolve around browsing in the neighbourhood market or sipping a drink in one of the quiet squares, though Gràcia also has an active cultural scene and nightlife of its own. Antoni Gaudí's surreal **Parc Güell**, on the northeastern fringes of Gràcia, is the single biggest draw, while in neighbouring **Horta** a

THE NORTHERN SUBURBS

couple more distinctive parks attract the curious with an hour or two to spare, notably the **Parc del Laberint** and its renowned maze.

To the northwest of the city centre, what was once the village of **Les Corts** is now indistinguishable from the rest of the modern city, save for the hallowed precincts of **Camp Nou**, FC Barcelona's stupendous football stadium and museum. North of here, past the university and across Avinguda Diagonal, the concentrated attractions of **Pedralbes** are worth half a day, while **Sarrià** just to the east is still more like a small town than a suburb, with a pretty main street and market to explore.

Perhaps the only rival to Parc Güell as a single-destination visit out of the centre is the city's new science museum, **CosmoCaixa**. This lies just below the ring road (the Ronda de Dalt), beyond which extend the Collserola hills whose highest peak – **Tibidabo**, reached by tram and funicular – should really be saved for a clear day. The views are the draw here, from the amusement park, peak-top church or nearby **Torre de Collserola**, while a pleasant walk winds west to **Vallvidrera**, a hilltop village with another funicular connection back towards the city. Finally, from the information centre of the nearby **Parc de Collserola**, you can hike in the pinewoods high above Barcelona and see scarcely a soul – perhaps the greatest surprise in this most surprising of cities.

Gràcia

Named after a long-destroyed fifteenth-century monastery, **Gràcia** was a village for much of its early existence before being annexed as a fully fledged suburb of the city in the late nineteenth century. Beginning at the top of Passeig de Gràcia, and bordered roughly by c/Balmes to the west and the streets above the Sagrada Família to the east, it's traditionally been home to arty and political types, students and the intelligentsia, though Gràcia also has a genuine local population (including one of the city's biggest Romany communities) that even today lends it an attractive small-town atmosphere. Consequently, its annual summer festival, the Festa Major every August (see p.222), has no peer in any other neighbourhood. Actual sights are few and far between, but much of the pleasure to be had here is serendipitous; wander the narrow, gridded eighteenth- and nineteenth-century streets, park yourself on a bench under a plane tree, catch a film or otherwise take time out from the rigours of city-centre life. You'll soon get the feel of a neighbourhood that – unlike some in Barcelona – still has a soul.

Around the neighbourhood

You may as well start where the locals start – first thing in the morning, shopping for bread and provisions in the **Mercat de la Llibertat** (Mon 8am–3pm, Tues–Thurs 8am–2pm & 5–8pm, Fri 7am–8pm, Sat 7am–3pm; closed afternoons in Aug), a block west of c/Gran de Gràcia. The building was revamped in 1893 by a former pupil of Gaudí, Francesc Berenguer i Mestrès, who sheltered its food stalls under a *modernista* wrought-iron roof. Two blocks to the north, **Rambla del Prat** has the finest surviving collection of *modernista* townhouses in the district, while a couple of blocks further north again stands Antoni Gaudí's first major private commission, the **Casa Vicens** (1883–85) at c/les Carolines 24 (ⓜFontana). Here he took inspiration from the Moorish style,

covering the facade in linear green-and-white tiles with a flower motif. The decorative iron railings are a reminder of Gaudí's early training as a metalsmith and, to further prove his versatility – and how Art Nouveau cuts across art forms – Gaudí also designed much of the mansion's furniture (though unfortunately you can't get in to see it).

From Casa Vicens, it's a five-minute walk east along c/Santa Agata, c/de la Providencia and then south into pretty **Plaça de la Virreina**, backed by its much-restored parish church of Sant Joan. This is one of Gràcia's favourite squares, with the *Virreina Bar* and others providing drinks and a place to rest and admire the handsome houses, most notably **Casa Rubinat** (1909), c/de l'Or 44, the last major work of Francesc Berenguer. Children and dogs, meanwhile, scamper around the small drinking fountain. Another short walk to the southwest, **Plaça del Sol** is the beating heart of much of the district's nightlife, though it's not quite so appealing during the day. It was redesigned rather soullessly in the 1980s, losing much of its attraction for older locals at least. Far more in keeping with Gràcia's overall tenor is **Plaça Rius i Taulet**, just to the south across Travessera de Gràcia. The thirty-metre-high clock tower was a rallying point for nineteenth-century radicals – whose twenty-first-century counterparts prefer to meet for brunch at the popular café *terrassas*.

At Plaça Rius i Taulet you're close to the main c/Gran de Gràcia. Walk south, and where the street becomes Passeig de Gràcia stands the **Casa Fuster**, on the left at no. 132 (ⓂDiagonal). Designed by Lluís Domènech i Montaner in

1908 (and now a luxury hotel, see p.170) it sports many of Domènech's most characteristic design features: a multi-columned building with chunky floral capitals, and – designed to fit the awkward corner it's built on – one concave and one convex tower.

Practicalities

Gràcia is close enough to the centre to walk to if you wish – around a thirty-minute hike from Plaça de Catalunya. **Getting there** by public transport means taking the FGC train from Plaça de Catalunya to Gràcia station, or buses #22 or #24 from Plaça de Catalunya up c/Gran de Gràcia, or the metro to either Ⓜ Diagonal (south) or Ⓜ Fontana (north). From any of the stations, it's around a five-hundred-metre walk to Gràcia's two central squares, Plaça del Sol and Plaça Rius i Taulet, in the network of gridded streets off the eastern side of c/Gran de Gràcia.

Parc Güell

From 1900 to 1914 Antoni Gaudí worked for Eusebi Güell (patron of Gaudí's Palau Güell, off the Ramblas) on the **Parc Güell** (daily: May–Aug 10am–9pm; April & Sept 10am–8pm; March & Oct 10am–7pm; Nov–Feb 10am–6pm; free), on the outskirts of Gràcia. This was Gaudí's most ambitious project after the Sagrada Família – on which he was engaged at the same time, commissioned as a private housing estate of sixty dwellings and furnished with paths, recreational areas and decorative monuments. It was conceived as a "Garden City" of the type popular at the time in England – indeed, Gaudí's original plans used the English spelling "Park Güell". In the end, only two houses were actually built, and the park was officially opened to the public instead in 1922.

Laid out on a hill, which provides fabulous views back across the city, the park is an almost hallucinatory expression of the imagination. Pavilions of contorted stone, giant decorative lizards, meandering rustic viaducts, a vast Hall of Columns (intended to be the estate's market), carved stone trees – all combine in one manic swirl of ideas and excesses, reminiscent of an amusement park. The Hall of Columns, for example, was described by Sacheverell Sitwell (in *Spain*) as "at once a fun fair, a petrified forest, and the great temple of Amun at Karnak, itself drunk, and reeling in an eccentric earthquake". Perhaps the most famous element – certainly the most widely photographed – is the long, meandering **ceramic bench** that snakes along the edge of the terrace above the columned hall. It's entirely decorated with a brightly coloured broken tile-and-glass mosaic (a method known as *trencadís*) that forms a dizzying sequence of abstract motifs, symbols, words and pictures. The ceramic mosaics and decorations found throughout the park were mostly executed by Josep Maria Jujol, who assisted on several of Gaudí's projects.

There are terrific views from the self-service **café**, which operates from one of the caverns adjoining the main terrace, but to escape the milling crowds you'll need to climb away from here, up into the wooded, landscaped gardens. At the very highest point – follow signs for "**Turó de les Tres Creus**" – on the spot where Gaudí had planned to place a chapel, three stone crosses top a stepped tumulus. It's from here that a 360-degree city panorama unfolds in all its glory.

At the main entrance on c/Olot, the fomer porter's lodge – and never can a porter have had more whimsical lodgings – is now the **Centre d'Interpretació** (daily 11am–3pm; €2; ℡932 856 899), offering a rather perfunctory introduction to the park's history, design and building methods used. Far better is the **Casa Museu Gaudí** (daily: April–Sept 10am–8pm; Oct–March 10am–6pm; €4, combined ticket with Sagrada Família €9; ℡932 193 811), a little way inside the park, designed and built in 1904 by one of Gaudí's other collaborators, Francesc Berenguer, and in which Gaudí was persuaded to live until he left to camp out at the Sagrada Família for good. Gaudí's ascetic study and bedroom have been kept much as they were in his day – there's an inkling of his personality in the displayed religious texts and pictures, along with a silver coffee cup and his death mask, made at the Sant Pau hospital. Other rooms display a diverting collection of furniture he designed for other projects – a typical mixture of wild originality and brilliant engineering, as well as plans and objects relating to the park and to Gaudí's life.

Park practicalities

If you have a choice, it's probably best to visit Parc Güell during the week, as weekends can be very busy indeed. The park straddles a steep hill and however you get there will involve an ascent on foot of some kind to reach the main section (see colour map 7 for approaches). The most direct route there is on **bus #24** from Plaça de Catalunya, Passeig de Gràcia or c/Gran de Gracia, which drops you on Carretera del Carmel at the eastern side gate by the car park. From Ⓜ Vallcarca you have to walk a few hundred metres down Avinguda de l'Hospital Militar until you see the mechanical escalators on your left, ascending Baixada de la Glória. Follow these – and the short sections of stepped path in between – right to the western-side park entrance (15min), from where you wind down a path to the main terrace. **Walking from Gràcia** (and Ⓜ Lesseps), turn right along Travessera de Dalt and then left up steep c/Larrard, which leads straight to the main entrance of the park on c/Olot (10min). The **Bus Turístic** stops at the bottom end of c/Larrard on c/la Mare de Deu de la Salut.

You'll have to walk back down c/Larrard to Travessera de Dalt for bus or metro connections back to the city, though **taxis** do hang about the main gates on c/Olot. There's a **café** with terrace seats in the park, while Carrer Larrard has several other little cafés, if you want to refuel on your way up or down, as well as a mini-market for picnic supplies.

Horta

To the north of Parc Güell spreads the neighbourhood of **Horta**, named for the gardens and country estates that once characterized the area. It's been developed beyond recognition over the last century, though there are some quiet spots to seek out, like the distinctive **Parc de la Creueta del Coll**. The Vall d'Hebron area, just to the east, was the site of another of the city's Olympic developments, based around the Velòdrom d'Horta, Barcelona's cycle stadium. It's behind here that the most extraordinary rural relic still survives; the hillside gardens and maze of the **Parc del Laberint**.

Parc de la Creueta del Coll

There couldn't be a greater contrast with Parc Güell than Horta's **Parc de la Creueta del Coll** (daily 10am–dusk; free), a *nou urbanisme* development by Olympic architects Martorell and Mackay, that was laid out on the site of an old quarry. There's a stand of palm trees by a small artificial lake, and concrete promenades under the sheer quarry walls, but lately it's all been allowed to go to the dogs (and feral cats) a bit and could do with a spruce-up. Still, you're greeted at the top of the park steps by an Ellsworth Kelly metal spike, while suspended by steel cables over a water-filled quarry is a massive concrete claw by the Basque artist Eduardo Chillida. **Bus** #28 from Plaça de Catalunya, up Passeig de Gràcia, stops just 100m from the park steps, or you can walk up Passeig de la Mare de Deu del Coll from Ⓜ Vallcarca in about twenty minutes (there's a neighbourhood map at the metro station).

Combining the park with a visit to Parc Güell is easy, too, though you'll need a keen sense of direction to find it from the rear exit of Parc Güell – it helps if you've climbed to the top of Güell's three-crosses hill and fixed in mind the quarry walls, which you can see across the valley. It's far easier to visit Parc de la Creueta del Coll first, then walk back down the main Passeig de la Mare de Deu del Coll until you see the signpost pointing down c/Balears (on your left) – from there, signposts guide you into Parc Güell the back way.

Parc del Laberint

Confronted by the roaring traffic on the Passeig Vall d'Hebron, it seems inconceivable that there's any kind of sanctuary to hand, but just a couple of minutes' walk from Ⓜ Mundet metro puts you at the gates of the **Parc del Laberint** (daily 10am–dusk; €2, free Wed & Sun. The former estate mansion is undergoing restoration, but the late eighteenth-century gardens are open for visits and are an enchanting spectacle. A series of paths, terraces, pavilions and water features embrace the hillside, merging with the pine forest beyond. At the very heart of the park is the famed topiary maze, El Laberint, created by the Marquis de Llupià i Alfarràs and designed as an Enlightenment puzzle concerning the forms of love. A statue of Eros in the centre is the reward for successfully negotiating the maze. Near the park entrance are a drinks kiosk, picnic area and children's playground.

At Ⓜ Mundet, use the Passeig Vall d'Hebron (Muntanya) exit. Walk up the main road against the traffic flow for one minute and turn left into the car park and grounds of the Velòdrom – the park entrance is immediately behind the cycle stadium, up the green slope.

Camp Nou: Museu del Futbol Club Barcelona

Within the city's Les Corts area, behind the university buildings, the magnificent **Camp Nou** football stadium of **FC Barcelona** will be high on the visiting list of any sports fan, and might well surprise even those indifferent to the game. Built in 1957, and enlarged to accommodate the

△ Parc del Laberint

1982 World Cup semi-final, the stadium seats a staggering 98,000 people in three steep tiers that provide one of the best football-watching experiences in the world – on a par with the famous Maracaña stadium in Brazil. The current team is the most exciting and succesful in Spain – packed full of international superstars – and were European Champions League winners in 2006. Still, trophies or not, it's more than just a football club to most people in the city. During the Franco era, it stood as a Catalan symbol, around which people could rally, and perhaps as a consequence FC Barcelona has the world's largest soccer club membership. The matches (played mostly on Sunday) can be an invigorating introduction to Catalan passions: if you can get a ticket (see p.000 for details), you're in for a treat.

Meanwhile, the stadium and the club's **Museu del Futbol** (Mon–Sat 10am–6.30pm, Sun 10am–2pm; museum only €5.50, including tour €9.90; ☎934 963 600) together provide a splendid celebration of Spain's national sport. The entrance is on Avinguda Arístides Maillol, through Gate (*Accés*) 9 (ⓂCollblanc/Maria Cristina & 10min walk); the Bus Turístic stops outside.

The all-inclusive ticket allows you on the **self-guided tour**, winding through the bowels of the stadium, through the changing rooms, out onto the pitch side and up to the press gallery and directors' box for stunning views. The **museum** is jammed full of silverware, memorabilia, paintings and sculpture, while photograph displays trace the history of the club back to 1901. There's also a gallery of the celebrated foreign players who have graced Barça's books, and it's not a new phenomenon: as early as 1911, there were five British players in the team. Finally, you're directed into the **FC Botiga Megastore**, where you can buy anything from a replica shirt down to a branded bottle of wine.

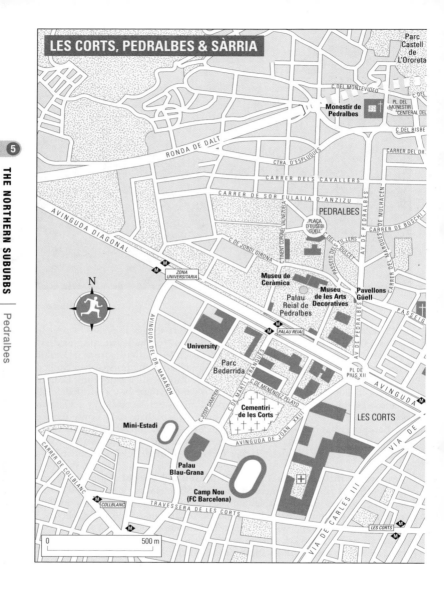

Pedralbes

The well-to-do residential neighbourhood of **Pedralbes** is largely one of wide avenues and fancy apartment buildings. Two interesting museums here (of decorative art and ceramics) occupy a former royal palace, the Palau Reial de

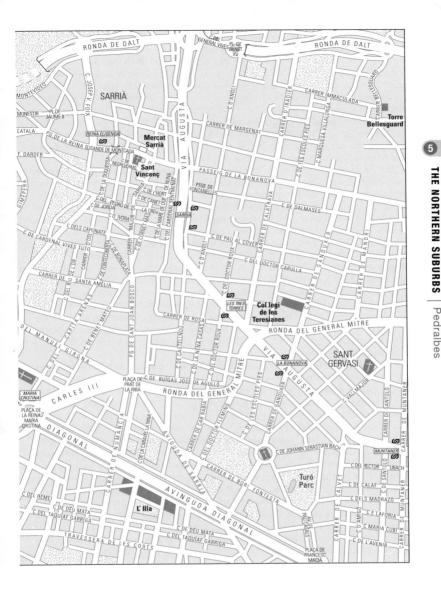

Pedralbes, while a half-day's excursion can be made of the trip by walking from the palace, past an early Gaudí creation, to the Gothic Monestir de Pedralbes.

Palau Reial de Pedralbes

Opposite the university on Avinguda Diagonal, formal grounds stretch up to the Italianate **Palau Reial de Pedralbes** (Ⓜ Palau Reial) – basically a large villa with pretensions. It was built for the use of the royal family on their visits to Barcelona, with funds raised by public subscription, and received its first such visit in 1926. However, within five years the king had abdicated and the palace somewhat lost its role. Franco kept it on as a presidential residence and it later passed to the city, which since 1990 has used its rooms to show off certain of its applied art collections. There are plans to shift the displays to a purpose-built design museum at Glòries, but for the foreseeable future the palace contains separate **museums of ceramics and decorative arts** (Tues–Sat 10am–6pm, Sun 10am–3pm; €3.50, first Sun of the month free; ☎932 805 024), both accessible on the same ticket, which you can also use within one month to get into the Museu Textil i d'Indumentària in La Ribera.

The bulk of the permanent exhibits at the **Museu de Ceràmica** (ⓦwww .museuceramica.bcn.es) range from the thirteenth to the nineteenth century, and include fine Moorish-influenced tiles and plates from the Aragonese town of Teruel, as well as a series of fifteenth- and sixteenth-century *socarrats* (decorated terracotta panels) from Paterno displaying demons and erotic scenes. Catalunya, too, has a long ceramics tradition, and there are entire rooms here of Catalan water stoups, jars, dishes, plates and bowls. Perhaps the most vivid examples of the polychromatic work coming out of Barcelona and Lleida workshops of the time are the two extensive *azulejo* panels of 1710, one showing a Madrid bullfight, the other the feasting and dancing taking place at a party centred on the craze of the period – hot-chocolate-drinking. In the modern section, Picasso, Miró and the *modernista* artist Antoni Serra i Fiter are all represented. The whole display is considerably more interesting than the bare recital of exhibits suggests, particularly if you're already fascinated by the diverse ceramic designs and embellishments that adorn so many of the city's buildings, old and new.

Across the corridor, the rooms of the **Museu de les Arts Decoratives** (ⓦwww.museuartsdecoratives.bcn.es) are arranged around the upper gallery of the palace's former throne room. This is a fair old romp from Romanesque art through to contemporary Catalan design, but there are some beautiful pieces here, starting with a pair of delicate thirteenth-century Andalusian boxes showing clear Arabic traits – these are two of the very earliest pieces in the collection. Side rooms showcase the various periods under the spotlight, with displays of highly polished Baroque and Neoclassical furniture contrasting with the varied Art Deco and *modernista* holdings. The highlight here has to be the four-metre-high stained-glass window of 1900, depicting the *sardana* being danced in a scene that looks back to medieval times for its inspiration. The entire latter half of the gallery concentrates on contemporary Catalan *disseny* (design), from chairs to espresso machines, lighting to sink taps, though there's not much context provided and in the end it's a bit like walking through the *Vinçon* design store and not being allowed to buy anything. English-language notes are provided if you'd prefer to put some names to goods and objects.

Pavellons Güell

A block east of the Palau Reial gardens, Avinguda Pedralbes heads north off the Diagonal up to the Monestir de Pedralbes. Just a couple of minutes up the avenue, you'll pass the **Pavellons Güell** on your left. Built as a summer residence for the family of Gaudí's patron, Eusebi Güell, the gatehouse, gardens and entrance were designed by Gaudí at the same time as he was working on the family's Palau Güell in the old town. The brick and tile buildings are frothy, whimsical affairs with more than a Moorish element to them, though it's the gateway that's the most famous element. An extraordinary winged dragon made of twisted iron snarls at the passers-by, its razor-toothed jaws spread wide in a fearsome roar. Backing up to pose for a photograph suddenly doesn't seem like such a good idea. During the week you can't go any further than the gate, but there are guided visits to see the stables, gatehouse and garden on (Mon, Fri, Sat & Sun 10.15am in English, plus 11.15am, 12.15pm & 1.15pm in Spanish/Catalan €5; more details on ☎902 076 621, ⊛www.rutadelmodernisme.com).

Monestir de Pedralbes

At the end of Avinguda Pedralbes, the Gothic **Monestir de Pedralbes** (Tues–Sat 10am–2pm, June–Sept 10am–5pm, Sun 10am–3pm; €4, free first Sun of the month; ☎932 039 282) is reached up a cobbled street that passes through a small archway set back from the road. Founded in 1326 for the nuns of the Order of St Clare, this is in effect an entire monastic village preserved on the outskirts of the city, within medieval walls and gateways that completely shut out the noise and clamour of the twenty-first century. It's a twenty-minute walk from Ⓜ Palau Reial, or ten minutes from FGC Reina Elisenda (frequent trains from Plaça de Catalunya). Alternatively, you can go directly by bus from the city centre (30min): the #22 from Plaça de Catalunya and Passeig de Gràcia stops outside, while the #64 from Ronda Sant Antoni and c/Aribau ends its run at the monastery.

The monastery

It took the medieval craftsmen a little over a year to prepare Pedralbes (from the Latin *petras albas*, "white stones") for its first community of nuns. The speed of the initial construction and the subsequent uninterrupted habitation by the Order helps explain the extreme architectural harmony. After 600 years of isolation the monastery was sequestered by the Generalitat during the Civil War and it later opened as a museum in 1983 – a new adjacent convent was built as part of the deal, where the Clare nuns still reside. The ensemble now forms part of the City History Museum.

The **cloisters** in particular are the finest in the city, built on three levels and adorned by the slenderest of columns, with the only sound the tinkling water from the fountain. Rooms opening off the cloisters give a clear impression of convent life, from the chapter house and austere refectory to a fully equipped kitchen and infirmary. Alcoves and day cells display restored frescoes, religious artefacts, furniture and utensils, while in the nuns' former dormitory – now given a black marble floor and soaring oak-beamed ceiling – are shown a selection of the rarer **treasures**. Whilst the nuns themselves eschewed personal trappings, the monastery acquired valuable art and other posessions over the centuries – including pieces of Gothic furniture claimed to be part of the founding queen's endowment. There are paintings by Flemish artists, an impressive series of so-called factitious altarpieces of the sixteenth century (made up of sections of different style and provenance) and some outstanding illuminated choir books.

The adjacent **church** (usually 11am–1pm & 5–8pm) is a simple, single-naved structure, which retains some of its original fourteenth-century stained glass. In the chancel, to the right of the altar, the foundation's sponsor, Elisenda de Montcada, wife of Jaume II, lies in a superb carved marble tomb. Widowed in 1327, six months after the inauguration of the monastery, Elisenda retired to an adjacent palace, where she lived until her death in 1364.

Sarrià

If *modernista* buildings are high on your agenda, the exteriors of a couple of other important Gaudí buildings can be seen in the **Sarrià** district, east of Pedralbes. Not far from the science museum (see below), the **Torre Belles-guard** (c/Bellesguard 16–20; FGC Avgda. del Tibidabo), built from 1900 to 1909 on the site of the early fifteenth-century palace of King Martin I (the last of the Catalan kings), is a neo-Gothic house of unremarkable proportions; the **Col.legi de les Teresianes** (c/Ganduxer 85; FGC Bonanova) was a convent school, embellished in 1888 by Gaudí with an iron gate and parabolic arches.

If you are going to poke around these nether reaches of Barcelona, you may as well venture into the heart of Sarrià itself. At the northern end of its narrow main street – c/Major de Sarrià (FGC Sarrià; c/Mare de Deu de Núria exit) – stands the much-restored church of **Sant Vicenç** (at Plaça de Sarrià; bus #64 from Pedralbes/Plaça Universitat also stops here on its way to and from the monastery). This flanks the main Passeig de la Reina Elisenda de Montcada, across which lies the neighbourhood market, **Mercat Sarrià** (open from 8am, closed Mon, Tues, Sat pm also closed afternoons all July & Aug), housed in a 1911 *modernista* red-brick building. Traffic-free c/Major de Sarrià runs downhill from here, past other surviving old-town squares, prettiest of which is **Plaça Sant Vicenç** (off c/Mañe i Flaquer), where there's a statue of the saint. If you make it this way, don't miss the *Bar Tomás* (see p.184), just around the corner on c/Major de Sarrià, for the world's best *patatas bravas*.

CosmoCaixa

A dramatic refurbishment in 2005 has left the city's science museum looking better than ever – it's an easy place to spend a couple of hours (longer with children), and can be seen on your way to or from Tibidabo. Partly housed in a converted *modernista* hospice (built in 1904–09 by Josep Domènech i Estapà), **CosmoCaixa** (Tues–Sun 10am–8pm; €3, children's activities €2, planetarium €2; ☏932 126 050, ⊛www.cosmocaixa.com) retains the original building but has added a stylish, light-filled public concourse and a huge underground extension with four subterranean levels. The main exhibits are all down on the bottom floor, centred on the enormous open-plan Sala de la Matèria (Matter Room), where hands-on experiments and displays investigate life, the universe and everything, "from bacteria to Shakespeare". Many of the exhibits, and their densely worded explanations, require a very large thinking cap – younger children are soon going to be zooming around the open spaces. But there's no denying the overall pull of the two big draws, namely the 100 tonnes of "sliced" rock in the Mur Geològic (Geological Wall) and, best of all, the **Bosc Inundat** – nothing less than a thousand square metres of real Amazonian rainforest, complete with croc-filled mangroves, anacondas, giant catfish and dozy capybaras (the world's largest rodent, the size of a family dog).

Other lower levels of the museum are devoted to **children's and family activities**, such as Toca Toca! (Touch Touch!) – handling animals, insects and plants – Clik (ages 3–6) and Flash (7–10), where science games and experiments are presented in a fun way. These activities all tend to be held at weekends and during school holidays – pick up a schedule when you arrive, or check the website. There are also daily shows in the **planetarium** (Spanish and Catalan only, but worth experiencing), a great gift shop, and a café-restaurant with outdoor seating beneath the restored hospital facade.

CosmoCaixa is at c/Teodor Roviralta 47–51, just below the city ring road, the Ronda del Dalt. The easiest way to get there is by FGC train from Plaça de Catalunya to **Avinguda del Tibidabo station**, and then walk up the avenue, turning left just before the ring road (10min) – or the Tramvia Blau or Bus Turístic can drop you close by.

Tibidabo and around

If the views from the Castell de Montjuïc are good, those from the heights of **Tibidabo** (550m) – which forms the northwestern boundary of the city – are legendary. On one of those mythical clear days, you can see across to Montserrat and the Pyrenees, and out to sea even as far as Mallorca. The very name is based on this view, taken from the Temptations of Christ in the wilderness, when Satan led him to a high place and offered him everything that could be seen: *Haec omnia tibi dabo si cadens adoraberis me* ("All these things will I give thee, if thou wilt fall down and worship me").

At the summit there's a modern church topped with a huge statue of Christ, and – immediately adjacent – a wonderful amusement park, where the rides and attractions are scattered around several levels of the mountaintop, connected by landscaped paths and gardens. A short walk away there are more views from the observation deck of a communications tower, while the nearby village of Vallvidrera offers an alternative route back to the city.

Tibidabo

The funicular (see overleaf) drops you right outside the gates of the **Parc d'Atraccions** (daily mid-May to Sept from 10am, Oct to mid-May weekends only from 10am, closes 6–11pm depending on season; days and hours may vary, contact ☎932 117 942, ⊛www.tibidabo.es; €11 or €22) – Barcelona's funfair that's been thrilling the citizens for nearly a century. It's a mix of traditional rides and a few more hi-tech attractions, and the most expensive entrance ticket allows unlimited access to everything; otherwise you're limited to a selection of the best rides and attractions, including the Museu d'Autòmates, a collection of coin-operated antique fairground machines in working order. If you want a real thrill, try the aeroplane ride, a Barcelona institution: it's been spinning since 1928.

You can get views of the city for free from the belvedere by the side of the park, and they are even more extensive if you climb the shining steps of the neighbouring **Templo Expiatorio de España** to the dramatic, wide balcony. Inside the church, also known as the Sagrat Cor (Sacred Heart), a lift (*ascensor*; daily 10am–2pm & 3–7pm; €2) takes you higher still, to just under the feet of Christ, from where the city, surrounding hills and sea shimmer in the distance.

Practicalities

Getting there can be a convoluted matter but it is also part of the attraction. First, take the FGC **train** (Tibidabo line) from the station at Plaça de Catalunya to Avinguda del Tibidabo. Emerging from the station escalators, cross the road to the tram and bus shelter at the bottom of the tree-lined avenue; the Bus Turístic stops here, too. An antique tram service, the Tramvia Blau (mid-June to mid-Sept daily 10am–8pm, rest of year Sat & Sun & holidays 10am–6pm, departures every 15–30min; €2.30 one way, €3.50 return; ⑨www.tramvia.org) then runs you up the hill to Plaça Doctor Andreu; on weekdays there's a bus service instead (Mon–Fri 7.45am–8.50pm, every 20min). By the tram and bus stop on Plaça Doctor Andreu there are several **café-bars and restaurants** – the views from *Mirablau* (p.206) are particularly fine – and a **funicular** station. When the Parc d'Atraccions is open, this has connections every 30min to Tibidabo at the top (€2 one way, €3 return). Alternatively, the special **Tibibus** runs direct to Tibidabo from Plaça de Catalunya, outside El Corte Inglés (Sat, Sun & holidays every 30min; plus Mon–Fri summer; €2.20).

Drinks and meals inside the park are pricey. Immediately outside the upper funicular station and park there's another restaurant, which is packed with families on Sundays. It's not that great, though it does have outdoor terrace seats. The best choice for a sandwich or simple meal is the *Marisa*, an inexpensive bar-restaurant on the road to Vallvidrera just below the Tibidabo car park. It's a three-minute walk from the upper funicular station and has a little concrete patio to the side with sweeping views.

Torre de Collserola and Vallvidrera

Follow the road from the Tibidabo car park and it's only a few minutes' walk to Norman Foster's **Torre de Collserola** (Wed–Fri 11am–2.30pm & 3.30–6pm, Sat & Sun 11am–6pm; April–Sept until 7pm; €5.25, also includes entrance to Mirador de Colón; ☎934 069 354, ⑨www.torredecollserola.com), a soaring communications tower high above the tree line, with a glass lift that whisks you up ten floors (115m) for yet more stunning views – 70km, they claim, on a good day.

Afterwards, you could just head back to Tibidabo for the funicular-and-tram ride back to the city, but to complete a circular tour it's more interesting to follow the large cobbled path near the tower's car park, which brings you out on the pine-clad edges of **Vallvidrera**, a wealthy suburban village perched on the flank of the Collserola hills – a twenty-minute walk all told from Tibidabo. There's another **funicular** station here (6am–midnight every 6–10min), connecting to Peu del Funicular, an FGC station on the Sabadell and Terrassa line from Plaça de Catalunya.

Vallvidrera's main square isn't obvious – if you turn left out of the funicular station and walk down the steep steps, Plaça de Vallvidrera is the traffic roundabout at the bottom. There are a couple of local **bar-restaurants** on its fringes, the most striking being *Can Josean* (closed Tues) with a simple bar at the front and a dining room at the rear, with views out over the city from the back tables.

Parc de Collserola

The **Parc de Collserola**, encompassing Tibidabo (its highest peak), is one of Barcelona's best-kept secrets. While many make the ascent to the amusement park and church, few realize that beyond stretches an area of peaks and wooded valleys roughly 17km by 18km, threaded by rivers, roads and paths. You can, in fact, walk into the park from Tibidabo and the Torre de Collserola, but it's better to start from the park's information centre, across to the east, above Vallvidrera, where hiking-trail leaflets and other information are available.

The **Centre d'Informació** (daily 10am–3pm; ☎932 803 552, ⓦwww .parccollserola.net) lies in oak and pinewoods, an easy, signposted ten-minute stepped walk up through the trees from the FGC Baixada de Vallvidrera station (Sabadell and Terrassa line from Pl. de Catalunya; 15min). There's an exhibition here on the park's history, flora and fauna, while the staff hand out English-language leaflets detailing the various walks you can make from the centre, ranging from a fifteen-minute stroll to the Vallvidrera dam to a couple of hours circling the hills. A bar-restaurant (with an outdoor terrace) provides snacks and meals, and sells bottles of water for hikers.

If you're here at the weekend, before you head off you might as well have a quick look inside the **Museu–Casa Verdaguer** (Sat, Sun & hols 10am–2pm; free; ☎932 047 805), housed in the Villa Joana, which sits just below the information centre. Jacint Verdaguer i Santaló (1845-1902), the Catalan Reniassance poet and priest, lived here briefly before his death, and the house has been preserved as an example of well-to-do nineteenth-century Catalan life. Extracts from his poetry enliven the climb up from the FGC station to the information centre and house.

Well-marked **paths** radiate from the information centre into the hills and valleys. Some – like the oak-forest walk – soon gain height for marvellous views over the tree canopy, while others descend through the valley bottoms to springs and shaded picnic areas. The walk touted as the most diverse is that to the **Font de la Buderalla**, a landscaped spring deep in the woods, beneath the Torre de Collserola. It's about an hour if you circle back to the information centre from here, but a good idea is to follow the signs for the Torre de Collserola and Vallvidrera once you reach the *font* (a further 20min). That way, you can return to Barcelona instead via the funicular from the village of Vallvidrera (see opposite), or even take in the views from the Collserola tower or Tibidabo before going back.

Out of the city

lthough there are plenty of traditional coastal bolt holes close to Barcelona, like Castelldefels to the south or the small towns of the Costa Maresme to the north, unquestionably the best local seaside destination is **Sitges**, half an hour to the south along the Costa Daurada. It's a charming resort with an international reputation, extremely popular with gay visitors and chic city-dwellers. Otherwise, the one essential excursion is to

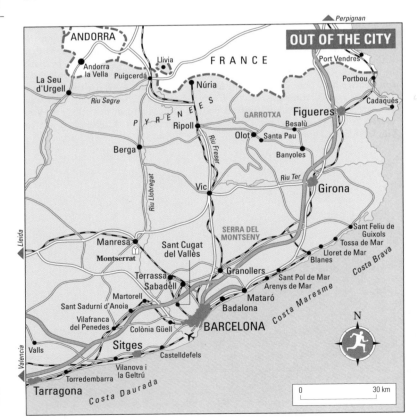

February–March
Carnival Sitges has Catalunya's best Carnival celebrations.

May
11 Cremada del Dimoni at Badalona: demon-burning, dancing and fireworks.
Third week Fires i Festes de la Santa Creu in Figueres – processions and music.
Corpus Christi (moveable feast, sometimes falls in early June): Festa de Corpus Christi in Sitges – big processions and streets decorated with flowers.

June
24 Dia de Sant Joan celebrated everywhere; watch out for things shutting down for a day on either side.
Last week Annual festival at Canet de Mar and Sant Cugat del Vallès.

July
Second week Annual festival at Arenys de Mar.

August
15 Annual festival at Castelldefels.
19 Festa de Sant Magí in Tarragona.
Last week: Festa Major in Sitges, to honour the town's patron saint, Sant Bartolomeu.
29 & 30 Festa Major in Vilafranca del Penedès, dedicated to Sant Felix, with human towers, dancing and processions – continues into the first two days of September.

September
Second Sunday Fira Gran in Sant Sadurní d'Anoia, the town's big annual festival.
23 Festa de Sant Tecla in Tarragona, with processions of *gegants* and human castles.

October
Second week Setmana del Cava – a sort of *cava* festival – is held in Sant Sadurní d'Anoia, well worth going out of your way for.

Montserrat, the extraordinary mountain and monastery 40km northwest of Barcelona, reached by a precipitous cable-car or mountain railway ride. However short your trip to the city, this is worth making time for, as it's a place of great significance for Catalans, not to mention being a terrific place for a hike in the hills.

If you enjoy Barcelona's varied church architecture, there's more to come, starting with Gaudí's inspired work at the **Colònia Güell**, a late nineteenth-century idealistic community established by the architect's patron Eusebi Güell. This is a half-day's outing, while a second half-day can be spent visiting the Benedictine monastery at **Sant Cugat del Vallès** and the complex of early medieval churches at **Terrassa**, all of them largely unsung and utterly fascinating. Another route out of the city, due west, leads through the wine-producing towns of **Sant Sadurní d'Anoia** and **Vilafranca del Penedès**, both of which can be seen in a pleasant day's excursion with enough time for a wine-tasting tour.

It's also straightforward to see something of Barcelona's neighbouring cities, all very different from the Catalan capital. To the south of Barcelona, beyond Sitges, lies **Tarragona**, with a compact old town and an amazing series of Roman remains; while to the north, inland from the coast, sits medieval **Girona**, perhaps the most beautiful of all Catalan cities, with its river, fortified walls and golden buildings. Both of these destinations are around an hour from Barcelona, and it's only the extreme northern town of **Figueres** that requires any lengthier a journey – entirely justified for anyone interested in seeing Catalunya's most indescribable museum, the renowned **Museu Dalí**.

Full **public transport** details are given below for each destination. Local and regional trains provide the most reliable service, and you can check current timetables with RENFE (☎902 240 202, ☒www.renfe.es) or FGC (☎932 051 515, ☒www.fgc.es). There are buses to most regional destinations, too, from the Estació del Nord bus station, though these usually take longer than the train. It really isn't worth renting a car unless you want to see a lot of what's described above in a short time. Each account also includes some **café and restaurant** recommendations, while if you feel like spending the night away from Barcelona it's best to contact the local tourist offices, whose details are provided. A visit to Barcelona's **Centre d'Informació de Catalunya** at Palau Robert (see p.28) might also be in order, to pick up maps, information and advice before you go.

Sitges

SITGES, 36km south of Barcelona, is definitely the highlight of the Costa Daurada – the great weekend escape for young Barcelonans, who have created a resort very much in their own image. It's also a noted gay holiday destination, with a nightlife to match and between June and September it seems like there's one nonstop party going on – which, in a way, there is. During the heat of the day, though, the tempo drops as everyone hits the beach, while out of season Sitges is delightful: far less crowded (indeed, empty in midweek), and with a temperate climate that encourages promenade strolls and old-town exploration. Note that Monday isn't the best day to come, as the three museums and many restaurants are closed.

The Town

It's the **beach** that brings most people to Sitges, with clean sands either side of the old-town headland – though these become extremely crowded in high season. For more space it's best to keep walking west along the promenade, passing a series of eight interlinked beaches that runs a couple of kilometres down the coast as far as the *Hotel Terramar*. There are breakwaters, beach bars, restaurants, showers and water sports facilities along the way, with the more notorious gay nudist beaches found at the far end – for these, keep on past *L'Antlantida* disco to the *Sun Beach Garden* (10min) and the small coves beyond.

There are scores of handsome restored **mansions** in town, largely built in the nineteenth century by wealthy merchants returned from the Americas – a walk along the prom reveals the best of them, adorned with wrought-iron balconies, stained-glass windows and ceramic decoration. The knoll overlooking the town beaches and marina is topped by the landmark Baroque **parish church** dedicated to Sant Bartolomeu, whose annual festival is celebrated in town in the last week of August. Behind, in the narrow streets of the old town, you'll find a series of late-medieval whitewashed mansions as well as the brick **Mercat Vell** (Old Market), the latter now an exhibition hall. One house on c/Fonollar contains the **Museu Cau Ferrat** (mid-June to Sept Tues–Sat 9.30am–2pm & 4–7pm, Sun 10am–3pm; Oct to mid-June Tues–Sat 9.30am–2pm & 3.30–6.30pm, Sun 10am–3pm; €3.50, combined ticket for all museums €6.40; ☎938 940 364),

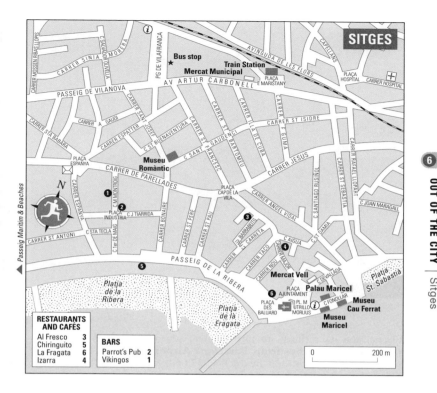

RESTAURANTS AND CAFÉS	
Al Fresco	3
Chiringuito	5
La Fragata	6
Izarra	4

BARS	
Parrot's Pub	2
Vikingos	1

the former house and workshop of the artist and writer **Santiago Rusiñol i Prats** (1861–1931), who moved here in 1891. Sitges flourished as an important *modernista* centre under his patronage – Rusiñol organized five *modernista* festivals between 1892 and 1899 – and the house contains a mixture of his own works and those by contemporaries, as well as various collected odds and ends, like the decorative ironwork Rusiñol brought back in bulk from the Pyrenees. Nearby, the **Museu Maricel** (same hours, price and contact details as Cau Ferrat) contains minor artworks, medieval to modern, and maintains an impressive collection of Catalan ceramics and sculpture. In July and August (usually two evenings a week) the main part of the mansion itself is open for guided tours, a short concert and drinks – the tourist office will have exact details.

The **Museu Romàntic** in the centre of town at c/Sant Gaudenci 1, off c/Sant Josep (same hours and price as Cau Ferrat; ☎938 942 969), occupies the stately rooms of a 1793 bourgeois house. Admission is by guided tour only (every 60min) and demonstrates the lifestyle of a rich Sitges family in the eighteenth and nineteenth centuries by displaying a wealth of period furniture and possessions, from divans to dolls.

Practicalities

Trains to Sitges leave Passeig de Gràcia or Barcelona Sants stations every twenty minutes, more frequently at peak times (destination Vilanova or St

△ Sitges

Vicenç) and it's a thirty- to forty-minute ride depending on the service. There's also a direct **bus from Barcelona Airport** (Mon–Fri hourly, Sat & Sun every 2–3hr with Mon-Bus, ☎938 937 060), which takes forty minutes. Although the Sitges nightlife might be legendary, the trains do you no favours, with the last departure back to Barcelona at around 10.30pm. However, there is an hourly **nightbus** from Passeig de Vilafranca by the tourist office (currently between midnight and 3am) which drops passengers on Ronda Universitat in Barcelona 50 minutes later. A taxi will cost at least €40.

The **Oficina de Turisme** (July to mid-Sept daily 9am–8pm; mid-Sept to June Mon–Fri 9am–2pm & 4–6.30pm; ☎938 945 004, ⊛www.sitgestur.com) is behind the Oasis shopping centre, up Passeig de Vilafranca, five minutes' walk from the station. There's a second office on c/Fonollar, opposite the Museu Cau Ferrat (July–Sept daily 10am–1.30pm & 5–9pm; Oct–June Wed–Fri 10.30am–1.45pm, Sat 11am–2pm & 4–7pm, Sun 11am–4pm; ☎938 110 611). You can pick up a town map, and restaurant and accommodation lists, from either office.

For picnic supplies visit the **Mercat Municipal** (Mon–Thurs 8am–2pm, Fri & Sat 8am–2pm & 5.30–8.30pm), close to the train station on Avinguda Artur Carbonell. Areas to explore for **cafés and restaurants** are the side streets off c/Major, or the beachfront for the more expensive seafood restaurants. *Izarra*, c/Major 20 (☎938 947 370), is a pint-sized Basque bar with tapas and meals, or for something fancier there's *Al Fresco*, c/Barrabeitg 4, just down the steps off c/Major (dinner only, closed Mon & Tues; ☎938 940 600), which serves Catalan fusion cuisine with main courses for €17–25 – the associated *Al Fresco Café* just on the corner of c/Major (open from 9am, closed Mon; ☎938 113 307) is good for breakfast and light meals. On the seafront there's a wide choice, starting with the *Chiringuito*, Pg. de la Ribera (☎938 947 596), claiming to be Spain's oldest

Carnival time

Carnival in Sitges (*Carnestoltes* in Catalan; Feb/March) is outrageous, thanks largely to the strong gay presence. It opens on the so-called Fat Thursday with the arrival of the Carnival King, following which there's a full programme of parades, masked balls, concerts, beach parties and sausage sizzles. The traditional *xatónada* gala dinners are named for the carnival dish, *xató*, a kind of salt-cod salad, which originates in Sitges. Carnival climaxes in Sunday night's Debauchery Parade and the even bigger Tuesday-night Extermination Parade, in which exquisitely dressed drag queens swan about the streets in high heels, twirling lacy parasols and coyly fanning themselves. Bar doors stand wide open, bands play, and processions and celebrations go on until dawn.

beach bar and offering grilled sardines, fried *chipirones* and calamari, sandwiches and snacks at budget prices. Every restaurant along the front does a paella with a promenade view, while typical of the new wave of classier seafood places is *La Fragata*, Pg. de la Ribera 1 (☎938 941 086), where catch-of-the-day choices like monkfish casserole, tuna tartare or grilled local prawns cost €15–25. The epicentre of local **nightlife** is c/Primer de Maig and c/Montroig, where café-*terrasas* like *Vikingos* and the staunchly gay *Parrot's Pub* are local fixtures.

Montserrat

The mountain of **Montserrat**, with its weirdly shaped crags of rock, vast monastery and deserted hermitage caves, stands just 40km northwest of Barcelona, off the road to Lleida. It's the most popular day-trip from the city, reached in around ninety minutes by train and then cable car or rack railway for a thrilling ride up to the monastery. Once there, you can visit the basilica and monastery buildings, and complete your day with a walk around the woods and crags, using the two funicular railways that depart from the monastery complex.

The mountain is one of the most spectacular of all Spain's natural sights, a saw-toothed outcrop left exposed to erosion when the inland sea that covered this area around 25 million years ago was drained by progressive uplifts of the earth's crust. Legends hang easily upon it. Fifty years after the birth of Christ, St Peter is said to have deposited an image of the Virgin (La Moreneta, the Black Virgin) carved by St Luke in one of the mountain caves. The icon was lost in the early eighth century after being hidden during the Moorish invasion, but reappeared in 880, accompanied by the customary visions and celestial music. A chapel was built to house it, and in 976 this was superseded by a Benedictine **monastery**, set about three-quarters of the way up the mountain at an altitude of nearly 1000m. Miracles abounded and the Virgin of Montserrat soon became the chief cult-image of Catalunya and a pilgrimage centre second in Spain only to Santiago de Compostela – the main **pilgrimages** to Montserrat take place on April 27 and September 8. For centuries, the monastery enjoyed outrageous prosperity, having its own flag and a form of extraterritorial independence along the lines of the Vatican City, and its fortunes declined only in the nineteenth century. In 1811 Napoleon's troops devastated the buildings, stole many of the treasures and "hunted the hermits like chamois along the cliffs". In 1835 the monastery was suppressed for supporting the wrong side in the civil war known as the First Carlist War. Monks were allowed to return nine years later, but by 1882 their numbers had fallen to nineteen. However, over the twentieth century Montserrat's popularity again became established. In addition to the tourists, tens of thousands of newly married couples come here to seek La Moreneta's blessing, while Montserrat has also become something of an important nationalist symbol for Catalans.

The monastery

The monastery itself is of no particular architectural interest, save perhaps in its monstrous bulk. Its various buildings – including hotel, post office, souvenir shop and even supermarket – fan out around an open square, and there are extraordinary mountain views from the terrace as well as from various other vantage points scattered around the complex.

Of the religious buildings, only the **Basilica** (daily 7.30am–8pm; free), dating largely from 1560 to 1592, is open to the public. **La Moreneta** (access 8–10.30am & noon–6.30pm), blackened by the smoke of countless candles, stands above the high altar – reached from behind, by way of an entrance to the right of the basilica's main entrance. The approach to this beautiful icon reveals the enormous wealth of the monastery, as you queue along a corridor leading through the back of the basilica's rich side-chapels. Signs at head height command "SILENCE" in various languages, but nothing quietens the line that waits to climb the stairs behind the altar and kiss the image's hands and feet. Your appreciation of the icon's noble features is likely to be limited to a quick glimpse as you file by. The best time to visit the basilica is when Montserrat's world-famous **boys' choir** sings (Mon–Fri 1pm, Sun & hols at noon & 6.45pm). The boys belong to the Escolania, a choral school established in the fourteenth century and unchanged in musical style since its foundation.

Near the entrance to the basilica, the **Museu de Montserrat** (daily 9am–5.45pm; €5.50) presents a few archeological finds brought back by travelling monks together with painting and sculpture dating from as early as the thirteenth century, including works by Caravaggio, El Greco, Tiepolo, Picasso, Dalí, Monet and Degas. Religious items are in short supply, as most of the monastery's valuables were carried off by Napoleon's troops. The joint ticket also gets you into the **Espai Audiovisual** (Mon–Fri 9am–5.45pm, Sat & Sun 9am–6.15pm), an interactive exhibition near the tourist office which tells you something of the life of a Benedictine community – around eighty brothers currently reside at the monastery.

Walks on the mountain

After you've poked around the monastery grounds, it's the walks around the woods and mountainside of Montserrat that are the real attraction. Following the tracks to various caves and the thirteen different hermitages, you can contemplate what Goethe wrote in 1816: "Nowhere but in his own Montserrat will a man find happiness and peace." The going is pretty good on all the tracks – most have been graded and some concreted – and the signposting is clear, but take a bottle of water and keep away from the edges. A map with walking notes is available from the Montserrat tourist office (see "Practicalities" opposite).

Two separate funiculars run from points close to the cable-car station, with departures every twenty minutes (daily 10am–6pm; weekends only in winter). One drops to the path for **Santa Cova** (€2.50 return), a seventeenth-century chapel built where the icon is said originally to have been found. It's an easy

The **vegetation** of the lower slopes of Montserrat is essentially Mediterranean forest – where fires have occasionally swept through, the burned patches have since been recolonized by Spanish gorse, rosemary and a profusion of grape hyacinths, early purple orchids and martagon lilies. Higher up, although apparently barren of vegetation, Montserrat's rounded turrets support a wide variety of fissure plants, not least of which is the lime-encrusting saxifrage *Saxifraga callosa* ssp. *catalaunica* – known to grow only at Montserrat and on the hills near Marseille. Plants more typical of the high Pyrenees also make their home here, including botanical gems such as ramonda and the handsome Pyrenean bellflower.

Birds of Montserrat include Bonelli's warblers, nightingales, serins and firecrests in the woodlands, while the burned areas provide refuge for Sardinian warblers and good hunting for Bonelli's eagles. Sant Jeroni, the highest point of Montserrat, is an excellent place to watch for peregrines, crag martins and black redstarts all year round, with the addition of alpine swifts in the summer and alpine accentors in the winter. On sunny days Iberian wall lizards emerge from the crevices to bask on rock faces.

walk there and back, which takes less than an hour. The other funicular rises steeply to the hermitage of **Sant Joan** (€6.10 return), from where it's a tougher forty-five-minute walk to the **Sant Jeroni** hermitage, and another fifteen minutes to the Sant Jeroni summit at 1236m. Several other walks are also possible from the Sant Joan funicular; perhaps the nicest is the simple (but steep) forty-five-minute circuit around the ridge that leads back down to the monastery.

Practicalities

To reach the Montserrat cable-car and rack-railway stations, take the **FGC train** (line R5, direction Manresa), which leaves from Plaça d'Espanya (ⓂEspanya) daily at hourly intervals from 8.36am. Get off at Montserrat Aeri (52min) for the connecting cable car, the **Aeri de Montserrat** (☎938 350 005, ⓦwww.aeridemontserrat.com) – you may have to queue for fifteen minutes or so, but then it's an exhilarating five-minute swoop up the sheer mountainside to a terrace just below the monastery. The alternative approach is by cog-wheel mountain railway, the **Cremallera de Montserrat** (☎902 312 020, ⓦwww .cremallerademontserrat.com), which departs from Monistrol de Montserrat (the next stop after Montserrat Aeri, another 4min); again, services connect with train arrivals from Barcelona, and take about twenty minutes to climb to the monastery. **Returning to Barcelona**, the R5 trains depart hourly from Monistrol de Montserrat (from 9.33am) and Montserrat Aeri (from 9.37am).

A desk and information board at Plaça d'Espanya station details all the combined fare options. Currently, a **return ticket** from Barcelona costs €12.60 (either for train and cable car or train and *cremallera*), and there are also two combined tickets: the **Trans Montserrat** (€18.40), which includes the metro, train, cable car/*cremallera*, unlimited use of the two funiculars and entry to the audiovisual exhibit; and the **Tot Montserrat** (€31), which includes the same plus museum entry and a self-service cafeteria lunch.

Drivers should take the A2 motorway as far as the Martorell exit, and then follow the N11 and C55 to the Montserrat turn-off – or they can park at either the cable-car or the rack-railway station and take the rides up instead. All-in cable-car/*cremallera*/Montserrat attraction combo tickets are available at the Cremellera station for drivers who park-and-ride. There is also a daily **bus tour** (€45) to Monsterrat from Barcelona with *Julià Tours* (Ronda Universitat 5 ☏933 176 454, information from any tourist office), but it can't compete for thrills with the train and aerial rides.

There's a tourist office at Montserrat, just up from the *cremallera* station, marked **Informació** (daily 9am–5.45pm, July–Sept until 7pm; ☏938 777 701, ⓦwww.montserratvisita.com), where you can pick up maps of the complex and mountain. They can also advise you about the accommodation options, from camping to staying at the three-star hotel.

There are plenty of places to eat, but all are relatively pricey and none particularly inspiring. They are also very busy at peak times. The most expensive **restaurant** is inside the *Hotel Abat Cisneros*, opposite the basilica, which is reasonably good but overpriced (meals €25–35). Cheaper, and boasting the best views, is the *Restaurant de Montserrat* (meals €15) in the cliff-edge building near the car park, though here and in the **self-service cafeteria**, one floor up and with the same good views, there's no *à la carte* choice – that is, you have to order a full meal – and the food can at best be described as adequate. The cafeteria is where you eat with the all-inclusive Tot Montserrat ticket. There's another self-service cafeteria near the upper cable-car station, a bar in the square further up, plus a patisserie and a supermarket, and there's a lot to be said for taking your own picnic and striking off up the mountainside – fresh *mató* (curd cheese) and honey is sold at stalls on the road up to the car park.

Sant Cugat and Terrassa

A series of remarkable churches lies on the commuter line out of the city to the northwest, the first in the dormitory town of **Sant Cugat del Vallès** – just twenty-five minutes from Barcelona – and the second (actually a group of three) another fifteen minutes beyond in the industrial city of **Terrassa**. You can easily see all the churches in a morning, but throw in lunch and this just about stretches to a day-trip, and it's not a bad ride in any case – after Sarrià, the train emerges from the city tunnels and chugs down the wooded valley into Sant Cugat. FGC trains run on the S1 line from Plaça de Catalunya, also stopping in Gràcia, with departures every ten to fifteen minutes.

Sant Cugat del Vallès

At **SANT CUGAT DEL VALLÈS**, the Benedictine **Reial Monestir** (Mon–Sat 9am–noon & 6–8pm, Sun 9am–8pm; free) was founded as far back as the ninth century, though most of the surviving buildings date from three or four hundred years later. Its fawn stone facade and triple-decker bell tower make a lovely sight as you approach from the square outside, through the gate, past the renovated Bishop's Palace and under a splendid rose window. Finest of all, though, is the beautiful twelfth-century Romanesque **cloister**, with noteworthy capital carvings of mythical beasts and biblical scenes. They have an unusual homogeneity, since they were all done by a single sculptor, Arnau Gatell. What were once the monastery's kitchen gardens lie across from the Bishop's Palace, though the formerly lush plots that sustained the brothers are now mere dusty gardens, albeit with views over the low walls to Tibidabo and the Collserola hills.

To reach the monastery, cross the road outside the train station and follow c/Valldoreix, taking the first right and then the first left (it's still c/Valldoreix), and then keep straight along the shopping street until you see the monastery bell tower (10min). Plaça Octavia, outside the monastery, has a **café–restaurant** with outdoor seating, and you'll pass plenty of other places to eat on your way.

Terrassa

TERRASSA, a large city with a population of 150,000, about 20km out of Barcelona, hides its treasures in the older part of town, a twenty-minute walk from the station (get off at Terrassa-Rambla, the last stop). Here, three pre-Romanesque churches, dating from the fifth to the tenth centuries, form an unusual complex built on the site of the former Roman town of Egara. It's known as the **Conjunt Monumental de les Esglésies de Sant Pere** (Tues–Sat 10am–1.30pm & 4–7pm, Sun 11am–2pm; free; ☏937 833 702) – not that you'll see any signs – and excavations are still ongoing, but the church doors are open for visits and someone should be around to give you an explanatory leaflet.

The largest church, **Sant Pere**, is the least interesting, with just a badly faded Gothic mural and a tenth-century mosaic fragment on view within its walls. **Santa Maria** is far better endowed, starting with a mosaic pavement outside that dates from the fifth century. The same date is given to the sunken baptismal font inside, while much later Gothic (fourteenth- and fifteenth-century) murals and altarpieces – one by Catalan master Jaume Huguet – are also on display. But it's the intervening building, the fifth-century baptistry of **Sant Miquel**, that's the most fascinating here. A tiny, square building of rough masonry, steeped in gloom, it has eight assorted columns supporting the dome, each with carved Roman or Visigothic capitals. Underneath sits the partially reconstructed baptismal bath, once octagonal, while steps lead down into a simple crypt.

To get there, turn right out of the station (Rambla Egara exit) and immediately right again into Plaça de Clavé, following c/Major up to Plaça Vella, where there are some outdoor **cafés**. The route then crosses the square, turns up c/Gavatxons and follows c/Sant Pere, c/Nou de Sant Pere and c/de la Gran Creu, finally crossing a viaduct to arrive at the entrance to the church complex.

Terrassa is also known for its *modernista*-style **industrial buildings** – the town was an important textile producer in the nineteenth century. The Ruta del Modernisme (p.28) provides an "industrial and *modernista* route" through town, while the local tourist office organizes guided tours (☏937 397 019, ⓦwww.terrassa.org/turisme).

Colònia Güell

Before work at the Parc Güell got under way, Antoni Gaudí had already been charged with the design of parts of Eusebi Güell's earliest attempts to establish a Utopian industrial estate, or *colònia* (colony), on the western outskirts of Barcelona. The **Colònia Güell** was very much of its time – more than seventy similar colonies were established along Catalan rivers in the late nineteenth century, using water power to drive the textile mills The concept was a familiar one in Britain, where enlightened Victorian entrepreneurs had long created idealistic towns (Saltaire, Bournville) to house their workers.

The Colònia Güell at Santa Coloma de Cervelló was begun in 1890 and, by 1920, incorporated over one hundred houses, a school, theatre and cultural association, plus the chapel and crypt for which Gaudí was responsible. The buildings were predominantly of brick and iron, sporting typical *modernista* Gothic and Moorish-style flourishes. The Güell company was taken over in 1945 and the whole complex closed as a going concern in 1973, though the buildings have since been restored – and, indeed, many are still lived in today.

There's an interpretive exhibition (with English notes) at the visitor centre, but by far the best way of appreciating the site is simply to stroll the streets, past the rows of terraced houses, whose front gardens are tended lovingly by the current inhabitants. Brick towers, ceramic panels and stained glass elevate many of the houses above the ordinary – like the private Ca l'Espinal (1900) by Gaudí's contemporary, Joan Rubió i Bellver. It is, though, Gaudí's **church** (May–Oct Mon–Sat 10am–2pm & 3–7pm, Sun 10am–3pm; Nov–April daily 10am–3pm), built into the pine-clad hillside above the colony, which alone deserves to be called a masterpiece. The crypt was designed to carry the weight of the chapel above, its palm-tree-like columns supporting a brick vault, and the whole resembling a labyrinth of caves fashioned from a variety of different stone and brick. The more extraordinary features of Gaudí's flights of fancy presage his later work on the Sagrada Família – like the original scalloped pews, the conch shells used as water stoups, the vivid stained glass, and the window that opens up like the wings of a butterfly. Despite appearances, the church was never actually finished – Gaudí stopped work on it in 1914 – and continuing restoration work aims to complete the outer walls, though Gaudí's planned forty-metre-high central dome is unlikely ever to be realized.

Practicalities

Take the **FGC train** S8 (direction Martorell; roughly every 15min) from Plaça d'Espanya to the small Colònia Güell station; the ride takes twenty minutes. From here, follow the painted blue footprints across the highway and into the *colònia* to the visitor centre (10min), the **Centre d'Acollida de Visitants** (May–Oct Mon–Sat 10am–7pm, Sun 10am–3pm; Nov–April daily 10am–3pm; ☎936 305 807, ⓦwww.elbaixllobregat.net/coloniaguell). You can walk around the *colònia* and see the church from the outside for free, though to visit the church interior you'll have to buy a ticket (€4) at the visitor centre – the church is open during the hours detailed above, but closed for visits during Mass on Sundays (11am & 1pm). There are **guided tours** available daily throughout the year, of either the church and estate (€8; 2hr) or the church on its own (€5; 30min), but you'll need to call the visitor centre in advance about the possibility since the service is only for groups.

It's a working village, so you'll find a bank and pharmacy, as well as two or three cafés and restaurants.

The wine region: L'Alt Penedès

Trains (Mon–Fri every 30min, Sat & Sun every 60min) from Plaça de Catalunya or Barcelona Sants run west from Barcelona into **L'Alt Penedès**, a region roughly halfway between the city and Tarragona, devoted to wine production.

It's the largest Catalan producer of still and sparkling wines, which becomes increasingly clear the further the train heads into the region, with vines as far as the eye can see on both sides of the track. There are two main towns to visit, both of which can easily be seen in a single day: **Sant Sadurní d'Anoia**, the closer to Barcelona (35min), is the self-styled Capital del Cava, home to around fifty producers of sparkling wine; **Vilafranca del Penedès**, ten minutes down the line, is the region's administrative capital and produces mostly still wine.

If you're serious about **visiting vineyards** it's a trip better done by car, as many of the more interesting boutique producers lie out in the countryside. Either of the towns' tourist offices can provide a good map pinpointing all the local vineyards as well as the rural farmhouse restaurants that are a feature of this region.

Sant Sadurní d'Anoia

SANT SADURNÍ D'ANOIA, built on land watered by the Riu Noya, has been an important centre of wine production since the eighteenth century. When, at the end of the nineteenth century, French vineyards suffered heavily from disease, Sant Sadurní prospered, though later it too succumbed to the same wasting disease – something remembered still in the annual September festival by the parade of a representation of the feared Philoxera parasite. The production of *cava*, for which the town is now famous, began only in the 1870s – an industry that went hand in hand with the Catalan cork business, established in the forests of the hinterland. Today, a hundred million bottles a year of *cava* – the Catalan *méthode champenoise* – are turned out by dozens of companies, many of which are only too happy to escort you around their premises, show you the fermentation process, and let you taste a glass or two.

The town itself is of little interest, but it hardly matters, since most people never get any further than the most prominent and most famous company, **Freixenet** (☎938 917 000, ⓦwww.freixenet.es), whose building is right outside the train station. Free **tours** operate from Monday to Thursday 9am–6pm, Friday 9am–1pm, and it's best to call and reserve a place. Many other compa-

△ Freixenet Cava company at Sant Sadurni d'Anoia

Cava

Cava is a naturally sparkling wine made using the *méthode champenoise*. The basic **grape** varieties of L'Alt Penedès are *macabeu*, *xarel.lo* and *parellada*, which are fermented to produce a wine base and then mixed with sugar and yeast before being bottled: a process known as **tiratge**. The bottles are then sealed hermetically – the **tapat** – and laid flat in cellars – the **criança** – for up to nine months, to ferment for a second time. The wine is later decanted to get rid of the sediment before being corked.

The *cava* is then **classified** according to the amount of sugar used in the fermentation: either *Brut* (less than 20g a litre) or *Sec* (20–30g); *Semisec* (30–50g) or *Dolç* (more than 50g). This is the first thing to take note of before buying or drinking: *Brut* and *Sec* are to most people's tastes and are excellent with almost any food; *Semisec* and *Dolç* are better used as dessert wines. To drink it at its best, serve *cava* at between 6° and 8°C, and remember – whatever your brain is telling you, and however swiggable that third bottle might be, it *is* alcoholic.

nies have similar arrangements, including the out-of-town **Codorníu** (☎938 183 232, ⊛www.codorniu.com) – the region's earliest *cava* producer – which has a fine building by *modernista* architect Josep Puig i Cadafalch as an added attraction.

Vilafranca del Penedès

As a town, **VILAFRANCA DEL PENEDÈS** is rather more interesting than Sant Sadurní. Founded in the eleventh century in an attempt to attract settlers to land retaken from the expelled Moors, it became a prosperous market centre. This character is still in evidence today, with a compact old town at whose heart lie narrow streets and arcaded squares adorned with restored medieval mansions.

From the train station, walk up to the main Rambla de Nostra Senyora and cut to the right up c/de Sant Joan to the enclosed Plaça de Sant Joan, which has a small daily produce **market**. A rather larger affair takes place every Saturday, when the stalls also stock clothes, household goods, handicrafts and agricultural gear. There's a **tourist office** at the back of the square, at c/Cort 14 (Mon 4–7pm, Tues–Fri 9am–1pm & 4–7pm, Sat 10am–1pm; ☎938 181 254, ⊛www.turismevilafranca.com). Behind here, in Plaça Jaume I, opposite the much-restored Gothic church of Santa Maria, the **Museu de Vilafranca** (Tues–Sat 10am–2pm & 4–7pm, Sun 10am–2pm; €3) is housed in a twelfth-century palace and worth visiting largely for its section on the region's wine industry. The experience culminates with a visit to the museum's tavern for a tasting.

The vineyards of Vilafranca are all out of town, though the largest and best known, **Torres** (Mon–Fri 9am–5pm, Sat 9am–6pm, Sun 9am–1pm; ☎938 177 487, ⊛www.torres.es), is only a three-kilometre taxi ride to the northwest, on the Sant Martí de Sarroca road. Also owned by Torres is boutique winemaker **Jean Leon** (Mon–Sat 9.30am–5.30pm, Sun 9.30am–1pm; tours €3; ☎938 995 512, ⊛www.jeanleon.com) at Torrelavit, closer to Sant Sadurní, whose American-modernist-inspired visitor centre is set in particularly bucolic surroundings.

The most agreeable place in town to **wine-taste** is *Inzolia*, c/de la Palma 21 (Mon 5–10pm, Tues–Sat 10am–2pm & 5–10pm), just off c/de Sant Joan, where a range of *cavas* and wines are sold by the glass. Nibbles are available, and there's a good wine shop attached. There are plenty of **restaurants** – the tourist office has a list – with the moderately priced *L'Hereu*, c/Casal 1 (☎938 902 217) particularly recommended, serving generous portions of country-style food with local wines. The restaurant is across the *rambla* from c/de Sant Joan, through the passageway.

The **Festa Major** (🖳www.festamajor.info), at the end of August and the first couple of days in September, brings the place to a standstill: dances and parades clog the streets, while the festival is most widely known for its display of *castellers* – teams of people competing to build human towers.

Tarragona

Majestically sited on a rocky hill, sheer above the sea, **TARRAGONA** is an ancient place: settled originally by Iberians and then Carthaginians, it was later used as the base for the Roman conquest of the peninsula, which began in 218 BC with Scipio's march south against Hannibal. The fortified city became an imperial resort and, under Augustus, "Tarraco" became capital of Rome's eastern Iberian province – the most elegant and cultured city of Roman Spain, boasting at its peak a quarter of a million inhabitants. The modern city provides a fine setting for some splendid Roman remains, and there's an attractive medieval part, too, while the rocky coastline below conceals a couple of reasonable beaches. It's worth noting that almost all Tarragona's sights and museums are **closed on Mondays**, though the old town and the exterior of some of the Roman remains can still be seen should you decide to visit then.

The City

The heart of the upper town is the sweeping **Rambla Nova**, a sturdy provincial rival to Barcelona's, lined with cafés and restaurants. Parallel, and to the east, lies the **Rambla Vella**, marking the start of the old town. To either side of the *rambles* are scattered a profusion of relics from Tarragona's Roman past, including various temples, and parts of the forum, theatre, circus and amphitheatre. The old encircling **Roman walls** still stand too, largely dating from the third and second century BC though erected on even older Iberian megalithic blocks; the sloping outer fortifications were added by the British in 1707 to secure the city during the War of the Spanish Succession. Unfortunately, the perimeter wall walk is currently closed to the public – the structures deemed unsafe after heavy rain and flooding.

At the heart of Tarragona lies the medieval old town, with the **Catedral** its focal point (Mon–Sat: June to mid-Oct 10am–7pm; mid-Oct to mid-Nov 10am–5pm; mid-Nov to mid-March 10am–2pm; mid-March to May 10am–1pm & 4–7pm; €2.40). It's a site of great antiquity, the Christian church being built over the site of the provincial Roman forum – in the main facade, a soaring Gothic portal is framed by Romanesque doors, surmounted by a cross and an elaborate rose window. Except for during services, entrance to the cathedral is through the lovely **cloisters** (*claustre*; signposted up a street to the left of the facade), where among several oddly sculpted capitals, one represents a cat's funeral being directed by rats.

Tarragona has several museums – dedicated to modern art, old weapons, port and harbour, and the noble Castellarnau family – but the only essential visit is to the **Museu Nacional Arqueològic** (June–Sept Tues–Sat 10am–8pm, Sun

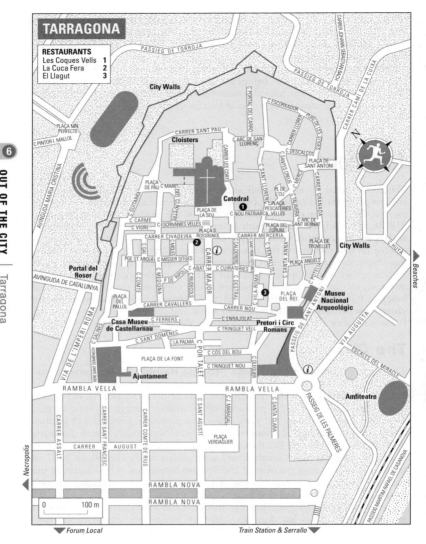

TARRAGONA

RESTAURANTS
Les Coques Vells 1
La Cuca Fera 2
El Llagut 3

City Walls

Cloisters

Catedral

Portal del Roser

Casa Museu de Castellarnau

Ajuntament

Museu Nacional Arqueológic

Pretori i Circ Romans

Amfiteatre

RAMBLA VELLA

RAMBLA NOVA

◀ Necropolis

▼ Forum Local

Train Station & Serrallo ▼

0   100 m

Beaches ▶

10am–2pm; Oct–May Tues–Sat 9.30am–1.30pm & 3.30–7pm, Sun 10am–2pm; €2.40), off Plaça del Rei. The huge collection is a marvellous reflection of the richness of imperial Tarraco, with thematic displays on the various remains and buildings around the city, as well as whole rooms devoted to inscriptions, mosaics, sculpture, ceramics and jewellery. This is likely to set you off on the trail of the local Roman sites, starting most spectacularly with the adjacent Roman Circus, whose vaults disappear back from the Rambla Vella into the gloom and under many of the surrounding buildings. The circus, as well as a Roman tower, the Pretori, can be visited together: the **Pretori i Circ Romans** (June–Sept

Tues–Sat 9am–9pm, Sun 9am–3pm; Oct–May Tues–Sat 9am–5pm, Sun 10am–3pm; €2.20) is entered from Plaça del Rei. Built at the end of the first century AD to hold chariot races, the Circ's vaults and chambers have been restored to spectacular effect, while the tower was a royal residence in medieval times. A lift takes you up to the roof for the best view in Tarragona, looking down over the **Amfiteatre** (June–Sept Tues–Sat 9am–9pm, Sun 9am–3pm; Oct–May Tues–Sat 9am–5pm, Sun 10am–3pm; €2), built into the green slopes of the hill nearby, to the coast below.

As provincial capital, Tarragona sustained both a ceremonial provincial forum (the scant remnants of which lie close to the cathedral in Plaça del Fòrum) and a **Fòrum Local** (June–Sept Tues–Sat 9am–9pm, Sun 9am–3pm; Oct–May Tues–Sat 9am–5pm, Sun 10am–3pm; €2.20), whose more substantial remains are on the western side of Rambla Nova, near the central market. This was the commercial centre of imperial Tarraco and the main meeting place for locals for three centuries – the evocative remains of the temple, some small shops, the Roman road and various house foundations can still be seen. Other remains lie further out of the centre, including those of the ancient **necropolis**, where both pagan and Christian tombs have been uncovered, spanning a period from the third to the sixth century AD. The site is largely closed, with only a small exhibition open to the public. More rewarding is a visit to the **Roman Aqueduct**, which brought water from the Riu Gayo, some 32km distant. The most impressive extant section, nearly 220m long and 26m high, lies in an overgrown valley, off the main road, in the middle of nowhere: take bus #5, marked "Sant Salvador" (every 20min from the stop outside Avgda. Prat de la Riba 11, off Avgda. Ramon i Cajal) – a ten-minute ride.

The closest beach to town is the long **Platja del Miracle**, over the rail lines below the amphitheatre, though nicer by far is **Platja Arrabassada**, a couple of kilometres further up the coast, reached by taking Via Augusta (off the end of Rambla Vella) and turning right at the *Hotel Astari* – a pleasant thirty-minute walk with gradually unfolding views of the beach and a few beach bars when you get there.

Practicalities

There are trains every thirty minutes from Passeig de Gràcia and Barcelona Sants and the journey takes just over an hour. Tarragona's **train station** is in the lower town: turn right out of the station and climb the steps ahead of you and you'll emerge at the head of the Rambla Nova, by the statue of Roger de Lluria (10min), from where the Rambla Vella and the old town are just a short walk around the balcony promenade. There are **taxis** outside the station.

The **Oficina de Turisme** is at c/Major 39 in the old town (July–Sept daily 9am–9pm; Oct–June Mon–Sat 10am–2pm & 4–7pm, Sun 10am–2pm; ☎977 250 795, ⊛www.tarragonaturisme.es). For the town museums and more information on the Roman sites, consult ⊛www.museutgn.com.

The pretty old-town squares, like Plaça del Rei, Plaça del Fòrum and Plaça de la Font are the best places for outdoor drinks. The latter in particular features more than a dozen **cafés, bars and restaurants** serving everything from *pinxtos* to pizzas. *La Cuca Fera*, Pl. Santiago Rossignol 5 (☎977 242 007; closed Tues, Wed & 3 weeks in Feb) serves moderately priced Catalan dishes with tables below the cathedral in one of Tarragona's loveliest backdrops. *El Llagut*, c/Natzaret 10 (☎977 228 938), on Plaça del Rei, is good for seafood, rice and *fideuà* dishes. Pricier is *Les Coques Vells*, c/Nou Patriarca (☎977 228 300; closed Sun & July), at around €40 a head for fine dining. Otherwise, a good place for lunch is down in **Serrallo**,

Tarragona's so-called fishermen's quarter, a fifteen-minute walk west along the industrial harbourfront from the train station. You'll get a tasty paella down here – try along c/Sant Pere, one block back from the harbour, at places like *Cal Marti* at no. 12 (℡977 212 384) and *Cal Brut* at no. 14 (℡977 241 405). The local workers eat at *La Calera* at no. 33 (℡977 245 631), where there's a budget no-choice *menú del dia*.

Girona

The ancient walled city of **GIRONA** stands on a fortress-like hill, high above the Riu Onyar. It's been fought over in almost every century since it was the Roman fortress of Gerunda on the Via Augusta and perhaps more than any other place in Catalunya it retains the distinct flavour of its erstwhile inhabitants. Following the Moorish conquest of Spain, Girona was an Arab town for over two hundred years, a fact apparent in the maze of narrow streets in the centre, and there was also a continuous Jewish presence here for six hundred years. By the eighteenth century, Girona had been besieged on 21 occasions, and in the nineteenth century it earned itself the nickname "Immortal" by surviving five attacks, of which the longest was a seven-month assault by the French in 1809. Not surprisingly, all this attention has bequeathed the city a hotchpotch of architectural styles, from Roman classicism to *modernisme*, yet the overall impression for the visitor is of an overwhelmingly beautiful medieval city. Its attraction is heightened by its setting, with the old and new towns divided by the river, which is crisscrossed by footbridges, with pastel-coloured houses reflected in the waters below.

The City

Although the bulk of modern Girona lies on the west side of the Riu Onyar, most visitors spend nearly all their time in the **old city**, over the river. This thin wedge of land contains all the sights and monuments, and it takes only half an hour or so to walk from end to end. It's worth noting that most of the museums and sights are **closed on Mondays**, though the city is emphatically still worth a visit if that's the only day you can manage.

Centrepiece of the old city is the **Catedral** (Tues–Fri 10am–8pm, Nov–March 10am–7pm, Sat 10am–4.30pm, Sun 2–8pm; €4, cloister and treasury free Sun; ⓦwww.lacatedraldegirona.com), a mighty Gothic structure approached by a magnificent flight of seventeenth-century Baroque steps. This area has been a place of worship since Roman times, and a Moorish mosque stood on the site before the foundation of the cathedral in 1038. Inside, there are no aisles, just one tremendous Gothic nave vault with a span of 22m, the largest in the world. This emphasis on width and height is a feature of Catalan-Gothic, with its "hall churches", of which, unsurprisingly, Girona's is the ultimate example. The displayed treasures of the cathedral include the famous eleventh century Creation Tapestry – the best piece of Romanesque textile in existence. But it's the exquisite Romanesque **cloisters** (1180–1210) that make the strongest impression, boasting minutely carved figures and scenes on double columns. There's a separate **Museu d'Art** (March–Sept Tues–Sat 10am–7pm; Oct–Feb Tues–Sat 10am–6pm; Sun all year 10am–2pm; €2) housed in the nearby Epis-copal Palace, which displays more fine work, notably an eleventh-century copy

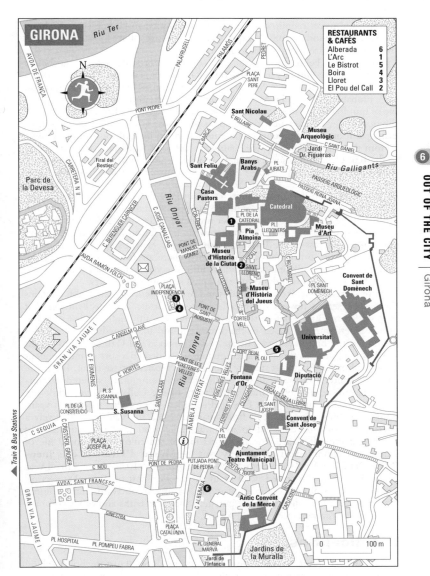

GIRONA

Riu Ter

AVDA DE FRANÇA

PALAFRUGELL

PALAMÓS

PEDRET

PLAÇA
SANT
PERE

PONT PEDRET

CARRETERA N II

Firal del
Bestier

Parc de
la Devesa

C. BERENGUER CARNICER

C. JOSÉ CANALEJAS

AVDA RAMÓN FOLCH

PLAÇA
INDEPENDENCIA

C ANSELM CLAVÉ

C F EIXIMENIS

C NORD

C HORTES

PL S'
SUSANNA

PL DE LA
CONSTITUCIÓ

C SÈQUIA

C CRISTÒFOL GRÒBER

PLAÇA
JOSEP PLA

C NOU

AVDA. SANT FRANCESC

GRAN VIA JAUME I

PL HOSPITAL

PL POMPEU FABRA

GINESTRA

PLAÇA
CATALUNYA

Jardí de
l'Infancia

Jardins de
la Muralla

Sant Nicolau

Museu
Arqueològic

C SANT DÁNIEL

Jardí
Dr. Figueras

Riu Galligants

Sant Feliu

Banys
Àrabs

PL.
JURATS

PASSEIG ARQUEOLÒGIC

Casa
Pastors

Catedral

PASSEIG REINA JOANA

PL DE LA
CATEDRAL

Pia
Almoina

PL.
LLEDONERS

Museu
d'Art

Museu
d'Història
de la Ciutat

SANT
LLORENÇ

Museu
d'Història
del Jueus

PL SANT
DOMÈNECH

Convent de
Sant
Domènech

PONT DE
MANUEL
GÓMEZ

PONT DE
SANT
AUGUSTÍ

PL
CORTEOI
VELL

Universitat

Riu Onyar

C SANTA CLARA

PONT DE LES
PEIXETERIES
VELLES

C.CORT REIAL

PL. OLI

Fontana
d'Or

Diputació

RAMBLA LLIBERTAT

FERRERIES VELLES

ESCALES DE LA LLEBRE

PL SANT
JOSEP

S. Susanna

Convent de
Sant Josep

PONT DE PEDRA

PUTJADA PONT
DE PEDRA

Ajuntament
Teatre Municipal

NOU DEL TEATRE

Antic Convent
de la Mercè

C ALBEREDA

PL GENERAL
MARVÀ

GRAN VIA JAUME I

▲ Train & Bus Stations

N

0   100 m

of Bede's works and an amazing martyrology from the monastery of Poblet in southern Catalunya.

Climb back down the cathedral steps for a view of one of Girona's best-known landmarks, the blunt tower of the church of **Sant Feliu** (Mon–Sat 10am–12.30pm & 4–6pm, Sun 10–11am; free). Shortened by a lightning strike in 1581 and never rebuilt, the belfry tops a hemmed-in church that combines Romanesque, Gothic and Baroque styles – a result of its long construction (between the thirteenth and sixteenth centuries).

Close to Sant Feliu, through the twin-towered Portal de Sobreportas below the cathedral, are Girona's so-called **Banys Arabs** (April–Sept Mon–Sat 10am–7pm, Sun 10am–2pm; Oct–March daily 10am–2pm; €1.50; @www.banysarabs. org), probably designed by Moorish craftsmen in the thirteenth century, a couple of hundred years after the Moors' occupation of Girona had ended. They are the best-preserved ancient baths in Spain after those at Granada, featuring three principal rooms for different temperatures, with an underfloor heating system.

From the cathedral square, the main street, Pujada Rei Marti, leads downhill to the Riu Galligants, a small tributary of the Onyar. The **Museu Arqueològic** (June–Sept Tues–Sat 10.30am–1.30pm & 4–7pm, Sun 10am–2pm; Oct–May Tues–Sat 10am–2pm & 4–6pm, Sun 10am–2pm; €1.80; @www.mac.es) stands on the far bank in the former church of Sant Pere de Galligants, a harmonious setting for displays of Roman statuary, sarcophagi and mosaics. The beautiful Romanesque cloisters contain heavier medieval relics, such as inscribed tablets and stones, including some bearing Jewish inscriptions. From the museum you can gain access to the **Passeig Arqueològic**, where steps and landscaped grounds lead up to the walls of the old city. There are fine views out over the rooftops and the cathedral, and endless little diversions into old watchtowers, down blind dead ends and around crumpled sections of masonry.

Quite apart from its Roman remains and Arab influences, Girona also contains the best-preserved **Jewish quarter** in western Europe. There is evidence that Jews settled in Girona before the Moorish invasion, although the first mention of a real settlement – based in the streets around the cathedral – dates from the end of the ninth century. The area was known as the **Call** and at its height was home to around three hundred people who formed a sort of independent town within Girona, protected by the king in return for payment. From the eleventh century onwards, however, the Jewish community suffered systematic persecution: in 1391 a mob killed forty of the Call's residents, while the rest were locked up until the fury had subsided. For the next hundred years, until the expulsion of the Jews from Spain in 1492, the Call was effectively a ghetto, its residents restricted to its limits and forced to wear distinguishing clothing if they did leave. For an impression of the cultural and social life of Girona's medieval Jewish community visit the **Museu d'Història dels Jueus** (May–Oct Mon–Sat 10am–8pm; Nov–April Mon–Sat 10am–6pm; Sun all year 10am–3pm; €2), signposted (Call Jueu) up the skinniest of stepped streets off c/de la Força. Amid the complex of rooms, staircases, courtyards and adjoining buildings were the synagogue, the butcher's shop, the baths and other community buildings and services.

Practicalities

Trains run every hour from Barcelona Sants (currently at 20 past the hour), calling at Passeig de Gràcia station, and take between 1hr 15min and 1hr 30min. Girona's **train station** lies across the river in the modern part of the city – walk down to Gran Via Jaume I and then turn right down c/Nou to reach the Pont de Pedra and the base of the old town (10min). There's also a taxi rank at the station.

The **Oficina de Turisme** (Mon–Fri 8am–8pm, Sat 8am–2pm & 4–8pm, Sun 9am–2pm; ☎972 226 575, @www.ajuntament.gi) is at Rambla de la Llibertat 1, on the river, near the Pont de Pedra. They can give you a useful map and have bus and train timetables for all onward and return services.

Girona's chic bars and restaurants are grouped on c/de la Força in the centre of the old city, as well as on and around Rambla de la Llibertat and on the parallel Plaça del Vi – the last two places being where you'll also find the best daytime **cafés** with outdoor seating. *L'Arc*, Pl. de la Catedral 9 (☏972 203 087), is a friendly bar serving snacks and sandwiches at the foot of the cathedral steps. Favoured old-town **restaurants** include *El Pou del Call*, c/de la Força 14 (☏972 223 774; closed Sun dinner), in the Jewish quarter, and the cheaper *Le Bistrot*, Pujada de Sant Domènec (☏972 218 803), which often has tables outside on the steps below the church. Considerably more expensive is the *Alberada*, c/Alberada 7 (☏972 226 002; closed all Sun, Mon dinner & Aug), for very fine Catalan dining. There's another dozen or so restaurants, serving sushi to seafood, just over the river in pretty **Plaça Independencia**. *Boira*, Pl. de la Independencia 17 (☏972 219 605), has arcade tables and upmarket Catalan food, while you won't score a cheaper *menú del dia* than at *Lloret*, Pl. de la Independencia 14 (☏972 213 671) – the food's reasonable enough, and the upstairs dining room has river and cathedral views.

Figueres and the Dalí museum

FIGUERES, a provincial town in the north of Catalunya with a population of some thirty thousand, would pass almost unnoticed were it not for the Museu Dalí, installed by Salvador Dalí in a building as surreal as the exhibits within. It's a popular day-trip from Barcelona, though you should make a reasonably early start since even the fastest trains take an hour and forty minutes to reach the town.

The museum is very much the main event in town (it's signposted from just about everywhere), though a circuit of the impressive walls of the seventeenth-century **Castell de Sant Fernand**, 1km northwest of the centre, the last bastion of the Republicans in the Civil War, helps fill in any spare time. In the centre, pavement cafés line the *rambla* and you can browse around the art galleries, clothes stores and gift shops in the pedestrianized streets and squares. There are a couple of other museums, too. The Museu de l'Empordà has some local Roman finds and work by local artists, while the Museu del Joguet is a toy museum with over three thousand exhibits from all over Catalunya, but really these are small beer when compared to the Dalí extravaganza.

Museu Dalí

The **Museu Dalí** (July–Sept daily 9am–7.45pm; Aug daily 9am–7.45pm & 10pm–1am; Oct–June Tues–Sun 10.30am–5.45pm; €10, night visits €11; ☏972 677 500; ⊛www.salvador-dali.org) is the most-visited museum in Spain after the Prado and Bilbao's Guggenheim, and appeals to everyone's innate love of fantasy, absurdity and participation. The museum is not a collection of Dalí's greatest hits – those are scattered far and wide. Nonetheless, what you do get beggars description and is not to be missed.

The building (a former theatre on Plaça Gala i Salvador Dalí) is an exhibit in itself, topped by a huge metallic dome and decorated with luminous egg shapes. It gets even crazier inside, where the walls of the circular courtyard are ringed by stylized mannequins preparing to dive from the heights – below

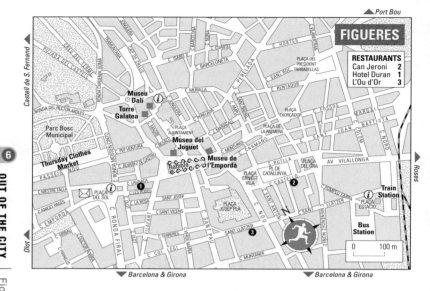

sits the famous *Rainy Cadillac*, where you can water the snail-encrusted occupants of a steamy Cadillac by feeding it with coins. In the Mae West Room an unnerving portrait of the actress is revealed by peering through a mirror at giant nostrils, red lips and hanging tresses, while elsewhere there's a complete life-sized orchestra, some of Dalí's extraordinary furniture (like the fish-tail bed), and ranks of Surrealist paintings – including one room dominated by the ceiling fresco of the huge feet of Dalí and Gala (his Russian wife and muse). The museum also contains many of Dalí's collected works by other artists, from Catalan contemporaries to El Greco, and there are temporary exhibitions, too, while your ticket also allows admission to see the **Dalí-Joies** – a collection of extraordinary jewels, designed in the Forties for an American millionaire and displayed here with Dalí's original drawings.

Practicalities

Trains depart hourly from Barcelona Sants and Passeig de Gràcia and take up to two hours to reach Figueres, depending on the service. Currently, the 7.50am, 9.20am or 10.20am from Sants (each taking 1hr 40min) are the best day-trip options. Alternatively, Figueres is just thirty to forty minutes by train from Girona, if you feel like combining the two towns. Arriving at the train station, you reach the centre of town simply by following the "Museu Dalí" signs (10min). There are small summer tourist information booths in Plaça Estació, with the main **Turisme** on Plaça del Sol (July–Sept Mon–Sat 9am–8pm, Sun 9am–3pm; Aug–June Mon–Fri 9am–3pm or later; ☎972 503 155, ⓦwww.figueresciutat. com), in front of the post office building.

A gaggle of tourist **restaurants** is crowded into the narrow streets around the Dalí museum, particularly along c/Jonquera, while the cafés on the *rambla* are good for snacks and sandwiches. To eat with the locals seek out *Can Jeroni*, c/Castelló 36 (☎972 500 983), a tiled tavern with country-style dishes and grills, or the pretty *L'Ou d'Or*, c/Sant Llatzer 16 (☎972 503 765; closed Sun), where

Salvador Dalí

Salvador Dalí (1904–89) was born in Figueres and gave his first exhibition in the town when he was just fourteen. Later expelled from the Royal Academy of Art in Madrid, he made his way to Paris, where he established himself at the forefront of the Surrealist movement. A celebrity artist in the US in the 1940s and 1950s, he returned eventually to Europe where, among other projects, he set about reconstructing Figueres' old municipal theatre, where he had held his first boyhood exhibition. This opened as the Museu Dalí in 1974, which Dalí then fashioned into an inspired repository for some of his most bizarre works. A frail man by 1980, controversy surrounds the artist's final years, particularly after he suffered severe burns in a fire in 1984, following which he moved into the Torre Galatea, the tower adjacent to the museum. Spanish government officials and friends fear that, in his senile condition, he was being manipulated. In particular, it's alleged that he was made to sign blank canvases – and this has inevitably led to the questioning of the authenticity of some of his later works. Dalí died in Figueres on January 23, 1989. His body now lies behind a simple granite slab inside the museum.

an uncomplicated *menú del dia* is served day and night – in either you'll be able to eat for around €15. The *Hotel Duran*, at c/Lausaca 5 (☎972 501 250, ⓦwww.hotelduran.com), at the top of the *rambla*, is the top choice in town, known for its excellent regional cuisine; it's expensive though there is a reasonable lunch-time *menú del dia*. On Tuesday, Thursday and Saturday, you'll coincide with the **fruit and veg market** in Plaça de Catalunya – if you have a choice, Thursday is best since there's also a huge **clothes market** on Passeig Nou.

Listings

Listings

Accommodation

Hotel rooms in Barcelona are among the most expensive in Spain and finding a vacancy can be very difficult, especially at Easter, in summer and during festivals or trade fairs. You're advised to book in advance – several weeks at peak times – especially if you want to stay at a particular place.

Places to stay go under a bewildering array of names – *pension, residencia, hostal, alberg, hotel* – though these are an anachronism and only **hotels and pensions** are recognized as official categories these days. These are all star-rated (hotels, one- to five-star; pensions, one- or two-star), but the rating is not necessarily a guide to cost, facilities or ambience. Private or en-suite "bathroom", for example, doesn't always mean exactly that – particularly in the cheaper pensions where your private facility might be a shower stall stuck in the corner of the room or a small added-on shower-and-toilet room.

Room rates vary wildly. The absolute cheapest double/twin rooms in a simple family-run pension, sharing an outside shower and toilet, cost around €45 (singles from €30), though for anything bearable (and certainly for anything with an en-suite shower) you'll really need to budget on a minimum of €60 a night. If you want heating in winter, summer air-conditioning, soundproofing, a TV and a lift to your room, there's a fair amount of choice around the €80–100 mark, while up to €150 gets you the run of decent hotels in most city areas. For Barcelona's most fashionable and exclusive hotels, room rates are set at European capital norms – from €250 to €400 a night. Right at the other end of the scale is the burgeoning number of city **youth hostels**, where a dorm bed goes for between €20 and €25.

Room rates quoted at the end of the reviews in this chapter reflect the official quoted cost of a double/twin room in high season (basically Easter to the end of Oct) – there's also a seven-percent tax, **IVA**, that is added to all accommodation bills. You'll often be able to get a cheaper room in the same establishment simply by asking – some places offer **discounts** in Jan, Feb and Nov, or for longer stays, while larger hotels have special rates in August (when business travel is scarce) or at weekends. Many hotels also have special Internet rates so it's always worth checking hotel websites, while if you don't mind arriving without a booking, same-day walk-in rates can offer substantial savings.

Breakfast isn't usually included in the price, unless specifically stated in our reviews – or unless offered as part of a special deal. However, it's usually available for an extra charge and, in many hotels, breakfast can be the most lavish of buffet spreads. These are not cheap though (around €10–15 per person), so if all you want is coffee and croissant it's better to go out to a café.

Balconies, views and noise

Almost all hotels and pensions in Barcelona have at least some rooms with a **balcony** over the street or square. These tend to be the lightest rooms in the building and, because of the obvious inherent attraction, they sometimes cost a little more than the other rooms. However, it can't be stressed enough that rooms facing onto Barcelona's streets are often noisy. Traffic is a constant presence (including the dawn street-cleaners) and, in a city where people are just getting ready to go out at 10pm, you can be assured of a fair amount of pedestrian noise too, particularly in the old town, and especially at weekends. Soundproofed windows and double-glazing deal partly with the problem, but you tend not to have this luxury in cheaper pensions – where throwing open the windows may be the only way to get some air in the height of summer anyway. Bring earplugs if you're at all concerned about having a sleepless night.

Alternatively, ask for an **internal room** (*habitación interior*). It's true that most buildings are built around a central air or lift shaft, and your view could simply be a lime-green wall 1m away and someone's washing line. However, some places are built instead around an internal patio, so your room might overlook a pot-plant terrace or garden – and you shouldn't get any street noise.

Credit cards are accepted almost everywhere, even in very modest places (though American Express isn't always) – pensions or hotels that don't accept cards are highlighted in the reviews.

Finally, don't be afraid to **ask to see the room** before you part with any money – even the swankiest places won't balk at showing you around. Standards vary greatly between places in the same category and it does no harm to check that you're not being stuck at the back in an airless box.

Making a reservation

You can book accommodation at the **city tourist offices**, but only in person on the day. However, you can book online through the tourist office website, or contact one of the other **reservation agencies** listed below.

Some agencies specialize in **apartment rentals**, available by the night, week or month. Prices for these compare well with mid-range hotels (starting at around €90–100 a night for a two-person studio), but make sure you're happy with the location (some are out in the more mundane suburbs) and understand all the costs – seasonal premiums, cleaning charges, utility bills and taxes can all push up the attractive quoted figure.

When booking directly at hotels and pensions, you may be asked for a **credit card** number to secure a room. At most hotels, the price won't be charged against your card until your stay, though some smaller pensions may take a deposit or charge you in advance.

Reservation agencies

Barcelona Apartment Rentals UK ☎0117/907 5060, ⊛www.barcelonaapartmentrentals.co.uk. A small range of quality apartments, mainly in the Eixample (some near the Sagrada Família) and Gràcia. Friendly, English-speaking service and advice from a born-and-bred *barcelonina*; airport pick-ups available.

Barcelona Living Barcelona ☎932 723 520 or 696 210 088, ⊛www.barcelonaliving.com. One-bed apartments in the Born (La Ribera), for short-term independent and corporate visitors.

Barcelona On-Line Barcelona ☎902 807 017 or 933 437 993/4, ⊛www.barcelona-on-line. es. Commission-free reservations for hotels, pensions and apartments in Barcelona and the local area. Call or use the online database.

Hotels Abroad UK ☏0845/330 2500, from outside the UK (+44)1689 882 500, ⓦwww.hotelsabroad.co.uk. Wide selection of Barcelona and Catalunya hotels.

Inside-BCN Barcelona ☏932 682 868 or 699 840 808, ⓦwww.inside-bcn.com. Small selection of stylishly renovated apartments (sleeping two to six) available in the Born or on Plaça Reial.

My Favourite Things Barcelona ☏637 265 405, ⓦwww.myft.net. Barcelona-based agency with an eye for unusual and offbeat accommodation, from boutique hotels to private bed and breakfasts in the city, or rural homestays and country retreats.

Tourist Flats BCN Barcelona ☏650 925 252, ⓦwww.flatsbcn.com. Old-town apartments sleeping two to ten, especially on and around the Ramblas.

Turisme de Barcelona Offices in Barcelona at Pl. de Catalunya; Pl. de Sant Jaume; Barcelona Sants; Barcelona Airport ☏932 853 833, ⓦwww.hotelsbcn.com. Same-day, commission-free accommodation bookings, in person only, or on the website. For office opening hours, see p.28.

Visit BCN.com UK ☏0871/990 3045, Barcelona ☏933 152 265, ⓦwww.visit-bcn.com. Wide range of private apartments for rent (by the night or longer), from lofts to *modernista* buildings.

Hotels and pensions

First things first: if you hanker after a **Ramblas** view, you're going to pay heavily for the privilege – generally speaking, there are much better deals to be had either side of the famous boulevard, often just a minute's walk away. Most of the very cheapest city accommodation is in the old town, in the **Barri Gòtic**, especially in the area bordered by c/dels Escudellers, Plaça de Sant Miquel and c/de la Boqueria, where there are loads of options, from basic pensions to three-star hotels. It's a heavily touristed district, but you should still be careful (without being paranoid) when coming and going after dark. As a general rule, anything to the north of c/de Ferran, especially around the cathedral, should be reliable and safe – in fact this area contains some of the city's most charismatic old-town hotels.

East of the Barri Gòtic, in **Sant Pere** and **La Ribera**, there are a number of safely sited budget and mid-range options, handy for the Picasso museum and Born nightlife area. The other main location for budget accommodation is on the west side of the Ramblas in **El Raval**, which still has its rough edges but is changing fast as the whole neighbourhood undergoes a massive face-lift.

North of Plaça de Catalunya, you're in the Eixample – the gridded nineteenth-century city – whose central spine, **Passeig de Gràcia**, has some of the city's most fashionable and luxurious hotels, often housed in converted palaces and mansions. The Eixample itself splits into Right (**Dreta**) and Left (**Esquerra**), and on either side there are some comparative bargains just a few minutes' walk from the *modernista* architectural masterpieces. Hotels near **Sants** station are convenient for Montjuïc and the metro system, and those further north in **Les Corts** for the Avinguda Diagonal shopping district. There's more fine accommodation on offer at the city's waterfront – at **Port Vell** at the end of the Ramblas, and at the **Port Olímpic** southeast of the old town – while new four- and five-stars abound much further out on the metro at the rather soulless **Diagonal Mar** conference and events site. If you don't mind being a metro ride from the museums and buildings, and like the idea of suburban living, then the northern district of **Gràcia** makes the best base – and you're only ever a short walk away from its excellent bars, restaurants and clubs.

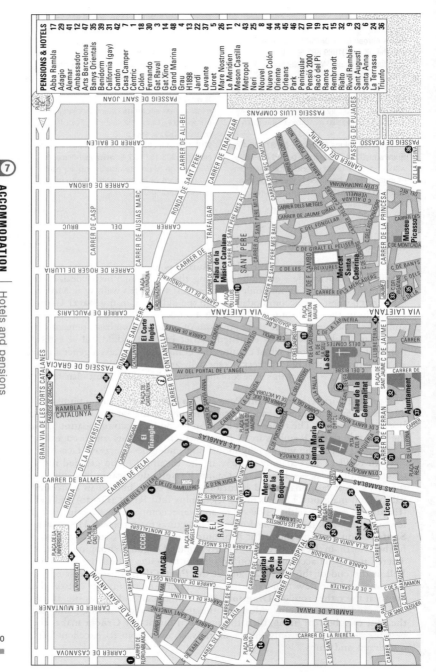

PENSIONS & HOTELS	
Abba Rambla	17
Adagio	29
Alemar	41
Ambassador	12
Arts Barcelona	47
Banys Orientals	35
Benidorm	39
California (gay)	31
Cantón	42
Casa Camper	7
Cèntric	1
Colón	18
Fernando	30
Gat Raval	3
Gat Xino	14
Grand Marina	48
Grau	4
H1898	13
Jardí	22
Levante	37
Lloret	5
Mare Nostrum	26
Le Meridien	11
Meson Castilla	2
Metropol	43
Neri	25
Nouvel	8
Nuevo Colón	44
Oriente	34
Orleans	45
Park	46
Peninsular	27
Pensió 2000	10
Racó del Pi	19
Ramos	21
Rembrandt	15
Rialto	32
Rivoli Ramblas	9
Sant Augustí	23
Santa Anna	24
La Terrassa	6
Triunfo	36

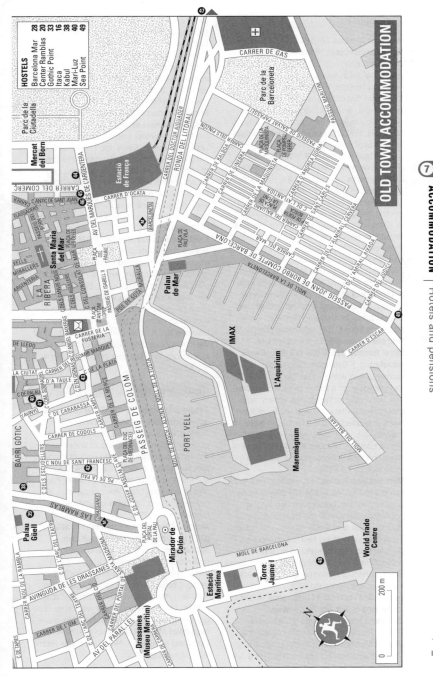

OLD TOWN ACCOMMODATION

HOSTELS	
Barcelona Mar	28
Center Ramblas	20
Gothic Point	33
Itaca	16
Kabul	38
Mari-Luz	40
Sea Point	49

ACCOMMODATION | Hotels and pensions

7

The Ramblas

Benidorm Ramblas 37 ☎933 022 054, ⓦwww.
hostalbenidorm.com; ⓜDrassanes. Refurbished pension opposite Plaça Reial that
offers real value for money, hence the tribes
of young tourists. Plain rooms available
for one to five people, all with bathtubs
or showers, and a balcony and Ramblas
view if you're lucky (and prepared to pay a
bit more). English spoken and left-luggage
service available. €60.

H1898 Ramblas 109 ☎935 529 552,
ⓦwww.nnhotels.es; ⓜCatalunya. One
of the grander buildings on the Ramblas,
the former HQ of the Philippines Tobacco
Company has been given a boutique refit,
adding five grades of rooms (the standard
is "Classic") in deep red, green or black, all
beautifully appointed. Public areas reflect
the period – 1898 – but there are some
stunningly updated spaces, like the neo-
colonial hall and lounge (and the fanciest
Starbucks in town), while facilities include
outdoor pool and spa, gym, bar and restaurant. Some suites even have their own
private pool, Jacuzzi and gardens. Same-
day rates from €150, otherwise from €250,
Ramblas views attract a supplement.

Lloret Ramblas 125 ☎933 173 366, ⓦwww.
hlloret.com; ⓜCatalunya. Gilt mirrors, old
paintings and wrinkled leather sofas in the
lounge speak of a faded glory for this one-
star hotel with rooms on the elderly side,
though the bathrooms and tile floors have
been upgraded. But the rooms all have TV,
heating, a/c, and many have Ramblas-facing balconies – as does the dining room
where continental breakfast is available (not
included). From €85.

Mare Nostrum Ramblas 67, entrance on c/Sant
Pau ☎933 185 340, ℻934 123 069; ⓜLiceu.
Cheery two-star pension whose English-
speaking management offers comfortable
double, triple and family rooms with satellite
TV and a/c – nothing flashy, but modern,
well kept and double-glazed against the
noise. Some come with balconies and street
views, others are internal. Simple breakfast
included. €66, en suite €75.

Le Meridien Ramblas 111, entrance on c/Pin-
tor Fortuny ☎933 186 200, ⓦwww
.barcelona.lemeridien.com; ⓜCatalunya.
Classy Ramblas hotel that's hosted the
likes of Madonna, Bruce Springsteen,
Michael Jackson and Pavarotti. There are

Mediterranean tones inside, plus wooden
floors, plasma-screen TVs and great
bathrooms, and a soothing hush, even in
Ramblas-facing rooms – though you don't
get a balcony or terrace unless you've
splashed out on a suite. Posted rates are
very high, though special deals are almost
always available. From €300.

Oriente Ramblas 45 ☎933 022 558 or 902 100
710, ⓦwww.husa.es; ⓜLiceu. If you're looking for somewhere traditional on the Ramblas, this historic three-star is your best bet
– mid-nineteenth-century style in the grand
public rooms and tastefully updated bedrooms, some with Ramblas views (though
these can be noisy). Single travellers don't
always do so well; specify that you want
space and light, as not all rooms have these
attributes. From €140.

Rivoli Ramblas Ramblas 128 ☎934 817 676,
ⓦwww.rivolihotels.com; ⓜCatalunya. The
elegant, soundproofed rooms in this stylish four-star hotel are variously furnished
(Art Deco to contemporary), but all come
with spacious bathrooms while the front
ones have Ramblas views. There's a lovely
rooftop terrace and bar, and guests can
also use the rooftop deck and small pool at
the cheaper sister hotel, the *Ambassador*,
just across the Ramblas in El Raval. From
€200.

Barri Gòtic

Adagio c/de Ferran 21 ☎933 189 061, ⓦwww.
adagiohotel.com; ⓜLiceu. Rooms on five
floors (there's a lift) have been given a thor-
ough refurbishment – parquet floors, satellite
TV, a/c, soundproofing and decent bathrooms – and a buffet breakfast is included,
so prices aren't bad for the location. Front
and side rooms have little balconies. Laundry service and car parking available on
request. From €90.

Alamar c/Comtessa de Sobradiel 1 ☎933
025 012, ℮pensioalamar@hotmail.com;
ⓜDrassanes. If you don't mind sharing a
bathroom then this makes a convenient
base. Thirteen simple rooms (including five
singles) have basin and double-glazing (no
TVs) and most have little balconies – space
is tight, but there's a friendly welcome, laundry service and use of a kitchen. No noise
requested after midnight, so it suits early-
birds and sightseers. No credit cards From
€36, July–Aug €45.

Cantón c/Nou de Sant Francesc 40 ☏ 933 173 019, Ⓦ www.hotelcanton-bcn.com; Ⓜ **Drassanes.** Refurbished one-star hotel that's only two blocks off the Ramblas and close to the harbour and Port Vell. Thirty rooms feature uniform blue-and-white trim curtains and bedspreads, high wooden headboards, central heating and a/c, fridge and wardrobe. Some bathrooms are a bit smarter than others, and some rooms have balconies (though they don't have much of a view – all are well-insulated against street noise. €65.

Colón Avgda. Catedral 7 ☏ 933 011 404, Ⓦ www.hotelcolon.es; Ⓜ **Jaume I.** Splendidly situated four-star hotel opposite the cathedral – rooms at the front throw open their windows onto balconies with superb views, while a pavement *terrassa* takes full advantage of its position. It's an old-money kind of place, with faithful-retainer staff and huge public salons. "Superior" rooms have an Edwardian lounge area and highly floral decor, though other rooms are more contemporary. From €250.

Fernando c/de Ferran 31 ☏ 933 017 993, Ⓦ www.hfernando.com; Ⓜ **Liceu.** Rooms at these prices fill quickly around here; that they're also light, modern and well kept by friendly people is a real bonus. All come with basin, shower and TV (some singles share facilities), while dorm accommodation is available on the top floor – these rooms sleep four to eight, some have an attached bathroom, and all are provided with lockers. All accommodation is a few euros cheaper outside July & Aug. Dorms €21, rooms €65.

Jardí Pl. Sant Josep Oriol 1 ☏ 933 015 900, Ⓦ www.hoteljardi-barcelona.com; Ⓜ **Liceu.** The location sells this place – overlooking the charming Plaça del Pi – which explains the steep prices for rooms that, though smart and modern, can be a bit bare and even poky. But the bathrooms have been nicely done and some rooms (the top ones have terraces) look directly onto the square. You can have breakfast here, but the *Bar del Pi* in the square is a better bet. Advance reservations essential. Interior rooms €80, exterior €86, terrace or balcony €96.

Levante Bxda. Sant Miquel 2 ☏ 933 179 565, Ⓦ www.hostallevante.com; Ⓜ **Jaume I.** A budget favourite, with fifty rooms – singles, doubles, twins, triples – on two rambling floors. Some have newer pine furniture, attached

bathrooms and balconies, so you may want to look at a couple before choosing. Communal bathrooms get pretty busy, staff can be scatty, and the comings and goings aren't to everyone's liking (*tranquilo* it isn't), but prices are very reasonable. Six apartments with kitchen and washing machine also available, sleeping five to seven people. €56, en suite €65, apartments €30 per person per day.

Metropol c/Ample 31 ☏ 933 105 100, Ⓦ www.hesperia-metropol.com; Ⓜ **Drassanes.** Stylish 2001 conversion of an older building that is slightly off the beaten old-town track – consequently, prices are better value than similar three-star places on the Ramblas. The lobby is a masterpiece of contemporary design, while rooms are understated but comfortable – street noise isn't too bad either, so opening the shutters onto c/Ample doesn't blast the earlugs first thing in the morning. From €120.

Neri c/de Sant Sever 5 ☏ 933 040 655, Ⓦ www.hotelneri.com; Ⓜ **Liceu/Jaume I.** Eighteenth-century palace that's given the boutique treatment to its 22 stylish rooms – gorgeous granite bathrooms, plasma-screen TVs, movies on demand, Internet access and CD/DVD player. Internal spaces are conducive to relaxation (courtyard, beamed library, tranquil roof terrace) and there's a good Mediterranean restaurant attached. Advance reservations essential. From €290, suites €360.

Nouvel c/Santa Anna 18–20 ☏ 933 018 274, Ⓦ www.hotelnouvel.com; Ⓜ **Catalunya.** Dating from 1917, this three-star has kept its handsome period details while updating most of the rooms. They differ in size but come with brass or wooden bedsteads, high ceilings, a/c and compact bathrooms with brown marble detailing – one has a Jacuzzi bath. It's best at the back, where rooms have little sunny terraces, and four spacious corner rooms at the front have curvacious double balconies. Be warned – the street might be pedestrianized, but it's not noise-free. Breakfast included. €170.

Racó del Pi c/del Pi 7 ☏ 933 426 190, Ⓦ www.h10.es; Ⓜ **Liceu.** Old-town mansion imaginatively converted into a three-star hotel. Stylish rooms – some flooded by skylights, other with balconies over the street – have wood floors and granite-and-mosaic bathrooms; there's a glass of *cava* on check-in, and although breakfast is extra there's free coffee and pastries during the day in the bar. Low-season last-minute rates as low as €100, otherwise €220.

🏃 **Rembrandt c/Portaferrissa 23** ☎ **933 181 011,** 🖥 **www.hostalrembrandt.com;** Ⓜ **Liceu.** The English-speaking owners have made a real effort to smarten this place up, adding prints to the walls, and matching furniture, cane chairs, heaters and fans to the simple tile-floored rooms (with or without private bathroom, no TVs). Some have a street-side balcony, quieter ones overlook the internal patio, while larger rooms are more versatile – one has a gallery (with single bed above the double) and large corner bath, while a rather Victorian-looking suite (two rooms split by hanging net curtain) can sleep two or four. It's a clean, safe old-town choice, with "pin-drop silence" requested after 11pm. Apartments also available nearby (c/Canuda 13, 🖥 www.apartrembrandt.com) offering en-suite single and double rooms with balcony, a/c, satellite TV and daily housekeeping. From €45, en suite €55, suite €70, apartment rooms €80.

Rialto c/de Ferran 42 ☎ **933 185 212,** 🖥 **www. gargallo-hotels.com;** Ⓜ **Jaume I.** Beyond the standard modern marble lobby, this turns out to be quite cosy inside – a three-star hotel that's more like a family-run concern, with carpeted corridors and heavy doors leading into updated period rooms with parquet flooring, oak furniture and country-style furnishings. There's a good buffet breakfast included in the price. From €100.

Santa Anna c/Santa Anna 23 ☎ **933 012 246;** Ⓜ **Catalunya.** So clean that the buffed corridors squeak. Attractive little rooms (with and without private shower room) on two floors, many with a small balcony onto the street or the rear. Room 202 has a private terrace, though its bathroom is down the hall. Singles are box-like but cheap. Not much English spoken, but it's such good value for the area it fills quickly. No credit cards.€45, en suite €55.

Port Vell

Grand Marina World Trade Centre, Moll de Barcelona ☎ **936 039 000,** 🖥 **www .grandmarinahotel.com;** Ⓜ **Drassanes.** Five-star comforts on eight floors overlooking the port. Most of the 235 rooms have enormous marble bathrooms with Jacuzzi baths and a separate dressing area. Public areas draw gasps, with commissioned works by Catalan artists and a rooftop pool with fantastic views. Winter-season and other special rates sometimes bring the price down to around €200; otherwise from €350.

El Raval

Abba Rambla Rambla de Raval 4 ☎ **935 055 400,** 🖥 **www.abbahoteles.com;** Ⓜ **Sant Antoni/ Liceu.** Three-star style on the Raval's up-and-coming rambla. Public areas, including the bar, are pretty cool and contemporary, rooms less so, though they are pleasing enough with wall-mounted flat-screen TVs and decent bathrooms. Rooms, bar and coffee shop all face the rambla. From €105.

Ambassador c/Pintor Fortuny 13 ☎ **933 426 180,** 🖥 **www.rivolihotels.com;** Ⓜ **Catalunya/ Liceu.** Just a minute off the Ramblas, this has a sunny rooftop deck with loungers, tiny pool and spa. Rooms have a/c and are soundproofed, though the lilac colour scheme, dark wood panelling and earthy marble bathrooms won't be to everyone's taste. The bar is great, an ornate cast-iron period piece in a contemporary setting. Official rates can almost always be beaten by calling or checking the website. From €160.

Casa Camper c/Elisabets 11 ☎ **933 426 280,** 🖥 **www.casacamper.com;** Ⓜ **Catalunya.** This upper Raval hotel, from trendy footwear chain Camper, is proof for some that designer style is fast disappearing up its own fundament in Barcelona. From outside it looks like a snooty art gallery or fashion store, while inside the 25 rooms have been given the boutique treatment by Fernando Amat of Vinçon fame. No one has the faintest idea what the weird house "eating space", *FoodBall*, is all about. Oh, and it's always full of matchstick models, so you'll never get a room. €235.

Cèntric c/Casanova 13 ☎ **934 267 573 or 902 014 881,** 🖥 **www.hostalcentric.com;** Ⓜ **Universitat.** Most.of the thirty rooms feature wood panelling and reasonable furniture, decent beds, and plenty of light; cheaper ones on the upper floors (no lift) share bathrooms, while some of the more expensive en-suite ones also have a/c. There's a sunny terrace at the rear. €60, en suite from €80.

Gat Raval c/Joaquín Costa 44, 2° ☎ **934 816 670,** 🖥 **www.gataccommodation.com;** Ⓜ **Universitat.** Going for the boutique end of the budget market, the *Gat Raval* has done its fashionable best with a rambling townhouse. Lime green is a recurring theme, from doors to bedspreads, while each room is broken down to fundamentals – chair, basin, wall-mounted TV, fan and heating, and signature back-lit street photograph and artwork that doubles as a reading light. Only six of the twenty-four rooms are ensuite, but communal facilities are good, and there are internal or street and MACBA views, Internet access, drinks machine and staff on duty 24/7. €66, en suite €75.

Gat Xino c/Hospital 149–155 T933 248 833, Ⓦ www.gataccommodation.com; Ⓜ Sant Antoni.The sister hotel to the *Gat Raval* shares the same signature style, facilities and colour scheme, but all 35 rooms here are en suite, while four suites have much more space, bigger bathrooms and less street noise (and one has a terrace). You also get a coffee, cereal and toast breakfast served in a patio area; there's 24hr staff and security. €80, suite €100, terrace suite €120.

Grau c/Ramelleres 27 ☎ 933 018 135, Ⓦ www.hostalgrau.com; Ⓜ Catalunya. A really friendly place, whose centrally heated rooms on several floors (no lift) have freshly painted walls and window shutters; renovated superior rooms also have balconies. There's a little lounge area, wireless Internet access, and breakfast available weekdays in the adjacent café-bar (a coffee-and-toast breakfast is included in room rates on weekdays in March, July & Aug). Six small private apartments in the same building (sleeping two, three or four, available by the night) offer a bit more independence. €55, standard en suite €70, superior €80, apartments from €85.

Meson Castilla c/Valldonzella 5 ☎ 933 182 182, Ⓦ www.mesoncastilla.com; Ⓜ Universitat. A throwback to 1950s rural Spain, with every inch carved, painted and stencilled, from the grandfather clock in reception to the wardrobe in your room. Large rooms with a/c (some with terraces), filled with country-style furniture, a vast rustic dining room (buffet breakfast included) and – best of all – a lovely tiled rear patio on which to read in the sun. Parking available. €130, terrace room €145.

Peninsular c/de Sant Pau 34 ☎ 933 023 138, Ⓦ www.hpeninsular.com; Ⓜ Liceu. This interesting old building originally belonged to a priestly order, which explains the slightly cell-like quality of the rooms. There's nothing spartan about the attractive galleried inner courtyard (around which the rooms are ranged), hung with dozens of plants, while breakfast is served in the arcaded dining room. €70.

Ramos c/Hospital 36 ☎ 933 020 723, Ⓦ www. hostalramos.com; Ⓜ Liceu. The best rooms here overlook either the quiet marble internal patio or the attractive Plaça de Sant Agusti. Partitioning has spoiled the proportions of some (those facing the square are the largest), but all have either half- or full-size bathtubs, polished tile floors and TV. It's something of a haven and very popular; some English is spoken. €75.

Sant Agustí Pl. Sant Agusti 3 ☎ 933 181 658, Ⓦ www.hotelsa.com; Ⓜ Liceu. Barcelona's oldest hotel is housed in a former seventeenth-century convent building on a restored square; the balconies overlook the trees and the namesake church. The appealing rooms have been modernized and air-conditioned, with the best located in the attic (supple-

---

Best hotels for...

Cheap rooms *Rembrandt* (p.164), *Pensió 2000* (p.166), *La Terrassa* (p.166).
Boutique beauty *Banys Orientals* (p.166), *Neri* (p.163), *Prestige* (p.172).
Dorm delight *Albergue Verge de Montserrat* (p.173), *Centric Point* (p.173), *Mari-Luz* (p.173).
Money no object *Arts Barcelona* (p.170), *Claris* (p.170), *Casa Fuster* (p.170).
Old-world lodgings *D'Uxelles* (p.167), *Meson Castilla* (p.165), *Peninsular* (p.165).
Rooftop pools *Ambassador* (p.164), *Grand Marina Hotel* (p.164), *Majestic* (p.170).
Rooms with a view *Condes de Barcelona* (p.167), *Gran Hotel La Florida* (p.172), *Torre Catalunya* (p.171).
Style on a budget *Eurostars Gaudí* (p.167), *Gat Raval/Xino* (p.164), *Goya Principal* (p.167).
Suite success *Australia* (p.170), *H1898* (p.162), *Palace* (p.170).

ment charged), from where there are rooftop views. Reservations essential. Breakfast is included. From €145.

La Terrassa c/Junta del Comerç 11 ☎933 025 174, ⓦwww.laterrassa-barcelona.com; ⓂLiceu. Ongoing renovations have smartened up this popular budget choice, and all 45 rooms on various floors (there's a lift) now have built-in closets, modern shower rooms, effective double-glazing, ceiling fans and heaters. They are fairly plain, and "basic-interior" rooms don't have much natural light, but "basic-" and "standard-exterior" rooms either face the street or the sunny courtyard (open to all guests), and some are more spacious than others. Interior rooms €46–50, basic and standard exterior €50–66, large exterior €76.

Sant Pere

Pensió 2000 c/Sant Pere Més Alt 6, 1° ☎933 107 466, ⓦwww.pensio2000.com; ⓂUrquinaona. As close to a family-run bed and breakfast as Barcelona gets – seven huge rooms (some overlook the Palau de la Música Catalana, across the street) in a welcoming mansion apartment strewn with books, plants and pictures. A third person could easily share most rooms (€20 supplement), while a choice of breakfasts (not included) is served either in your room or on the internal patio. Laundry service available. €50, en suite €65.

La Ribera

Banys Orientals c/de l'Argenteria 37 ☎932 688 460, ⓦwww.hotelbanysorientals.com; ⓂJaume I. Funky boutique hotel with 43 minimalist rooms and some more spacious duplex suites next door. Hardwood floors, crisp white sheets, sharp marble bathrooms and urban-chic decor – not to mention the bargain prices – make it a hugely popular choice, so advance reservations are essential. The attached restaurant, *Senyor Parellada*, is a great find too. €100, suites €125.
Nuevo Colón Avgda. Marquès de l'Argentera 19, 1° ☎933 195 077, ⓦwww.hostalnuevocolon.com; ⓂBarceloneta. In the hands of the same friendly family for over seventy years, with twenty-six spacious rooms painted yellow and kitted out with directors' chairs, good quality beds, new tiling and double glazing. Front rooms are very sunny, as is

the lounge and terrace, all with side views to Ciutadella park. There are also three self-catering apartments available (by the night) in the same building, which sleep up to six. €45, en suite €60, apartments €150.
Orleans Avgda. Marquès de l'Argentera 13, 1° ☎933 197 382, ⓦwww.hostalorleans.com; ⓂBarceloneta. Rooms on two floors of a tranquil family-run pension. Public areas and rooms are kept spick-and-span, and twins and doubles have TV, desk and chair, and heating in winter (summer air-con attracts a daily supplement). Front rooms with balconies face França station and the busy main road, so you'll get some noise here; other rooms are internal, while some sleep three or four. From €55.
Park Avgda. Marquès de l'Argentera 11 ☎933 196 000, ⓦwww.parkhotelbarcelona.com; ⓂBarceloneta. A classy update for this elegant, modernist 1950s building starts with the chic bar and lounge, and runs up the feature period stairway to rooms in fawn and brown with parquet floors, marble bathrooms and beds with reading lights. It's pricey for a three-star, but there's real style here, augmented by the new-wave *Abac* restaurant on the premises. From €150.
Triunfo Pg. de Picasso 22 ☎933 150 860, ⓦwww.atriumhotels.com; ⓂJaume I/Arc de Triomf. Small one-star hotel right opposite Ciutadella park (your balcony view) and convenient for the Born nightlife. All rooms are en suite with a/c and though no breakfast is served you're hardly pushed for cafés in this neighbourhood. €75, park view €85.

Port Olímpic

Arts Barcelona c/Marina 19–21, Port Olímpic ☎932 211 000, ⓦwww.ritzcarlton.com/hotels/barcelona; ⓂCiutadella-Vila Olímpica. See colour map 6. 33 floors of five-star-plus designer luxury, with fabulous views of the port and sea from every angle. Service and standards are first-rate (there's a team of butlers on call) and the highly pleasing rooms feature floor-to-ceiling windows with remote-controlled blinds, thick carpets and robes, enormous marble bathrooms, multi-entertainment centres and fresh flowers. Seafront gardens encompass an open-air pool and hot tub, there's a forty-third-floor spa, while dining is courtesy of the contemporary Mediterranean *Enoteca* restaurant, the more informal *Arola*, and several other café, bar and terrace areas. Special rates start at around €200, otherwise from €400.

Passeig de Gràcia and Dreta de l'Eixample

▽ The Claris Hotel rooftop pool

Claris c/Pau Claris 150 ☎ 934 876 262, ⓦ www.derbyhotels.es; Ⓜ Passeig de Gràcia. Very select luxury five-star hotel, from the incense-scented marble lobby complete with authentic Roman mosaics to the hugely appealing rooms ranged around a soaring, water-washed atrium. It even has it's own private antiquities museum. If there's a gripe, it's that there's not a lot of room space for your euro, but the staff couldn't be more accommodating, there's a rooftop terrace pool, a great bar, and excellent restaurant, *East* 47. From €350.

Condes de Barcelona Pg. de Gràcia 73–75 ☎ 934 450 000, ⓦ www.condesdebarcelona .com; Ⓜ Passeig de Gràcia. Straddling two sides of c/Mallorca, the *Condes* is fashioned from two former palaces; the north side has kept its interior marblework and wrought-iron balconies, but there's little difference between the rooms in either building, which are all classily turned out in contemporary style, some with Jacuzzi and balcony, and some with views of Gaudí's La Pedrera. The best deals are those on the south-side seventh-floor exterior, with fantastic private terraces but charging standard room rates. There's also a pretty roof terrace and plunge pool, bar and restaurant. From €250.

D'Uxelles Gran Via de les Corts Catalanes 688 ☎ 932 652 560, ⓦ www.hotelduxelles .com; Ⓜ Girona/Tetuan. Elegant nineteenth-century townhouse rooms feature high ceilings, wrought-iron bedsteads, antique mirrors, tiled floors and country-decor bathrooms – some also have balconies and little private patios (it's quietest at the back of the building). Prices are very reasonable, especially in winter, and extra beds can be placed in many rooms – a few rooms are also available in another building at Gran Via 667. €100.

Eurostars Gaudí c/Consell de Cent 498–500 ☎ 932 320 288, ⓦ www .eurostarshotels.com; Ⓜ Monumental. An excellent four-star choice within walking distance of the Sagrada Família. The angular hotel doesn't overdo the Gaudí theme, staff are really helpful and the comfortable rooms feature contemporary furniture, marble bathrooms, black-out curtains and flat-screen TV. Standard room prices are very reasonable, while junior suites on the eighth floor boast a terrace with loungers and views of the Gaudí church and distant hills. Buffet breakfast included. From €109, suites €120–200.

Girona c/Girona 24, 1° ☎ 932 650 259, ⓦ www .hostalgirona.com; Ⓜ Urquinaona. Has a positively baronial stairway and things are scarcely any less impressive inside the family-run pension – corridors laid with rugs, polished wooden doors, paintings and restored furniture. A fair choice of rooms, either with full bathroom or just shower (plus some bathroom-less singles), internal or with balcony – some open onto a peaceful patio. From €50, en suite €70.

Goya/Goya Principal c/de Pau Claris 74, 1° ☎ 933 022 565, ⓦ www.hostalgoya .com; Ⓜ Urquinaona. Upgraded mansion building with ten pension rooms, not all en suite, and nine more modern ones on the floor below in *Goya Principal* (formerly the owners' own apartment), which have been fitted with laminate flooring, a/c, stylish bed linen and pleasant bathrooms – the three largest (and most expensive) open directly onto a terrace. There are attractive sitting areas, and free coffee and tea available, on both floors. *Goya* €50, en suite €65; *Goya Principal* €65, en suite €70, terrace rooms €90.

Gran Hotel Havana Gran Via de les Corts Catalanes 647 ☎ 934 121 115, ⓦ www

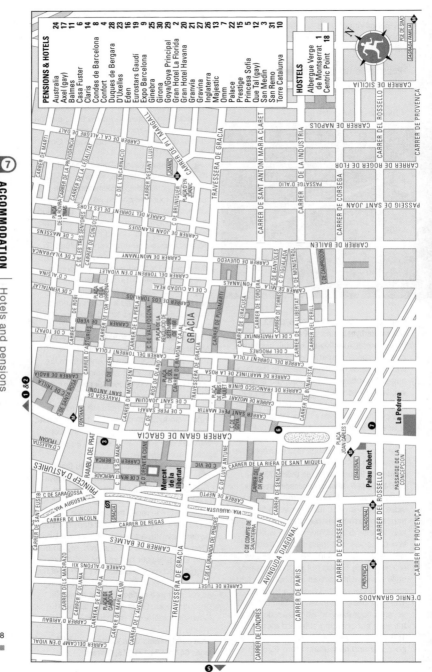

PENSIONS & HOTELS	
Australia	24
Axel (gay)	17
Balmes	11
Casa Fuster	6
Claris	14
Condes de Barcelona	8
Confort	4
Duques de Bergara	28
D'Uxelles	23
Eden	16
Eurostars Gaudí	19
Expo Barcelona	9
Ginebra	25
Girona	30
Goya/Goya Principal	29
Gran Hotel La Florida	2
Gran Hotel Havana	20
Gravina	21
Granvia	27
Inglaterra	26
Majestic	13
Omm	7
Palace	22
Prestige	15
Princesa Sofía	5
Que Tal (gay)	12
San Medin	3
San Remo	31
Torre Catalunya	10

HOSTELS	
Albergue Verge de Montserrat	1
Centric Point	18

169

.granhotelhavana.com; ⓂGirona. The nineteenth-century facade has been retained but everything else in this four-star hotel is contemporary in style, from the tadpole-shaped atrium to the Italian marble bathrooms. Rooms are on the sober side, but there's a comfortable atrium bar from which to plan the next day's outing. From €120.

Granvía Gran Via de les Corts Catalanes 642 Ⓣ933 181 900, Ⓦwww.nnhotels.es; ⓂCatalunya/Passeig de Gràcia. An attractive townhouse, built for a nineteenth-century banking family, with swish lobby and public rooms exuding old-style comfort. You may be less lucky with your own room, as some of the accommodation is cramped, but there's a lovely roof terrace. Prices are pretty reasonable for a three-star hotel given that a/c, full bath and satellite TV come as standard. €130.

Majestic Pg. de Gràcia 68 Ⓣ934 881 717, Ⓦwww.hotelmajestic.es; ⓂPasseig de Gràcia. Big, traditional hotel, refitted in muted colours to provide a tranquil base. *Objets* and limited-edition art adorn the public areas, and the rooms – bigger than many in this price bracket – have been pleasantly refurbished, but the absolute clincher is the rooftop pool and deck, with amazing views over the rooftops to the Sagrada Família. *Drolma* restaurant is highly rated while the high quoted room rates can almost always be beaten (bringing spacious junior suites into the equation) – at weekends and in summer they fall by up to twenty percent. €380.

Omm c/Rosselló 265 Ⓣ934 454 000, Ⓦwww. hotelomm.es; ⓂDiagonal. The black-and-grey designer experience that is Omm isn't to everyone's taste and can seem a bit oppressive, but matters improve inside the immaculate, minimalist, open-plan rooms – everyone gets a balcony, with the quietest rooms sited at the rear. The fearsomely handsome staff thaw after a while, as you glide effortlessly from the studiously chic bar to the Michelin-starred *Moo* restaurant. From €300.

Palace Gran Via de les Corts Catalanes 668 Ⓣ935 101 130, Ⓦwww.hotelpalacebarcelona .com; ⓂPasseig de Gràcia. What used to be the *Ritz*, and dating from 1919, this is still one of the benchmarks for city luxury. Formally attired staff jump to your every command, while your domain extends to opulent lounges, a terrace garden, health club, bar and *Caelis* restaurant with cuisine by Michelin-starred chef Romain Fornell. Deluxe rooms (there's no such thing as "standard" here) are either traditional (with four-posters) or more contemporary, and the suites are simply sensational. From €400.

Prestige Pg. de Gràcia 62 Ⓣ932 724 180 or 902 200 414, Ⓦwww.prestigepaseodegracia.com; ⓂPasseig de Gràcia. A redesign of a 1930s Eixample building has added achingly fashionable minimalist rooms, an Oriental-style internal patio garden and the *Zeroom*, a lounge with wireless Internet facility and style library. It's almost a parody of itself it's so cool, but the staff keep things real and pride themselves on their city know-how. "Functional" (standard) rooms are a bit less impressive (no views), so upgrade if you can. From €250.

San Remo c/Ausias Marc 19, 2° Ⓣ933 021 989, Ⓦwww.hostalsanremo.com; ⓂUrquinaona. The doubles aren't a bad size for the money and the small tiled bathrooms are pretty good for this price range. There's a/c and double-glazing, but even so you'll get more peace at the back – though the internal rooms aren't nearly as appealing as those with balconies. The seven rooms include one decently priced single. €60.

Rambla de Catalunya and Esquerra de l'Eixample

Australia Ronda Universitat 11, 4° Ⓣ933 174 177, Ⓦwww.residenciaustralia.com; ⓂUniversitat. The owner is well into her third decade looking after visitors and treats everyone kindly – you'll need to reserve at least a fortnight in advance in summer. Three of the four rooms have basins and balconies, and share two nice bathrooms (hairdryers provided); the other is a suite with private bathroom, a/c, TV, fridge and coffee-making machine. Rooms will take a third person (for an extra €12–20, depending on season), or there are four more spacious twin and double "Tasmanian" suites just across the road, also with full facilities. €53, suites €70.

Balmes c/Mallorca 216 Ⓣ934 511 914, Ⓦwww. derbyhotels.es; ⓂPasseig de Gràcia. Boutique three-star hotel with sharp-as-a-knife dining and bar facilities, classy rooms with parquet floors and leather sofas, and some larger duplexes available. A couple of ground-floor rooms have their own terrace overlooking the lush patio garden, complete with swimming pool and bar, and on your way in and out every day you can browse the African art and sculpture in the lobby. Last-minute rates as low as €100, otherwise €200, duplex €260.

Duques de Bergara c/Bergara 11 ☎933 015 151, ⊛www.hoteles-catalonia.com; Ⓜ **Catalunya**. This handsome late nineteenth-century building, designed by Gaudí's mentor Emili Sala, has had a complete makeover as a four-star hotel. Rooms have a bright, contemporary air, with parquet floors, brown marble bathrooms and little sitting areas – upgrade to a junior suite and you get jet-black marble and a Jacuzzi bath, lounge area and huge TV. It's set in a small side street, but there are Catalunya views from some balconies, and a small first-floor outdoor pool and terrace. Offers from €99, otherwise from €200, suites €300.

Eden c/Balmes 55, 1° ☎934 526 620, ⊛www.hostaleden.net; Ⓜ **Passeig de Gràcia**. Eager-to-please staff and a wide choice of simply furnished rooms, but overpriced given its student-dorm atmosphere and occasional rough edges. Make sure you get a room facing the back patio for a quiet night, though you'll want to avoid the odd one that doesn't have a window. Plenty of facilities attract a backpacker crowd – fridges in rooms, TV and DVD lounge, free Internet access, 24hr reception, laundry and coffee machine – and discounts are available for winter and longer stays. €50, en suite €70.

Ginebra Rambla de Catalunya 1, 3° ☎933 171 063, ⓔhotelginebra@telefonica.net; Ⓜ **Catalunya**. Even on a budget, if you spend a bit more you get a bit more space – a dozen good-sized rooms with handsome old furniture, bathrooms you can turn round in for a change, pot plants, cappuccino machine and small bar. All rooms come with TV and a/c, and some have impressive views of Plaça de Catalunya – be sure to ask for one with a balcony. €75.

Gravina c/Gravina 12 ☎933 016 868, ⊛www.hotel-gravina.com; Ⓜ **Universitat**. The old-style facade deceives, for this is a contemporary three-star update and pretty good value for money. It's fairly quiet (off the main road), while comfort levels are high – toiletries, robes and hairdryers in the bathrooms, neat little window-side armchairs, artwork in the public areas, and a buffet breakfast included in the price. Offers from €99, otherwise from €150.

Inglaterra c/Pelai 14 ☎935 051 100, ⊛www.hotel-inglaterra.com; Ⓜ **Universitat**. The boutique little sister to the

Majestic has an excellent location, and harmoniously toned rooms and snazzy bathrooms. Space is at a premium, but some rooms have cute private terraces, others street-side balconies (and very effective double-glazing). Best of all is the romantic roof-terrace – and guests can use the *Majestic's* pool. Three-night-for-two offers run Dec-Feb and July–Aug, special rates from €99, otherwise from €119.

Sants

Expo Barcelona c/Mallorca 1-23 ☎936 003 020, ⊛www.expogrupo.com; Ⓜ **Sants-Estació**. The interior has been upgraded, and the bright, spacious rooms at this four-star are very good value for money. Each has a sliding window onto a capacious terrace and the best have views across to MNAC on Montjuïc. There's also a rooftop pool, a good buffet breakfast, and the metro right on your doorstep. The hotel is around the back of the Torre Catalunya (see below), just a minute from Sants station. From €80.

Torre Catalunya Avgda. de Roma 2–4 ☎936 006 999, ⊛www.expogrupo.com; Ⓜ **Sants-Estació**. The landmark four-star-deluxe hotel outside Sants station towers over the surrounding buildings, which means the large, light rooms have sweeping views from all sides. Rooms above the twelfth floor are superior in terms of views and services, but all are elegantly turned out in earth tones and boast huge beds, flat-screen TVs and very good bathrooms. Breakfast is a buzz – an extensive buffet served on the twenty-third floor, accompanied by panoramic views – with the adjacent contemporary Catalan restaurant, *Visual*, another reason to linger. There's a spa with indoor pool, and guests can also use the sister *Expo's* outdoor pool. From €100, superior rooms from €125.

Les Corts

Princesa Sofia Pl. Pius XII 4 ☎935 081 000, ⊛www.expogrupo.com; Ⓜ **Maria Cristina**. A classic – one of the first five-star hotels in town thirty years ago – and well placed for shoppers, with wide-ranging city views from the upper floors. It still exudes old-school charm (the concierges know everything) though the warm-toned rooms, massages and treatments in the Aqua Diagonal Wellness Centre, pool (with retractable roof) and superior club rooms and lounges offer a more contemporary experience – the Barcelona football team stays and eats here before every home match. An immense buffet breakfast is served in the *Contraste* restaurant – which also has a pretty patio for summer dining. From €140, club rooms from €210.

Gràcia

Casa Fuster Pg. de Gràcia 132 ☎ 932 553 000, ⓦ www.hotelcasafuster.com; Ⓜ **Diagonal.** Modernista architect Domènech i Montaner's magnificent Casa Fuster (1908) is the backdrop for five-star-deluxe luxury with service to match. Rooms are in earth tones, with huge beds, smart bathrooms, flat-screen TVs and remote-controlled light and heat, while public areas make full use of the architectural heritage – from the magnificent pillared lobby bar to the panoramic roof terrace and pool. There's also a contemporary restaurant, *Galaxó*, plus fitness centre, sauna and 24hr room service. From €370. **Confort** Trav. de Gràcia 72 ☎ 932 386 828, ⓦ www.mediumhoteles.com; FGC Gràcia/ Ⓜ **Fon-**

tana. Handy for uptown shopping or Gràcia nightlife, this modern two-star has far more character than most, with chic little rooms, a dining room (buffet breakfast served) and attractive terrace. €120.

San Medín c/Gran de Gràcia 125 ☎ 932 173 068, Ⓔ sanmedin@telefonica.net; Ⓜ **Fontana.** Well-located pension with a dozen rooms, most with shower. The affable owner is busily renovating but he can't stop the traffic, so for a decent night's sleep you'll want to ask for an interior room. €65.

Tibidabo

Gran Hotel La Florida Carreterra Vallviderera a Tibidabo 83–93, 7km from the centre ☎ 932 593 000, ⓦ www.hotellaflorida.com. Describing itself as an "urban resort", the five-star, hillside *Gran Hotel* re-creates the glory days of the 1950s, when it was at the centre of Barcelona high society. Its terraces and pool all have amazing views, while some rooms and suites have a private garden or terrace and a Jacuzzi – sea-view rooms are charged at a premium. There's also a spa, restaurant, and poolside bar. From €370.

Youth hostels

The number of youth hostels in Barcelona has expanded rapidly in recent years. Some traditional backpacker dives survive here and there, but they have largely been superseded by purpose-built modern hostels with ensuite dorm rooms as well as private rooms. They compare well in price with budget rooms in the very cheapest pensions, and Internet access, self-catering kitchens, common rooms and laundry facilities are standard. If you don't have your own sleeping bag or sheet sleeping bag, most places can rent them to you. Rates given below indicate the low-season and high-season range, and some places offer discounts for longer stays. Security is pretty good at most hostels, with staffed reception desks and 24hr access commonplace, but you should still always use the lockers or safes provided. You only need an International Youth Hostel Federation (IYHF) card for a couple of places, but you can join on check-in.

Barri Gòtic

Itaca c/Ripoll 21 ☎ 933 019 751, ⓦ www .itacahostel.com; Ⓜ **Jaume I.** Bright and breezy converted house close to the cathedral, with spacious rooms (sleeping eight or twelve) with lockers and balconies. Dorms are mixed, though there is a six-bed women-only dorm and private rooms avail-

able. No TV lounge, but there's a kitchen and coffee machine, and breakfast available. Dorms €18–21, private rooms €48–60.

Kabul Pl. Reial 17 ☎ 933 185 190, ⓦ www .kabul-hostel.com; Ⓜ **Liceu.** A budget travellers' haven in the heart of the old town, with pool table and terrace, and weekly pub crawls to help you get acquainted. A big, monastic-style common room-cum-bar overlooks the square. It has a reputation as a bit of a party place, but it's safe and welcoming enough. Rooms vary in size and number of beds (sleeping four to twenty, no private rooms) and the price includes breakfast. No phone reservations in summer. €17–24.

Mari-Luz c/de la Palau 4, 2° ☎ & ℱ933 173 463, ⓦwww.pensionmariluz.com; Ⓜ Jaume I/Liceu. This old mansion, on a quieter-than-usual Barri Gòtic street, has a more personal touch than the huge new hostels in town. Someone's been to IKEA for furniture and there are contemporary art prints on the walls, central heating, laundry facilities and a small kitchen. It can be a tight squeeze when full as there are thirty-five dorm beds in variously sized rooms (some en suite), plus seven inexpensive doubles with shared bathrooms. Their restored apartments a few minutes' walk away in the Raval offer more space. Dorms €15–19, rooms €48.

El Raval

Barcelona Mar c/de Sant Pau 80 ☎933 248 530, ⓦwww.youthostel-barcelona.com; Ⓜ Paral.lel/Drassanes. Large, rather clinically furnished hostel with lots of beds, on the fringe of the Rambla de Raval. Dorms – in six-, eight-, ten-, fourteen- or sixteen-bedded rooms – are mixed, and beds are ship's-bunk-style with a little curtain for privacy. €18–23, includes continental breakfast.
Center Ramblas c/Hospital 63 ☎934 124 069, ⓦwww.center-ramblas.com; Ⓜ Liceu. Very popular 200-bed hostel, 100m from the Ramblas, and equipped with lounge, bar, laundry, Internet access, travel library, luggage storage and more. Heated and a/c dorms – sleeping three to ten – have flagged floors and individual lockers. IYHF membership is required (you can join on the spot). Price includes breakfast. No credit cards. Under-25s €16–19, over-25s €19–23.

La Ribera

Gothic Point c/Vigatans 5 ☎932 687 808, ⓦwww.gothicpoint.com; Ⓜ Jaume I. A grand downstairs communal area shows off the building's dramatic proportions, and there's a great roof terrace. Rooms have fourteen bunks and en-suite bathrooms and each bed has its own bedside cabinet and read-

ing light. Lockers, left-luggage and tours available. Open 24hr. Dorms €18–21, includes breakfast and free Internet.

Barceloneta

Sea Point Pl. del Mar 1–4 ☎932 247 075, ⓦwww.seapointhostel.com; Ⓜ Barceloneta. Neat little modern bunk rooms sleeping six or seven, with an integral shower-bathroom and big lockers in each one. The attached café, where you have breakfast, looks right out onto the boardwalk and palm trees. Open 24hr. Dorms €18–21, includes breakfast and free Internet.

Eixample

Centric Point Pg. de Gràcia 33 ☎932 312 045, ⓦwww.centricpointhostel. com; Ⓜ Passeig de Gràcia. Bills itself as "one of the most spectacular hostels in Europe" and it's hard to disagree, with around 450 beds spread across several floors of a refurbished *modernista* building. Good-quality private twins, doubles, triples and quads are available, all with wardrobe, shower room, balcony and views, while dorms (all en suite, most also with balcony) sleep up to fourteen. Facilities are first-rate, with bar, kitchen, wireless Internet, laundry and roof terrace with spectacular views of Gaudí's Casa Batlló. Prices include continental breakfast and free Internet access. Dorms €17–23, private rooms €70–90.

Horta

Albergue Verge de Montserrat Pg. de la Mare de Déu del Coll 41–51 ☎932 105 151, ⓦwww.tujuca.com; Ⓜ Vallcarca (follow Avgda. República d'Argentina, c/Viaducte de Vallcarca and then signs) or bus #28 from Pl. de Catalunya stops just across the street. Stunning converted mansion with tile and stained-glass interior, gardens, terrace and city views – a long way out, but close to Parc Güell. Dorms sleep four, six, eight or twelve, and there are all the usual facilities plus a local restaurant just around the corner or meals provided. IYHF membership required; five-night maximum stay; reception open 8am–3pm & 4.30–11pm; main door closes at midnight, but opens every 30min thereafter. Dorms €19–23, includes breakfast.

Eating

G ood cafés, tapas bars and restaurants are easily found all over the city, though you'll probably do most of your eating where you do most of your sightseeing, in the old town, particularly in the **Barri Gòtic**. However, if you step no further than the Ramblas, or the streets around the cathedral, you are not going to experience the best of the city's cuisine – in the main tourist areas food and service can be indifferent and prices high.You need to be a bit more adventurous, and explore the back streets of **La Ribera**, **El Raval** and **Poble Sec**, where you'll find excellent restaurants, some little more than hole-in-the-wall cafés or traditional taverns, others surprisingly funky. In the **Eixample** prices tend to be higher all round, though you'll find plenty of bargains in cafés and restaurants aimed at lunching workers. **Gràcia**, further out, is a nice place to spend the evening, with plenty of good mid-range restaurants. For fish and seafood you're best off in **Port Vell** by the Palau de Mar, in the harbourside **Barceloneta** district or at the **Port Olímpic**.

Cafés and fast food

There are thousands of **cafés** in Barcelona – you're rarely more than a step away from a coffee fix or a quick sandwich. In terms of what's available to eat and drink, there's often little difference between a bar and a café, but the places detailed in this section have been chosen for their food or ambience.You might be able to get a full meal, but they are more geared towards breakfast, snacks and sightseeing stops. Many are classics of their kind – century-old cafés or unique neighbourhood haunts – while others specialize in certain types of food and

---

Starting the day

Unless you're staying somewhere with a decent buffet breakfast spread, you may as well pass up the overpriced coffee-and-croissant option in your hotel and join the locals in the bars, cafés and patisseries. A couple of euros should get you a hot drink and a brioche, croissant or sandwich just about anywhere – many advertised deals run until noon. *Ensaimadas* (pastry spirals) are a popular choice, and *xocolata amb xurros* (*chocolate con churros* – long, fried tubular doughnuts with thick drinking chocolate) is a good cold-weather starter. A slice of *truita* (*tortilla*), ham or cheese – in a *flauta* (thin baguette) also makes an excellent breakfast. The traditional country breakfast is *pa amb tomàquet* (*pan con tomate*) – bread rubbed with tomato, olive oil and garlic, perhaps topped with some cured ham or sliced cheese. For toast, ask for *torrades* (*tostadas*).

Best for...

Al fresco dining Agua (p.193), Bar Ra (p.190), El Cangrejo Loco (p.194).
Breakfast Bagel Shop (p.175), Kasparo (p.179), Laie Llibreria Café (p.179).
Cheap eats Bar Salvador (p.188), Casa Delfin (p.188), L'Económic (p.187).
Catch of the day Arrel del Born (p.189), Els Pescadors (p.195), Mar de la Ribera (p.189).
Classy café society Café d'Estiu (p.175), Café de l'Opera (p.178), Valor (p.181).
Ethnic artistry Emu (p.197), Habibi (p.196), El Japonés (p.195).
Fusion sensations Ànima (p.191), Biblioteca (p.191), Santa Maria (p.189).
Money no object Àbac (p.189), Comerç 24 (p.189), Jean Luc Figueras (p.197).
Romantic assignations Café de l'Acadèmia (p.186), El Salón (p.185), Octubre (p.197).
Tapas Bar Pinotxo (p.182), Cal Pep (p.182), Quimet i Quimet (p.183).
Traditional classics Can Culleretes (p.185), Los Caracoles (p.186), Set Portes (p.189).
Unique experiences Casa Fernandez (p.197), Espai Sucre (p.189), Flash, Flash (p.196).

drink. Most are open long hours – from 7am or 8am until midnight, or much later in some cases – so whether it's coffee first thing or a late-night nibble, you'll find somewhere to cater for you.

A quick primer will help you sort out what's what in the café world. A **forn** is a bakery, a **pastisseria** a cake and pastry shop, both often with cafés attached. A **xocolateria** specializes in chocolate, including the drinking kind. In a **granja** or **orxateria**, more like milk bars than regular cafés, you'll be able to sample traditional delights like *orxata* (*horchata*, tiger-nut drink), ice cream, and *granissat* (*granizado*, a crushed ice drink flavoured with orange, lemon or coffee).

Pizza, burger, felafel and **kebab** and **cappuccino** joints are ubiquitous, especially around the Ramblas and on the main streets in the Eixample. Most major international chains are represented, while **local and Spanish chains** include: *Pans & Company* and *Bocatta*, for hot and cold baguette-based sandwiches and salads; *Fresh and Ready* for deli, sandwiches and juices; *Il Caffè di Roma*, serving coffee and other hot drinks, pastries and ice creams; the classier *Aroma* cafés; and the warehouse-style *Café di Francesco* for coffee (with added alcohol or cream combinations), thirty types of tea, and croissants.

Ramblas and the Barri Gòtic

Antiga Casa Figueras Ramblas 83 ☎933 016 027, ⓦwww.escriba.es; Ⓜ**Liceu.** Serves pastries from the Escribà family business in a *modernista* pastry shop, with a few tables inside and out. Many people rate this as the best bakery in Barcelona. Mon–Sat 9am–3pm & 5–8.30pm.

Bagel Shop c/Canuda 25 ☎933 024 161; Ⓜ**Catalunya.** Funky yellow café that first introduced the bagel to Barcelona – there's cream cheese and smoked salmon, plus many others, including one rubbed with tomato, olive oil, garlic and salt for the local crowd. Bagel-and-coffee breakfast runs until noon (or choose pancakes and maple syrup), and there's brunch on Sunday and devilish chocolate brownies. Mon–Sat 9.30am–9.30pm, Sun 11am–4pm.

Bar del Pi Pl. Sant Josep Oriol 1 ☎933 022 123; Ⓜ**Liceu.** Best known for its terrace tables in one of Barcelona's prettiest squares. Service can be slow – not that anyone's in a hurry in this prime people-watching spot. Mon–Sat 9am–11pm, Sun 10am–10pm; closed two weeks in Jan & Aug.

Café d'Estiu Pl. de Sant Iu 5–6 ☎933 103 014; Ⓜ**Jaume I.** A summer-only café housed on the delightful interior terrace of the Museu Marès. Relax with the newspapers during the day, or come for the candlelit evenings. April–Oct Tues–Sun 10am–10pm.

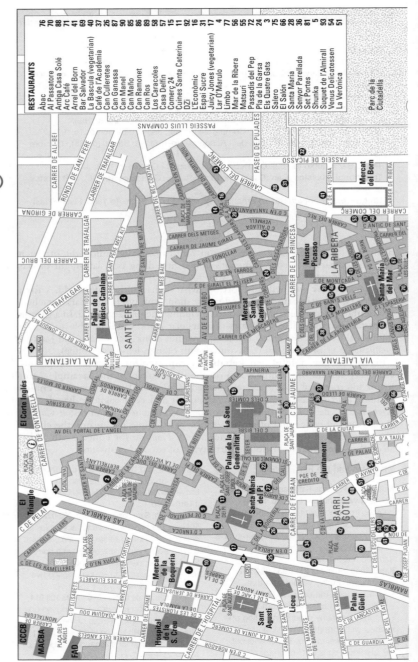

RESTAURANTS	
Abac	76
Al Passatore	70
Antiga Casa Solé	88
Arc Café	71
Arrel del Born	41
Bar Salvador	69
La Bascula (vegetarian)	40
Café de l'Acadèmia	37
Can Culleretes	26
Can Ganassa	87
Can Manel	90
Can Maño	85
Can Ramonet	86
Can Ros	89
Los Caracoles	58
Casa Delfin	57
Comerç 24	15
Cuines Santa Caterina	11
DZi	92
L'Economic	16
Espai Sucre	31
Juicy Jones (vegetarian)	17
Lar O'Marulo	4
Limbo	77
Mar de la Ribera	56
Matsuri	55
Passadis del Pep	72
Pla de la Garsa	24
Els Quatre Gats	3
Salero	75
El Salón	66
Santa Maria	28
Senyor Parellada	36
Set Portes	81
Shunka	5
Suquet de l'Almirall	93
Venus Delicatessen	54
La Verónica	51

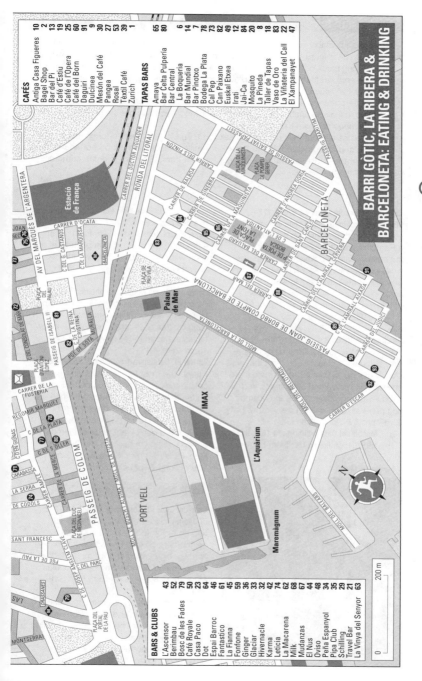

BARRI GÒTIC, LA RIBERA & BARCELONETA: EATING & DRINKING

⑧ EATING

CAFÉS
Antiga Casa Figueres	10
Bagel Shop	2
Bar del Pi	13
Café d'Estiu	19
Café de l'Òpera	25
Café del Born	60
Daguiri	91
Dulcinea	9
Mesón del Café	30
Pangea	27
Rosal	53
Tèxtil Café	39
Zurich	1

TAPAS BARS
Amaya	65
Bar Celta Pulperia	80
Bar Central	6
La Boquería	14
Bar Mundial	7
Bar Pinotxo	78
Bodega La Plata	73
Cal Pep	82
Can Paixano	49
Euskal Etxea	12
Irati	84
Jai-Ca	20
Mosquito	8
La Pineda	18
Taller de Tapas	83
Vaso de Oro	22
La Vinateria del Call	47
El Xampanyet	

BARS & CLUBS
L'Ascensor	43
Berimbau	52
Bosc de les Fades	79
Café Royale	50
Casa Paco	23
Dot	64
Espai Barroc	46
Fantàstico	61
La Fianna	45
Fontone	59
Ginger	36
Glaciar	33
Hivernacle	32
Karma	42
Leticia	74
La Macarena	62
Milk	68
Mudanzas	67
El Nus	44
Oviso	48
Peña Espanyol	34
Pipa Club	35
Schilling	29
Travel Bar	21
La Vinya del Senyor	63

Estació de França

CARRER DEL DOCTOR AIGUADER
RONDA DEL LITORAL
CARRER DELS PINZÓN
CARRER DE BALBOA
CARRER DE GINEBRA
CARRER DE LA MAQUINISTA
CARRER DE L'ATLÀNTIDA
PLAÇA DE LA BARCELONETA
CARRER DE SANT CARLES
CARRER DE SANT MIQUEL
CARRER DE L'ALMIRALL CERVERA
CARRER DE L'ALMIRALL AIXADA
CARRER DEL JUDICI
CARRER DE GINEBRA
CARRER DE BALUARD
CARRER DE POETA BOSCÀ
PLAÇA DE LA FONT
BARCELONETA
CARRER D'ANDREA DORIA
PASSEIG DE SALVAT PAPASSEIT
PASSEIG MARÍTIM
PLAÇA DE LA ARGODLLINISTA
PLAÇA DE POMPEU GENER

Palau de Mar
PASSEIG JOAN DE BORBÓ COMTE DE BARCELONA
MOLL DE LA BARCELONETA
CARRER D'ESCAR
MOLL DELS PESCADORS
MOLL DE LES BALEARS

IMAX
L'Aquàrium
PORT VELL
Maremàgnum
MOLL DE BOSCH I ALSINA / MOLL DE LA FUSTA
PASSEIG DE COLOM
MOLL DE LA FUSTA

PLAÇA DEL PALAU
AV DEL MARQUÈS DE L'ARGENTERA
CARRER D'OCATA
C DE CASTAÑOS
C DE LA MARQUESA
BARCELONETA
PLAÇA DE PAU VILA
PASSEIG DE ISABEL II
PGE DE SOTA MURALLA
C DE LA REINA CRISTINA

PLAÇA DEL DUC DE MEDINACELI
CARRER DE LA FUSTERIA
REGOMIR MARQUET
C DE LA PLATA
C DE S OLLER
CARABASSA
LA SERRA
DE CODOLS
SANT FRANCESC
PGE DE LA PAU
C DE JOSEP ANSELM CLAVÉ
C DEL PARC
PLAÇA DEL PORTAL DE LA PAU
MONTSERRAL
DRASSANES
LES
C PER GIGNÀS
JOAN REC
PLAÇA DE MONT LÓPEZ
CARRER ANTE
CARRER DE LA MERCÈ
CARRER DEL DUC DE MEDINACELI
DEL CONSOLAT DE MAR
PLAÇA DEL PALAU

200 m

N

177

Coffee is invariably espresso – ask for a *café sol* (*café solo*) or simply *un café*. A slightly weaker large black coffee is called a *café americano*. A *tallat* (*cortado*) is a small strong black coffee with a dash of steamed milk; a larger cup with more hot milk is a *café amb llet* (*café con leche*). Black coffee is also frequently mixed with brandy, cognac or whisky, all such concoctions being called *cigaló* (*carajillo*); liqueur mixed with white coffee is a *trifásico*. Decaffeinated coffee (*descafeinat*, *descafeinado*) is available, usually in sachet form, though increasingly you can get the real thing – ask for it *de màquina* (from the machine*)*.

Tea comes without milk unless you ask for it, and is often insipid (often just a tea-bag in a cup of hot water). If you do ask for milk, chances are it'll be hot and UHT. Better are the infusions that you can get in most bars, like mint (*menta*), camomile (*camomila*) and lime (*tila*).

Café de l'Opera Ramblas 74 ⓣ933 177 585, Ⓦwww.cafeoperabcn.com; Ⓜ Liceu. If you're going to pay through the nose for a Ramblas seat, it may as well be at this famous old café-bar, which retains its late nineteenth-century decor as well as a bank of sought-after pavement tables. It's not a complete tourist-fest, though – locals pop in throughout the day and night for coffee, cakes, snacks and tapas. Daily 8.30am–2am.

Dulcinea c/Petritxol 2 ⓣ932 311 756; Ⓜ Liceu. Traditional *granja* specializing in hot chocolate, slathered in cream if you like it that way, plus all manner of pastries, *mel i mato* (curd cheese with honey) and other treats. A dickie-bow-wearing waiter patrols the beamed and panelled room bearing a silver tray. Daily 9am–1pm & 5–9pm; closed Aug.

Mesón del Cafe c/Llibreteria 16 ⓣ933 150 754; Ⓜ Jaume I. Offbeat bar where you'll probably have to stand to sample the pastries and the excellent coffee – including a cappuccino laden with fresh cream – though there is a sort of cubbyhole at the back with a few tables. The bar attracts all sorts of local characters. Mon–Sat 7am–11pm.

Pangea c/Banys Nous 4, no phone; Ⓜ Liceu. Stop by this hole-in-the-wall for one of their fantastic fruit smoothies and juices, stuffed veggie pittas or salads – the sofas and low tables are open to the pavement. Daily 10am–2am.

Zurich Pl. Catalunya 1 ⓣ933 179 153; Ⓜ Catalunya. The most famous meet-and-greet café in town, right at the top of the Ramblas underneath El Triangle shopping centre. It's good for croissants and breakfast sandwiches and there's a huge terrace, but sit inside if you don't want to be bothered by endless rounds of buskers and beggars. Mon–Fri 8am–11pm, Sat & Sun 10am–11pm, June–Sept until 1am.

La Ribera

Café del Born Pl. Comercial 10 932 683 272; Ⓜ Jaume I. No gimmicks, no dodgy art and no fusion food – just a successful neighbourhood café-bar with wooden floors, a high ceiling and a simple Mediterranean menu. Sunday brunch is popular. Mon–Thurs & Sun 9am–1am, Fri & Sat 9am–3.30am.

Rosal Pg. del Born 27, no phone; Ⓜ Jaume I. The *terrassa* at the end of the Born gets the sun all day, making it a popular meeting place, though it's also packed on summer nights. Menu specials here are couscous or curry combinations, and if you can raise

▽ Meson del Café

a smile from the staff you're on a roll. Daily 9am–2am.

Tèxtil Café c/de Montcada 12–14 ☎ 932 682 598, ⓦ www.textilcafe.com; Ⓜ **Jaume I.** Set inside the shady, cobbled medieval courtyard of the Museu Textil i d'Indumentaria. Serves hummus, tzatziki, quiche, salads, chilli, lasagne and big sandwiches, plus a lunchtime *menú del dia*. There are Sunday jazz nights (9.30pm; €4) with the Barcelona Swing Serenaders, for which you'll need to book ahead. Tues–Thurs & Sun 10am–midnight, Fri & Sat until 2am.

Barceloneta

Daguiri c/Grau i Torras 59 ☎ 932 215 109, ⓦ www.daguiri.com; Ⓜ **Barceloneta.** Seaside caff with a breezy terrace overlooking the beach. Food is along the lines of tzatziki and hummus, sandwiches and salads, and there's a large range of teas. Mon–Fri 11.30am–1am, Sat & Sun 10.30am–1am; Nov–March closed Tues & Wed.

El Raval

Buenas Migas Pl. Bonsuccés 6 ☎ 933 183 708, ⓦ www.buenasmigas.com; Ⓜ **Catalunya.** You can eat in either the cosy rustic interior or on the traffic-free *terrassa*. The menu is wide-ranging – foccaccia slices and pizza wedges, cakes and pastries, but also seasonal pastas, salads and soups. There's a Barri Gòtic branch near Plaça del Rei. Daily 10am–midnight.

Granja de Gavà c/Joaquim Costa 37 ☎ 933 175 883; Ⓜ **Universitat.** This traditionally tiled café has an arty air – witness the daubs on the walls, the 3m-high woman on the bar and the weekly poetry readings and other events. It's a relaxed spot – proclaiming "No TV, just good music" – and serves up sandwiches, crepes, salads, juices and shakes. Mon–Fri 8am–1am, Sat 8am–2.30am.

Granja M. Viader c/Xuclà 4–6 ☎ 933 183 486; Ⓜ **Liceu.** The oldest milk bar (*granja*) in town is a great breakfast stop, tucked away down a narrow alley just off c/del Carmé, with a pavement plaque outside for services to the city. Sr. Viader was the proud inventor of "Cacaolat" (a popular chocolate drink, but you could also try the *mel i mató* (curd cheese and honey) *llet Mallorquina* (fresh milk with cinnamon and lemon rind). Mon 5–8.45pm, Tues–Sat 9am–1.45pm & 5–8.45pm.

Kasparo Pl. Vicenç Martorell 4 ☎ 933 022 072; Ⓜ **Catalunya.** Sited in the arcaded corner of a quiet square off c/Bonsuccés, this tiny bar and *terrassa* is popular with locals who come to let their kids play in the adjacent playground. Sandwiches, tapas and assorted *platos del dia* are on offer – such as hummus and bread, vegetable quiche, couscous or pasta. There's also muesli, Greek yoghurt, and toast and jam for early birds. Daily 9am–midnight; closed Jan.

Mendizábal c/Junta de Comerç 2, no phone; Ⓜ **Liceu.** Don't look for a bar – there isn't one. This cheery stand-up counter opposite the Hospital de la Santa Creu dispenses juices, shakes, beer and sandwiches to passing punters. The lucky ones grab a table over the road in the little square. Daily 10am–midnight, June–Sept until 1am.

Poble Nou

El Tío Ché Rambla Poble Nou 44–46 ☎ 933 091 872, ⓦ www.eltioche.com; Ⓜ **Poble Nou, or bus #36 from** Ⓜ **Barceloneta.** Famous old *orxateria* in a down-to-earth neighbourhood that's a bit off the beaten track – though you can stroll up easily enough from Bogatell beach (15min). Four generations of the same family have overseen the business since 1940 – choose from orange or lemon *granissat*, *orxata*, *torrons* (almond fudge), hot chocolate, coffee, croissants and sandwiches. Daily 10am–midnight; reduced hours in winter.

Eixample

Café del Centre c/Girona 69 ☎ 934 881 101; Ⓜ **Girona.** Formerly a casino, later converted into a café, but retaining its *modernista* decor. It's a couple of blocks from the tourist sights, but a good stop for *pa amb tomàquet,* coffee, or lunchtime *platos del día*. Mon–Fri 7am–1am, Sat 7pm–1am.

Forn de Sant Jaume Rambla de Catalunya 50 ☎ 932 160 229; Ⓜ **Passeig de Gràcia.** The windows are piled high with goodies from this classic old *pastisseria* and *bomboneria* – croissants, cakes and sweets are either to take away or eat at the busy little adjacent café. Mon–Sat 9am–9pm.

Laie Llibreria Café c/Pau Claris 85 ☎ 933 027 310, ⓦ www.laie.es; Ⓜ **Urquinaona.** Head up the stairs in front of the bookshop, and your choice is the bar and mezzanine seating or

EATING | Cafés and fast food

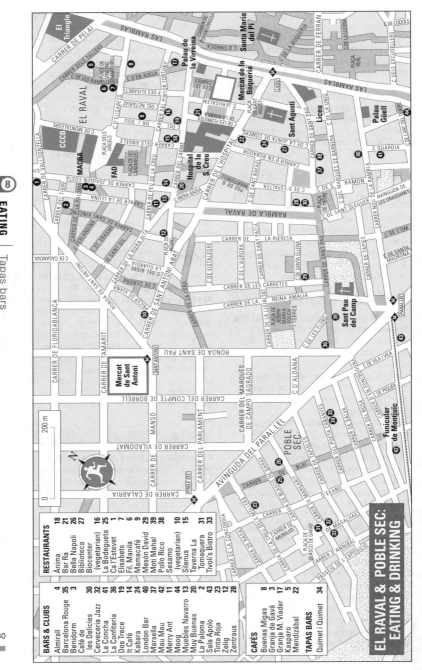

the roomier salon at the back. The weekday buffet breakfast spread is popular, and there are set lunch and dinner deals, à la carte dining, and magazines (*National Geographic* to *Marie Claire*) to browse. Also branches in the Caixa Forum art gallery and L'Illa shopping centre. Mon 9am–9pm, Tues–Sat 9am–1am.

Valor Rambla de Catalunya 46 ⊤934 876 246; ⓜPasseig de Gràcia. Ornate uptown chocolate specialist, serving the gentle folk since 1881. A warming hot choc and *xurros* sends you happily on your way on a

chilly morning. Mon–Thurs 8.30am–1pm & 3.30–11pm, Fri–Sun 9am–midnight.

Gràcia

Mos Via Augusta 112 ⊤932 371 313; FGC Plaça Molina. Self-service designer café – graze the sleek counters, picking up a croissant or tuna turnover, or maybe one of the cooked dishes, pasta servings or seasonal salads, then repair upstairs, helping yourself to coffee from the *màquina* (regular or decaf). Finish off with a handmade chocolate, a house speciality. Daily 7am–10pm.

Tapas bars

Tapas are not a particularly Catalan phenomenon, and most **tapas bars** in the city are run by people from other parts of Spain, especially Galicia and the Basque country. That's not to say the tapas bars aren't any good – far from it – and jumping from bar to bar, with a bite to eat in each, is as good a way as any to spend the evening. It never works out particularly cheaply though – crawling the tapas bars for dinner is going to cost you at least as much as eating in a medium-priced restaurant, say €25 a head.

Most **traditional tapas bars** – like those in the Barri Gòtic, near the harbour, or in Barceloneta – have their own specialities, so look at what the locals are eating before diving in. More contemporary places serve what's styled "creative tapas", mixing in Asian and Far Eastern dishes and flavours, while others specialize in **Basque-style** *pintxos*, which are bite-sized slices of baguette piled with various combinations of meat, cheese or fish held together with a cocktail stick – you're charged by the number of sticks on your plate when you've finished. More Catalan in execution are the city's **llesqueries**, more like upmarket wine bars. A *llesca* is a thick slice of country bread which is toasted, rubbed with garlic and tomato, and sprinkled with olive oil, and better known as *pa amb tomàquet* (bread with tomato). It's accompanied by cured ham or cold cuts, slices of cheese, *escalivada* (roasted pepper, onion and aubergine) and other salads.

Ramblas and the Barri Gòtic

Amaya Ramblas 20–24 ⊤933 026 138 (bar), 933 021 037 (restaurant), ⓦwww .restauranteamaya.com; ⓜDrassanes. A Ramblas fixture since 1941 – restaurant on one side, tapas bar on the other, both serving Basque seafood specialities, including octopus, baby squid, clams, mussels, anchovies and prawns. The bar offers the cheapest and most enjoyable introduction to the cuisine, otherwise main dishes in the restaurant cost €14–20. Bar daily 10am–12.30am; restaurant daily 1.30–4pm & 8.30pm–midnight.

Bar Celta Pulpería c/de la Mercè 16 ⊤933 150 006; ⓜDrassanes. This no-nonsense brightly lit Galician tapas bar specializes in octopus, fried *pimientos* (peppers) and heady regional

wine. Eat at the U-shaped bar or at tables in the back room. It's best to ask prices as you go here – the food's good but the bill has a habit of mounting up, especially for out-of-towners. Mon–Sat 10am–1am.

Bar Central La Boqueria Mercat de la Boqueria, Ramblas 91, no phone; ⓜLiceu. The gleaming chrome stand-up bar in the central aisle is the venue for ultra-fresh market produce, served by blue-smocked staff who work at a fair lick. Breakfast, snack or lunch, it's all the same to them – salmon cutlets, sardines, calamari, razor clams, hake fillets, sausages, pork steaks, asparagus spears and the rest, plunked on the griddle and sprinkled with salt. Breakast costs just a few euros or it's €5–10 for a main dish and a drink. Mon–Sat 6.30am–4pm.

Bar Pinotxo Mercat de la Boqueria, Ramblas 91 ☎933 171 731; ⓂLiceu. The market's most renowned refuelling stop – just inside the main entrance on the right – attracts traders, chefs, tourists and celebs, who stand three deep at busy times. A *tallat* and a grilled sandwich is the local breakfast of choice, or let the cheery staff steer you towards the tapas and daily specials. Mon–Sat 6am–5pm; closed Aug.

Bodega La Plata c/de la Mercè 28 ☎933 151 009; ⓂDrassanes. An old-town classic with a marble counter open to the street and dirt-cheap wine straight from the barrel. Anchovies are the speciality (salted and laid over cut tomatoes or deep-fried, like whitebait), attracting an enthusiastic local crowd, from businessmen to pre-clubbers. Daily 10am–4pm & 8–11pm.

Irati c/Cardenal Casañas 17 ☎933 023 084; ⓂLiceu. Crowded brick-walled Basque bar that has been around longer than most – locals still think favourably of the *pintxos*, which run the gamut from country sausage to smoked salmon. There's a seasonally changing Basque menu in the restaurant (mains around €20). Daily noon–1am; *pintxos* served noon–3pm & 7–11pm.

La Pineda c/del Pi 16 ☎933 024 393; ⓂLiceu. On a street of boutiques and gift shops survives this old-fashioned grocery store, with a tiny bar and a few tables at the back where the old guys and curious tourists hang out. *Pa amb tomàquet* plus selections from the cured hams suspended over the counter are the things to eat. Mon–Sat 9am–3pm & 6–10pm.

Taller de Tapas Pl. Sant Josep Oriol 9 ☎933 018 020, Ⓦwww.tallerdetapas.com; ⓂLiceu. More restaurant than bar, the fashionable "tapas workshop" sucks in tourists with its pretty location by the church of Santa Maria del Pi – there's a year-round outdoor terrace. The open kitchen turns out market-fresh tapas, with fish a speciality at dinner, so you might get griddled tuna, sautéed razor clams, anchovies from L'Escala or cod fish-cakes. Prices are high, but the food's reliable. There is another branch in the Born at c/Argentería 51. Daily noon–midnight, Fri & Sat until 1am.

La Viñatería del Call c/Sant Domènec del Call 9 ☎933 026 092; ⓂJaume I. The wood-table tavern is principally an eating place – with a long menu of *pa amb tomàquet*, cheese, ham, *escalivada*, fish,

fried peppers and much more – but it's also a great late-night bar, with a serious wine list and jazz and flamenco sounds as a backdrop. If you want to eat, especially at weekends, it's best to reserve a table. Mon–Sat 6pm–1am.

Sant Pere

Bar Mundial Pl. de Sant Agustí el Vell 1 ☎933 199 056; ⓂJaume I. Simple eighty-year-old neighbourhood bar, famous for its seafood tapas and meals. Tues–Fri 11am–4pm & 8–11.30pm, Sat noon–4pm & 8.30pm–midnight, Sun noon–3.30pm; closed 2 weeks in Aug.

Mosquito c/dels Carders 46 ☎932 687 569, Ⓦwww.mosquitotapas.com; ⓂJaume 1. Delicious pan-Asian tapas including fragrant noodle salads, potato *chaat*, chicken *tikka* skewers and crispy *pakoras*, each around €5. Add friendly service, Fair Trade coffee and world music for a winning mixture. Tues–Sun 5pm–2am.

La Ribera

Cal Pep Pl. de les Olles 8 ☎933 107 961, Ⓦwww.calpep.net; ⓂBarceloneta. There's no equal in town for fresh-off-the-boat and out-of-the-market tapas, and though prices can be high (a meal will cost €30–40 a head, including drinks) it's definitely worth it. If you don't want to queue, get there on opening for a seat at the bar. After a quick tutorial from the waiter, sit back and enjoy fried shrimp, hot green peppers, grilled seabass, Catalan sausage and beans, baby squid and chickpeas, and other classics – all overseen by Pep himself bustling up and down the counter. Mon 8pm–midnight, Tues–Sat 1.30–4pm & 8pm–midnight; closed Aug.

Can Paixano c/Reina Cristina 7 ☎933 100 839; ⓂBarceloneta. Unmarked stand-up bar (next to *Bazar Internacional*) where the drink of choice (all right, the only drink) is champagne. Don't go thinking sophistication – it might come in traditional champagne saucers (the sort of thing Dean Martin used to stack in a pyramid and then pour wine over), but this is a counter-only joint where there's fizz, tapas and tapas-in-sandwiches, and that's your lot. And who could want more? Mon–Sat 9am–10.30pm.

Euskal Etxea Pl. de Montcada 1–3 ☎933 102 185; ⓂJaume I/Barceloneta. The bar at the

EATING

⑧

front of the local Basque community centre is great for *pintxos*-picking – graze from the counter and then hunker down around the huge barrel-tables. There's a pricier restaurant out back with more good Basque specialities. Mon 6.30pm–midnight, Tues–Sat noon–4pm & 6.30pm–midnight; restaurant opens 1.30pm & 8.30pm.

El Xampanyet c/de Montcada 22 ☎933 197 003; Ⓜ **Jaume I/Barceloneta.** Traditional blue-tiled bar doing a roaring trade in sweet sparkling *cava* and *sidra.* Salted anchovies are the house speciality, but there's also marinaded tuna, spicy mussels, sun-dried tomatoes, sliced meats and cheese, and *pa amb tomàquet.* As is often the way, the drinks are cheap and the tapas turn out to be rather pricey, but there's usually a good buzz about the place. Tues–Sat noon–4pm & 7–11.30pm, Sun noon–4pm; closed Aug.

Barceloneta

Jai-Ca c/Ginebra 13 ☎932 683 265; Ⓜ **Barceloneta.** There's often a bit of a scrum in this traditional local bar, but you can usually get a view of the tapas list on the wall or just check what your neighbour's having – perhaps some razor clams or plump anchovies. Meanwhile, the fryers in the kitchen work overtime, turning out crisp baby squid and little green peppers scattered with salt. Take your haul to a tile-topped cane table, or outside onto the tiny street-corner patio. Daily 10am–11pm.

Vaso de Oro c/Balboa 6 ☎933 193 098; Ⓜ **Barceloneta.** If you can get in this corridor of a bar you're doing well (Sun lunch is particularly busy), and there's no menu or list, so order the *patatas bravas,* some thick slices of fried sausage and a dollop of tuna salad and you've touched all the bases. Tall schooners of own-brewed beer come either light or dark. Daily 9am–midnight.

Poble Sec

Quimet i Quimet c/Poeta Cabanyes 25 ☎934 423 142; Ⓜ **Paral.lel.** The neighbourhood's best tapas joint, with bottles stacked five shelves high – there's a chalkboard menu of twenty wines by the glass – and little plates of food served from the minuscule counter. Order a roast onion, a marinaded mushroom or two, stuffed cherry tomatoes, grilled aubergine and anchovy-wrapped olives – classy finger food for the discerning nibbler. Tues–Sat noon–4pm & 7–11pm, Sun noon–4pm; closed Aug.

Eixample

Els Barrils c/d'Aribau 89 ☎934 531 091; Ⓜ **Provença.** Hanging hams and barrels set a rustic tone inside whilst the stuffed boar and moose keep watch on punters tucking into good, country-style tapas – cured meats a speciality. A *menú del dia* is also available, while a sheltered *terrassa* provides a breath of fresh air. Daily 9am–2am; closed Tues, and first two weeks in July.

La Bodegueta Rambla Catalunya 100 ☎932 154 894; Ⓜ **Diagonal.** Long-established basement bodega with *cava* by the glass, a serious range of other wines, and good ham, cheese, anchovies and *pa amb tomàquet* to soak it all up. In summer you can sit outside at the *rambla* tables. Daily 8am–2am; closed mornings in Aug.

Casa Alfonso c/Roger de Llúria 6 ☎933 019 783, Ⓦ www.casaalfonso.com; Ⓜ **Urquinaona.** It's about half-past 1930 in *Alfonso's* – bar and *xarcuteria* up front, country-style wood-panelled dining room at the rear. Alongside the tapas are two-person platters (like mixed cheeses or smoked fish) or selections from the grill, served with garlic or *romesco* sauces. Mon–Fri 9am–1am, Sat noon–1am.

Celler de Tapas Pl. Universitat 5 ☎933 176 488, Ⓦ www.cellerdetapas.com; Ⓜ **Universitat.** Offers a bit more refinement than your average tapas joint, with creative nibbles (sautéed wild mushrooms, grilled cuttlefish and cod brandade) delivered swiftly from a sleek open kitchen. You can make more of a meal of it at the dining room tables. Daily 8am–midnight.

Cerveseria Catalana c/de Mallorca 236 ☎932 160 368; Ⓜ **Passeig de Gràcia.** This place is serious about its tapas and its beer – the counters are piled high, supplemented by a blackboard list of daily specials, while the walls are lined with bottled brews from around the world. It's mostly an after-work kind of place, though lunchtime is always busy too. Daily 9am–1am.

Ciudad Condal Rambla de Catalunya 18 ☎933 181 997; Ⓜ **Passeig de Gràcia.** Cavernous city pit stop that caters for all needs. Breakfast sees the bar groan under the weight of a dozen types of crispy baguette sandwich, piled high on platters, supplemented by a cabinet of croissants and pastries, while the tapas selection ranges far and wide, *patatas bravas* to octopus. Daily 7.30am–1.30am.

dine at tables as well as stand at the bar. Tues–Sat 8.30pm–midnight, Sun 1–3.30pm & 8.30pm–midnight.

Gràcia

El Roble c/Luis Antunez 7, corner c/de la Riera de Sant Miquel ☎ 932 187 387; Ⓜ Diagonal. Roomy L-shaped bar on a busy corner with locals popping in for a snack and a chat. Large tapas selection served promptly to your table (order at the bar; there's a list on the wall) or nudge your way up to the counter and peruse the day's specials. Mon–Sat 7am–midnight; closed Aug.

Sureny Pl. de la Revolució 17 ☎ 932 137 556; Ⓜ Fontana. For a more gourmet experience in Gràcia – a changing list of seasonal tapas dishes at middling to high prices. It's good for a relaxed meal because you can

Sarrià

Bar Tomás c/Major de Sarrià 49 ☎ 932 031 077; FGC Sarrià. It requires a special trip to the 'burbs (12min by train from Pl. Catalunya FGC station) but it has to be done for a taste of the *patatas bravas* of the gods – a dish of fried potatoes with garlic mayo and *salsa picante*. It's not all they serve in this utterly unassuming, white-Formica-table bar, but it might as well be, as that's what the queues are for. They fry between noon and 3pm and 6pm and closing so if it's *bravas* you want, note the hours. Daily except Wed 8am–10pm; closed Aug.

Restaurants

Most restaurants in Barcelona serve a mixture of local **Catalan** and more mainstream Spanish food. The feature on p.188 provides a rundown of specialities, while for a **menu reader** turn to p.284. **Regional Spanish** and **colonial Spanish** cuisine is fairly well represented, too, from Basque and Galician to Cuban and Filipino, while traditionally the fancier local restaurants have tended towards a refined Catalan-French style of dining. This has been superseded recently by the two dominant trends in **contemporary Spanish cooking**, namely the food-as-chemistry approach pioneered by superchef Ferran Adrià (see p.190) and the more accessible tendency towards so-called **fusion** cuisine (basically Mediterranean flavours with exotic touches). Other specialist places to note are the city's *marisqueries* (*marisquerias*), which concentrate on fish and seafood, and the traditional taverns where grilled chicken and meats are the house speciality. The range of **foreign and ethnic** restaurants is not as wide as in other European cities, with Italian, Chinese, Middle Eastern and Indian and Pakistani food providing the main choices, though the cuisines of Latin America, North Africa, Southeast Asia and Japan are also represented.

Nearly all restaurants offer a three-course **menú del dia** (menu of the day) at lunchtime (usually Mon–Fri), with the cheapest starting at about €8, rising to €12 in fancier places. In many restaurants the price includes a drink, so this can be a real bargain. At night, the set menus aren't generally available but eating out is still pretty good value and you'll be able to dine in a huge variety of restaurants for around €25 a head – though you can, of course, pay a lot more. If your main criteria are price and quantity, look for a **buffet restaurant** (*Fresc Co* has several outlets, and there are many others), where €8–10 gets you unlimited access to the hot and cold *buffet lliure* (free buffet). In other bars or cafés, budget meals often come in the form of a *plat combinat* (*plato combinado*, combined plate), of things like eggs, steak, calamari or chicken with fries and salad. Be warned that many cheaper restaurants and cafés might not provide a written **menu**, with the waiter merely reeling off the day's dishes at bewildering speed. To ask for a menu, request *la carta*.

Opening hours for restaurants are generally 1pm to 4pm and 8.30pm to 11pm, though most locals don't eat lunch until 2pm and dinner at 9pm or

10pm. However, in tourist and entertainment zones like Maremàgnum and the Port Olímpic, restaurants tend to stay open all day and will serve on request. A lot of restaurants **close on Sundays or Mondays, on public holidays and throughout August** – check the listings for specific details but expect changes, since many places imaginatively interpret their own posted opening days and times.

If there's somewhere you'd particularly like to eat – certainly at the more fashionable end of the market – you should **reserve a table**. Some places are booked solid for days, or weeks, in advance. Finally, all restaurant menus should make it clear whether the seven-percent **IVA** tax is included in the prices or not.

Ramblas and the Barri Gòtic

Inexpensive

Venus Delicatessen c/Avinyó 25 ☎933 011 585; Ⓜ Liceu/Jaume I. Mediterranean cuisine available throughout the day and night. It's good for vegetarians, with things like lasagne, couscous, moussaka and salads mostly meat-free, and all costing around €5–9. Mon–Sat noon–midnight.

Moderate

Arc Café c/Carabassa 19 ☎933 025 204, Ⓦ www.arccafe.com; Ⓜ Drassanes. One of the old town's best contemporary brasseries presents a seasonally changing à la carte menu that's a smorgasbord of Mediterranean and fusion flavours. Best of all, meals are served nonstop all day. Daily 1pm–1am, Fri & Sat until 2am.

Can Culleretes c/Quintana 5 ☎933 173 022; Ⓜ Liceu. Supposedly Barcelona's oldest restaurant (founded in 1786), serving good-value Catalan food in traditional surroundings. Local families come in droves, especially for celebrations or for Sunday lunch. Tues–Sat 1.30–4pm & 9–11pm, Sun 1.30–4pm.

Matsuri Pl. Regomir 1 ☎932 681 535, Ⓦ www. matsuri-restaurante.com; Ⓜ Jaume I. Creative Southeast Asian cuisine, concentrating on Thai-style noodles, soups, curries, salads, and sushi and sashimi. Tastes are very definitely Catalan in execution – nothing too spicy or adventurous – but it's a relaxed place to eat, with friendly staff. Mon–Thurs 1.30–3.30pm & 8.30–11.30pm, Fri & Sat 1.30–3.30pm & 8.30pm–midnight.

El Salón c/L'Hostal d'en Sol 6–8 ☎933 152 159; Ⓜ Jaume I. This is a really charming place for a cosy dinner, with candlelit tables in a Gothic dining room with imaginative seasonal Mediterranean cooking. The *menú del dia* is available at night too, and offers real value for money, puddings are a highlight and there's a bar (until 2am) that encourages lingering into the small hours. Mon–Sat 1.30–4.30pm & 8.30pm–midnight; closed two weeks in Aug.

La Verònica c/d'Avinyo 30 ☎934 121 122; Ⓜ Jaume I. Delicious pizzas (all bar one vegetarian) and inventive salads – such as *escalivada* on your dough, and sunflower seeds, red cabbage, onions and olives with mixed greens on the side. Tables outside on funky Plaça George Orwell catch the sun during the day; at night there's a bit of a gay scene. Daily noon–1am; closed two weeks in Feb and two weeks in Aug.

The restaurants listed below are the pick of the specifically vegetarian places in Barcelona, but you'll also be able to eat well in many regular tapas bars and modern Catalan brasseries and restaurants. Some salads and vegetable dishes are strictly vegan – like *espinacs a la Catalana* (spinach, pine nuts and raisins) and *escalivada* (roasted aubergine, onions and peppers). Otherwise, there are plenty of Middle Eastern, Indian and Pakistani restaurants, where you can order veg curries or a falafel-stuffed pitta, while Italian restaurants are always a reliable stand-by. The **websites** ⓦ www.sincarne.net and ⓦ www.vegdining.com are useful for listings and reviews in Barcelona.

Arco Iris c/Roger de Flor 216, Eixample ☏ 934 582 283; Ⓜ Verdaguer. Simple café near the Sagrada Família serving a low-cost, four-course lunchtime veggie *menú del dia* (drinks extra). Typically, you'll start with a cream of vegetable soup or consommé, and finish with fresh fruit. Mon–Sat 1–4pm; closed Aug. Inexpensive.

L'Atzavara c/Muntaner 109, Eixample ☏ 934 545 925; Ⓜ Provença. This lunch-only spot is a bit more gourmet than many similar places, with a choice of half a dozen starters and soups, and three or four mains (stuffed peppers, say, or a vegetarian *fideuà*) and puds. Mon–Sat 1–4pm. Inexpensive.

La Bascula c/Flassaders 30, La Ribera ☏ 933 199 866; Ⓜ Jaume I. An old chocolate factory in the back-streets has been given a hippy-chic makeover – bar at the front, with echoing dining room at the rear. The food is great, with speciality stuffed pasta and *empanadas* made daily, plus gourmet sandwiches, crepes, dipping platters, salads, and dozens of teas, coffees, organic wines, juices and shakes. No credit cards. Tues–Sat 1pm–midnight. Moderate.

Biocenter c/Pintor Fortuny 25, El Raval ☏ 933 014 583; Ⓜ Liceu. One of the longest-running Raval veggie places, with a restaurant-bar across the road from the original health-food store. The fixed-price menú del dia starts serving at 1pm, with soup and a trawl through the salad bar for a first course, followed by market-fresh mains. Mon–Sat 9am–5pm. Inexpensive.

Illa de Gràcia c/Sant Domènec 19, Gràcia ☏ 932 380 229; Ⓜ Diagonal. Sleek vegetarian dining room where the food is a cut above – think grilled tofu, stuffed aubergine gratin or wholewheat spaghetti *carbonara*. The veggie lasagne is a weekend special and the tofu burger also comes highly recommended. Tues–Fri 1–4pm & 9pm–midnight, Sat & Sun 2pm–midnight; closed mid-Aug to mid-Sept. Inexpensive.

Juicy Jones c/Cardenal Casañas 7, Barri Gòtic ☏ 933 024 330; Ⓜ Liceu. Veggie and vegan restaurant and juice bar with a *menú del día* that touches all corners of the world – cashew, carrot and coriander soup could be followed by pumpkin-stuffed gnocchi. The restaurant inhabits a mural-and-graffiti-splashed cellar at the back – juices are squeezed and soya milkshakes whizzed at the front bar. No credit cards. Daily 10am–midnight. Inexpensive.

Sesamo c/Sant Antoni Abat 52, El Raval ☏ 934 416 411; ⓦ www.sesamo-bcn.com; Ⓜ Sant Antoni. Innovative vegetarian cooking that will please the most discerning palate. The recipe: fresh, organic ingredients and influences from all over the globe. Mon & Wed–Sat 1–3.30pm & 9–11.30pm, Sun 8.30–11pm.

Expensive

Café de l'Acadèmia c/Lledó 1 ☏ 933 198 253; Ⓜ Jaume I. Creative Catalan cooking in a romantic stone-flagged restaurant, with lovely summer *terrassa* in the medieval square outside. Dishes range from confit of *bacallà* with spinach and pine kernels, or aubergine terrine with goat's cheese, plus grills, fresh fish and rice dishes. Prices are very reasonable (mains €10–16)

and it's always busy, so dinner reservations are essential. A no-choice *menú del dia* is a bargain for the quality; breakfast is served too. Mon–Fri 9am-noon, 1.30–4pm & 8.45–11.30pm; closed two weeks in Aug.

Los Caracoles c/Escudellers 14 ☏ 933 023 185; Ⓜ Liceu/Drassanes. A cavernous Barcelona landmark with spit-roast chickens turning on grills outside, dining rooms on various floors adorned with chandeliers and oils, and an open kitchen straight out of Mervyn Peake's "Gormenghast". The restaurant name means "snails", a house speciality, and the chicken's good too. There's a full Catalan/Spanish menu in a multitude of languages. Service can be chaotic, to say the least, and the best that can be said about the whole affair sometimes is that it's been an experience – you certainly won't forget it. Daily 1pm–midnight.

Limbo c/de la Mercè 13 ☎933 107 699; Ⓜ **Liceu**. Designer restaurant with an intimate feel, presenting an eclectic menu of seasonal fusion cuisine – tuna with stilton, say, or Thai noodles and curries. Mon–Thurs & Sun 9pm–midnight, Fri & Sat 9pm–1am.

Els Quatre Gats c/Montsió 3 ☎933 024 140, Ⓦ www.4gats.com; Ⓜ **Catalunya**. The *modernista*-designed haunt of Picasso and his contemporaries – the lofty interior has rich furnishings, tiles and paintings, and was the setting for Picasso's first public exhibition. Now it's a pricey Catalan restaurant and bar aimed squarely at tourists that some find a bit disappointing, foodwise at least. Daily 1pm–1am.

Shunka c/Sagristans 5 ☎934 124 991; Ⓜ **Jaume I**. Locals think this is the best Japanese restaurant in the old town – it's certainly always busy, so it's essential to make an advance reservation. The open kitchen and the bustling staff are half the show, while the food's reliably good – sushi to udon noodles, plus more esoteric specials like a memorable baked aubergine with red-bean sauce. Mon–Fri 1.30–3.30pm & 8.30–11.30pm, Sat & Sun 2–4pm & 8.30–11.30pm; closed two weeks in Aug.

Sant Pere

Inexpensive

🏃 **L'Econòmic** Pl. de Sant Agustí Vell 13 ☎933 196 494; Ⓜ **Jaume I**. The beauti-

fully old tiled dining room dates back to 1932, and makes the perfect surrounding for a hearty three-course set lunch, served up, as the name implies, for a very reasonable price. Well-cooked standards (grilled pork or chicken escalopes, a fish of the day) alternate with finer fare – like a pasta salad with black olive paste and salmon. It's nearly always full, but you can wait outside under the arcades until a table is free. No credit cards. Mon–Fri 12.30–4.30pm; closed Aug.

Lar O'Marulo c/Bou de Sant Pere 13 ☎933 105 798; Ⓜ **Urquinaona**. A popular lunchtime-only place for local workers. There is a choice of eight starters and eight mains, plus dessert and wine, at a knock-down price. The food is straightforward and Spanish, fresh from the market, and it's a busy, chatter-filled dining room. Mon–Fri 12.30–4.30pm.

Moderate

🏃 **Cuines Santa Caterina** Mercat Santa Caterina, Avgda. Francesc Cambó s/n ☎932 689 918, Ⓦ www.cuinessantacaterina.com; Ⓜ **Jaume I**. The new neighbourhood market has a ravishing open-plan restaurant, with refectory tables set under soaring wooden rafters. The food touches all bases – pasta to sushi, Catalan rice dishes to Thai curries – with daily specials rolling along an airport-style departure board above the open kitchen. Portions aren't enormous, but they're not expensive either (most things cost €8–10 – or you can just drink and munch superior tapas at the horseshoe bar. Bar daily 9am–midnight, restaurant 1–4pm & 9pm–midnight.

Pla de la Garsa c/Assaonadors 13 ☎933 152 413; Ⓜ **Jaume I**. Seventeenth-century stone-and-beam house that's a relaxing place to sip wine, and eat pâté, cheese, sliced meats and other refined fare. Daily 8pm–2am.

Learn to cook with the experts

The **Aula Gastronómica Boqueria** (Boqueria Cookery School), at the back of the Boqueria market, runs a weekly programme of cooking classes, demonstrations and children's sessions. It's a great way to learn more about Catalan food, though you'll have to be prepared to be instructed in Catalan or Spanish. Sessions cost up to €50, and you can get a current programme by calling ☎933 040 272 or checking the Boqueria website Ⓦ www.boqueria.info (click on "Aula").

Traditional Catalan food places heavy emphasis on meat, olive oil, garlic, fruit and salad. The cuisine is typified by a willingness to mix flavours, so savoury dishes cooked with nuts or fruit are common, as are salads using both cooked and raw ingredients.

Meat is usually either grilled and served with a few fried potatoes or salad, or – like ham – cured or dried and served as a starter, or in sandwiches. Grilled sausage served with a pool of stewed haricot beans is a classic menu item in traditional taverns. Stewed veal and other casseroles are common, while poultry is often mixed with seafood (chicken and prawns) or fruit (chicken or duck with prunes or pears) for tastes very definitely out of the Spanish mainstream. In season, **game** is also available, especially partridge, hare, rabbit and boar.

Surprisingly, fresh **fish and seafood** is almost always expensive, since much of it is imported despite the local fishing industries up and down the Catalan coast. However, you'll be offered hake, tuna, squid or cuttlefish even in cheap restaurants, and the local anchovies are superb. Cod is often salted and turns up in *esquiexada*, a summer salad of *bacallà* (salt cod), tomatoes, onions and olives. Fish stews are a speciality in certain restaurants, though the mainstays of seafood restaurants throughout the city are the rice- and noodle-based dishes. **Paella** comes originally from Valencia, but as that region was historically part of Catalunya, the dish has been enthusiastically adopted as Catalunya's own. More certainly Catalan is **fideuà**, thin noodles served with seafood in a flat pan – you stir in the fiery *all i olli* (garlic mayonnaise) provided. **Arròs negre** (black rice) is another local delicacy: rice cooked with squid in squid ink.

Vegetables rarely amount to more than a few French fries or boiled potatoes with the main dish, though vegetable dishes do appear on some menus, like Catalan spinach (tossed with raisins and pine nuts) or *samfaina*, a ratatouille-like stew. Spring is the season for **calçots**, huge spring onions, which are roasted whole and eaten with a spicy *romesco* dipping sauce. Autumn sees the arrival of **wild mushrooms**, mixed with rice, omelettes, salads or scrambled eggs. In winter, a dish of **stewed beans or lentils** is also a popular starter, almost certainly flavoured with bits of sausage, meat and fat. Or you can start your meal with a **salad** or a platter of sliced, cured meats and cheese.

The best dessert is often fresh **fruit**, especially in summer, when you can expect a choice of melon, peach, apricot, pear and orange. There's always *crème caramel* (*flan* in Catalan) – fantastic when home-made – though *crema Catalana* is the local choice, more like a crème brûlée, with a caramelized sugar coating. Or you might be offered *músic*, nuts and dried fruit served with a glass of sweet *moscatel* wine.

Check the **food glossary**, p.284, for help when faced with a restaurant menu; it gives all the basic food words and plenty of Catalan specialities, too. For details of **how to cook** Catalan food, see p.266.

La Ribera

Inexpensive

Bar Salvador c/dels Canvis Nous 8 ⓣ933 101 041; Ⓜ Jaume I/Barceloneta. Everything in this simple workers' café costs around €5, which is why tables are packed at lunch, but you don't have to wait long. Fillets of fish in egg batter, grilled steak with potato wedges, chickpeas with sausage or garlic chicken are examples from a changing menu of six or seven starters, six or seven mains and a few classic puds. Lunch starts at 1.30pm – before that, it's filled crusty sandwiches for Catalan breakfast. Mon–Fri 9am–5pm.

Casa Delfin Pg. del Born 36 ⓣ933 195 088; Ⓜ Jaume I/Barceloneta. Old-school paper-tablecloth bar-restaurant that packs in the locals for a cheap-and-cheerful *menú del dia* – up to ten fish and ten meat choices, from grills to stews, topped off by home-made desserts or fruit. Add a coffee and the whole blowout shouldn't top €12. Mon–Sat 8am–5pm; closed Aug.

Moderate

Al Passatore Pl. del Palau 8 ⓣ 933 197 851; Ⓜ **Barceloneta.** The pizzas are immense, and definitely the main event as other dishes are frequently disappointing. In good weather you'll need to get your name on the list if you want an outdoor table – but the fast turnover means there's usually space here, in the bigger branch across the square at no. 11, or at one of the other city locations (including Port Olímpic). Mon–Wed 1pm–12.30am, Thurs–Sun 1pm–1am.

Mar de la Ribera c/Sombrerers 7 ⓣ 933 151 336; Ⓜ **Jaume I.** A cosy little place around the back of Santa Maria del Mar serving the best Galician-style seafood at decent prices. Try any of the steaks and fillets – hake, salmon, tuna, sole, calamari – dressed with oil, garlic and chopped parsley, accompanied by tasty platters of grilled vegetables. Mixed fried fish and paella are also highly recommended. Mon 8–11.30pm, Tues–Sat 1–4pm & 8–11.30pm.

Salero c/Rec 60 ⓣ 933 198 022; Ⓜ **Barceloneta.** A crisp, modern space fashioned from an old cod warehouse – if white is your colour, you'll enjoy the experience with the kind of clientele that shops in the nearby boutiques. The food's largely Asian, such as an aubergine, coconut and pumpkin curry or a *mee goreng* (fried noodle) of the day. Weekend reservations advised. Mon–Fri 1.30–4pm & 9pm–midnight, Sat 9pm–1am.

Senyor Parellada c/Argenteria 37 ⓣ 933 105 094; Ⓜ **Jaume I.** Utterly gorgeous renovation of an eighteenth-century building has kept the arcaded interior and splashed the walls yellow. Food is traditional Catalan through and through – *sepia* (cuttlefish) and *bacallà* (cod), home-style cabbage rolls, duck with figs, a *papillote* of beans with herbs – served from a long menu that doesn't bother dividing starters from mains. Most dishes cost between €7 and €12, while more than a dozen puds await those who struggle through. Daily 1–4pm & 8.30pm–midnight.

Expensive

Arrel del Born c/Fusina 5 ⓣ 933 199 299, Ⓦ www.arreldelborn.com; Ⓜ **Barceloneta.** Lovely, light-filled restaurant with a warehouse-style interior, opposite the old Born market. Fish is the speciality here, caught by the owner's uncle, and the rice dishes are fantastic. The service is charming, and prices are very reasonable for the quality. Mon–Sat

1–4pm & 8.30pm–midnight, Sun 1–4pm.

Espai Sucre c/de la Princesa 53 ⓣ 932 681 630, Ⓦ www.espaisucre.com; Ⓜ **Jaume I.** The "Sugar Space" takes the current fad for food deconstruction off at a tangent by serving pretty much just dessert-inspired creations by Jordi Butrón, who assembles flavours and textures with the skill of a magician. There's a three-course or five-course seasonally changing pudding menu, with a small selection of savoury "mains" to pad out the experience. Check the website for a schedule of dessert demos and hands-on courses. Tues–Sat 9pm–midnight; closed Aug.

Santa Maria c/Comerç 17 ⓣ 933 151 227, Ⓦ www.santamania.biz; Ⓜ **Jaume I.** Paco Guzmán's new-wave tapas bar has a glass-fronted kitchen turning out taste sensations – such as Catalan sushi, octopus confit, yucca chips, or quail with salsa. Around €40 should get you a filling range of dishes, finishing on a high note with the famous "Dracula" dessert – a shot glass of strawberry and vanilla cream flavours with pop-rocks that sets off crackles in your head. Tues–Sat 1.30–3.30pm & 8.30pm–12.30am; closed two weeks in Aug.

Set Portes Pg. d'Isabel II 14 ⓣ 933 192 950 or 933 193 033, Ⓦ www.grup7portes.com; Ⓜ **Barceloneta.** A wood-panelled classic with the names of its famous clientele much to the fore – they've all eaten here, Errol Flynn to Yoko Ono. The decor in the "Seven Doors" has barely changed in 170 years and, while very elegant, it's not exclusive – you should book ahead, though, as the queues can be horrendous. The renowned rice dishes are fairly reasonably priced (€12–17), but for a full meal you're looking at around €40 a head, plus drinks. Daily 1pm–1am.

Very expensive

Àbac c/del Rec 79 ⓣ 933 196 600, Ⓦ www.restaurantabac.com; Ⓜ **Barceloneta.** The minimalist domain of top chef Xavier Pellicer, who refines Catalan food in ever more imaginative ways – for example, roast partridge served with pears, or lamb in vanilla milk, for well-out-of-the-ordinary dining. Of course, it all comes at a price (more than €80 a head) but it's rated as one of the city's best gourmet experiences. Mon 8.30–11pm, Tues–Sat 1.30–4pm & 8.30–11pm; closed two weeks in Jan & three weeks in Aug.

Comerç 24 c/Comerc 24 ⓣ 933 192 102, Ⓦ www.carlesabellan.com; Ⓜ **Jaume I.** Chef Carles

The best chef in the world, by common consent, is Catalan. **Ferran Adrià**, a self-taught chef from Barcelona, presides over *El Bulli* (Ⓦ www.elbulli.com), his triple-*Michelin*-starred restaurant just outside the town of Roses on the Costa Brava. Dinner here costs €200 a head, but it's barely worth worrying about the price because the tables are booked solid until the next millennium. It's strange, because what Adrià does is less like cooking and more like chemistry, spending the winter months each year when the restaurant is closed refining his techniques in his Barcelona "laboratory". He is the man responsible for breaking down dishes into their constituent ingredients and then playing with them – turning food into foam, distilling vegetable essence into gelatin blocks, injecting a seafood reduction into Rice Krispies, or adding herbs, cheese or even perfume to ice cream. You're either going to think this is fantastic or plain ridiculous but Adrià has spawned a generation of regional Spanish chefs – Jordi Vilà, Paco Guzmán, Andoni Luis Aduriz, Carles Abellan, Ramon Freixa, Xavier Pellicer, Sergi Arola – who are challenging contemporary tastes in an equally inventive fashion.

Abellan presents "glocal" cooking (a mixture of global and local) dishes from around the world, interpreted locally by a master of invention. In an oh-so-cool stripped-down warehouse interior the meal comes tapas-style, mixing flavours and textures with seeming abandon but to calculated effect (such as *foie gras* and truffle hamburger, shot glasses of frothy soup, tuna *sashimi* on pizza). Prices are high (around €70 a head), but this is as good as contemporary dining in the city gets. Reservations advised. Tues–Sat 1.30–3.30pm & 8.30pm–12.30am; closed two weeks in Aug possible.

Passadís del Pep Pl. del Palau 2 Ⓣ **933 101 021;** Ⓜ **Barceloneta.** One of La Ribera's hidden secrets, down a passageway on the square, with no sign and hardly visible from the street. To compound matters there is no menu; instead you are offered wonderfully prepared shellfish, landed at local ports, and fish dishes that depend on the catch. Reservations essential; expect to pay at least €70 a head. Tues–Sat 1.30–4pm & 9–11.30pm; closed Aug.

El Raval

Inexpensive

Bar Ra Pl. de la Garduña 3 Ⓣ **933 014 163,** Ⓦ **www.ratown.com;** Ⓜ **Liceu.** Extremely hip restaurant-bar behind the Boqueria market, with a groove-ridden music policy and a sunny patio, serving up eclectic world cuisine for breakfast, lunch and dinner. You can just drop in for a drink outside meal times, and Sunday brunch is a buzz. Mon–Sat 9am–2am.

Elisabets c/d'Elisabets 2 Ⓣ **933 175 826;** Ⓜ **Catalunya.** Reliable Catalan home cooking served at cramped tables in a jovial brick-walled dining room. Locals breakfast on a sandwich and a glass of wine, the hearty lunchtime *menú del dia* is hard to beat for price, or you can just have tapas and drinks at the bar. No credit cards. Meals Mon–Sat 1–4pm, bar open Mon–Thurs & Sat 7.30am–11pm, Fri 7.30am–2.30am; closed Aug.

Mesón David c/de les Carretes 63 Ⓣ **934 415 934;** Ⓜ **Paral.lel.** Down-to-earth Galician bar-restaurant that's a firm favourite with neighbourhood families who bring their kids before they can walk. The weekday *menú* is a steal – maybe some lentil broth followed by a grilled, butterflied trout and home-made *flan* – though it's the octopus and the *combinado Gallego* ("ham, salami, ear") that has the locals purring. There's a bang on the clog-gong for anyone who tips. Daily except Wed 1–4pm & 8pm–midnight; closed Aug.

Moti Mahal c/de Sant Pau 103 Ⓣ **933 293 252,** Ⓦ **www.motimahalbcn.com;** Ⓜ **Paral.lel.** Indian restaurants have sprouted all over the Raval in recent years, and most don't cut it in British eyes, as spicing is toned down for the local market. The Moti Mahal is considered one of the more authentic places with a typical menu of biryanis, tandoori dishes and curries in various styles and strengths. Daily except Tues 1–4pm & 8pm–midnight.

Pollo Rico c/de Sant Pau 31 Ⓣ **934 413 184;** Ⓜ **Liceu.** Barcelona's original greasy spoon has been here forever and, while it's not to everyone's taste, if you're in the market for good spit-roast chicken, limp fries and a glass of rot-gut, served in double-quick time, this is the place. The upstairs dining room is a tad more sophisticated (only a tad) – either way, you'll be hard pushed to spend €12 from a long menu of Spanish and Catalan staples. No credit cards. Daily 10am–midnight; closed Wed.

Moderate

Ànima c/dels Angels 6 ☎ **933 424 912;** Ⓜ **Liceu.** Only the presence of tables and waiters give the game away – otherwise the slab walls, exposed ducts and smoked glass chairs shriek contemporary art gallery. Seasonally influenced fusion food comes immaculately presented in deep tureens, and staff are informal and charming. Lunch is a treat (it'll cost you three or four times as much at night), especially if you can get a table outside. Mon–Sat 1–4pm & 9pm–midnight.

Ca l'Estevet c/Valldonzella 46 ☎ **933 024 186;** Ⓜ **Universitat.** It's had its heyday, with scarcely a celebrity photo dating later than the 1980s (including a fresh-faced Gary Lineker). But the chatty English-speaking owner works the room with gusto, glad-handing locals and tourists alike, and talking up the short menu. Entrecôte and the *cabri-to* (goat) are the house specials, otherwise it's a market-led daily changing menu. Portions aren't huge, but this is a reliable place for a decent meal. Mon–Sat 1.30–4pm & 8.30–11.30pm; closed two weeks in Aug.

Fil. Manila c/de les Ramelleres 3 ☎ **933 186 487;** Ⓜ **Catalunya.** There's a token effort at bamboo cladding, but this resolute mom-and-pop Filipino establishment is little more than an extension of the family kitchen – the radio or TV provides background, and the kids are fed alongside customers. Sizzling is what the menu does best, but there are warming soups, grilled fish in banana leaves, sautéed meat or fish with garlic sauce, barbecued pork ribs – all good hearty stuff. No credit cards. Daily 11am–4.30pm & 7.30pm–1am; closed Tues.

Mamacafé c/del Dr Joaquim Dou 10 ☎ **933 012 940;** Ⓜ **Catalunya.** It looks like a spruced-up boiler room – aluminium ducts, concrete floor, bare colourwashed walls – but the contemporary Mediterranean food has its moments and the atmosphere is laid back. Mains cover everything from a house ham-

burger to salmon with Indonesian-style rice. Mon–Sat 1–4pm & 8pm–midnight.

Expensive

Biblioteca c/Junta del Comerç 28 ☎ **934 126 221;** Ⓜ **Liceu.** One of the less austere, more agreeable of Barcelona's current dining hot spots – the name's a nod to the library of cookbooks on display. Fish might be cooked Japanese- or Basque-style, lamb given the local treatment (with parsnip and turnip), or venison pie served with a market-fresh veg purée. Meals cost around €40, though the lunchtime *menú del dia* (Tues–Fri) provides a simpler experience. Tues–Sat 1–4pm & 9pm–midnight; closed two weeks in Aug.

Silenus c/dels Àngels 8 ☎ **933 022 680;** Ⓜ **Liceu.** Very arty place near MACBA (it's not a menu, it's a "short treatise") presenting some unique dishes – squid with broad beans and *foie gras*, for example, or even fillets of that well-known Catalan marsupial, the kangaroo. The interior is very now, very Barcelona (distressed walls, leather banquettes, and white tablecloths laid on marble tables). Mon–Thurs 1.30–4pm & 8.30–11.30pm, Fri & Sat 8.30pm–12.30am.

Poble Sec

Moderate

Bella Napoli c/Margarit 14 ☎ **934 425 056;** Ⓜ **Paral.lel/Poble Sec.** The pizzas – the best in the city – come straight from the depths of a beehive-shaped oven, or there's a big range of *antipasti*, pastas, *risotti* and veal *scaloppine*, with almost everything priced between €8 and €12. It's all authentically Neapolitan, right down to the cheery waiters and cheesy pop music, and a regular Italian clientele tells you what a find this is. Tues–Sun 1.30–4.30pm & 8.30pm–12.30am.

La Bodegueta c/de Blai 47 ☎ **934 420 846;** Ⓜ **Poble Sec.** Catalan taverna with food like mother used to make – a relaxed Sunday lunch here brings local families out in force. It is a *torrades*, salads and grills in a good-natured, red-check-tablecloth-and-barrels kind of place – try the excellent grilled veg platter. Tues–Sun 1–4pm & 8.30pm–midnight.

Taverna La Tomaquera c/Margarit 58, no phone; Ⓜ **Paral.lel/Poble Sec.** Sit down in this chatter-filled tavern and the *pa amb*

Hotel restaurants

Some of the city's fanciest Michelin-starred cooking is going on in its hotel restaurants, epitomized by the designer space that is **Moo** (c/Rosselló 265, ☏934 454 000; closed Sun), Felip Llufriu's restaurant at the über-fashionable *Hotel Omm*. At Gaig in the stylish *Hotel Cram* (c/Aragó 214, ☏934 291 017; closed Sun) it's renowned minimalist chef Carles Gaig at the helm, while Madrid-based Sergi Arola lends his name to the *Hotel Arts'* **Arola** (c/Marina 19–21, ☏934 838 090), where designer tapas is the name of the game. Meanwhile, **East 47** at Hotel Claris (c/Pau Claris 150, ☏934 874 647) brings New York style to the city, serving creative Mediterranean cuisine under the gaze of a line of Warhol self-portraits. Prices are high at all these destination-dining spots (€80–100 a head and upwards), and reservations are essential, but there's one hotel restaurant in the city where you can walk right in and that won't break the bank. It's not the food at the Hotel **España** (c/de Sant Pau 9–11, ☏933 181 758) that's the draw, rather the famed *modernista* dining room designed by Domènech i Montaner (see p.57) – the lunchtime *menú del dia* is the best way to experience one of Barcelona's landmark buildings.

tomàquet arrives with a dish of olives and two quails' eggs – and there any delicacy ends as the chefs set to hacking steaks and chops from great sides and ribs of meat. The grilled chicken will be the best you've ever had, and the entrecôtes are enormous, while the locals limber up with an appetizer of pan-fried snails with *chorizo* and tomato. No credit cards. Tues–Sat 1.30–3.45pm & 8.30–10.45pm; closed Aug.

Tivoli's Bistro c/Magalhaes 35 ☏934 414 017, ⓦwww.tivolisbistro.com; Ⓜ Paral.lel/Poble Sec. Home-style Thai cuisine, toned down for local tastes but reasonably priced and run by a nice Catalan-Thai couple, who also organize cooking classes. A set meal (dishes change monthly) is delivered to your table, usually incorporating a starter or two, a red or green curry, a vegetable and fish dish, and Thai noodles. Tues–Fri 8.30–11.30pm, Sat 1.30–3.30pm & 8.30–11.30pm; closed 1st week Jan, & Aug to mid-Sept.

Barceloneta

Inexpensive

Can Ganassa Pl. de Barceloneta 4–6 ☏932 216 739; Ⓜ Barceloneta. Extensive range of tapas and snacks on Barceloneta's central square. It's a real all-dayer – card school over coffee, brandy and tortillas in the morning, a cheap and cheerful *menú del dia* at lunchtime, and more expensive seafood dinners if you want. It's a bit rough-and-ready inside, but tables sprout in the square in summer. Daily except Wed 9am–11pm; closed Nov.

Can Maño Barceloneta ☏933 193 082. There's rarely a tourist in sight in this old-fashioned locals' diner. Fried or grilled fish is the thing, such as sardines, mullet and calamari, though there are some daily specials and basic meat dishes, rough house wine and absolutely no frills. It's an authentic experience, which is likely to cost you less than €12 a head. No credit cards. Mon–Fri noon–5pm & 8.30–11pm, Sat noon–5pm; closed Aug.

Moderate

Can Manel Pg. Joan de Borbó 60 ☏932 215 013; Ⓜ Barceloneta. An institution since 1870, which fills very quickly, inside and out, because the food is both good and reasonably priced. Paella, *fideuà* and *arròs a banda* are staples, while grilled fish always costs more. A weekday lunchtime *menú* keeps the cost down, but there's usually not much fish or seafood choice on this. Daily 1–4pm & 8pm–midnight.

Can Ros c/Almirall Aixada 7 ☏932 215 049; Ⓜ Barceloneta. This is one of the best places to sample paella, *arròs negre* or a *fideuà*, all of which cost around €12. The tables are packed in close together, upstairs and down, but it's a comfortable, no-hurry kind of place. Daily 1–5pm & 8pm–midnight; closed Wed.

dZi Pg. Joan de Borbó 76 ☏932 212 182; Ⓜ Barceloneta. It's pronounced "zhee", which is a Tibetan sacred stone, but the food is Southeast Asian (mainly Chinese, Malaysian and Japanese) either served in the serene dining room or outside on the shady *terrassa*. Yu-shian pork with aubergine or Formosa-style shrimps with ginger are great bets, with green-tea ice cream amongst the desserts. Daily 1–4pm & 8pm–midnight.

Expensive

Antiga Casa Solé c/Sant Carles 4 ⓣ 932 215 012, Ⓦ www.restaurantcansole.com; Ⓜ Barceloneta. Founded in 1903, it was here that *sarsuela* (Catalan fish stew) was invented. Since then, the quiet, formal *Casa Solé* has been dishing up market-fresh fish and seafood, either in stews or casseroles or simply grilled, sautéed or mixed with rice – baked squid and grilled cod are both house specialities. Count on a good €40 a head. Tues–Sat 1.30–4pm & 8.30–11pm, Sun 1.30–4pm; closed two weeks in Aug.

Can Ramonet c/Maquinista 17 ⓣ 933 193 064; Ⓜ Barceloneta. Reputedly the oldest restaurant in the port area, it has the added attraction of a shady *terrassa*. The food's good – splendid paella, plus whatever's fresh from the market that day – and though full meals can be pricey, you can always just hunker down in the front bar where the tapas are piled high on wooden barrels. Daily 1–4pm & 8pm–midnight; closed Sun dinner & Aug.

Suquet de l'Almirall Pg. Joan de Borbó 65 ⓣ 932 216 233; Ⓜ Barceloneta. Let the restaurant do the work for you by plumping for one of the set-menu deals that rattle through the highlights – say, seven tapas samplers with *arròs* to follow. You don't have to have the works though – sweet peppers with anchovies, or a dish of steamed mussels, provide reason enough to linger in the shrub-fronted suntrap *terrassa*. Tues–Sat 1–4pm & 9–11pm, Sun 1–4pm.

Port Olímpic

Moderate

Agua Pg. Marítim 30 ⓣ 932 251 272, Ⓦ www.aguadeltragaluz.com; Ⓜ Ciutadella-Vila Olímpica. Much the nicest boardwalk restaurant, perfect for brunch, though if the weather's iffy you can opt for the sleek, split-level dining room. The menu is seasonal, contemporary Mediterranean – grills, *risotti*, pasta – and the prices are pretty fair, so it's usually busy. Daily 1.30–4pm (Sat & Sun until 5pm) & 8.30–midnight, Fri & Sat until 1am.

Expensive

Bestial c/Ramon Trias Fargas 2–4 ⓣ 932 240 407, Ⓦ www.bestialdeltragaluz.com; Ⓜ Ciuta-

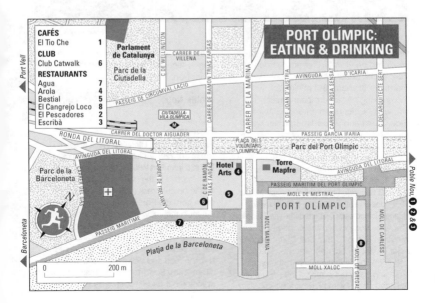

CAFÉS
El Tio Che   1
CLUB
Club Catwalk   6
RESTAURANTS
Agua   7
Arola   4
Bestial   5
El Cangrejo Loco   8
El Pescadores   2
Escribà   3

PORT OLÍMPIC: EATING & DRINKING

Port Vell

Parlament de Catalunya
Parc de la Ciutadella
PASSEIG DE CIRCUMVAL·LACIÓ
CIUTADELLA-VILA OLÍMPICA Ⓜ
CARRER DE WELLINGTON
CARRER DE VILLENA
CARRER DE RAMON TRIAS FARGAS
CARRER DE LA MARINA
AVINGUDA D'ICARIA
C. DE JOAN D'ÀUSTRIA
CARRER DE ROSA SENSAT
C. DE L'ARQUITECTE SERT

RONDA DEL LITORAL
CARRER DEL DOCTOR AIGUADER
PLAÇA DELS VOLUNTARIS OLÍMPICS
PASSEIG GARCIA FARIA
Parc del Port Olímpic

AVINGUDA DEL LITORAL
Parc de la Barceloneta
CARRER DE L'ATLÀNTIDA
CARRER DE TRELAWNY
C. DE RAMON TRIAS FARGAS
Hotel Arts ❹
Torre Mapfre
AVINGUDA DEL LITORAL
PASSEIG MARÍTIM DEL PORT OLÍMPIC
MOLL DE MESTRAL
N
❻ ❺
PASSEIG MARÍTIM
❼
PORT OLÍMPIC
MOLL MARINA
MOLL DE CARLESS I
Barceloneta
Platja de la Barceloneta
MOLL XALOC
❽
MOLL DE GREGAL
Poble Nou ❶ ❷ & ❸

0   200 m

△ Eating out in Bar Ra

della-Vila Olímpica. Near Frank Gehry's fish you'll find an elevated terrace-garden in front of the beach, great for lunch. Inside the decor is sharp and minimalist, while the cooking's Mediterranean, mainly Italian, with dishes given an original twist. Rice, pasta and wood-fired pizzas are in the €9–13 range, with other dishes up to €20. At weekends you can drink at the bar until 3am. Daily 1.30–4pm (Sat & Sun until 5pm) & 8.30pm–midnight, Sat & Sun until 1am.

🏃 El Cangrejo Loco Moll de Gregal 29–30, upper level ☎932 211 748, ⓦwww. elcangrejoloco.com; Ⓜ Ciutadella-Vila Olímpica. The large outdoor terrace or huge picture windows at the "Crazy Crab" offer panoramas of the local coast and marina. The fish and shellfish are first-rate, with the catch changing daily, but a mixed fried-fish plate or broad beans with prawns are typically

Catalan starters. The paella can be thoroughly recommended too, and the service is spot-on. Daily 1pm–1am.

Poble Nou

Expensive

Escribà Ronda del Litoral 42, Platja Bogatell ☎932 210 729; Ⓜ Ciutadella-Vila Olímpica, or bus #36 from Port Vell. Glorified beach shack – a xiringuito in the parlance – that's enough off the beaten track (a 20min walk along the prom from the Port Olímpic) to mark you out as in the know. The paellas and fideuàs (from €13–16) fly out of the kitchen; daily fish specials are more like €20, and there's a ten percent terrace surcharge, but what the hell: the food and views are great. Tues–Sat 11am–1am, Sun 11am–4pm; restricted hours in winter, but usually open weekend lunch.

Very expensive

Els Pescadors Pl. del Prim 1 ☎932 252 018, ⓦwww.elspescadors.com; ⓜPoble Nou. Considered something of a pilgrimage for fish-lovers, a meal here should certainly include a house special *fideuà* or a Catalan classic like cod with *samfaina* – though that's only just scratching the surface of a wide-ranging menu. The restaurant is hidden away in a pretty square with gnarled trees in the back alleys of Rambla de Poble Nou. Daily 1–4pm & 8pm–midnight.

Eixample

Inexpensive

La Flauta c/d'Aribau 23 ☎933 237 038; ⓜUniversitat. One of the city's best-value lunch menus sees potential diners queueing for tables daily – get there before 1pm. It's a handsome bar-restaurant of dark wood, deep colours and black-clad staff, but it's completely unstuffy – the name's a nod to the house speciality gourmet sandwiches (a *flauta* is a thin baguette), which together with inventive tapas are served all day and night at the bar. Lunch depends on what's available that day at the market. Mon–Sat 8am–1am.

Marrakech c/Mallorca 10 ☎934 240 741; ⓜSants Estació. Excellent little back-of-bar restaurant, around the corner from the Moroccan consulate (opposite the *Expo Barcelona* hotel). You'll have to ignore the TV, but the dips, kebabs, tagines and couscous are all delicious, with nothing costing more than around €8. Daily 1–4pm & 8pm–midnight.

El Mussol c/Aragó 261 ☎934 876 151, ⓜPasseig de Gràcia; branch at c/de Casp 19 ☎933 017 610, ⓜCatalunya/Passeig de Gràcia. Big rustic diners of the type that's all the rage in the city, known for their meat and vegetables *a la brasa*, most of which run between €5 and €10. *Calçots* (big spring onions) are a spring speciality, while snails are on the menu all year round. There are also *torrades*, tapas, home-made desserts – the usual Catalan menu – and it opens early for sandwich-and-croissant breakfasts for city workers. Meals daily 1pm–1am.

O Pote Pl. del Dr. Letamendi 29 ☎934 541 881, ⓜPasseig de Gràcia/Universitat. For a cheap uptown meal in a convivial atmosphere this family-run Galician bar-restaurant might

just do the trick. Fried and grilled fish and seafood is the speciality, from baby squid to garlic prawns, served on paper tablecloths with no airs or graces. Mon–Sat 1–4pm & 8–11pm.

Moderate

El Glop de la Rambla Rambla de Catalunya 65 ☎934 870 097, ⓦwww.elglopdelarambla.com, ⓜPasseig de Gràcia; **Braseria El Glop** c/de Casp 21 ☎933 187 575, ⓦwww.braseriaelglop.com, ⓜCatalunya. Reliable Catalan tavern-style diners, with a changing daily menu of *torrades*, salads, rice, pasta and grills, attracting an grab-it-and-go city clientele. Daily 1–4pm & 8pm–1am.

La Muscleria c/Mallorca 290 ☎934 589 844; ⓜVerdaguer. Barcelona's mussels specialist, with a score of sauces and toppings on pots and platters, accompanied by some of the best fries in the city, plus Asturian cider or Galician and Penedès wines. Sautéed clams, *pulpo*, fried *chipirones* or calamares are offered as starters, and there are a few salad-and-snack plates offered, but basically, if bivalves don't appeal, you're in the wrong place. The black-and-terracotta basement is no place for a quiet tête-à-tête either. Mon–Fri 1–4pm & 8.30pm–midnight, Sat 8.30pm–1am.

El Japonés Ptge. de la Concepció 2 ☎934 872 592, ⓦwww.grupotragaluz.com/japones; ⓜDiagonal. Designer-style – gun-metal grey interior, staff-in-black service – at moderate prices gives this minimalist Japanese restaurant the edge over its more traditional rivals. Tick your sushi, sashimi, tempura and noodle choices from the long menu and hand it to the waiter. Mon–Thurs & Sun 1.30–4pm & 8.30pm–midnight, Fri & Sat 1.30–4pm & 8.30pm–1am.

Radio-Ohm c/Muntaner 55 ☎934 5 13 609; ⓜUniversitat. A few shops in this old electrical retailers' district still survive – this one has been given a new lease of life as a Mediterranean-fusion restaurant, but retains a few nods to its old trade in the lighting and decor. Lunch is busy – the menú del dia includes a soup and salad bar – while at night the seasonally changing menu offers three courses for €25. Mon–Sat 1–4pm & 9pm–midnight.

La Tramoia Rambla de Catalunya 15 ☎934 123 634, ⓦwww.grupcacheiro.com; ⓜCatalunya/Passeig de Gràcia. Fashionable eatery for anything from a coffee and croissant to

⑧

EATING | Restaurants

a filling meal. Snack downstairs on tapas and *torrades* or head upstairs for Catalan brasserie food, including meat, fish and seasonal vegetables straight from the grill. It's a bit on the pricey side, but the staff are very accommodating and it's a handy meeting point. Daily 7.30am–1.30am.

Expensive

O'Nabo de Lugo c/de Pau Claris 169 ⊕ **932 153 047;** Ⓜ **Diagonal.** A la carte meals in this renowned Galician seafood restaurant can easily top €40, but arrive at lunch for the cut-price *menú del dia* and you'll get to sample standards like thick, meaty broth or *boutifarra* and potatoes; for more choice (and for some fish), trade up to the *menú especial*. The gruff, waistcoated waiters tend to know the locals by name but show the same generosity to all, leaving the wine bottle on your table for refills. Mon–Sat 1–4pm & 8.30pm–midnight.

Thai Gardens c/Diputació 273 ⊕ **934 879 898;** Ⓜ **Passeig de Gràcia.** Barcelona's favourite Thai restaurant is an over-the-top experience of fountains and gilded elephants. Authenticity loses its way here and there, but the weekday lunch deal is popular while an English-language menu highlights things like a creamy prawn and vegetable curry or spicy ground pork with Thai basil. Daily 1.30–4pm & 8.30–midnight, until 1am at weekends.

🏃 **Tragaluz Ptge. de la Concepció 5** ⊕ **934 870 621,** Ⓦ **www.grupotragaluz.com/tragaluz;** Ⓜ **Diagonal.** Attracts beautiful people by the score, and the classy Mediterranean-with-knobs-on cooking, served under a glass roof (*tragaluz* means "skylight") doesn't disappoint. Mains cost €16–22, though cheaper eats are served downstairs courtesy of the *Tragarràpid* menu (served daily 1pm–midnight), where *fajitas* or a club sandwich cater for those fresh off the *modernista* trail (La Pedrera is just across the way). Daily 1.30–4pm & 8.30pm–midnight, Thurs–Sat until 1am.

Very expensive

Casa Calvet c/de Casp 48 ⊕ **934 124 012;** Ⓜ **Urquinaona.** Dining in Gaudí's wonderfully decorated townhouse is a glam night out. A seasonally changing, modern Catalan menu runs the gamut from simple (shrimp with home-made pasta and parmesan) to elaborate (duck livers with a balsamic vin-

egar reduction), and the desserts – some of which you have to order on arrival – are an artwork in themselves. Mon–Sat 1–3.30pm & 8.30–11.30pm; closed two weeks in Aug.

Cinc Sentits c/Aribau 58 ⊕ **933 239 490,** Ⓦ **www.cincsentits.com;** Ⓜ **Passeig de Gràcia/ Universitat.** Dishes are assembled with great flair in this contemporary "tasting restaurant" – wild fish with black-olive compôte and lemon marmalade is typical – and though some find the whole experience a bit overly formal there's no doubting the skill in the "Five Senses" kitchen. A business lunch is realistically priced, while for €75 you have the run of the tasting menu and accompanying wines. Mon 1.30–3.30pm, Tues–Sat 1.30–3.30pm & 8.30–11pm.

Gorria c/de la Diputacio 421 ⊕ **932 451 164,** Ⓦ **www.restaurantegorria.com;** Ⓜ **Monumental.** This elegant family-owned restaurant serves the finest seasonal Basque cuisine, like *pochas de Sanguesa* (a sort of white-bean stew), clams and hake in salsa verde, or wood-grilled lamb and suckling pig. Prices are steep, but this is regional Spanish cooking of the highest order. Mon–Sat 1–3.30pm & 9–11.30pm; closed Aug.

Gràcia

Inexpensive

🏃 **Flash, Flash c/de la Granada del Penedès 25** ⊕ **932 370 990,** Ⓦ **www.grup7portes. com;** Ⓜ **Diagonal.** A classic 1970s survivor, *Flash, Flash* does tortillas (most €5–6) – served any way you like, from plain and simple to elaborately stuffed or doused in salsa, with sweet ones for dessert. If that doesn't grab you, there's a small menu of salads, soups and burgers. Either way, you'll love the original white leatherette seating and monotone "models-with-cameras" Pop-Art photography – very Austin Powers. Daily 1pm–1.30am, bar open 11am–2am.

La Gavina c/Ros de Olano 17 ⊕ **934 157 450;** Ⓜ **Fontana.** This wacky pizzeria, known locally as "Els Angels" – due to the fact that the only sign is a series of *putti* pasted over the door – is a Gràcia legend. Arrive after 8pm and you will have a long wait, but no reservations are accepted. Tues–Sun noon–1am.

Habibi c/Gran de Gràcia 7 ⊕ **932 179 545;** Ⓜ **Diagonal.** Bright and breezy North African dining room with a summer *terrassa*.

The Plat Habibi gives you a taste of all the house specials – from a minty tabbouleh to lamb and chicken *schawarma* – and the *maghmour* (chickpeas with aubergine and mint) is excellent. Add a fresh-squeezed juice (there's no alcohol served), a home-made dessert and a mint tea and you're still unlikely to spend more than €15. Mon–Fri 1pm–1am, Sat 2–4.30pm & 8pm–1am.

Nou Candanchu Pl. Rius i Taulet 9 ☎ **932 377 362;** Ⓜ **Fontana.** Sit beneath the clock tower in summer and choose from the wide selection of local dishes – tapas and hot sandwiches but also steak and eggs, steamed clams and mussels, or cod and hake cooked plenty of ways. It's managed by an affable bunch of young guys, and there's lots of choice for €8–12. Daily except Tues 7am–1am, Fri & Sat until 3am.

Moderate

Emu c/Guilleries 17 ☎ **932 184 502;** Ⓜ **Fontana.** Emu's Australian owner-chef cooks up the most authentic Southeast Asian food in town, properly spiced and properly fiery. The short menu changes constantly – but expect Thai curry with kangaroo – and all the wines are blockbuster Aussies, with Aboriginal art to match. There are only a few tables (it's as much bar as restaurant), so go before 9.30pm or book. Mon–Thurs 7pm–2am, Fri & Sat 7pm–3am, meals served 8.30pm–midnight; Nov–March Thurs–Sat 7pm–2 or 3am.

Octubre c/Julian Romea 18 ☎ **932 182 518;** Ⓜ **Diagonal.** For romance and the food to go with it, it's hard to beat this warm, rustic little charmer. The Catalan menus are seasonal but constants are the sensational desserts and the good-value prices – around €25 for three courses. Mon–Fri 1.30–3.30pm & 9–11pm, Sat 9–11pm; closed Aug.

La Singular c/Francesc Giner 50 ☎ **932 375 098;** Ⓜ **Diagonal.** The tiniest of kitchens turns out refined Mediterranean food at budget prices – think sticky pork ribs with strawberry

sauce on mash, seasonal salads, or a daily paella or *fideuà* dish. It's a cornerstone of the neighbourhood, with a friendly atmosphere, but there are only nine tables and a line of seats at the bar, so go early. Mon–Fri 1–4pm & 9pm–midnight; closed Sat lunch & Sun.

Taverna El Glop c/Sant Lluís 24 ☎ **932 137 058,** Ⓦ **www.tavernaelglop.com;** Ⓜ **Joanic.** The rusticity (stone-flagged floors, beams, baskets of garlic) stops just the right side of parody and the lunch *menú* is one of the city's best deals; otherwise expect to spend €15–20 a head for grills and other tavern specials, prepared in front of you on the open kitchen ranges, while waiters scurry back and forth bearing vast slabs of meat and *torrades*. At the weekend you may have to wait for a table. Tues–Sun 1–4pm & 8pm–1am.

Very expensive

Jean Luc Figueras c/Santa Teresa 10 ☎ **934 152 877;** Ⓜ **Diagonal.** Michelin-starred Franco-Catalan cooking of the highest calibre, at the highest prices – reckon on at least €100 a head. It's a very sophisticated place that's first port of call for most dedicated foodies. The menu changes with the seasons and market availability. Mon–Sat 1.30–3.30pm & 8.30–11.30pm; closed Aug.

Sant-Gervasi

Moderate

Casa Fernandez c/Santaló 46 ☎ **932 019 308,** Ⓦ **www.casafernandez.com; FGC Gràcia.** The long kitchen hours are a boon for the bar-crawlers in this neck of the woods. It's a contemporary place featuring market cuisine, snappily served, though they are specialists in – of all things – fried eggs, either served straight with chips or add Catalan sausage, foie gras or other bespoke accompaniments. Daily 1pm–1.30am.

EIXAMPLE, GRÀCIA & SARRIÀ-SANT GERVASI : EATING & DRINKING

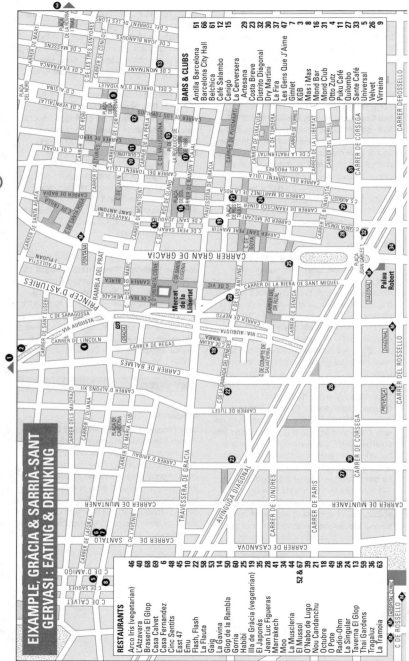

RESTAURANTS

Arco Iris (vegetarian)	46
L'Atzavara	40
Braseria El Glop	68
Casa Calvet	69
Casa Fernandez	6
Cinc Sentits	48
East 47	45
Emu	10
Flash, Flash	22
La Flauta	58
Gaig	53
La Gavina	14
Glop de la Rambla	50
Gorria	60
Habibi	25
Illa de Gràcia (vegetarian)	19
El Japonés	35
Jean Luc Figueras	28
Marrakech	41
Moo	34
La Muscleria	44
El Mussol	52 & 67
O'Nabo de Lugo	39
Nou Candanchu	21
Octubre	18
O Pote	49
Radio-Ohm	56
La Singular	24
Taverna El Glop	13
Thai Gardens	59
Tragaluz	36
La Tramoia	63

BARS & CLUBS

Antilla Barcelona	51
Barcelona City Hall	66
Belchica	61
Café Salambo	12
Canigó	15
La Cerversera	29
Artesana	23
Costa Breve	32
Distrito Diagonal	30
Dry Martini	37
La Fira	47
Les Gens Que J'Aime	7
Gimlet	3
KGB	8
Mas i Mas	16
Mond Bar	31
Mond Club	4
Otto Zutz	11
Puku Café	27
Quilombo	33
Sante Café	5
Universal	26
Velvet	9
Virreina	

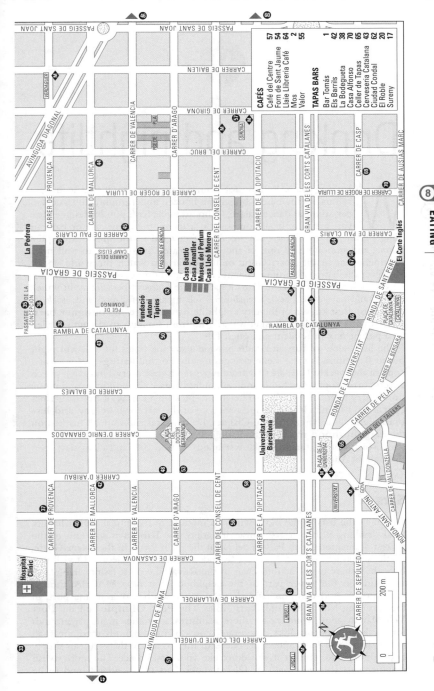

CAFÉS
Café del Centre	57
Forn de Sant Jaume	54
Llaie Llibreria Café	64
Mos	2
Valor	55

TAPAS BARS
Bar Tomás	1
Els Barrils	42
La Bodegueta	38
Casa Alfonso	70
Celler de Tapas	65
Cerveseria Catalana	43
Ciudad Condal	62
El Roble	20
Sureny	17

Drinking and nightlife

Whatever you're looking for from a night out, you'll find it in Barcelona, somewhere – bohemian boozer, underground club, cocktail bar, summer dance palace, techno temple, Irish pub or designer bar, you name it. If all you want is a drink, then any café or bar can oblige. Some of the finest cafés are already covered in the previous chapter, *Eating*, and undoubtedly one of the city's greatest pleasures is to pull up a pavement seat in the Barri Gòtic or in Gràcia and watch the world go by. However the bar scene proper operates at a different pace, and with a different set of rules. Specialist **bars** in Barcelona include *bodegas* (specializing in wine), "pubs" and *cerveserías* (beer), *xampanyerías* (champagne and *cava*) and *coctelerías* (cocktails). Best known of the city's nightlife haunts are its hip **designer bars**, while there's a stylish **club scene** that goes from strength to strength fuelled by a potent mix of resident and guest DJs.

The lists below of bars and clubs provide a starting point for a decent night out in Barcelona, but the scene changes rapidly. For full **listings**, get hold of a copy of the weekly *Guia del Ocio* from newsstands (out every Thursday), which covers current openings, hours and club nights. Bars, cafés, boutiques and music stores carry flyers, and you'll also be able to pick up an array of free magazines containing bar and club news and reviews. For the lowdown on **gay and lesbian** nightlife in Barcelona, see Chapter 11. Bars and clubs are all marked on the **neighborhood maps** in the Eating chapter.

It's worth noting, that – unlike restaurants – most bars and clubs stay open throughout August.

Bars

Generally, the bars in the old town are a mixture of traditional tourist haunts, local drinking places or fashionista hangouts. **La Ribera** is still one of the hottest destinations, with Passeig del Born the main focus. In the **Barri Gòtic**, it's the streets around c/d'Avinyó, c/Escudellers and Plaça George Orwell that have their share of the action. Over in the **Raval**, the most fashionable places are found in the upper part of the neighbourhood near MACBA, though you can still find tradition (and sleaze) further south, closer to the port, in the surviving bars of the old Barri Xines. The **Port Olímpic** and the **Port Vell** Maremàgnum complex are more mainstream summer-night playgrounds for locals and tourists alike. There are scores of bars in both these areas, all either themed or fairly mundane, but with the advantage that you can simply hop from one to another if you don't like your first choice. The more stylish designer bars (*bars modernos*) or DJ-led music bars (*bars musicals*) tend to be

Alcoholic drinks

The **beer** (*cervesa* in Catalan, *cerveza* in Spanish) in Barcelona is lager, with the two main brands you'll see everywhere being Damm's Estrella and San Miguel. Voll Damm is a stronger lager, Bock Damm a darker one, or you might also see draught *cervesa negra*, a black fizzy lager with a bitter taste. Beer generally comes in 300ml bottles, while, on draught, a *caña* is a small glass, a *caña grande* or a *jarra* is a larger one, whilst the *tubo* is a tall, cylindrical glass.

Wine (*vino*, *vi*), either red (*tinto*, *negre*), white (*blanco*, *blanc*) or rosé (*rosado*, *rosat*), is the invariable accompaniment to every meal. In bars, cafés and budget restaurants, it's whatever comes out of the barrel, or the house bottled special (ask for *vin* or *vi de la casa*). If you want to try this year's local wine, ask for *vi novell*. Catalan wine is mostly excellent; the wine-making industry is centred on the Alt Penedès and Priorat regions, with other local wine-making regions found in Empordà and around Lleida. The champagne-like *cava* from Sant Sadurní d'Anoia (see p.143) is definitely worth sampling. You'll also see a lot of standard Spanish wines, most notably Rioja, while the Galician and Basque bars and restaurants in the city serve wines from their own regions. The classic Andalucian wine, **sherry** – *vino de Jerez* – is served chilled or at *bodega* temperature, a perfect drink to wash down tapas. The main distinctions are between *fino* or *Jerez seco* (dry sherry), *amontillado* (medium) and *oloroso* or *Jerez dulce* (sweet), and these are the terms you should use to order.

In mid-afternoon – or even at breakfast – many Catalans take a *copa* of **liqueur** with their coffee (for that matter, many of them drink wine and beer at breakfast, too). The best – certainly to put in your coffee – is **brandy** (*coñac*), mostly from the south and often deceptively smooth. If you want a brandy from Catalunya, look for Torres or Mascaró. For other spirits, always specify *nacional* if you want to avoid getting an expensive foreign brand. The current drink of choice for the cool crowd is **absinthe**, served in a variety of old-town bars.

concentrated mainly in the **Eixample** and the streets to the west of **Gràcia**, particularly on c/Santaló and c/Marià Cubí in **Sant Gervasi**.

Local bars are licensed to stay open usually until 11pm, although some keep going until 3am. Music bars usually go until 2am or 3am, after which you'll have to resort to a club.

Barri Gòtic

L'Ascensor c/Bella-fila 3 ☎ 933 185 347; Ⓜ **Jaume I.** Sliding antique wooden lift doors announce the entrance to "The Lift", but it's a no theme bar – just an easy-going local hangout, great for a late-night drink. Daily 6.30pm–3am.

Bosc de les Fades Ptge. de la Banca 5 ☎ 933 172 649, Ⓦ www.museocerabcn.com; Ⓜ **Drassanes.** Tucked away in an alley off the Ramblas, beside the entrance to the wax museum, the "Forest of the Fairies" is festooned

with gnarled plaster tree trunks, hanging branches, fountains and stalactites. It's a bit

▽ El Bosc de les Fades

Barcelona has embraced the "English" pub and "Irish" bar with a vengeance, and every *barri* has a place where the stag and hen boys and girls can feel right at home. On the whole, there's little to choose between them, though they come into their own when only a pint of Guinness, a singalong-a-pub band or the match on the big screen will do. By common consent, the **Black Horse** (c/d'Allada Vermell 16, Sant Pere ☎ 932 683 338; Ⓜ Jaume I) is best, with an off-the-beaten-track neighbourhood feel, despite being just a few minutes from the Picasso museum, while the same can be said of the **Michael Collins** (Pl. Sagrada Família 4, Eixample ☎ 934 591 964; Ⓜ Sagrada Família), across from Gaudí's church. The old-town pubs see a more transient tourist crowd – at least at **Molly's Fair City** (c/de Ferran 7–9, Barri Gòtic ☎ 933 424 026; Ⓜ Liceu) there's the original modernista decor to admire. Uptown expats and hotel guests favour **Kitty O'Shea's** (c/Nau Santa Maria 5–7, Les Corts ☎ 932 803 675; Ⓜ Maria Cristina), while for nightly knees-ups and big-screen sports make for the Port Olímpic's **Kennedy Irish Sailing Club** (Moll de Mestral, Port Olímpic ☎ 932 210 039; Ⓜ Ciutadella-Vila Olímpica).

cheesy, and it's a huge hit with the twenty-something crowd who cuddle up in the dark recesses. Mon–Fri & Sun 10.30am–1am, Sat 10.30am–2am.

Café Royale c/Nou de Zurbano 3 ☎ 934 121 433; Ⓜ **Liceu**. Sleek lounge bar where all the beautiful people get together to show off their best moves to the Latin jazz, soul and funky tunes. Arrive after midnight and you'll have to join the queue; come too early and you'll be on your own. Daily 6pm–2.30am.

Ginger c/Palma Sant Just 1 ☎ 933 105 309; Ⓜ **Jaume I**. Imparting a certain 1970s style, *Ginger* serves cocktails, wine and creative tapas to a chilled-out clientele. Tues–Sat 7pm–3am; closed two weeks in Aug.

Glaciar Pl. Reial 3 ☎ 933 021 163; Ⓜ **Liceu**. At this traditional Barcelona meeting point the terrace seating in the square is packed out most sunny evenings and at weekends. Mon–Thurs 4pm–2am, Fri & Sat 4pm–3am, Sun 9am–2am.

Leticia c/de Codols 21 ☎ 933 020 074; Ⓜ **Drassanes**. Backstreet bar that fancies itself as an art space – a large-scale video projection on the wall, changing exhibitions and the like. It's got mellow sounds and a laidback clientele – the sofa at the back is the seat in demand. Daily except Tues 7pm–3am.

🏃 **Milk c/Gignàs 21** ☎ 932 680 922; Ⓜ **Jaume I**. Irish-owned bar and bistro that's quickly carved a niche as a welcoming neighbourhood hangout – nothing flashy, but decent food and cocktails backed by a

funky soundtrack. Mon–Fri 7pm–3am, Sat 1pm–3am, Sun noon–3am.

Oviso c/Arai 5, Pl. George Orwell, no phone; Ⓜ **Drassanes**. It couldn't really be anywhere else – the essence of the urban square outside is reflected in the young grunge crowd which frequents this mural-clad café-bar. The food's good too and it's open for breakfast onwards. Daily 10am–2.30am, Fri & Sat until 3am.

Peña Espanyol Ptge. de Madoz, no phone; Ⓜ **Liceu**. Fans of Barcelona's "other" football club, l'Espanyol, gather here and even if you're not into sport this is undoubtedly the best bar in Pl. Reial, with stunning views over the square. Look for the name "Penya Central" on the buzzer of the first door around the corner from the *Quinze Nits* restaurant, ring the bell and go up to the first floor. Everybody is welcome. Daily 3pm–2am.

Pipa Club Pl. Reial 3 ☎ 933 024 732, ⓦ www.bpipaclub.com; Ⓜ **Liceu**. A bit like a Victorian English pub, with its wood-panelled rooms, pool table and battery of regulars. Historically a pipe-smoker's private club, it's a jazzy, late-night kind of place – ring the bell for admission and make your way up the stairs. Nonmembers usually welcome daily 10pm–3am.

Schilling c/de Ferran 23 ☎ 933 176 787, ⓦ www.cafeschilling.com; Ⓜ **Liceu**. In the European "grand-café" style, with high ceilings, big windows and an upmarket feel. It has a loyal gay following, but it's a mixed, chilled place to meet up, grab a bite and

a *copa* and move on. Mon–Sat 10am–
2.30am, Sun noon–2.30am.
Travel Bar c/Boqueria 27 ☏ 933 425 252,
ⓦ www.travelbar.com; Ⓜ Liceu. Backpacking
Catalans have brought their experiences
home to provide a bar where travellers can
hang out and meet like-minded souls, sign
up for walking, biking or drinking tours,
check their email, practise their Spanish
and generally chill out. Mon–Thurs & Sun
10am–1am, Fri & Sat 10am–2am.

El Raval

🏃 **Almirall c/de Joaquin Costa 33** ☏ 933
189 917; Ⓜ Universitat. Dating from
1860, Barcelona's oldest bar – check out
the *modernista* doors and counter – is a
venerated leftist hangout, not to mention a
great place to kick off an evening of more
intense bar-hopping. Daily 7pm–3am.
Benidorm c/de Joaquin Costa 39 ☏ 933 178
052; Ⓜ Universitat. Imagine. . . if your elderly
aunt turned her parlour into a bar, dimmed
the lights, and invited all her young friends.
That, in a nutshell, is *Benidorm*, just a little bit cheesy and none the worse for that.
Daily 7pm–3am.
🏃 **Café de les Delícies Rambla de Raval 47**
☏ 934 415 714; Ⓜ Liceu. One of the first
off the blocks in this revamped neighbourhood, and still the best – cute and cosy,
mellow and arty, with a summer terrace and
food for sharing. Daily 7pm–2am.
La Confitería c/de Sant Pau 128 ☏ 934 430
458; Ⓜ Paral.lel. This old *modernista* bakery
and confectioner's with a carved wood bar,
murals, chandeliers and mirrored cabinets
is now a popular drinks stop. Mon–Sat
8pm–3am, Sun 7pm–2am.
It Café c/de Joaquin Costa 4 ☏ 934 430 341;
Ⓜ Sant Antoni. A "drinks and sofas" bar that
runs down the checklist with ease – scuffed
floors, cast-iron pillars, mood music and
comfy seats. Mon–Wed 4pm–1am, Thurs–
Sat 4pm–3am, Sun 6pm–midnight.
Kabara c/Junta de Comerç 20 ☏ 934 127 698;
Ⓜ Liceu. Blood-red arts-scene bar and
multicultural space with odds-and-ends
furniture, music most nights (DJs, bands
and open-mic sessions) and a chilled-out
atmosphere. Hours are variable, but currently Tues–Thurs & Sun 8.30pm–2am, Fri &
Sat 8.30pm–3am; closed Aug.
London Bar c/Nou de la Rambla 34 ☏ 933
185 261, ⓦ www.londonbarbcn.com; Ⓜ Liceu.

Opened in 1910, this well-known *modernista* bar attracts a mostly tourist clientele
these days, but it's still worth looking in at
least once. It puts on jazz, swing, blues or
tango gigs most nights; the music starts at
12.30am. Tues–Thurs & Sun 7.30pm–4am,
Fri & Sat 7.30pm–5am; closed two weeks
in Aug.
Marsella c/de Sant Pau 65 ☏ 934 427 263;
Ⓜ Liceu. Authentic, atmospheric, 1930s
bar where absinthe is the drink of choice.
It's frequented by a spirited mix of local
characters and young trendies, all looking
for a slice of the old Barri Xines. Mon–Sat
10pm–3am.
Merry Ant c/Peu de la Creu 23, no phone;
Ⓜ Sant Antoni. Barn doors open into a DIY
bodger's delight – bar, seats and tables
have all been fashioned from cannibalized
furniture and junk-shop debris. It's a bit
studied, and fiendishly cool, but La Hormiga
Feliz (the sign you might see on the door
from time to time) has a certain eccentric
charm. Tues–Sun 7pm–3am.
Muebles Navarro c/Riera Alta 4–6 ☏ 607 188
096; Ⓜ Sant Antoni. Café-bar that occupies
various rooms in a converted furniture
store, hence the name, "Navarro Furniture".
Tues–Thurs & Sun 6pm–midnight, Fri & Sat
6pm–3am; closed two weeks in Aug.
🏃 **Muy Buenas c/del Carme 63** ☏ 934 425
053; Ⓜ Liceu. Arguably the Raval's
nicest watering-hole, with a hip, eager-to-
please staff making things go with a swing.
It's got a restored *modernista* interior, a long
marble trough functioning as the bar, and
beer pulled from antique beer taps. Mon–
Sat 7.30am–2.30am, Sun 7pm–2.30am.
🏃 **Zelig c/del Carme 116** ☏ 934 415 622;
Ⓜ Sant Antoni. The photo-frieze on
granite walls and a fully stocked cocktail bar
make it very much of its *barri* but *Zelig* stands
out from the crowd – two Dutch owners offer
a chatty welcome, a tendency towards 1980s
sounds and a slight whiff of camp. Tues–Sun
7pm–2am, Fri & Sat until 3am.

Sant Pere

Casa Paco c/d'Allada Vermell 10 ☏ 935 073 719;
Ⓜ Jaume I. Casual, hip bar that's a hit on
the weekend DJ scene – the tag line "not
a disco, just a bar with good music" says it
all. Plus there's a great terrassa under the
palm trees outside. Mon–Fri 9am–2am, Sat
& Sun noon–3am.

La Ribera

Berimbau Pg. del Born 17 ☎933 195 378; Ⓜ**Jaume I/Barceloneta.** The oldest Brazilian bar in town, still a good place for authentic sounds and killer cocktails. Daily 6pm–2.30am.

Espai Barroc c/de Montcada 8 ☎933 100 673; Ⓜ**Jaume I.** One of a series of handsome mansions along c/de Montcada, Palau Dalmasses is open in the evenings as a rather grand bar which could double as a Peter Greenaway film set. Every Thursday there's live opera, Baroque or chamber music (€20, first drink included). Tues–Sat 8pm–2am, Sun 6–10pm.

🏃 **La Fianna c/Banys Vells 19** ☎933 151 810, ⓦwww.lafianna.com; Ⓜ**Jaume I.** Flickering candelabras, parchment lampshades, rough plaster walls and deep colours set the Gothic mood in this stylish lounge-bar that offers "a taste of the East". Relax on cushions for a drink, or book ahead to eat – the fusion-food restaurant is open from 8.30pm or it's a popular Sunday brunch spot. Mon–Thurs 6pm–1.30am, Fri & Sat 6pm–3am, Sun 2pm–1.30am.

Hivernacle Pg. de Picasso, Parc de la Ciutadella ☎932 954 017; Ⓜ**Arc de Triomf.** Quiet, relaxing *terrassa* set amongst the palm trees inside the nineteenth-century glass conservatory. It's a genteel spot for coffee, drinks, fancy tapas or fine Catalan dining, with live music and jazz nights a couple of times a week. Daily 10am–midnight.

Mudanzas c/Vidreria 15 ☎933 191 137; Ⓜ**Barceloneta.** A relaxed feel (especially if you can hide yourself away in the cosy upper room) attracts the locals, while those in the know come for the wide selection of rums from around the world. Daily 10pm–2.30am.

El Nus c/Mirallers 5 ☎933 195 355; Ⓜ**Jaume I.** Still has the feel of the shop it once was, down to the antique cash register, though it's now a kind of jazz-bar-cum-gallery – a quiet, faintly old-fashioned, late-night place. Daily except Wed 7.30pm–2.30am.

La Vinya del Senyor Pl. Santa Maria 5 ☎933 103 379; Ⓜ**Jaume I.** Nook-and-cranny wine bar with tables right outside the lovely church of Santa Maria del Mar. The wine list runs to novel length – a score of them also available by the glass – and there are oysters, smoked salmon and other classy tapas. Tues–Thurs noon–1am, Fri & Sat noon–2am, Sun noon–midnight.

Port Vell

Luz de Gas Moll de Diposit, in front of Palau de Mar ☎932 097 711, ⓦwww.luzdegas.com; Ⓜ**Barceloneta.** Sip a chilled drink on the polished deck of the moored boat, and soak up some great marina and harbour views. Queues form on hot days, when every parasol-shaded seat is taken, but it's especially nice at dusk as the city lights begin to twinkle. March–Oct daily noon–3am.

Poble Sec

Barcelona Rouge c/Poeta Cabanyes 21 ☎934 424 985; Ⓜ**Paral.lel.** It's red all right – it couldn't be more red, in fact, inside this laid-back cocktail emporium playing downtempo jazz, trip hop and other dreamy beats. Tues–Sat 11pm–3am.

Cervecería Jazz c/Margarit 43 ☎934 433 259; Ⓜ**Poble Sec.** Grab a stool at the carved bar and shoot the breeze over an imported beer. It's an amiable place, and the music policy embraces reggae and other mellow sounds, not just jazz. Mon–Sat 7pm–2.30am.

🏃 **Tinta Roja c/Creu dels Molers 17** ☎934 433 243, ⓦwww.tintaroja.net; Ⓜ**Poble Sec.** Highly theatrical tango bar with a succession of crimson rooms dripping with ornamentation leading through to a stage at the back. There's cabaret and live music (tango, rumba and Cuban) – often free – a couple of nights a week, though special shows are €10. Wed, Thurs & Sun 8pm–1.30am, Fri & Sat 8pm–3am.

Eixample

🏃 **Belchica c/Villaroel 60** ☎934 514 902; Ⓜ**Urgell.** Barcelona's first Belgian beer bar, which guarantees a range of decent brews. It's not a theme bar – unless you count drinking in what resembles a boiler room – just an enjoyable locals' bar playing electronica, new jazz, lounge, reggae and other left-field sounds. Mon–Fri 3pm–3am, Sat 8pm–3am, Sun 8pm–1am.

Dry Martini c/Aribau 166 ☎932 175 072; Ⓜ**Diagonal/Provença.** White-jacketed bar-tenders, dark wood and brass, cigar smoke heavy in the air, middle-aged paunches – it could only be the city's legendary uptown cocktail bar. To be fair, though, no one mixes drinks better and the regulars aren't the one-dimensional business types you might expect. Mon–Thurs 1pm–2.30am, Fri & Sat

Drinks with Gaudí

Some cool rhythms, champagne, and a setting on the roof terrace of one of Gaudí's most extraordinary buildings makes for an extremely agreeable summer's night. The weekend event known as **La Pedrera de Nit** provides all of this, though you'll need to make reservations well in advance. See p.106 for all the details.

1pm–3am, Sun 6.30pm–2.30am.

La Fira c/Provença 171, no phone; Ⓜ Provença. One of the city's most bizarre drinking emporiums comes complete with old-fashioned fairground rides and circus paraphernalia. Sit at the bar fashioned from a circus awning or cosy up in the dodgem cars – but come at the weekend for any kind of crowd or atmosphere. Tues–Thurs & Sun 11pm–3am, Fri & Sat 11pm–5am.

Les Gens Que J'Aime c/Valencia 286 ☏ 932 156 879; Ⓜ Passeig de Gràcia. It takes your eyes a while to adjust as you descend into the intimate *fin-de-siècle* interior of red velvet, dimmed lights and soulful mood music. As a refuge from the club scene, it's very pleasant for a relaxing drink. Daily 7pm–2.30am.

Quilombo c/d'Aribau 149 ☏ 934 395 406; Ⓜ Diagonal. Unpretentious music bar – just a bare box of a room really – that's rolled with the years since 1971, with live guitarists, South American bands and a clientele that joins in enthusiastically. Mon–Thurs & Sun 9pm–3am, Fri & Sat 7.30pm–3.30am.

Sante Café c/Comte d'Urgell 171 ☏ 933 237 832; Ⓜ Hospital Clínic. A minimalist-style place that's more of a café during the day but chills out at night, with DJs at the weekend. Mon–Fri 8am–3pm, Sat & Sun 5pm–3am; closed Aug.

Gràcia

Café Salambo c/Torrijos 51 ☏ 932 186 966, Ⓦ www.cafesalambo.com; Ⓜ Joanic. Neighbourhood drink-and-meet spot with something of a colonial feel. The pre- and post-cinema crowd pops in for coffee, sandwiches and meals, and there are lots of wines and *cava* by the glass. Upstairs, you can shoot pool. Daily noon–2.30am.

🏃 **Canigó** Pl. de la Revolucio 10, no phone; Ⓜ Fontana. Family-run neighbourhood bar now entering its third generation. It's not much to look at, but it's a Gràcia institution, packed out at weekends with a young, hip and largely local crowd, meeting to chew the fat. Tues–Sun 11am–midnight.

La Cervesera Artesana c/Sant Agustí 14 ☏ 932 379 594, Ⓦ www.lacervesera.net; Ⓜ Diagonal. Skip the city's "Irish" bars in favour of this Catalan brewpub serving a house IPA (Iberian Pale Ale) and stout made on the premises, plus a whole host of other speciality and bottled beers. Mon–Sat 6pm–1am.

Mond Bar Pl. del Sol 21 ☏ 932 720 910; Ⓜ Diagonal/Fontana. Every night a different resident DJ plays the newest beats in the bar where "pop will make us free". The bar is an apéritif for the *Mond Club*. Daily 8.30pm–3am.

Puku Café c/Guilleries 10 ☏ 936 013 237, Ⓦ www.puku-café.com; Ⓜ Fontana. Come early and it's a relaxed place for a bite to eat and a drink – there's a fine range of wines by glass or bottle. At weekends it morphs into an equally chilled electro-lounge as "indietronica" DJs take the helm. Sun–Wed 5pm–1am, Thurs 5pm–2am, Fri & Sat 5pm–3am.

🏃 **Virreina** Pl. de la Virreina 1 ☏ 932 379 880; Ⓜ Fontana. Popular local bar with seats outside in one of Gràcia's loveliest squares. A great place to enjoy hard-to-find Trappist beers from Belgium. Mon–Thurs & Sun 10am–1am, Fri & Sat 10am–2am.

Sarrià-Sant Gervasi

Gimlet c/Santaló 46 ☏ 932 015 306; FGC Muntaner. A favourite in summertime, when the tables outside are packed with the local beautiful people, who come here for snacks and cocktails. Daily 7.30pm–2.30am.

🏃 **Mas i Mas** c/Marià Cubí 199 ☏ 932 094 502, Ⓦ www.masimas.com; FGC Muntaner. Cornerstone of the uptown bar scene and, in their own words, "a cross between a cocktail bar and a dancehall". The music policy is blues, acid jazz, hip hop and house, and the crowd is young and funky. Daily 7pm–3am.

Universal c/Marià Cubí 182 ☏ 932 013 596, Ⓦ www.grupocostaeste.com; FGC Muntaner. A classic designer bar that's been at the cutting edge of Barcelona style since 1985 – and there are still queues. Be warned: they operate a strict door policy here and

if your face doesn't fit you won't get in.
Mon–Sat 11pm–5am.

Mirablau Pl. del Dr Andrea, Avgda. Tibidabo
T 934 185 879; FGC Avgda. del Tibidabo &

Tramvia Blau or taxi. Unbelievable city views
from a chic bar by the tram and funicular
terminus. By day a great place for coffee
and views, at night a rich-kid disco-tunes
stamping ground. Daily 11am–5am.

Clubs

The main city-centre **neighbourhoods** for clubbing are the Barri Gòtic,
Raval, Eixample and Gràcia, though it's actually the peripheral areas where
you'll find the bulk of the big-name warehouse and designer venues. Poble
Nou, Poble Sec, Sants and Les Corts might not attract you during the day, but
they'll be high on the list of any seasoned clubber, as will the otherwise tourist
fantasy village of Poble Espanyol in Montjuïc. Meanwhile the Port Olímpic has
a number of high-profile clubs alongside the myriad music bars.

Admission prices are difficult to predict: some places are free or free before
a certain time, others charge a few token euros' entry, a few only charge if there's
live music, while in several entry depends on what you look like rather than
how much is in your pocket. Those that do charge tend to fall into the €10–20
range, though this usually includes your first drink. If there is free entry, don't be
surprised to find that there's a minimum drinks charge of anything up to €10.

Note that the distinction between a music-bar and a club is between a **closing time** of 2am or 3am and at least 5am. Many of those listed below stay
open until 6am or 7am at weekends – fair enough, as they've usually barely got
started by 3am.

Dot c/Nou de Sant Francesc 7 T 933 027 026;
Ⓜ **Drassanes.** Tiny bar, tiny dance floor, with
a music policy changing nightly – electronica, deep beats, Brazilian, funk. Mon–Thurs
& Sun 11pm–2.30am, Fri & Sat 11pm–3am.
Fantastico Ptge. dels Escudellers 3 T 933 175
411, wwww.fantasticoclub.com; Ⓜ **Drassanes.**
A cheery dive for the pop and indie crowd
who want to listen to Franz Ferdinand,
Kaiser Chiefs and the like. Wed–Sat
10.30pm–3am.

Fonfone c/dels Escudellers 24 T 933 171
424, Ⓦ **www.fonfone.com;** Ⓜ **Drassanes.**
Cunningly designed, beautifully lit bar
attracting a young crowd into fast, hard
music, though it changes mood with satin
soul and best-of-Eighties nights. Daily
10pm–3am.
Karma Pl. Reial 10 T 933 025 680; Ⓜ **Liceu.** A
stalwart of the scene, this studenty basement place can get claustrophobic at times.
Sounds are Indie, Britpop and US college,
while a lively local crowd mills around the
square outside. Tues–Sun midnight–5am.

**La Macarena c/Nou de Sant Francesc
5, no phone** Ⓦ **www.macarenaclub.com;**
Ⓜ **Drassanes.** Once a place where flamenco
tunes were offered up to La Macarena, the
Virgin of Seville. Now it's a heaving, funky,
electronic temple with a tolerant crowd
– they have to be, as there's not much
space. Mon–Thurs & Sun 11pm–4am, Fri &
Sat 11pm–5am.

La Concha c/Guardia 14 T 933 024 118;
Ⓜ **Drassanes.** The Arab–flamenco fusion
throws up a great atmosphere, worth
braving the slightly dodgy area for. Drag
performances on Fri and Sat at midnight are
the big draw, with uninhibited dancing to flamenco and *rai* afterwards. Daily 5pm–3am.
Dos Trece c/del Carme 40 T 933 017 306,
Ⓦ **www.dostrece.net;** Ⓜ **Liceu.** Small club
under a stylish upper Raval bar-restaurant
where local musicians and DJs take care
of the ambience. Every night is different,
though the crowd is always young and cool.
Daily 11.30pm–4am.

First it was bars in pool halls and archery ranges, followed in quick order by the invasion of the Irish bar and the gentle creep of the lounge scene. Barcelona always has another fad up its sleeve, and now it's upscale dining-and-dancing, as exemplified by the beautiful-people hangouts **Sugar Club** (World Trade Centre, Port Vell ⓣ935 088 325, Ⓜ Drassanes), **CDLC** (Pg. Marítim 32, Port Olímpic ⓣ932 240 470, Ⓜ Ciutadella-Vila Olímpica) and **Shôko** (Pg. Marítim 36, Port Olímpic ⓣ932 259 203, Ⓜ Ciutadella-Vila Olímpica). The clientele is A-list celeb, well-heeled tourist and local rich kid, not adverse to dining out and kicking back in like-minded company. **Salsitas** (c/Nou de la Rambla 22, El Raval ⓣ933 180 840, Ⓜ Liceu) was one of the first to spot the potential, with house sounds breaking out after midnight once the tables were cleared – and the Salsitas group now operates some of the flashest gastro-clubs in town, including **Danzarama** (Gran Via de les Corts Catalanes 604, Eixample ⓣ933 425 070, Ⓜ Universitat) and the very classy **Danzatoria** (Avgda. Tibidabo 61 ⓣ902 888 115, FGC Avgda. del Tibidabo), a superb mansion with bar, restaurant and gardens set high on the hill above the city.

Moog c/Arc del Teatre 3 ⓣ933 017 282, Ⓦ www.masimas.com; Ⓜ Drassanes. Influential club playing techno, electro, drum 'n' bass, house, funk and soul to an up-for-it crowd. Daily midnight–5am.

🏃 **La Paloma** c/Tigre 27 ⓣ933 016 897, Ⓦ www.lapaloma-bcn.com; Ⓜ Universitat. Fabulous 1903-era ballroom and concert venue where old and young alike are put through their rumba and cha-cha-cha steps from 6pm to 9.30pm. After 11.30pm, dancers climb onto the stage, and DJs take their positions. Club nights vary – funk and soul to electro and indie – but there's always quite a crowd. Thurs–Sat 6pm–5am, Sun 6–10pm.

Zentraus Rambla de Raval 41 ⓣ934 438 078, Ⓦ www.zentraus.com, Ⓜ Liceu/Paral.lel. Tues–Sat 9pm–3am. Minimalist dance club with the best in electronic sounds supplied by local and visiting DJs. Tues–Thurs 10pm–2.30am, Fri & Sat 10pm–3am.

Port Olímpic

Club Catwalk c/Ramon Trias Fargas 2–4 ⓣ932 216 161, Ⓦ www.clubcatwalk.net; Ⓜ Ciutadella-Vila Olímpica. The portside club of choice for the beautiful of Barcelona, playing house or funk and r&b to well-heeled locals and visitors. Thurs–Sun midnight–5am.

Poble Nou

🏃 **Razzmatazz** c/dels Almogavers 122 & c/Pamplona 88 ⓣ932 720 910, Ⓦ www. salarazzmatazz.com; Ⓜ Bogatell/Marina. Razz-

matazz hosts the biggest in-town rock gigs at weekends (the concert hall capacity is 3000), after which the former warehouse (now also incorporating *The Loft*) turns into "five clubs in one". Resident DJs spin Indie, rock, pop, techno, electro, retro and more, and one price gets you entrance to all the bars. Fri & Sat 1–5am.

Montjuïc

La Terrazza Avgda. Marquès de Comillas, Poble Espanyol ⓣ934 231 285, Ⓦ www .nightsungroup.com; Ⓜ Espanya. Open-air summer club that's *the* place to be. Non-stop dance, house and techno, though don't get there until at least 4am, and be prepared for the style police. May–Oct Thurs–Sat midnight–7am.

Poble Sec

Mau Mau c/Fontrodona 33 ⓣ934 418 015; Ⓦ www.maumaunderground.com; Ⓜ Paral.lel. Great underground lounge-club, cultural centre and chillout space with comfy sofas, nightly film and video projections, exhibitions, and a roster of guest DJs playing deep, soulful grooves. Strictly speaking it's a private club, but membership is only €5 and they tend to let foreign visitors in anyway. Thurs 11pm–2.30am, Fri & Sat 11pm–3.30am, Sun 6.30–11.30pm.

🏃 **Sala Apolo** c/Nou de la Rambla 113 ⓣ934 414 001, Ⓦ www.sala-apolo. com; Ⓜ Paral.lel. Former ballroom, now concert venue with two stages, which hosts an eclectic series of club nights – from Wednesday's Canibal Sound Sistem (reggae, latin, hip-hop and funk) to Friday and Saturday nights' longstanding pumping house/techno/electro Nitsa Club (Ⓦwww.nitsa.com). Wed midnight–5am, Thurs–Sat 12.30–5am.

Eixample

Antilla Barcelona c/Aragó 141–143 ☎934 512 151, Ⓦwww.antillasalsa.com; Ⓜ**Hospital Clinic/Urgell**. Caribbean tunes galore, with rumba, son, salsa, merengue and mambo. There are live bands, fantastic cocktails and even dance classes. Mon–Fri 11pm–5am, Sat & Sun 10pm–6am.

Barcelona City Hall Rambla de Catalunya 2–4 ☎932 380 722; Ⓜ**Catalunya**. Hosts some of the most varied club nights around, from 1980s hits to the latest house sounds. Daily midnight–5am.

Costa Breve c/d'Aribau 230 ☎934 142 778, Ⓦwww.costabreve.net; Ⓜ**Diagonal**. Late-night funk, pop, dance and soul "discoteca" that attracts an uptown crowd ready for a bit of serious boogieing. Thurs–Sat midnight–6am.

Distrito Diagonal Avgda. Diagonal 442 ☎934 154 635, Ⓦwww.distritodiagonal.com; Ⓜ**Diagonal**. A hot weekend venue for house and garage, plus one-off party nights. Fri midnight–4.30am, Sat 10pm–4.30am.

🏃 **Velvet c/Balmes 161** ☎932 176 714; Ⓜ**Diagonal**. One of the few survivors of the first wave of stylish dance-bars in the 1980s, this lavish creation of designer Alfredo Arribas was inspired by the velveteen excesses of film-maker David Lynch. Daily 10.30pm–4.30am.

Sants

Space Barcelona c/Tarragona 141–147 ☎934 268 444, Ⓦwww.spacebarcelona.com; Ⓜ**Tarragona**. With the Balearic electro-beat big in Barcelona, it wasn't a surprise when offshoots of the actual Ibiza clubs appeared

on the scene too, as here in the city's own Space. Fri & Sat midnight–6am.

Gràcia

KGB c/Alegre de Dalt 55 ☎932 105 906; Ⓜ**Joanic**. This warehouse bar and club was the first with the industrial look back in the 1980s. It was a well-known techno haunt, though current gigs and music policy aren't so rigid now. Daily 10pm–5am.

Mond Club Sala Cibeles, c/Corsega 363 ☎932 720 910, Ⓦwww.mondclub.com; Ⓜ**Diagonal**. Old ballroom converted into a stylish Friday-night club, with a bit of everything thrown into the mix – punk, glam, electronica and guest DJs. At the time of writing, *Mond* was contemplating a move to Thursday night at *Club Fellini*, Ramblas 27 – check the website for details.

Otto Zutz c/de Lincoln 15 ☎932 380 722, Ⓦwww.ottozutz.com; Ⓜ**FGC Gràcia**. Still one of the most fashionable places in the city, this three-storey former textile factory has a shed-load of pretensions. With the right clothes and face, you're in; you may or may not have to pay, judging on how impressive you are or on the day of the week. Tues–Sat midnight–6am.

Les Corts

🏃 **Bikini c/Deu i Mata 105, off Avgda. Diagonal** ☎933 220 800, Ⓦwww.bikinibcn.com; Ⓜ**Les Corts/María Cristina**. This traditional landmark of Barcelona nightlife (behind the L'Illa shopping centre) offers a regular diet of great gigs followed by club sounds, from house to Brazilian, according to the night. Tues–Sun midnight–5am.

Pacha Avgda. Dr. Marañon 17 ☎933 343 233, Ⓦwww.clubpachabcn.com; Ⓜ**Zona Universitaria**. More Ibizan club culture in the latest superclub to transfer from beach to Barcelona. A roster of international name DJs are present year-round. Thurs–Sat midnight–6am, Sun 10pm–2am.

Festive Barcelona

Decorated floats and costumed giants inch down crowded streets, teams of red-shirted men clamber on each other's shoulders, sweets are hurled to children, fireworks burst into the sky and the drummers are going crazy – it's festival time in Barcelona, and you can forget all about a decent night's sleep. In a city with two patron saints, a dozen neighbourhoods each with their own *festa*, and a full cultural and music calendar, there will be something going on whenever you visit.

There's a month-by-month run-down of festivals on pp.220–223

A *gegant*

Festes de Santa Eulàlia

The depths of winter are interrupted by a sharp burst of festivities in honour of Eulàlia, the young Barcelona girl who suffered a beastly martyrdom by the Romans for refusing to renounce her Christianity. She's a revered patron of the city, her saint's day falling on **February 12**, around which are held several days' worth of events and celebrations with a focus on children and families. Celebrations take place in Plaça de Sant Jaume, outside the town hall in the Barri Gòtic, where you'll be able to see the saint in parade with other *gegants* (giants), as well as the usual fire-running, dancing, concerts and firework displays throughout the neighbourhood. It's also an appropriate time to visit La Seu, Barcelona's old-town cathedral, whose crypt (open to view) contains the saint's venerated remains in a marble sarcophagus.

Dia de Sant Jordi

April 23 is **St George's Day**, dedicated to Catalunya's dragon-slaying patron saint. It's a day of national identity – the Catalan flag appears everywhere and red roses (the colour of the dragon's blood) are the bloom of choice, with the two coming together at the Palau de la Generalitat, the home of the Catalan government. The saint's day has been entwined over the years with two other occasions, so that it's also a kind of local Valentine's Day (traditionally, men give their sweethearts a rose…) and International Book Day (…and receive a book in return). You'll be hard pushed to escape stumping up for either as you run the gauntlet of stalls down the Ramblas.

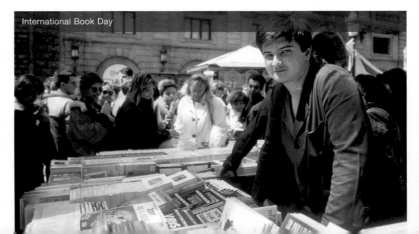
International Book Day

Dia de Sant Joan

St John's Day (June 24) is the quietest saint's day of the year in the city – largely because everyone has been up all of the previous night for the famed **Nit del Foc** (Night of Fire), which involves massive bonfires and fireworks across the city. It marks a hedonistic welcome to summer, with *cava* (champagne) parties in full swing in every neighbourhood and pyrotechnics on Montjuïc and Tibidabo. The traditional place to end the night is on the beach, watching the sun come up, thankful that the dawning day is a public holiday.

Grec

The Barcelona Festival

Since the 1970s, the summer's foremost **arts and music festival** (formerly known as the Grec) has centred its performances on Montjuïc's open-air Greek theatre. Cut into the hillside on the site of an old quarry, this is a dramatic location for cutting-edge Shakespearean productions or events by Catalan avant-garde performance artists like La Fura del Baus, while music ranges from the likes of Phillip Glass to Taj Mahal, and African rap to Spanish singer-songwriters. There are also concerts, plays and dance productions at the CCCB and city theatres – in total, around fifty different events held over a six-week period from the end of June. The city council's cultural information office at Palau de la Virreina on the Ramblas is the best stop for information and tickets.

Castles in the sky

The *anxaneta* tops the *castell*

Guaranteed to draw crowds at every festival are the teams of **castellers** – castle-makers – who pile person upon person, feet on shoulders, to see who can construct the highest, most aesthetically pleasing tower. It's an art that goes back over 200 years, combining individual strength with mutual cooperation – perhaps this is why it was discouraged as an activity under Franco. Nowadays, it's very popular once again, with societies known as *colles* in most Catalan towns who come together to perform at annual festivals and events. There's a real skill to assembling the *castell*, with operations directed by the *cap de colla* (society head) – the strongest members form the crowd at the base, known as the *pinya*, with the whole edifice topped by an agile child, the *anxaneta*, who lifts their palm above their head to "crown" the castle. Ten human storeys is the record.

Dancing the sardana in Plaça de Sant Jaume

Celebrating Catalan-style

Central to any Catalan festival is the parade of **gegants**, the overblown five-metre-high giants with a costumed frame (to allow them to be carried) and papier-mâché or fibreglass heads. Barcelona has its own official city *gegants* of King Jaume and his queen, while each neighbourhood cherishes its own traditional figures, from elegant noblewomen to turban-clad sultans – the Barri Gòtic's church of Santa Maria del Pi has some of the most renowned. Come festival time they congregate in the city's squares, dancing cumbersomely to the sound of flutes and drums, and accompanied by smaller, more nimble figures known as **capgrossos** (bigheads) and by outsized lions and dragons. Also typically Catalan is the **correfoc** (fire-running), where brigades of drummers, fire-breathing dragons and demons with firework-flaring tridents cavort in the streets. It's as devilishly dangerous as it sounds, with intrepid onlookers attempting to stop the dragons passing, as firecrackers explode all around – approach with caution.

Festes de la Mercè

The single biggest annual festival, held around September 24, is dedicated to **Our Lady of Mercy**, co-patroness of the city, whose image is paraded from the church of La Mercè in the Barri Gòtic near the port. It's an excuse for a solid week of merrymaking and mayhem, culminating in spectacular pyrotechnics along the seafront. Every unique element of a Catalan festival can be seen at some stage during the Mercè – firework-toting demons chasing onlookers through the streets, human castle-builders reaching for the sky, processions of lumbering giants, and locals linking hands in the traditional circle-dance, the *sardana* (see p.211). If that wasn't enough, there are outdoor concerts across the city, fun runs, harbour swims and bicycle races, children's events and family activities, and even free admission to city museums and galleries on the saint's day itself.

10

Entertainment

As you would expect from a city of this size, Barcelona has a busy entertainment calendar – throughout the year there will be something worth catching, whether it's a rock gig, cabaret show or night at the opera. The **music** scene is particularly strong, with jazz, rock and flamenco to the fore, and Catalans like their **cinema** and **theatre**; even if you don't speak Catalan or Spanish there's no need to miss out, since many cinemas show films in their original language, while Catalan performers have always steered away from the classics and gone for the innovative, so the city boasts a long tradition of street and performance art. Barcelona excels in the **visual arts**, too – from traditional exhibitions of paintings to contemporary photography or installation works – and dozens of arts centres and galleries put on varied shows throughout the year.

A useful first stop for tickets and information is the **Palau de la Virreina**, Ramblas 99 (Mon–Sat 10am–8pm, Sun 11am–3pm; ☎933 017 775; ⓂLiceu). **ServiCaixa** (☎902 332 211, Ⓦature www.servicaixa.com) and **Tel-Entrada** (☎902 101 212, Ⓦwww.telentrada.com) are the main advance booking agencies for music, theatre, cinema and exhibition tickets. There's also a handy ticket desk on the ground floor of **FNAC** (Mon–Sat 10am–10pm), the books and music megastore in El Triangle shopping centre, Plaça de Catalunya.

The main clubs, concert halls and venues are listed below, but for up-to-date art, music and culture information, the city council's Institute of Culture website, Ⓦwww.bcn.es/canalcultura (English version available), is invaluable – it covers every aspect of art and culture in the city, with links to daily updated arts stories and a comprehensive calendar of events. Otherwise, the best **listings magazine** is the weekly *Guía del Ocio* (Ⓦwww.guiadelociobcn.com), online or from any newspaper stand. There's also a free monthly "Cultural Agenda" guide in English published by the Ajuntament, available from tourist offices and the Palau de la Virreina.

The year's big arts and culture crossover festival is the summer **Barcelona Festival** (formerly the Grec), featuring a wealth of music, theatre and dance. Other specific festivals are highlighted in the relevant sections below – for full details turn to the festival calendar in Chapter 12.

Classical, contemporary and opera

Most of Barcelona's **classical** music concerts take place in the *modernista* Palau de la Música Catalana or at the purpose-built, contemporary L'Auditori, while **opera** is performed at its traditional home, the Gran Teatre del Liceu on the Ramblas. Many of the city's churches, including the cathedral and

Santa María del Mar, also host concerts and recitals, while other interesting venues with concert programmes include the historic Saló del Tinell in the Ajuntament, Palau Robert, FNAC Triangle at Plaça de Catalunya, Caixa Forum, the Fundació Joan Miró and CCCB (these two particularly for contemporary music), and the Teatre Mercat de les Flors.

Notable **festivals** include the Festival de Música Antiga (May) and the Festa de la Música (June 21), while there are free concerts in Barcelona's parks each summer, the so-called **Clàssics als Parcs**. L'Auditori is the main venue for Nous Sons ("New Sounds"), the annual contemporary music festival (March–April), and there's also Gràcia's experimental and electronic music festival, known as LEM (October).

L'Auditori c/Lepant 150, Eixample ☎932 479 300, ⊛www.auditori.org; Marina/Monumental. The city's main contemporary concert hall is home to the Orquestra Simfònica de Barcelona i Nacional de Catalunya (OBC), whose weekend concert season runs Sept–May. L'Auditori also puts on other orchestral and chamber works, jazz and world gigs, and music for children and families. Under-26s with ID get fifty-percent discount on all tickets, 1hr before performances. The Bus de les Arts runs back to Pl. de Catalunya after concerts. Box office Mon–Sat noon–9pm, Sun 1hr before performance.

Casa Elizalde c/València 302, Eixample ☎934 880 590, ⊛www.casaelizalde.com; Passeig de Gràcia. Small-scale classical concerts and recitals held once a week at the cultural centre, usually with free entry.

Gran Teatre del Liceu Ramblas 51–59, Raval ☎934 859 900, ⊛www.liceubarcelona.com; Liceu. One of Europe's finest opera houses

hosts a wide-ranging programme of opera and dance productions, plus other concerts and recitals including the extremely popular *sessions golfes* (late-night concerts). Make bookings well in advance for all concerts and productions. Box office Mon–Fri 2–8.30pm, Sat 1hr before performance. For more on the building, see p.52.

Palau de la Música Catalana c/Sant Francesc de Paula 2, off c/Sant Pere Més Alt, Sant Pere ☎932 957 200, ⊛www.palaumusica.org; Urquinaona. The extravagantly decorated Catalan concert hall is home to the Orfeó Català choral group, and venue for concerts by the Orquestra Ciutat de Barcelona among others, though there's a broad remit here – over a season you can catch anything, from *sardanes* to pop concerts. Concert season Oct–June. Box office Mon–Sat 10am–9pm, Sun 1hr before performance. See p.70 for tours of the building.

Dance

Barcelona is very much a **contemporary dance** city, with regional, national and international performers and companies appearing regularly at theatre venues like the Mercat de les Flors, TNC, Teatre Lliure and Institut del Teatre – the latter, the city's theatre and dance school, has its own youth dance company, IT Dansa. For most visitors, however, dance in Barcelona means either watching (or joining in with) the Catalan national dance, the **sardana**, or catching a **flamenco** show. Although its home is indisputably Andalucia, flamenco also has deep roots in and around Barcelona, courtesy of its *andaluz* immigrants – unless you're looking for a showy night out, the pricey, tourist-oriented *tablaos* (flamenco and dinner shows) are best passed up in favour of the smaller clubs and restaurants that put on performances.

Dance venue

Mercat de les Flors c/de Lleida 59, Poble Sec ☎934 261 875, ⊛www.mercatflors.org; Poble Sec. The city's old flower market was for

years a fringe-style venue for music, dance and theatre. From 2007 it will steer a new course as a "national centre for movement arts", with dance the central focus of its programme.

Flamenco clubs

Flamenco Barcelona c/Marqués de Barberà 6, El Raval ☎934 436 680, ⓦwww.flamencobarcelona.com; Liceu. Authentic performances (Tues–Sat 8pm; €10) in a flamenco workshop (courses available) and club that harks back to the 1960s glory days of Catalan flamenco.

El Tablao de Carmen Poble Espanyol, Montjuïc ☎933 256 895, ⓦwww.tablaodecarmen.com; Espanya. The long-standing *tablao* in the Poble Espanyol at least looks the real deal, sited in a replica Andalucian street and featuring a variety of flamenco styles from both seasoned performers and new talent. Prices start at around €30 for the show and a drink, rising to €60 and upwards for the show plus dinner. Advance reservations essential. Tues–Sun from 9.30pm.

Tarantos Pl. Reial 17, Barri Gòtic ☎933 191 789, ⓦwww.masimas.com; Liceu. Some purists are sniffy about the experience, but for a cheap flamenco taster you can't beat *Tarantos* – a couple of rows of seats and a small bar in front of a stage where young singers, dancers and guitarists perform nightly at 8.30pm, 9.30pm & 10.30pm. Entry is just €5, you can stay as long as you like, and when the flamenco's finished the club sounds begin in adjacent *Jamboree* (see "Live music" on p.213).

Sardana performances

Sardanes Populars *Sardanes* are danced all year round every Sunday at noon, outside the cathedral, La Seu, in Plaça de la Seu (Ⓜ Jaume I). There are also usually performances on Saturday at 6.30pm from Easter until the end of October.

Film

All the latest films reach Barcelona fairly quickly, though at most of the larger cinemas and multiplexes (including the Maremàgnum screens at Port Vell) they're usually shown dubbed into Spanish or Catalan. However, several cinemas do show mostly **original-language** (*versión original* or V.O.) foreign films; the best are listed below. Tickets cost €6–7, and most cinemas have one night (usually Mon or Wed) – *el día del espectador* – when entry is **discounted**, usually to around €5. Many cinemas also feature **late-night** screenings (*madrugadas*) on Friday and Saturday nights, which begin at 12.30 or 1am. Every July there's

The sardana

The origins of the **sardana**, the Catalan national dance, are obscure, though similar folk dances in the Mediterranean date back hundreds if not thousands of years. It was established in its present form during the mid-nineteenth-century *Renaixança* (Renaissance), when Catalan arts and culture flourished, and was so identified with expressions of national identity that public dancing of *sardanes* was banned under the Franco regime. Sometimes mocked elsewhere in Spain, Catalans claim it to be truly democratic – a circle-dance open to all, danced in ordinary clothes (though some wear espadrilles) with no restriction in age or number. The dancers join hands, heads held high, arms raised, and though it looks deceptively simple and sedate it follows a precise pattern of steps, with shifts in pace and rhythm signalled by the accompanying *cobla* (band) of brass and wind instruments. This features typically Catalan instruments like the *flabiol* (a type of flute), and both tenor and soprano oboes, providing the characteristic high-pitched music. A strict etiquette applies to prevent the circle being broken in the wrong place, or a breakdown in the steps, and some of the more serious adherents may not welcome an intrusion into their circle by well-meaning first-timers. But usually visitors are encouraged to join the dance, especially at festival times, when the *sardana* breaks out spontaneously in the city's squares and parks. The **Federació Sardanista de Catalunya** (ⓦwww.fed.sardanista.com) publishes a calendar of dances and events on its website.

a giant-screen **open-air cinema** at Montjuïc castle (Wed & Fri night; @www .salamontjuic.com) – bring a picnic.

The city hosts several small **film festivals** throughout the year, including an international festival of independent short films, plus festivals devoted specifically to animation, women's, gay and lesbian, and African film. The Generalitat's Filmoteca (see below) is often the venue for festival screenings. The sci-fi and horror fest that is the **Festival Internacional de Cinema de Catalunya** (@www.cinemasitges.com) is held in nearby Sitges in October.

Cinemas

Filmoteca Avgda. de Sarrià 33, Eixample @934 107 590, @http://cultura.gencat.net/filmo; **Hospital Clinic.** Run by the Generalitat, the Filmoteca shows three or four different films (often foreign, and usually in V.O.) every night – themed programming and retrospectives are its stock-in-trade. Tickets are just €2.70 per film, or there's an €18 pass allowing entry to ten films.
Icaria-Yelmo c/de Salvador Espriu 61, Vila Olímpica @932 217 585, @www.yelmocineplex. es; **Ciutadella-Vila Olímpica.** No fewer than fifteen screens showing V.O. movies at a comfortable multiplex just a few minutes' walk from the Port Olímpic. Late-night screenings Fri & Sat; discount night Mon.
Méliès c/Villaroel 102, Eixample @934 510 051; **Urgell.** A repertory cinema specializing in V.O. showings, with three to five different films daily in its two *salas*. Discount night Mon.
Verdi c/Verdi 32, and Verdi Park, c/Torrijos 49, Gràcia @932 387 990, @www.cines-verdi.com; **Fontana.** Sister cinemas in adjacent streets showing art-house V.O. movies from around the world. Late-night films at Verdi on Fri & Sat; discount night Mon.

Live music

Major **rock, pop and indie** bands include Barcelona on their tours, playing either at sports stadium venues (at the Palau Sant Jordi on Montjuïc and the Velòdrom d'Horta) or at the city's bigger clubs, like *Razzmatazz, Sala Apolo, La Paloma, Bikini, KGB* and *Otto Zutz* (all listed). Tickets for these run from €20 to €50, depending on the act, though there are cheaper gigs (€5–20) almost every night of the year at a variety of smaller clubs and bars. The city's pretty hot on **jazz, Latin** and **blues**, too, while **folk, roots** and **world music** aficionados need to scour the club gig lists for home-grown and touring talent alike. All sorts of city venues, museums, galleries and institutions have **live music programmes** too – Caixa Forum (see p.89) is particularly well regarded, while the books-and-music chain **FNAC** (@www.clubcultura.com) sponsors gigs and events at the concert halls at its stores at Plaça de Catalunya, L'Illa Diagonal and L'Illa Diagonal Mar. The **websites** @www.atiza.com and @www.barcelonarocks.com provide a rundown of the Barcelona music scene, with gig calendars, band profiles and reviews.

Tickets for major gigs are available from the main **ticket agencies** (see chapter introduction); in addition, there's a concert ticket desk in the Plaça Catalunya FNAC store (@Catalunya), while the music shops along c/dels Tallers (just off the Ramblas; @Catalunya) also sell gig tickets.

The big annual **music festivals** start with the Generalitat's summer-long Barcelona Festival (formerly known as the Grec), while techno, rock and indie heads focus on Primavera Sound (May) and Sónar (June). Singer-songwriters are showcased every year at Barnasants (Feb–March), while for jazz fans the main event is the Festival de Jazz (Nov–Dec), though there's also the jazz and Latin-tinged Festival de Guitarra (April–May).

Centre Artesà Tradicionàrius (CAT) Trav. de Sant Antoni 6–8, Gràcia ☎ 932 184 485 ⓦ www. tradicionarius.com; Fontana. Folk and world gigs and recitals by Catalan and visiting performers, usually Fri around 10pm (though the bar is open nightly). Sponsors an annual international folk and traditional dance festival between Jan & April.

Harlem Jazz Club c/Comtessa de Sobradiel 8, Barri Gòtic ☎ 933 100 755; Jaume I. Small, usually jam-packed venue for mixed jazz styles, from African and gypsy to flamenco and fusion. Live music 10.30pm & midnight (Sat & Sun 11.30pm & 1am); it's best to get advance tickets for the second spot. Cover charge up to €6. Closed Aug.

▽ Harlem Jazz Club

Jamboree Pl. Reial 17, Barri Gòtic ☎ 933 191 789, ⓦ www.masimas.com; Liceu. There's a really good range of jazz gigs here, from traditional to modern (9pm & 11pm; €8–10), with an additional jazz, funk and hip-hop jam session (Mon 10pm; €3). Best of all, every night you can stay on for the club,

playing funk, swing, hip-hop and R&B from around midnight until 5am.

Jazzroom-La Cova del Drac c/Vallmajor 33, Sant Gervasi ☎ 933 191 789, ⓦ www.masimas.com; FGC Muntaner. One of Barcelona's best jazz clubs serves up live music Tues–Sat from 11pm – some of the bigger names play here. Cover charge €10–20 depending on the act. Closed Aug.

Jazz Sí Club c/Requesens 2, El Raval ☎ 933 290 020, ⓦ www.tallerdemusics.com; Sant Antoni. Good, inexpensive gigs in a small club and bar associated with the music school. Every night from 9pm there's something different: rock, blues and jam sessions, plus jazz, *mestiza*, *son cubano* and flamenco.

Luz de Gas c/Muntaner 246, Eixample ☎ 932 097 711, ⓦ www.luzdegas. com; Diagonal. Live music (rock blues, soul, jazz and covers) every night around midnight. Foreign acts appear regularly, too, mainly jazz-blues types but also old soul acts and up-and-coming rockers.

La Sala Castello Avgda. Francesc Cambó 36, Sant Pere ⓦ www.salacastello.com. Gigs, album presentations and guest appearances by indie, rock and pop artists, in association with Discos Castelló music stores – check the website for schedules.

Sidecar Pl. Reial 7, Barri Gòtic ☎ 933 021 586, ⓦ www.sidecarfactoryclub.com; Liceu. Hip bar – pronounced "See-day-car" – with nightly gigs and DJs. It's a good place to catch local rock, indie, roots and fusion acts, with admission for most gigs around €5–12. Tues–Sun 8pm–4am, gigs usually at 10pm.

Theatre and cabaret

The **Teatre Nacional de Catalunya** (Catalan National Theatre) was specifically conceived as a venue to promote Catalan productions, and features a repertory programme of translated classics (such as Shakespeare in Catalan), original works and productions by guest companies from Europe. The other big local theatrical project is the **Ciutat del Teatre** (Theatre City) on Montjuïc, which incorporates the fringe-style Mercat de les Flors, the progressive Teatre Lliure and the Institut del Teatre theatre and dance school. The centre for commercial theatre is Avinguda Paral.lel and the nearby streets. Some theatres draw on the city's strong **cabaret** tradition – more music-hall entertainment than stand-up comedy, and thus a little more accessible to non-Catalan or Spanish speakers. For **children's theatre**, see p.239.

It may not have the global influence of 1980s Manchester or 1990s Seattle, but the *mestiza* sound of twenty-first century Barcelona is causing quite a stir – a cross-cultural fusion of rock, reggae, rap, hip-hop, rai, son, flamenco, rumba and electronica. Its heartland is the immigrant melting-pot of the Raval district, whose postcode – **08001** – lends a name to the sound's hippest flagbearers. Also typically "Raval" is the collective called **Cheb Balowski**, an Algerian-Catalan fusion band, while **Macaco** draw on their South American heritage with their characteristic mix of rumba, ragga and hip-hop. The biggest star on the scene is the Parisian-born, Barcelona-resident **Manu Chao**, whose infectious, multi-million-selling album *Clandestino* (1998) kick-started the whole genre. He's widely known abroad now, and has influenced many Barcelona bands, including the world music festival favourites **Ojos de Brujo** (Eyes of the Wizard), who present a fusion reinvention of flamenco and Catalan rumba. Other hot sounds are being hatched by the ska-tinged acoustic roots outfit **Dusminguet**, the Latin American dub and reggae band **GoLem System**, the Latin fusion merchants **Radio Malanga** and the rock-and-rumba duo, **Estopa**. Street and hip-hop freestyle bands also have a loyal local following, with **Payo Malo** and **LA Kinky Beat** the names to check. Lots of these artists play regularly in Barcelona, and there's more information on the useful *mestiza* portal Ⓦwww.radiochango.com. Meanwhile, you can hear all the above – and more – on three great samplers, *Barcelona Raval Sessions* (K Industria), *Barcelona Raval Sessions 2* (Satelite K) and *Barcelona Zona Bastarda* (K Industria).

A free monthly magazine **Teatre BCN** (Ⓦwww.teatrebcn.com) carries listings and reviews (in Catalan). **Tickets** are available from the box offices at the Palau de la Virreina (Ramblas 99), or the usual agency outlets. Same-day **half-price tickets** (Tiquet-3) for some shows can be bought at the Caixa de Catalunya desk (Mon–Sat 11am–9.30pm) in the Plaça de Catalunya tourist office.

The summer Barcelona Festival always has a strong theatre and dance programme – many performances are at the open-air **Teatre Grec** on Montjuïc. June's Mataró de l'Espectacle at the Mercat de les Flors is also worth catching, a two-day marathon of theatrical performances.

Theatre venues

Café Teatre Llantiol c/Riereta 7, El Raval ☎933 299 009, Ⓦwww.llantiol.com; Paral.lel/Sant Antoni. Cabaret café-theatre whose varied shows (9pm & 11pm) feature a mix of mime, song, poetry, clowns, magic and dance. It is also the venue of the once-a-month Giggling Guiri (Ⓦwww.gigglingguiri.com) stand-up comedy night (in English). Closed Mon.

Institut del Teatre Pl. Margarida Xirgu s/n, Poble Sec ☎932 273 900, Ⓦwww.institutdelteatre.org; Poble Sec. Regular performances of all kinds at the school for dramatic arts and dance.

Teatre Lliure Pl. Margarida Xirgu, Poble Sec ☎932 289 747, Poble Sec; Ⓦwww.teatrelliure.com. The "Free Theatre" performs the work of contemporary Catalan and Spanish playwrights, as well as reworkings of the clas-

sics, from Shakespeare to David Mamet; it also hosts visiting dance companies, concerts and recitals. Some productions have English subtitles.

Teatre Nacional de Catalunya (TNC) Pl. de les Arts 1, Glòries ☎933 065 700, Ⓦwww.tnc.es; Glòries. Intended to foster Catalan works, the national theatre – built as a modern emulation of an ancient Greek temple – features major productions by Catalan, Spanish and European companies, as well as smaller-scale plays, experimental works and dance productions.

Teatre Poliorama Ramblas 115, El Raval ☎933 177 599, Ⓦwww.teatrepoliorama.com; Catalunya. Specializes in modern drama (Catalan and translation) and musicals, often utilizing the talents of offbeat companies like Tricicle and Dagoll Dagom (see box, opposite).

Teatre Romea c/Hospital 51, El Raval ☎933 181

Catalan theatre companies

Els Comediants (ⓦ www.comediants.com) – a travelling collective of actors, musicians and artists, established in 1971, who use any open space as a stage to celebrate "the festive spirit of human existence".

La Cubana (ⓦ www.lacubana.es) is a highly original company that started life as a street theatre group, though has since moved into television and theatre proper. It still hits the streets occasionally, taking on the role of market traders in the Boqueria or cleaning cars in the street in full evening dress.

Dagoll Dagom (ⓦ www.dagolldagom.com) specializes in hugely theatrical, over-the-top musicals.

La Fura del Baus (Vermin of the Sewer; ⓦ www.lafura.com) are performance artists who aim to shock and lend a new meaning to audience participation. They've subsequently taken on opera, cabaret, film and installations, lending each a wild, challenging perspective.

Els Joglars (ⓦ www.elsjoglars.com) present political theatre, and are particularly critical of the Church and government, who come in for regular satirical attacks.

Teatre Nu (Naked Theatre; ⓦ www.teatrenu.com) was founded in 1991 by young Catalan actors who wanted to bring theatre back to its essence and "provoke social, moral and ideological dialectic between the audience and public".

Tricicle (ⓦ www.tricicle.com) – a very successful three-man mime, circus and theatre group – has branched off into film and television, but always places its humour "somewhere between reality and the absurd".

431, ⓦ www.fundacioromea.org; **Liceu**. Has an emphasis on contemporary Catalan and Spanish playwrights, and pan-European productions, and gives space to new theatre groups and radical directors.

Visual arts

Barcelona has dozens of private art galleries and exhibition halls, in addition to the temporary displays on show in its art centres, museums and galleries. **Major venues** with regularly changing art exhibitions include Caixa Forum, CCCB, MACBA and Fundació Antoni Tàpies for contemporary art; Espai 13 at Fundacío Joan Miró for young experimental artists; MNAC and La Pedrera for blockbuster international art shows; FAD for industrial and graphic art, design, craft and architecture; and the Centre d'Art Santa Mònica for contemporary Catalan art and photography. A few more specialist places are listed below.

▽ Teatre Nacional de Catalunya

Commercial galleries cluster together in the **Barri Gòtic**, on c/de Montcada and Passeig del Born near the Museu Picasso, and c/Petritxol near the cathedral; in **El Raval** c/Àngels and c/Doctor Dou near the MACBA; in the **Eixample** Passeig de Gràcia, c/Consell de Cent and Rambla Catalunya. Note that most commercial galleries are closed on Sundays, Mondays and in August. The weekly *Guía del Ocio* and the Associació Art Barcelona (ⓦwww.artbarcelona.es) have gallery listings and exhibition news. In spring **photography** fans should look out for the Primavera Fotogràfica, when photography exhibitions are held at various venues around the city.

Art and cultural centres

Capella de l'Antic Hospital de la Santa Creu c/de l'Hospital 56, El Raval ☎934 427 171, ⓦwww.bcn.es/virreinaexposicions; Liceu. Contemporary art of all kinds, though often a platform for work by young Barcelona artists.

Fundació Foto Colectania c/Julian Romea 6, Gràcia ☎932 171 626, ⓦwww.colectania.es; Fontana. Spanish and Portuguese photography shows, with works from the 1950s onwards.

Palau Robert Pg. de Gràcia 107, Eixample ☎932 388 091, ⓦwww.gencat.net/probert; Diagonal. Puts on a wide range of shows, all with a Catalan connection.

Palau de la Virreina Ramblas 99, Barri Gòtic ☎933 017 775, ⓦwww.bcn.es/virreinaexposicions; Liceu. Modern art and photography shows in two galleries.

Sala d'Art Jove de la Generalitat c/Calabria 147, Eixample ☎934 838 383; Rocafort. The Generalitat's youth art space.

Commercial galleries

Galleria Joan Prats Rambla de Catalunya 54, Eixample ☎932 160 290, ⓦwww.galeriajoan-prats.com; Passeig de Gràcia. Contemporary Catalan artists and photographers.

H2O c/Verdi 152, Gràcia ☎934 151 801, ⓦwww.h2o.es; Fontana. Design, photography, contemporary art.

Iguapop c/del Comerç 15, La Ribera ☎933 100 735, ⓦwww.iguapop.net; Jaume I. Unique Born gallery showcasing street art, graffiti and photography – the window is usually a hoot.

Kowasa c/de Mallorca 235, Eixample ☎934 873 588, ⓦwww.kowasa.com; Provença. Traditional and contemporary photography and photographic art.

Metrònom c/Fusina 9, La Ribera ☎932 684 298, ⓦwww.metronom-bcn.org; Jaume I. Contemporary art, photography and multimedia exhibits.

Sala Pares c/Petritxol 5–8, Barri Gòtic ☎933 187 020, ⓦwww.salapares.com; Liceu. Hosted Picasso's first show and now dedicated to nineteenth- and twentieth-century Catalan art.

Gay and lesbian Barcelona

There's a vibrant gay and lesbian scene in Barcelona, backed up by an established organizational infrastructure and a generally supportive city council. Information about the scene is pretty easy to come by, while locals and tourists alike are well aware of the lure of Sitges, forty minutes south by train and mainland Spain's biggest gay resort.

The expression for the gay scene in Spanish is *"el ambiente"*, which simply means "the atmosphere" – it's the name of the useful section in the weekly listings magazine *Guía del Ocio*, which lists gay and lesbian bars, clubs, restaurants and other services.

We've picked out the best of bars, clubs, restaurants and hotels aimed specifically at a gay and lesbian clientele. They're scattered across the city, though there's a particular concentration of bars, restaurants and clubs in the so-called **Gaixample**, the "Gay Eixample", an area of a few square blocks just northwest of the main university in the Esquerra de l'Eixample. Bear in mind that you'll also be welcome at plenty of other nominally straight Barcelona dance bars and clubs – for full listings, see Chapter 9.

For up-to-date **information** and other advice on the scene, you can contact any of the organizations listed below, or call the **lesbian and gay city telephone hotline** on ☎900 601 601 (Mon–Fri 6–10pm only). *Guía del Ocio* (out every Thursday) can put you on the right track for bars and clubs, though there's also a good free **magazine** called *Nois* (ⓦwww.revistanois.com), which carries an up-to-date review of the scene. For full listings and other links, the web portal ⓦwww.gaybarcelona.net is extremely useful, while ⓦwww.gays-abroad.com is a forum and chat site for gay men living in or visiting Barcelona.

Biggest event of the year is **Carnival** in Sitges (see p.134), while there's the Barcelona International Gay and Lesbian **Film Festival** every October. The city's annual lesbian and gay **pride march** is on the nearest Saturday to June 28, starting at Plaça Universitat. Barcelona has also been chosen as the host of the July 2008 **Eurogames** (ⓦwww.eurogames.info), the European Gay and Lesbian Sports Championships.

Useful contacts

Ca la Dona c/de Casp 38, Eixample ☎934 127 161, ⓦwww.caladona.org; Ⓜ Urquinaona. A women's centre with library and bar, used for meetings by various feminist and lesbian organizations; information available to callers.

Casal Lambda c/Verdaguer i Callis 10 ☎933 195 550, ⓦwww.lambdaweb.org; Ⓜ Urquinaona. A gay and lesbian group with a wide range of social, cultural and educational events.

Front d'Alliberament Gai de Catalunya (FAGC) c/Verdi 88, Gràcia ☎932 172 669; Ⓜ Fontana. Association for gay men, with a library, meetings and events.

Shops and services

Antinous c/Josep Anselm Clavé 6, Barri Gòtic ☎933 019 070, ⓦ www.antinouslibros.com; Ⓜ Drassanes. Gay bookshop with useful contacts and information board – there's a café at the back. Closed Sun.

Cómplices c/Cervantes 2, Barri Gòtic ☎934 127 283, ⓦ www.libreriacomplices.com; Ⓜ Liceu. Exclusively gay and lesbian bookshop; also magazines and DVDs. Closed Sun.

Rainbow c/Diputació 191 ☎934 520 504, ⓦ www .rainbowviajes.com; Ⓜ Universitat. Gay and lesbian travel agency offering hotels, resorts and holidays worldwide, including Spain.

Accommodation

Outlet4Spain ☎938 102 711, ⓦ www .outlet4spain.com. Gay-run accommodation agency, offering to find you gay-friendly hotels, villas, apartments and flat-shares in Barcelona and Sitges; the website's in English.

Hotel Axel c/d'Aribau 33, Eixample ☎933 239 393, ⓦ www.hotelaxel.com; Ⓜ Universitat. A snazzy hotel set in the Gaixample, with stylishly appointed rooms in which designer fabrics, complimentary beauty products, flat-screen TVs and Internet access come as standard. Relaxation is taken care of in the restaurant and bar, library corner, chillout area, terrace pool and sauna, and there's a fitness centre and massage treatments available. From €170.

Hotel California c/Rauric 14, Barri Gòtic ☎933 177 766, ⓦ www.hotelcaliforniabcn.com; Ⓜ Liceu. Tucked down a side street that crosses c/de Ferran, this friendly hotel has nicely colour-coordinated rooms with TV, air-conditioning and full bathrooms, breakfast included in the price. There are some internal rooms, and all are double-glazed, but even so, you never quite escape the weekend noise in this part of town. From €85.

Hostal Que Tal c/Mallorca 290, Eixample ☎934 592 366, ⓦ www.quetalbarcelona.com; Ⓜ Passeig de Gràcia/Verdaguer. Pretty rooms, with and without private bath, in a good uptown location. It's a nice, if modest, choice, with an attractive courtyard patio. No credit cards. From €60, en suite from €75.

Cafés and bars

Aire c/Valencia 236, Eixample ☎934 515 812, ⓦ www.arenadisco.com; Ⓜ Passeig de Gràcia. The hottest, most stylish lesbian bar in town is a surprisingly relaxed place for a drink and a dance to pop, house and retro sounds. Gay men welcome too. Thurs–Sat 11pm–3am, July & Aug also Tues & Wed.

Átame c/Consell de Cent 257, Eixample ☎934 549 273; Ⓜ Universitat. Contemporary music bar with a change of pace, from early evening drinks and gentility to late-night hot sounds. Daily 8pm–2am.

Dietrich c/Consell de Cent 255, Eixample ☎934 517 707; Ⓜ Universitat. This well-known music bar and "teatro-café" serves food until midnight, with drag shows, acrobats and dancers punctuating the DJ sets. Daily 6pm–2.30am.

▽ Café Dietrich

D-Mer c/Plató 13, Sant Gervasi ☎932 016 207, ⓦ www.d-mer.com; FGC Muntaner. Sleek uptown music and dance bar, a strictly lesbian space. Thurs–Sat 11pm–3am.

Punto BCN c/Muntaner 63–65, Eixample ☎934 536 123, ⓦ www.arenadisco.com; Ⓜ Universitat. A Gaixample classic that attracts an uptown crowd for drinks, chat and music – it's a popular trysting place. Friday night is party night. Daily 6pm–2am.

Zeltas c/Casanova 75, Eixample ☎934 541

Restaurants

Barcelona has several gay- and lesbian-friendly or gay- and lesbian-run restaurants, where you'll be assured of a warm welcome and sympathetic atmosphere. **Miranda** (c/Casanova 30, Eixample ☎934 535 249, ⓦwww.mirandabarcelona.com; ⓜUniversitat; reservations advised; closed Mon) probably has the highest profile, serving around-the-world bistro dishes (around €25 à la carte) to the accompaniment of singing drag queens, trapeze acts and contortionists. **dDivine** (c/Balmes 24, Eixample ☎933 172 248, ⓦwww.ddivine.com; ⓜUniversitat; closed Mon & Tues) also offers dinner and a live drag show. More relaxed, moderately priced gay-friendly eateries include the New York-style **Castro** (c/Casanova 85, Eixample ☎933 236 784, ⓦwww.castrorestaurant.com; ⓜUniversitat; closed Sat lunch & Sun) and fusion-Italian **Iurantia** (c/Casanova 42, Eixample ☎934 547 887, ⓦwww.iurantia.com; ⓜUniversitat; closed Sat lunch & Sun).

902, ⓦwww.zeltas.net; ⓜUrgell. Pumped-up house-music bar for the pre-club crowd. Wed–Sun 11pm–3am.

Clubs

As well as the gay clubs reviewed below, the two biggest gay club nights in the city are Gay Day (Sunday, at Space Barcelona, ⓦwww.gaydaybcn.com) and Gay T Dance (Sunday, at Sala Apolo, ⓦwww.gaytdance.com).

Arena Madre c/Balmes 32, Eixample ☎934 878 342, ⓦwww.arenadisco.com; ⓜPasseig de Gràcia. The "mother" club sits at the helm of the Arena empire, all in the same block (pay for one, get in to all) – frenetic house and chart at *Arena Madre* (Tues–Sat 12.30–5am, Sun 7pm–5am), high disco antics at *Arena Classic* (c/de la Diputació 233; Fri & Sat

12.30–5am), more of the same plus dance, R&B, pop and rock at the more mixed *Arena VIP* (Grand Via de les Corts Catalanes 593; Fri & Sat 12.30–6am), and the best in house at *Arena Dandy* (Grand Via de les Corts Catalanes 593; Fri & Sat 12.30–6am).
Metro c/Sepúlveda 158, Eixample ☎933 235 227, ⓦwww.metrodiscobcn.com; ⓜUniversitat/Urgell. A gay institution in Barcelona, with cabaret nights and other events midweek. Extremely crowded at weekends in its two rooms playing either current dance and house or retro disco. Mon–Thurs & Sun midnight–5am, Fri & Sat midnight–6am.
Salvation Ronda de Sant Pere 19–21 ☎933 180 686, ⓦwww.matineegroup.com; ⓜUrquinaona. Huge Ibiza-scene gay club playing the best in European house, and promoting all sorts of parties, events and performances. Fri–Sun midnight–5am.

Festivals and holidays

Almost any month you choose to visit Barcelona you'll coincide with a saint's day, festival or holiday, and it's hard to beat the experience of arriving to discover the streets decked out with flags and streamers, bands playing and the entire population out celebrating. Traditionally, each neighbourhood celebrates with its own *festa*, though the major ones – like Gràcia's Festa Major and the Mercè – have become city institutions. Each is different, but there is always music, dancing, traditional costume, fireworks and an immense spirit of enjoyment – for more, see the colour section. The religious calendar has its annual highlights too, with Carnaval, Easter and Christmas a big time for parades, events and festivities across the city. Meanwhile, biggest and best of the annual arts events are the Generalitat's summer Barcelona Festival and the ever-expanding Sónar extravaganza of electronic music and multimedia art.

There's a **month-by-month calendar** below of the best annual festivals, holidays, trade fairs and events, though it's not an exhaustive list. Tourist offices have more information about what's going on at any given time; or call into the cultural information office at the **Palau de la Virreina**, Ramblas 99, or check out the Ajuntament's useful **website** (@www.bcn.es/cultura). It's worth noting that during the most popular festivals you'll find it difficult to find a bed, so it pays to book your accommodation well in advance. Incidentally, not all **public holidays** coincide with a festival, but many do – there's a complete list on p.40. In addition, saints' day festivals – indeed all Catalan celebrations – can vary in date, often being observed over the weekend closest to the dates given.

January

Cap d'Any New Year's Eve Street and club parties, and mass gatherings in Pl. de Catalunya and other main squares. You're supposed to eat twelve grapes in the last twelve seconds of the year for twelve months of good luck. Next day, Jan 1, is a public holiday.

Cavalcada de Reis Afternoon of Jan 5 This is when the Three Kings (who distribute Christmas gifts to Spanish children) arrive by sea at the port and ride into town, throwing sweets as they go. The parade begins at the port at about 5pm on Jan 5; the next day is a public holiday.

Festa dels Tres Tombs Jan 17 Costumed horseback parade through the Sant Antoni neighbourhood, with local saint's day festivities to follow.

February

Festes de Santa Eulàlia Feb 12 The signal for a week's worth of music, *sardanes*, children's processions, *castellers* and fireworks in honour of one of Barcelona's two patron saints, the thirteen-year-old girl martyred by the Romans. See colour section for more.

Carnaval/Carnestoltes Week before Lent, sometimes in March Costumed parades, dances, concerts, open-air barbecues and other traditional carnival events in every city neighbourhood. However, it's Sitges, p.137, which has the best Catalan celebrations.

Barnasants Dates vary, Feb–March, @ www.

barnasants.com A singer-songwriter festival (Catalan/Spanish, plus Brazilian and Latin American artists), with around 50 gigs held over six weeks in city clubs and concert venues.

March/April

Festes de Sant Medir de Gràcia First week in March, ⓦ**www.santmedir.org** Horse-and-carriage parade around Pl. Rius i Taulet in Gràcia, before heading to the Sant Medir hermitage in the Collserola hills. Later, the procession returns to Gràcia, where sweets are thrown to children along c/Gran de Gràcia.

Setmana Santa Easter, Holy Week Religious celebrations and services at churches throughout the city. Special services are on Thurs and Fri in Holy Week at 7–8pm, Sat at 10pm; there's a procession from the church of Sant Agustí on c/de l'Hospital (El Raval) to La Seu, starting at 4pm on Good Friday; and Palm Sunday sees the blessing of the palms at La Seu. Public holidays on Good Friday and Easter Monday.

Dia de Sant Jordi St George's Day, April 23 Celebrating Catalunya's patron saint and coinciding with the International Day of the Book, with book and flower stalls throughout the city. Men are traditionally presented with a book while women in turn are presented with a rose (although, in recent years, modernization has demanded books for women as well). See colour section for more.

Feria de Abril Last week in April, ⓦ**www.fecac. com** The region's biggest Andalucian festival, with ten days of food, drink and flamenco. Marquees are erected at the Fòrum plaza (Diagonal Mar).

May

Dia del Treball May 1 May Day/Labour Day is a public holiday, with union parades along main city thoroughfares.

Saló Internacional del Còmic Second week, ⓦ**www.ficomic.com** The International Comic Fair takes place over three days, with stalls, drawing workshops and children's activities at one of the city's exhibition halls.

Dia de San Ponç May 11 Saint's day, celebrated by a market running along c/de l'Hospital in the Raval, with fresh herbs, flowers, cakes, aromatic oils and sweets.

Festival de Música Antiga Usually first two weeks Medieval and Baroque groups from around the world, with paying concerts in larger venues, but free fringe shows outdoors in old-town squares.

Barcelona Poesia Usually second week Week-long poetry festival with readings and recitals in venues across the city. It incorporates the Jocs Floral (Floral Games), a revived medieval Catalan poetry competition, while Spanish and foreign poets converge for the International Poetry Festival at the Palau de la Música Catalana.

Primavera Sound Usually last week, ⓦ**www.pri-maverasound.com** Three-day music festival at the Parc del Fòrum (Diagonal Mar) attracting top international names in the rock, indie and electronica world.

Festival de Flamenco de Ciutat Vella Usually last week, ⓦ**www.tallerdemusics.com** Annual old-town flamenco bash, organized by the Taller de Músics (music workshop) and centred on the CCCB. Five days of guitar recitals, singing and dancing, plus DJ sessions and chill-out zone, and lectures and conferences on all matters flamenco.

June

Marató de l'Espectacle Entertainment Marathon, ⓦ**www.marato.com** A nonstop, two-day marathon of rapid-fire performances of theatre, dance, cabaret, music and children's shows, which takes place in and around the Mercat de les Flors theatre.

Festa de la Música June 21, ⓦ**www.fusic. org/fm** Every year on this day, scores of concerts are held in squares, parks, civic centres and museums across the city – buskers to orchestras, folk to techno.

Verbena/Dia de Sant Joan June 23–24 The "eve" and "day" of St John herald probably the wildest celebrations in the city, with a "night of fire" of bonfires and fireworks (particularly on Montjuïc), drinking and dancing. Coca de Sant Joan, a sweet flatbread, and *cava* are the traditional accompaniments to the merriment – see colour section for more. The day itself (June 24) is a public holiday.

Sónar Dates vary, ⓦ**www.sonar.es** The three-day International Festival of Advanced Music and Multimedia Art is Europe's biggest and most cutting-edge electronic music and multimedia festival, attracting up to 100,000 visitors. Sónar by day centres on events at MACBA/CCCB; by night the action shifts to out-of-town L'Hospitalet, with all-night buses running from the city to the Sónar bars and clubs. Separate day, night and general tickets available – buy well in advance.

Barcelona Festival June–Aug, ⓦwww .barcelonafestival.com Starting in the last week of June (and running throughout July and into Aug), this is the city's main performing arts festival, with a strong programme of theatre, music and dance productions, many staged at Montjuïc's Teatre Grec. See colour section for more.

July

Summercase Barcelona Two days in July, dates vary, ⓦwww.summercase.com With simultaneous indie, rock and electronica gigs held in Barcelona and Madrid, this is the summer version of November's big-name indie festival.

August

Festa Major de Gràcia Mid-Aug, ⓦwww.fes- tamajordegracia.org A fine example of what was once a local festival in the erstwhile village of Gràcia, with music, dancing, decorations, fireworks, giants and human castles in the streets and squares.

Festa Major de Sants Last week of Aug, ⓦwww. festamajordesants.org A week's worth of traditional festivities in an untouristed neighbourhood, in the streets behind Barcelona Sants station.

September

Moda Barcelona Second week, ⓦwww. moda-barcelona.com Barcelona Fashion Week is the year's big couture event, with catwalk shows and exhibitions, including Gaudí Hombre (for men) and Gaudí Mujer (women).

Diada Nacional Sept 11 Catalan national day, commemorating the eighteenth-century defeat at the hands of the Bourbons. It's a public holiday in Barcelona, and special events include the city's more radical Catalan regionalists throwing bricks through burger-bar windows, fighting with the police and showing their patriotism by spraying graffiti on every available space.

Festes de la Mercè Sept 24 Huge annual festival dedicated to another of Barcelona's patron saints, the Virgin of Mercè, and celebrated for a week around this date (Sept

24 is a public holiday). Highlights include costumed giants, breathtaking firework displays, and competing teams of castellers – see colour section for more. The concurrent alternative music festival, known as BAM (ⓦwww.bcn.es/bam), puts on free rock, world and fusion gigs around the old town and at Diagonal Mar Fòrum during Mercè week.

Festa Major de Sant Miquel/Barceloneta Last week Traditional festivities on the waterfront as Barceloneta celebrates its saint's day with fireworks, parades, castellers, music and dancing.

October

LEM Throughout Oct, ⓦwww.gracia-territori. com Experimental and electronic music festival organized by the Gràcia Territori Sonor collective, with free or cheap concerts and events held in Gràcia's bars, cafés and galleries.

Festival de Tardor Ribermúsica Third week in Oct, ⓦwww.ribermusica.org Wide-ranging three-day music festival held in the Born, with free concerts in historic and picturesque locations.

Festival de Jazz Last week in Oct and through Nov, ⓦwww.the-project.net The annual jazz festival attracts big-name solo artists and bands to the clubs and concert halls, as well as smaller-scale street concerts.

November

Tots Sants All Saints' Day, Nov 1 When the Spanish remember their dead, with cemetery visits and special meals, it's traditional to eat roast chestnuts (*castanyes*), sold by street vendors, sweet potatoes and *panellets* (almond-based sweets). It's also a public holiday.

Wintercase Barcelona End of Nov; ⓦwww. ⓦintercase.com Gloom-mongers, mullets and guitar-merchants celebrate at this one-night indie music showcase, with similar one-night gigs also held in Madrid, Valencia and Bilbao.

December

Fira de Santa Llúcia Dec 1–22 For more than 200 years the Christmas season has seen a special market and crafts fair outside the cathedral.

Nadal/Sant Esteve Dec 25–26 Christmas

Day and St Stephen's Day are both public holidays, which Catalans tend to spend at home – the traditional gift-giving is on Twelfth Night (Jan 6).

Sports and outdoor activities

B arcelona is well placed for access to the sea and mountains, which is one of the reasons it was picked for the 1992 Olympics. A spin-off from the games was an increased provision of top-quality sports and leisure facilities throughout Catalunya. However, while there are scores of sports centres and swimming pools in the city, there aren't actually that many that will appeal to tourists or casual visitors. Most people are content to hit the city beaches or take off for a hike or jog in the surrounding hills of the Parc de la Collserola.

Attending the big match, whatever that might be, is a different matter. **Tickets** for all major sporting events can be bought from the usual agencies, **ServiCaixa** (☎902 332 211, ⊛www.servicaixa.com) or **Tel-Entrada** (☎902 101 212, ⊛www.telentrada.com). The main source of information about municipal sports facilities is the Ajuntament's **Servei d'informació Esportiva** (☎934 023 000 or 010, ⊛www.bcn.es, look under "Esports"), which has a drop-in office (Direcció d'Esports) on Montjuïc at Avgda. de l'Estadi 30–40 (Ⓜ Espanya), at the side of the Bernat Picornell swimming pool.

Basketball

Second only to football in popularity, basketball has been played in Barcelona since the 1920s. Games are usually played September to June at weekends – you'll often catch the tail-end of one on TV in a bar – with most interest in the city's two main teams. **Club Joventat de Badalona**, founded in 1930, were European champions in 1994, while **FC Barcelona** (an offshoot of the football club as early as 1926) finished runners-up five times before finally becoming European champions in 2003. Tickets to games are fairly inexpensive (up to €30), and it's easiest to go and watch FC Barcelona, as Badalona is out in the sticks. The team plays at the Palau Blaugrana, adjacent to the Camp Nou, which is where you have to go to buy tickets (go the day before the game) - see "Football" overleaf for main stadium contact details.

Cycling

Cycling as transport is something of a novel concept for Barcelonans, though to be fair the city authorities are doing their best by rapidly laying out rights of way along many of the most heavily trafficked streets. However, the population at large has yet to adapt, as the cycle paths are often ignored by cars or clogged with pedestrians, indignantly reluctant to give way to two-wheelers. Currently, there are around 130km of cycle paths throughout the city, with plans to double the network by 2010.

The best way to see the city by bike – certainly as a first-time visitor – is to take a **bike tour** (see Basics, p.33); bikes and equipment will be provided. If you would rather go on your own, you can **rent a bike** from one of the outlets listed in the Directory on p.242. A map detailing current **cycle paths** is available from the tourist office, or consult the city council's website Ⓦwww.bcn.es/bicicleta, which has useful information about cycling in the city (in English). The nicest place to get off the road is in the **Parc de la Collserola** (p.130), where there are bike trails for varying abilities through the woods and hills. Montjuïc is another popular place for mountain-biking – there's a weekend rental outfit up behind the castle. Bikes are allowed on the metro, on FGC trains, and on the Montjuïc and Vallvidrera funiculars.

The city hosts a variety of annual **cycling events**. The Semana Catalana at the end of March is the big regional race (suspended in 2006, but due to return in 2007), while the Tour of Spain (Vuelta España) also usually passes through Catalunya. In Barcelona itself, May sees the Bicycle Fiesta – a week's worth of rides and events – while September is another big month, with races during the Mercè festival and a day during the city's "Mobility Week" dedicated to cycling. In October, there's the Escalada a Montjuïc, an annual international hill-climb race on Montjuïc.

Football

In Barcelona, football is a genuine obsession, with support for the local giants, **FC** (Futbol Club) **Barcelona**, raised to an art form. The team plays at the splendid Camp Nou stadium in the north of the city and, even if you don't coincide with a game, the stadium's football museum alone is worth the trip. All the details are on p.123. The other local team – though not to be compared – is **RCD** (Reial Club Deportiu) **Espanyol**, whose games are currently played at the Olympic stadium on Montjuïc, though they are due to move to a new 40,000-seater stadium being built at Cornellà, west of the city centre.

The season runs from late August until May, with games usually played on Sundays (though sometimes on other days). You'll have little problem getting a **ticket** to see an Espanyol game: either just turn up on the day, or buy them up to three days in advance from the stadium ticket office. It's also fairly straightforward to get tickets for FC Barcelona. The Camp Nou seats 98,000, which means it's only really full for big games against rivals like Real Madrid, or for major European ties. For all other games, some tickets are put on general sale a week before each match (and may be available at ticket booths on the day), or try ServiCaixa. Touts and season-ticket holders at the ground also offer spare tickets for most matches. The cheapest seats at both grounds start at €20, though for a typical league game at Barcelona you're more likely to end up paying €30–40 (and be seated *very* high up).

Team contacts

FC Barcelona Camp Nou, Avgda. Arístides Maillol ☎934 963 600, Ⓦwww.fcbarcelona.com; ⓂCollblanc/Maria Cristina.

RCD Espanyol Estadi Olímpic, Pg. Olímpic 17–19 ☎932 927 700, Ⓦwww.rcdespanyol. com; ⓂEspanya, then free shuttle bus from Pl. d'Espanya on match days.

Horse riding

The municipal riding school on Montjuïc offers lessons and courses for adults (beginners especially welcome), children and disabled people, or you can just have a taster with an hour-long riding session from around €15.

Riding school

Escola Municipal d'Hípica La Foixarda Avgda. Montanyans 1, Montjuïc ☎934 261 066;

ⓂEspanya, then bus #50. Office open Mon–Fri 4.30–9.30pm.

Ice-skating

There are a couple of ice rinks in the city, including one at FC Barcelona's Camp Nou stadium, and a seasonal rink at the Parc del Fòrum at Diagonal Mar. At the Roger de Flor rink there's a bar from where you can watch the action. It's a good idea to have someone check hours and restrictions before you go, as weekends and holidays especially can see the rinks inundated with children.

Ice rinks

Pavelló Pista Gel Camp Nou, c/Arístides Maillol 12 ☎934 963 600; ⓂCollblanc/Maria Cristina. Morning and afternoon skating sessions daily throughout the year, times vary. Admission €10, including skate rental.

Skating Pista de Gel c/Roger de Flor 168, Eixample ☎932 452 800, Ⓦwww.skatingbcn.com; ⓂTetuan. Morning and afternoon skating sessions daily throughout the year, times vary. Admission €11, including skate rental.

Roller blading/skating/skateboarding

The Passeig Marítim and Port Olímpic area (Ⓜ Ciutadella-Vila Olímpica) see heavy **skate and blade** traffic, while other popular runs include Arc de Triomf (Ⓜ Arc de Triomf), Parc Joan Miró (Ⓜ Tarragona) and Barceloneta, next to the Palau del Mar (Ⓜ Barceloneta). The Fòrum site down at Diagonal Mar (Ⓜ El Marseme Forum) has acres of wide open space. You're supposed to keep off all marked cycle paths. Meanwhile, *the* place for **skateboarders** is the piazza outside MACBA, the contemporary art gallery in the Raval.

Running and jogging

The **Passeig Marítim** (Ⓜ Ciutadella-Vila Olímpica) is the best place for a seafront run – there's a five-kilometre promenade from Barceloneta all the way to the River Besòs, with a fitness circuit on the way at Mar Bella beach. To get off the beaten track, you'll need to head for the heights of Montjuïc or the Parc de la Collserola.

There's a half-marathon (Mitja Marató de Barcelona) held in the city every February or March, while the full **Barcelona Marathon** (Marató Barcelona; application forms and details on Ⓦ www.barcelonamarathon.com) takes place in the last week of March on a course that weaves right through the city centre, past many famous landmarks. On the day there's also a shorter 10km race, plus street entertainment for spectators and a runners' trade show at the Fira exhibition hall. There are more road races during the September Mercè festival, while **La Cursa**, the annual twelve-kilometre run (June) organized by El Corte Inglés, attracts thousands onto the streets.

Sports centres

Every city neighbourhood has a sports centre, most with swimming pools but also offering a variety of other sports, games and activities. Schedules and prices vary, so it's best to contact the centres directly for any sport you might be interested in. Most have a general daily admission fee (around €15) if all you want is a swim and use of the gym. A couple of the more useful centres are listed below, but for a full rundown call ☏ 010 or consult the sports section database on Ⓦ www.bcn.es.

Poliesportiu Marítim Pg. Marítim 33, Vila Olímpica ☏ 932 240 440, Ⓦ www.claror.org; Ⓜ Ciutadella-Vila Olímpica. Large complex by the Port Olímpic with a pool, gym and sauna, plus a wide range of organized activities, games and treatments, from aerobics, dance and yoga to indoor biking, beach tennis and hydrotherapy. Mon–Fri 7am–midnight, Sat 8am–9pm, Sun 8am–5pm.

Poliesportiu Municpal Frontó Colom Ramblas 18, Barri Gòtic ☏ 933 023 295, Ⓦ www.fronto-colom.com; Ⓜ Drassanes. Centrally situated sports centre with pool and gym, where you can see traditional Spanish *frontón* (handball) or Basque *jai alai*, reputedly fastest sport in the world. Mon–Fri 7.30am–10.30pm, Sat 9am–8pm, Sun 9am–2.30pm.

Swimming

The city **beaches** are fine for a stroll across the sand and an ice cream, but the water's none too welcoming and you'd do best to save your swimming for the region's coastal beaches (Sitges is the best) or one of Barcelona's many municipal **pools**. There are scores of them, but we've picked out three of the best below. You may be required to show your passport before being allowed in, and you'll need to wear a swimming cap. If you're hardy enough, the annual Christmas swimming cup involves diving into the port on December 25 and racing other like-minded fools.

Swimming pools

Club Natació Atlètic Barceloneta Pl. del Mar, Barceloneta ☎932 210 010, Ⓦ www.cnab.org; Ⓜ **Ciutadella-Vila Olímpica.** One indoor pool, two outdoor, plus bar, restaurant and gym facilities. Mon–Fri 6.30am–11pm, Sat 7am–11pm, Sun 8am–5pm (until 8pm mid-May to Sept). Daily admission for nonmembers is around €8.

Piscina Municipal de Montjuïc Avgda. Miramar 31, Montjuïc ☎934 430 046; **Funicular de Montjuïc.** The city's most beautiful outdoor pool, high on Montjuïc. Mid-June to mid-Sept, daily 11am–6.30pm. Admission €4.50.

Piscines Bernat Picornell Avgda. de l'Estadi 30–40, Montjuïc ☎934 234 041, Ⓦ www.picornell.com; Ⓜ **Espanya, then bus #50.** Remodelled and expanded for the Olympics, the fifty-metre indoor pool is open all year, while the outdoor pool is open to the public from June to September. Nudist sessions all year on Sat night, plus Sun pm Oct–May. Indoor pool and other facilities Mon–Fri 7am–midnight, Sat 7am–9pm, Sun 7.30am–4pm; outdoor pool usually 9am–9pm. Outdoor €4.50, indoor €8.50, includes gym and sauna.

Tennis

The main municipal tennis centre at Vall d'Hebron is the best place to play. Unlike many clubs in the city, you can rent courts by the hour without being a member. There are asphalt and clay courts, costing around €15 an hour, plus a pool, gym and café. Rackets are available for rent. Other municipal tennis courts are listed on Ⓦ www.bcn.es, while for private clubs consult the website of the Federació Catalana de Tennis (Ⓦ www.fctennis.org). One of these, the Reial Club de Tennis Barcelona-1899 (Ⓦ www.rctb1899.es), hosts the **Barcelona Open** every April.

Tennis courts

Centre Municipal de Tenis Pg. Vall d'Hebron 178–196, Vall d'Hebron ☎934 276 500; Ⓜ **Montbau.** Public hours Mon–Fri 8am–11pm, Sat & Sun 8am–9pm.

Watersports

Courses and instruction in catamaran and laser sailing, kayaking and windsurfing, from two hours to two days, are available from the Port Olímpic's sailing club, Centre Municipal de Vela. At Base Nàutica, by Mar Bella beach, you can rent catamarans and windsurfers, and there's a popular bar

▽ Windsurfing

here as well. Prices at either vary considerably, but you can expect to pay around €35 for a couple of hours' windsurfing or €200 for a two-day elementary sailing course.

Watersports centres

Base Nàutica de la Mar Bella Avgda. Litoral ☎ 932 210 432, ⓦ www.basenautica.org; Ⓜ Ciutadella-Vila Olímpica, then bus #41. Daily 9.30am–9pm.

Centre Municipal de Vela Moll de Gregal, Port Olímpic ☎ 932 257 940, ⓦ www .vela-barcelona.com; Ⓜ Ciutadella-Vila Olímpica. Mon–Fri 9am–9pm, Sat & Sun 9am–8pm.

⑬

SPORTS AND OUTDOOR ACTIVITIES

Shopping

W hile for sheer size and scope Barcelona cannot compete with Paris or other fashion capitals, it is one of the world's most stylish cities – architecture, fashion and decoration are thoroughly permeated by Catalan *disseny* (design). All of this makes for great shopping, from designer clothes and accessories to crafts and household goods. Moreover, Barcelona is an undeniably pleasant place to shop: the wide boulevards of the Eixample, the pedestrianized old-town streets and the classic markets all encourage lengthy browsing.

Many visitors will find the city to be relatively cheap for a lot of items, and even more so if you coincide with the **annual sales** (*rebaixes, rebajas*) that follow the main fashion seasons – mid-January until the end of February, and throughout July and August. Non-EU residents can get a VAT refund on each purchase over the value of €90; look for the "Tax-Free Shopping" logo in stores.

Shop **opening hours** are typically Monday to Saturday 10am to 1.30/2pm and 4.30 to 7.30/8pm. though all the bigger shops stay open over lunchtime, while smaller shops close on Saturday afternoons or may vary their hours in other ways. **Major department stores and shopping malls** open Monday to Saturday 10am–10pm, though the cafés, restaurants and leisure outlets in

---

Where to shop

The best **general shopping area** for clothes, souvenirs, arts and crafts is the Barri Gòtic, particularly between the upper part of the Ramblas and Avinguda Portal de l'Àngel. Established designer and high-street fashion is at home in the Eixample, along Passeig de Gràcia, Rambla de Catalunya and c/de Pelai, as well as along Avinguda Diagonal in Les Corts. Hot **new designers and boutiques** – including shoe, street- and skatewear specialists – can be found in La Ribera, around Passeig del Born (c/Flassaders, c/Rec, c/Calders, c/Espartería, c/Vidrería, c/Bonaire), but also down c/d'Avinyó in the Barri Gòtic, between c/del Carme and MACBA in El Raval, and along c/Verdi in Gràcia. For **secondhand and vintage clothing**, stores line the whole of c/de la Riera Baixa (El Raval), with others nearby on c/del Carme and c/de l'Hospital, and on Saturdays there's a street market here. More bargains are in the **remainder stores, wholesalers and discount outlets** found along c/Girona in the Eixample, between the Gran Via and Ronda Sant Pere.

For **antiques** – books, furniture, paintings and artefacts – you need to trawl c/de la Palla, c/Banys Nous and surrounding streets in the Barri Gòtic, best combined with the antique market on Thursdays in front of the cathedral. **Delis and specialist food shops** tend to be concentrated around the Passeig del Born in La Ribera. Independent **music and CD stores** are concentrated on c/dels Tallers (El Raval), just off the top of the Ramblas. And don't forget the city's **museums and galleries**, where you'll find reasonably priced items ranging from postcards to wall-hangings.

malls are usually open on Sunday too. All the stores below are open in August unless otherwise stated. Barcelona's daily food **markets**, all in covered halls, are open from Monday to Saturday, 8am–3pm and 5pm–8pm, though the most famous, La Boqueria on the Ramblas, opens throughout the day.

Antiques

L'Arca del Avia c/Banys Nous 20, Barri Gòtic ℡933 021 598, ⊛www.larcadelavia.com; ⓂLiceu. Catalan brides used to fill up their nuptial trunk (*arca*) with embroidered bed linen and lace. Period (eighteenth to early-twentieth century) costumes can be hired or purchased as well – Kate Winslet's *Titanic* costume came from here. Closed Aug.

Bulevard dels Antiquarius Pg. de Gràcia 55–57, Eixample ℡932 154 499, ⊛www .bulevarddelsantiquaris.com; ⓂPasseig de Gràcia. An arcade with over seventy shops full of antiques of all kinds. Closed Sat in Aug.

Las Tres Ranas c/Nou de Sant Francesc 17, Barri Gòtic ℡932 703 068; ⓂDrassanes. Beautifully restored furniture and period objects combined with some of their own designs.

Urbana c/Còrsega 258, Eixample ℡932 187 036; ⓂDiagonal. Shop selling restored mirrors, fireplaces and other fittings rescued from demolition. The other branch, at c/Sèneca 13, Gràcia, (ⓂDiagonal), does the same with old furniture.

Arts and crafts

Art Escudellers c/Escudellers 23–25, Barri Gòtic ℡934 126 801, ⊛www .escudellers-art.com; ⓂLiceu. Enormous shop selling a wide range of ceramics, glass, jewellery and decorated tiles from different regions of Spain. Shipping can be arranged, and there's also a gourmet wine and food section.

Baraka c/dels Canvis Vells 2, La Ribera ℡932 684 220; ⓂBarceloneta. All things Morroccan – *objets*, gifts, rugs, lamps, basketware, books and music.

La Caixa de Fang c/Freneria 1, Barri Gòtic ℡933 151 704; ⓂJaume I. This has very good-value ceramics and recycled glassware. It's off Bxda. Llibreteria, behind the cathedral.

Cereria Subirà Bxda. Llibreteria 7, Barri Gòtic ℡933 152 606; ⓂJaume I. Barcelona's oldest shop (founded 1760) has a beautiful interior, selling unique hand-crafted candles.

Kitsch Pl. de Montcada 10, La Ribera ℡933 195 768; ⓂJaume I. Known for its papier-mâché models – matadors, flamenco dancers, pierrots and other characters – which are all unique. Also handmade paper fans.

Papirum Bxda. Llibreteria 2, Barri Gòtic ℡933 105 242; ⓂJaume I. For all your writing needs – hand-painted paper, draughtsman's pens, leather-bound notebooks and more.

2 Bis c/Bisbe 2 bis, Barri Gòtic ℡933 150 954; ⓂJaume I. Gift and souvenir store with interesting ceramics, glassware, papier-mâché models, masks and mobiles.

Craft workshops

Crafts have always been central to Barcelona's industry, with a history dating back to the Middle Ages. To learn and practise a certain craft, you had to be a member of a guild, while many of the street names in the Born (ⓂJaume I/Barceloneta), particularly, refer to the crafts once practised there; eg c/de la Argenteria, silversmith's street, c/Mirallers, the street where they used to make mirrors, or c/Sombrerers, where hats (*sombreros*) were made. Over the last decade or so, neighbourhoods like the Born, El Raval and Poble Nou have once again become craft centres as empty buildings and warehouses have been opened up as workshops. Some artists work behind closed doors, while others have a space at the front where they sell their limited series or unique pieces.

A good way to see the workshops is to coincide with the **Tallers Oberts**, or open workshops (⊛www.tallersoberts.org), usually held over the last two weekends of May, when there are studio visits, exhibitions, guided tours and other events. Or contact My Favourite Things (see p.33 for details), who can organize a workshop tour on request, introducing you directly to selected artists.

Books

General

BCN c/Roger de Llúria 118, Eixample ☎ 934 577 692, ⓦ www.bcnbooks.com; Ⓜ Diagonal. Good selection of English-language novels and the city's best place for teaching materials.

Casa del Llibre Pg. de Gràcia 62, Eixample ☎ 932 723 840, ⓦ www.casadellibro.com; Ⓜ Passeig de Gràcia. Barcelona's biggest book emporium, with lots of English titles.

Elephant Books c/Creu dels Molers 12, Poble Sec ☎ 934 430 594, ⓦ www.lfantbooks.4t.com; Ⓜ Poble Sec. Only stocks English-language books, with cheap prices for current novels, classics, children's books and secondhand. A small café at the back serves English tea, home-made brownies, cakes and cookies.

Laie c/Pau Claris 85, Eixample ☎ 933 181 739, ⓦ www.laie.es; Ⓜ Passeig de Gràcia. Excellent selection of humanities and literature and lots of English-language titles. There's a café-restaurant upstairs.

Art, design and photography

Kowasa c/de Mallorca 235, Eixample ☎ 932 158 058, ⓦ www.kowasa.com; Ⓜ Provença. The city's best bookstore for photography and photographic art.

Museu Nacional d'Art de Catalunya Palau Nacional, Montjuïc ☎ 936 220 376, ⓦ www.mnac.es; Ⓜ Espanya. MNAC has the city's widest selection of books on Catalan art, architecture, design and style.

Ras c/Doctor Joaquim Dou 10, El Raval ☎ 934 127 199, ⓦ www.actar.es; Ⓜ Liceu. Specializes in books and magazines on graphic design, architecture and photography. The exhibitions here are always worth a look.

Comics and graphic books

Norma Comics Pg. de Sant Joan 9, Eixample ☎ 932 448 423, ⓦ www.normacomics.com. Spain's best comic and graphic-novel shop, for everything from manga to the caped crusader, plus DVDs and all kinds of related items.

Secondhand

Hibernian Books c/Montseny 17, Gràcia ☎ 932 174 796, ⓦ www.hibernian-books.com; Ⓜ Fontana. Barcelona's secondhand English bookstore has around 30,000 titles in stock – you can part-exchange, and the January sale is great for giveaway bargains.

Travel, guides and maps

Altaïr Gran Via de les Corts Catalanes 616, Eixample ☎ 933 427 171, ⓦ www.altair.es; Ⓜ Universitat. Travel superstore with a huge selection of travel books, guides, maps and world music; there's also an Altaïr outlet at Palau Robert, Pg. de Gràcia 107, that specializes in Catalan maps, guides and travel books.

Llibreria Quera c/Petritxol 2, Barri Gòtic ☎ 933 180 743, ⓦ www.llibreriaquera.com; Ⓜ Liceu. The most knowledgeable place in town for Catalan and Pyrenean maps and trekking guides. Closed Sat in Aug.

Clothes, shoes and accessories

Designer fashion

Adolfo Domínguez c/Ribera 16, La Ribera ☎ 933 192 159, Ⓜ Barceloneta; Pg. de Gràcia 32, Eixample ☎ 934 874 170, Ⓜ Passeig de Gràcia; ⓦ www.adolfodominguez.com. Superior men's and women's designs from the well-known *gallego* designer – he also branches out into casual youth and children's wear.

Agua del Carmem c/Bonaire 5, La Ribera ☎ 932 687 799; Ⓜ Barceloneta. Original designs by Rona, limited series, kitschy but stylish.

Antonio Miró c/Consell de Cent 349, Eixample ☎ 934 870 670, ⓦ www.antoniomiro.es Ⓜ Passeig de Gràcia. The showcase for Barcelona's most innovative designer, Antonio Miró, especially good for classy men's suits, though now also branding jeans, accessories, fragrances and household design. Closed Mon in Aug.

Black Jazz c/del Rec 28, La Ribera ☎ 933 104 236; Ⓜ Jaume I. Typical of the neighbourhood, this snazzy boutique gathers together the hottest names in men's designer fashion.

Camisería Pons c/Gran de Gràcia 49, Gràcia ☎ 932 177 292; FGC Gràcia. A showcase for contemporary Spanish fashion designers.

Cuca Fera c/Cremat Gran 9, La Ribera ☎ 932 683 710; Ⓜ Jaume I. Original children's clothing, from T-shirts to matching outfits – it's down the alleyway behind the Picasso Museum.

Custo Barcelona Pl. de les Olles 7, La Ribera ☎ 932 687 893, Ⓜ Barceloneta; and c/Ferran 36, Barri Gòtic ☎ 933 426 698, Ⓜ Liceu; ⓦ www.custo-barcelona.com. Where the stars get their T-shirts. Hugely colourful and highly priced designer tops, sweaters and casual wear for men and women.

Daniela Yavich Pl. del Pi 14, Barri Gòtic ☏933 428 510, ⓦwww.danielayavich.com, ⓂLiceu. Argentinian designer producing clothes from interesting, colourful fabrics.

Giménez & Zuazo c/Elisabets 20, El Raval ☏934 123 381, ⓂCatalunya; and c/del Rec 42, La Ribera ☏933 106 743, ⓂJaume I; ⓦwww.gimenezzuazo.com. Two collections a year of cutting-edge women's fashion that's funky and informal.

Janina Rambla de Catalunya 94, Eixample ☏932 150 484, ⓂDiagonal; and Avgda. Paul Casals 8, Eixample ☏932 020 693, FGC Muntaner. Barcelona's premier lingerie stockist, with own-label designs, swimwear and sleepwear, plus items by other designers.

Jean-Pierre Bua Avgda. Diagonal 469, Eixample ☏934 397 100, ⓦwww.jeanpierrebua.com; ⓂDiagonal. The city's temple for fashion victims: a postmodern tribute to Yamamoto, Gaultier, Miyake, Galliano, McQueen, Westwood, Miró and others.

Loft Avignon c/d'Avinyó 22, Barri Gòtic ☏933 012 420; ⓂLiceu. If ever a shop was an indicator of how the neighbourhood's changing, it's this – the once-seedy backstreet fast becoming a byword for where-it's-at fashion. International designer labels (Helmut Lang, JP Gaultier, Vivienne Westwood) and high prices abound.

Naifa c/Doctor Joaquim Dou 11, El Raval ☏933 024 005, ⓂLiceu. Original, colourful, informal, very reasonably priced men's and women's clothing.

Natalie Capell, Atelier de Moda c/Banys Vells 4, La Ribera ☏933 199 219; ⓂJaume I. Her own very elegant designs, in 1920s- and 1930s-style.

High-street fashion

Mango Pg. de Gràcia 8–10, Eixample ☏934 121 599, ⓂPasseig de Gràcia; Pg. de Gràcia 65, Eixample ☏932 157 530, ⓂPasseig de Gràcia ; plus others, ⓦwww.mango.es. Now available worldwide, Barcelona is where Mango began and prices here are cheaper than in North America and other European countries. See also Mango Outlet on p.234.

Zara Pg. de Gràcia 16, Eixample ☏933 187 675, ⓦwww.zara.com; ⓂPasseig de Gràcia; plus others. Trendy but cheap seasonal fashion for men, women and children from the Spanish chain. The Pg. de Gracia branch is the flagship store.

Jewellery and accessories

Atalanta Manufactura Pg. del Born 10, La Ribera ☏932 683 702; ⓂJaume I. Naturally dyed and painted silk and linen, including lovely scarves and wallhangings.

Joaquín Berao Rambla de Catalunya 74, Eixample ☏932 150 091, ⓦwww.joaquinberao.com;

△ Designer shopping on Passeig del Born

Ⓜ **Passeig de Gràcia**. Avant-garde jewellery by a Madrid designer in a beautifully presented shop.

Mandarina Duck Pg. de Gràcia 44, Eixample ℡ 932 720 364; Ⓜ **Passeig de Gràcia**. Funky, colourful travel bags, backpacks, handbags and other carriers.

Obach Sombrería c/del Call 2, Barri Gòtic ℡ 933 184 094; Ⓜ **Liceu**. An excellent selection of hats and caps of all types, from berets to stetsons.

🏃 **Rafa Teja Atelier** c/Santa Maria 18, La Ribera ℡ 932 377 059; Ⓜ **Jaume I**. A browser's delight for gorgeous silk scarves, mohair wraps and Chinese-style silk jackets and dresses.

Leather

Loewe Pg. de Gràcia 35, Eixample ℡ 932 160 400, ⓦ www.loewe.com, Ⓜ **Passeig de Gràcia**; Avgda. Diagonal 570, Eixample, Ⓜ **Diagonal**. Superb leather jackets, coats, gloves and other accessories at heart-stopping prices.

⑭ Secondhand, vintage and discount outlets

Contribucions c/Riera de Sant Miquel 30, Gràcia ℡ 932 187 140; Ⓜ **Diagonal**. Discount outlet for Spanish and Italian designer labels. Closed two weeks Aug.

Lailo c/Riera Baixa 20, El Raval ℡ 934 413 749; Ⓜ **Liceu**. Secondhand and vintage clothes shop that's usually worth a look, with a massively wide-ranging stock. Fancy-dress costumes for rent at the back.

Le Swing c/Riera Baixa 13, El Raval no phone; Ⓜ **Liceu**. Vintage fashion, from the 1950s onwards, with a rapid turnover.

Mango Outlet c/Girona 37, Eixample ℡ 934 122 935; Ⓜ **Girona**. Last season's Mango gear at unbeatable prices, with items starting at just a few euros.

Stockland c/Comtal 22, Barri Gòtic ℡ 933 180 331; Ⓜ **Urquinaona**. A bargain-hunter's dream. Top-name haute couture at thirty- to sixty-percent discounts.

Shoes

Camper c/Pelai 13-37, El Triangle, Eixample, Ⓜ **Catalunya**; Rambla de Catalunya 122, Eixample, Ⓜ Ⓜ **Diagonal**; plus others; ℡ 902 364 598, ⓦ www.camper.com. Spain's favourite shoe store opened its first shop in Barcelona in 1981. Providing hip, well-made, casual city footwear at a good price has been the cornerstone of its success.

Czar Pg. del Born 20, La Ribera ℡ 933 107 222; Ⓜ **Jaume I**. A galaxy of running shoes, pumps, sneakers, bowling shoes and baseball boots – if your Starsky and Hutch Adidas SL76s have worn out, they can sell you another pair.

La Manual Alpargatera c/d'Avinyó 7, Barri Gòtic ℡ 933 010 172, ⓦ www.lamanualalpargatera .com; Ⓜ **Liceu**. This traditional workshop makes and sells *alpargatas* (espadrilles) to order, as well as producing other straw and rope work.

Muxart c/Rosselló 230, Eixample ℡ 934 881 064, Ⓜ **Diagonal**; Rambla de Catalunya 47, Eixample ℡ 934 677 423, Ⓜ **Catalunya**; ⓦ www .muxart.com. Barcelona's top-class shoe designer, pricey gems for men and women.

Department stores and shopping malls

Bulevard Rosa Pg. de Gràcia 55, entrances on Rambla de Catalunya, c/de Valencia and c/ d'Aragó, Eixample ℡ 933 090 650, ⓦ www .bulevardrosa.com; Ⓜ **Passeig de Gràcia**. Barcelona's first shopping arcade features over one hundred shops, specializing in chic designer gear, shoes and accessories.

Centre Comercial Barcelona Glòries Avgda. Diagonal 208 at Pl. de les Glòries Catalanes, Eixample ℡ 934 860 404, www.lesglories.com; Ⓜ **Glòries**. Huge 230-store mall with all the national high-street fashion names (H&M, Zara, Bershka, Mango) as well as children's wear, toys and games, ice-cream parlours, a dozen bars, cafés and restaurants, and a cinema complex.

El Corte Inglés Pl. de Catalunya 14, Eixample ℡ 933 063 800, Ⓜ **Catalunya**; Avgda. del Portal de l'Angel 19–21, Barri Gòtic ℡ 933 063 800,

Tomb Bus

The Tomb Bus shopping line service connects Pl. de Catalunya with the Diagonal (Pl. Pius XII), an easy way to reach the uptown L'Illa and El Corte Inglès shopping centres. Departures are every 7min (Mon–Fri 7am–9.38pm, Sat 9.10am–9.20pm); tickets (available on the bus) are €1.35 one way, €5.40 for one day's unlimited travel.

Ⓜ Catalunya; plus uptown branches at Avgda. Diagonal 471, 545 & 617, Eixample, Ⓜ María Cristina; Ⓦ www.elcorteingles.es. The city's biggest department store – visit the flagship Pl. de Catalunya branch for nine floors of clothes, accessories, cosmetics, household goods, toys and top-floor café; while for music, books, computers and sports gear, head for the Portal de l'Angel branch.

Diagonal Mar Avgda. Diagonal 3, Diagonal Mar Ⓣ 902 530 300, Ⓦ www.diagonalmarcentre. es; Ⓜ Maresme Forum or T4 tram. The city's newest major mall (the largest in Catalunya) anchors the Diagonal Mar zone, and features the usual high-street suspects (El Corte Inglés, H&M, Zara, Mango, Sephora and FNAC) plus designer clothes and accessories, cafés, restaurants and a cinema.

L'Illa Avgda. Diagonal 545–559, Eixample Ⓣ 934 440 000, Ⓦ www.lilla.com; Ⓜ María Cristina. The landmark uptown shopping mall is stuffed full of designer fashion (including the local Custo), plus Camper (shoes), FNAC (music and books), Sfera (cosmetics), Decathlon (sports), El Corte Inglés (a department store), Caprabo (a supermarket) and much more.

Maremàgnum Moll d'Espanya, Port Vell Ⓣ 932 258 100, Ⓦ www.maremagnum.es; Ⓜ Drassanes. The harbour's complex features mainly souvenir, leisure and sportswear shops – including an official FC Barcelona store – alongside restaurants, bars, fast-food joints and a multi-screen cinema.

El Mercadillo c/Portaferrissa 17, Barri Gòtic Ⓣ 933 018 913; Ⓜ Liceu. Double-decker complex of shops selling skate-, club- and beachwear and shoes – look out for the camel marking the entrance. There's a bar upstairs with a nice patio garden.

El Triangle Pl. de Catalunya 4, Eixample Ⓣ 933 180 108; Ⓜ Catalunya. Shopping centre at the top of the Ramblas, dominated by the flagship FNAC store, which specializes in books (good English-language selection), music CDs and computer software. Also has a Habitat, Sephora for cosmetics, various clothes shops, plus magazines and a café on the ground floor.

Design, decorative art and household goods

BD Ediciones de Diseño c/Mallorca 291, Eixample Ⓣ 934 586 909, Ⓦ www.bdbarcelona.com; Ⓜ Diagonal. The building is by Domènech i Montaner while the interior is filled with the very latest in furniture and household design. Also reproductions of classic furniture by Gaudí, Dalí and Eames. Closed Aug.

Dom c/de Provença 249, Eixample Ⓣ 934 871 181, Ⓜ Diagonal; c/d'Avinyo 7, Barri Gòtic Ⓣ 933 425 591, Ⓜ Liceu; Ⓦ www.id-dom.com. Original, amusing household and personal items at affordable prices – whether it's alarm clocks or bouncy chairs.

Ganivetería Roca Pl. del Pi 3, Barri Gòtic Ⓣ 933 021 241; Ⓜ Liceu. Handsome old shop, dating from 1911, selling a big range of knives, cutlery, corkscrews and other household goods – including a fine array of gentlemen's shaving gear.

Germanes Garcia c/Banys Nous 15, Barri Gòtic Ⓣ 933 186 646; Ⓜ Liceu. Enormous warehouse-showroom devoted to the art of basket-, raffia- and wickerware – cradles to tables, plantholders to wardrobes.

Gotham c/Cervantes 7, Barri Gòtic Ⓣ 934 124 647, Ⓦ www.gotham-bcn.com; Ⓜ Jaume 1. The place to come for retro furniture, lighting and accessories from all periods from the 1930s to the 1970s, plus original designs. Closed Sat in Aug.

Indio c/del Carme, El Raval Ⓣ 933 175 442; Ⓜ Catalunya. The most traditional place in town to buy linen, pillows, blankets, sheets and tablecloths – the *modernista* facade, long cutting counters, wood panels and marble floor survive from its nineteenth-century glory days.

Pilma Avgda. Diagonal 403, Eixample Ⓣ 934 161 399, Ⓜ Diagonal; c/de Valencia 1, Eixample Ⓣ 932 260 676, Ⓜ Tarragona; Ⓦ www .pilma.com. Immerse yourself in stylish household furniture, lighting, and kitchen and bathroom accessories.

Vinçon Pg. de Gràcia 96, Eixample Ⓣ 932 156 050, Ⓦ www.vincom.com; Ⓜ Passeig de Gràcia. The grandaddy of household style, pioneered by Fernando Amat – known as the Spanish Terence Conran. It's a fantastic building, never mind what's on sale, and there are temporary art and design exhibitions.

Vitra Pl. Comercial 5, La Ribera Ⓣ 932 687 219, Ⓦ www.vitra.com; Ⓜ Jaume I. Home and workplace furniture specialist with stunning chairs by the likes of Frank O. Gehry, Philippe Starck, Charles and Ray Eames, and Ron Arad.

Food and drink

There's a full list of city markets at ⓦwww .mercatsbcn.com. The ones picked out below are all covered more fully in the guide. The main local supermarket chain is Caprabo (ⓦwww.caprabo.es), though most branches are located in residential neighbourhoods, away from the tourist sights. The most convenient downtown supermarket is that in the basement of El Corte Inglés (Pl. de Catalunya), and there's also the fairly basic Champion at Ramblas 113.

Daily food markets

Mercat de la Barceloneta Pl. de la Font, Barceloneta; ⓜBarceloneta.
Mercat de la Concepció c/de Valencia, Eixample; ⓜPasseig de Gràcia.
Mercat de la Llibertat Pl. de la Llibertat, Gràcia; ⓜFontana.
Mercat Sant Antoni Ronda de Sant Pau/Ronda de Sant Antoni, Eixample; ⓜSant Antoni.
Mercat Sant Josep/La Boqueria Ramblas; ⓜLiceu.
Mercat Santa Caterina Avgda. Francesc Cambó 16, Sant Pere; ⓜJaume I.

Specialist food stores

La Casa del Bacalao c/del Comtal 8, Barri Gòtic ☏933 016 539; ⓜCatalunya. Just goes to show what window dressing can do for the humblest of products – in this case, a beautifully presented display of salt cod (sealed to take home, if you decide to buy).
🏃 **Casa Gispert** c/Sombrerers 23, La Ribera ☏933 197 535, ⓦwww.casagispert.com; ⓜJaume I. Roasters of nuts, coffee and spices for over 150 years – it's a truly delectable store with some tantalizing smells, and there are gourmet deli items available too.
Colmado Quilez Rambla de Catalunya 63, Eixample ☏932 152 356; ⓜPasseig de Gràcia. Classic Catalan grocery, windows and shelves piled high with tins, preserves, bottles, jars and packets, plus a groaning *xarcuteria* counter.
🏃 **Formatgeria La Seu** c/Dagueria 16, Barri Gòtic ☏934 126 548, ⓦwww .formatgerialaseu.com; ⓜJaume I. The best farmhouse cheeses from independent producers all over Spain. The owner, who's

Scottish, will introduce you into the world of cheese with Saturday cheese-tastings – or you can taste before you buy at any time. Closed Mon & Aug.
Origens 99,9% c/Vidrería 6–8, La Ribera ☏933 107 531; ⓜJaume I. The original deli-tavern has now been franchised at new city locations, but it's still a good place to browse for Catalan gourmet items and specialities: pâtés, sauces, olive oil, vinegar, *turron* and more.
Papabubble c/Ample 28, Barri Gòtic ☏932 688 625, ⓦwww.papabubble.com; ⓜDrassanes. Candidate for "only in Barcelona" – groovy young things rolling out home-made candy to a chillout soundtrack. Closed Aug.

Wine

Vila Viniteca c/Agullers 7–9, La Ribera ☏932 683 227, ⓦwww.vilaviniteca.es; ⓜBarceloneta. Very knowledgeable specialist in Catalan and Spanish wines. Pick your vintage and then nip over the road for the deli part of the operation.

Markets

Antiques Avgda. de la Catedral, Barri Gòtic; ⓜJaume I. Every Thurs; closed Aug from 9am. The tourist location outside the cathedral attracts high prices. Better for bargains is the market on the Port Vell harbourside (ⓜBarceloneta) at weekends from 11am.
Art Pl. Sant Josep Oriol, Barri Gòtic; ⓜLiceu. The square is filled with stalls and easels every weekend from 10am: featuring still lives to harbour views.
Christmas Avgda. de la Catedral, and surrounding streets, Barri Gòtic; ⓜJaume I. Traditional decorations, gifts, Christmas trees and more at the annual Fira de Santa Llúcia; daily Dec 1–22, 10am–9pm.
Coins, books and postcards Mercat Sant Antoni, Ronda de Sant Pau/Ronda de Sant Antoni, Eixample; ⓜSant Antoni. Every Sun 9am–2pm. Finish off with a *vermouth negre* in the *Tres Tombs* bar.
Coins and stamps Pl. Reial, Barri Gòtic; ⓜLiceu. Specialist dealers and collectors do battle every Sun 10am–2pm.
Farmers' market Pl. del Pi, Barri Gòtic; ⓜLiceu. First and third Fri, Sat & Sun of the month – honey, cheese, cakes and other produce; also during the Festa de la Mercè in Sept, and the Festa de Sant Ponç in c/de l'Hospital on May 11.
Flea market Els Encants, c/Dos de Maig, northwest side of Pl. de les Glòries Catalanes,

Eixample; Ⓜ Glòries/Encants. Every Mon, Wed, Fri & Sat 9am–6pm, plus Dec 1–Jan 5 Sun 9am–3pm, for clothes, jewellery, antiques, junk and furniture. Get there before lunch for the best of the action.

Flowers and birds Ramblas; Ⓜ Liceu. Stalls present daily; flowers also in abundance at Mercat de la Concepció, c/de Valencia, Eixample.

Museums, galleries and attractions

L'Aquàrium Moll d'Espanya, Port Vell; Ⓜ Drassanes or Barceloneta. A fish-related extravaganza, from the mundane (T-shirts, stationery, posters, games, toiletries) to cult must-haves (Mariscal-designed bathroom transfers).

CosmoCaixa c/Teodor Roviralta 47–51, Tibidabo; FGC Avgda. del Tibidabo. The science museum shop is the place to buy space jigsaws, planet mobiles, model lunar-rovers, dinosaur kits, star charts, natural history books.

Les Muses el Palau c/Sant Pere Més Alt 1, Sant Pere; Ⓜ Urquinaona. Shop associated with the Palau de la Música Catalana, just across the square – *modernista*-styled porcelain, jewellery and crystal plus art supplies, artistic reproductions and choral music CDs.

Museu d'Art Contemporani de Barcelona Pl. dels Àngels, El Raval; Ⓜ Universitat. Designer aprons, espresso cups, T-shirts, posters, gifts and toys, plus art and design books.

Museu Barbier-Mueller c/de Montcada 14, La Ribera; Ⓜ Jaume I. The pre-Columbian art museum shop has a wide range of ethnic artefacts, from wall-hangings and jewellery to terracotta pots and figurines. Definitely the place to pick up your panama hat.

Museu Textil i d'Indumentaria c/de Montcada 12, La Ribera; Ⓜ Jaume I. Funky jewellery, silk ties, candles, kitchen aprons, bags and other design-led gifts and trinkets.

Music

Casa Beethoven Ramblas 97, El Raval ☎933 014 826, ✆www.casabeethoven.com; Ⓜ Liceu. Wonderful old shop selling sheet music, CDs and music reference books – not just classical, but rock, jazz and flamenco too. Closed Aug.

Discos Castelló c/Tallers 3 ☎933 182 041; **Tallers 7** ☎933 025 946; **Tallers 9** ☎934 127 285; **Tallers 79** ☎933 013 575, El Raval, Ⓜ Catalunya; ✆www.discoscastello.es. Major local music retailer with separate stores for classical (no. 3), general (no. 7), hip-hop, rock,

pop and merchandise (no. 9), jazz and 70s pop/rock (no. 79).

Espai Licei Ramblas 51, El Raval ☎934 859 913; Ⓜ Liceu. The shop in the Liceu opera house has the widest range of opera CDs and DVDs in the city, plus branded T-shirts, ceramics, and other souvenirs.

🏃 **Etnomusic c/del Bonsuccés 6, El Raval** ☎933 011 884, ✆www.etnomusic.com; Ⓜ Catalunya. World-music specialist, especially good for reggae, Latin and all types of South American music.

Wah Wah Discos c/Riera Baixa 14, El Raval ☎934 423 703, ✆www.wah-wahsupersonic .com; Ⓜ Liceu. Vinyl heaven for record collectors' – rock, indie, electronica, blues, folk, prog, jazz, soul and rarities of all kinds.

Sports

Botiga del Barça FC Barcelona, Camp Nou, Les Corts ☎934 090 271, Ⓜ María Cristina; **Maremàgnum, Moll d'Espanya, Port Vell** ☎932 258 045, Ⓜ Drassanes. You can buy Barça shirts anywhere on the Ramblas, but for official merchandise the stadium megastore has it all – including that all-important lettering service for the back of the shirt that elevates you to the squad.

Decathlon c/de la Canuda 20, at Pl. Vila de Madrid, Barri Gòtic ☎933 426 161, ✆www .decathlon.es; Ⓜ Catalunya; plus others. They've got sports and equipment for 63 sports in the old-town megastore, so you're bound to find what you want. Also bike rental and repair.

Toys, magic, costume and party wear

🏃 **Almacen Marabi c/Flassaders 30, La Ribera** ☎686 187 645; Ⓜ Jaume I. Handmade finger dolls, mobiles, puppets and animals.

El Ingenio c/Rauric 6–8, Barri Gòtic ☎933 177 138, ✆www.el-ingenio.com; Ⓜ Liceu. Juggling, magic and street-performer shop with a *modernista* storefront – also carnival costumes and masks.

El Rey de la Magica c/Princesa 11, La Ribera ☎933 193 920; Ⓜ Jaume I. Spain's oldest magic shop contains all the tricks of the trade, from rubber chickens to Dracula capes.

Xalar Bxda. Llibreteria 4, Barri Gòtic ☎933 150 458; Ⓜ Jaume I. Designer and hand-crafted toys – traditional games, dolls' houses, toy theatres and puppets.

Children's Barcelona

aking your children to Barcelona doesn't pose insurmountable travel problems, but it's as well to be aware of the potential difficulties before you go. Below we've pointed out some of the things you might find tricky, as well as providing a few pointers for a smooth stay. Once you're happily ensconced, and have cracked the transport system, you'll find that not only will your children be given a warm welcome almost everywhere you go, but in many ways the city appears as one huge playground, whether it's a day at the beach or a daredevil cable-car ride. There's plenty to do for children of all ages, much of it free or inexpensive, while if you coincide with one of Barcelona's festivals (see Chapter 12 for full details) you'll be able to join in with the local celebrations, from sweet-tossing and puppet shows to fireworks and human castles. "Children's attractions" rounds up the best of the options for keeping everybody happy; for sporting suggestions and outdoor activities, see Chapter 13.

Public transport

With very young children, the main problem is using **public transport**, especially the metro, which seems almost expressly designed to thwart access to pushchairs and buggies. Most stations are accessed by stairs or escalators, and there are steps and stairs within the system itself, making it difficult for single travellers with young children to get around easily. Even with two adults, you often face a stiff climb out of stations with the pushchair. However, the stations on line 2 – including Passeig de Gràcia and Sagrada Família – are accessible by lift from street level, and many FGC stations have lifts to the platforms too, including Catalunya, Espanya (for Montserrat trains) and Avdga. del Tibidabo (for Tibidabo). If travelling by bus, try to stick to disabled-accessible routes, on which the buses will have room to handle a buggy. Children under 4 **travel free** on public transport, while there are reduced prices for tickets on the sightseeing Bus Turístic and the cable cars.

Products, clothes and services

Disposable **nappies** (diapers), **baby food, formula milk** and other standard items are widely available in pharmacies and supermarkets, though not necessarily with the same range or brands that you will be used to at home. Organic baby food, for example, is hard to come by – you can sometimes find the odd jar in a health-food store – and most Spanish non-organic baby foods contain small amounts of sugar or salt. If you require anything specific for your baby or child, it's best to bring it with you or check with the manufacturer about equivalent brands.

For relatively cheap, well-made babies' and children's **clothing** Prénatal (ⓦ www.prenatal.es) has an excellent range, and there are branches all over the city. Or go to Galeries Malda (c/Portaferrissa 22, Barri Gòtic) or El Corte Inglés (Pl. de Catalunya 14, Eixample) for children's and babies' clothes and designer labels.

Most establishments are baby-friendly in the sense that you'll be made very welcome if you turn up with a child in tow. Many museum cloakrooms, for example, will be happy to look after your pushchair as you carry your child around the building, while restaurants will make a fuss of your little one. However, specific facilities are not as widespread as they are in the UK or USA. **Baby-changing areas** are relatively rare, except in department stores and shopping centres, and even where they do exist they are not always up to scratch. By far the best is at El Corte Inglés, while El Triangle and Maremàgnum have pull-down changing tables in their public toilets.

Restaurants, accommodation and babysitting

Local restaurants tend not to offer **children's menus** (though they will try to accommodate specific requests), highchairs are rarely provided, and restaurants open relatively late for lunch and dinner. Despite best intentions, you might find yourself eating in one of the international franchise restaurants, which tend to be geared more towards families and open throughout the day.

Suitable **accommodation** is easy to find, and most hotels and pensions will be welcoming. However, bear in mind that much of the city's budget accommodation is located in buildings without lifts; while, if you're travelling out of season, it's worth noting that some older-style pensions don't have heating systems – and it can get cold. If you want a cot provided, or baby-listening and sitting services, you'll have to pay the price of staying in one of the larger hotels – and, even then, never assume that these facilities are provided, so always check in advance. You'll pay from around €10–12 per hour for **babysitting** if arranged through your hotel, or contact Tender Loving Canguros (from €7 per hour plus fee; call Mon–Sat 9am–9pm, ⓦ www.tlcanguros.com), whose nannies and babysitters all speak English.

Children's attractions

If you've spent too much time already in the showpiece museums, galleries and churches, any of the suggestions below should head off a children's revolt. Most have been covered in the text, so you can get more information by turning to the relevant page. Admission charges are almost always reduced for children, though the cut-off age varies from attraction to attraction.

Cinema, shows and theatre

Cinema Children's film sessions are held at the Filmoteca (see p.212), Sun 5pm.
Font Màgica The sound and light show in front of the Palau Nacional on Montjuïc (p.88) is always a hit, though it starts quite late.

Imax Port Vell Three different screens showing giant screen and 3D documentaries on nature, space and the human body. See p.83.
Statues and street theatre The Ramblas is one big outdoor show for children, with human statues (p.49) a speciality, not to mention buskers, pavement artists, magi-

cians, and food, bird and flower markets.
Theatre There are children's puppet shows, music, mime and clowns at the **Fundació Joan Miró** (Avgda. Miramar 71–75, Montjuïc ℡934 439 470, Ⓦwww.bcn.fjmiro.es; ⓂEspanya & bus #50), with performances Sat 5.30pm & Sun 11.30am &1pm. **Jove Teatre Regina** (c/Sèneca 22, Gràcia ℡932 181 512, Ⓦwww.jtregina.com; ⓂDiagonal) puts on music and comedy productions for children (Sat & Sun 5.30pm).

Museums and attractions

L'Aquàrium Adults might find the Aquarium a bit of a disappointment, but there's no denying its popularity with children. Under-4s get in free, and there are discounts for four- to twelve-year-olds. See p.82.

Museums Museums with a special interest for children include **Cosmocaixa** (Science Museum; p.128); the **Museu del Football Club Barcelona** (FC Barcelona Museum; p.123); **Museu d'Història de la Ciutat** (City History Museum; p.61); **Museu de Cera** (Wax Museum; p.53); **Museu de Zoología** (Zoology Museum; p.75); and **Museu Marítim** (Maritime Museum; p.80).

Poble Espanyol Open-air "museum" of Spanish buildings, craft demonstrations, gift shops, bars and restaurants. Family ticket available. See p.90.

Parc Zoològic All the usual suspects, plus children's zoo and dolphin shows; free for under-3s, discounts for under-12s. See p.76.

▽ Street entertainer on Las Ramblas

Parks and gardens

Gardens Top *Rough Guide* choice is the **Parc del Laberint** in Horta (p.122), where the hillside gardens, maze and playground provide a great day out.

Parks In the city, the **Parc de la Ciutadella** (p.74) has the best range of attractions, with a boating lake and a zoo. Older children will love the bizarre gardens and buildings of Gaudí's **Parc Güell** (p.120), while the **Parc de Collserola** (p.130) is a good target for a walk in the hills and a picnic. At **Parc del Castell de l'Oreneta** (daily 10am–dusk), behind Pedralbes monastery, there are miniature train rides and pony rides on Sundays; it's at the end of c/Montevideo (take bus #66 from Pl. Catalunya or #64 from Pl. Universitat to the end of the line and walk up Avgda. d'Espasa).

Playgrounds Most city kids use the squares as playgrounds, under parental supervision. In **Gràcia**, Plaça de la Virreina and Plaça de Rius i Taulet are handsome traffic-free spaces with good bars with attached *terrassas*. Wherever your children play, however, you need to keep an eagle eye out for dog dirt. In the old town, the nicest dog- and traffic-free playground is in **Plaça de Vicenç Martorell**, in El Raval, where there are some fenced-off swings in front of a great café, *Kasparo*.

Rides and views

Bike tours Join a group bike tour for a safe way to see the sights on two wheels. See p.33.

Cable cars The two best rides in the city are the cross-harbour cable car (p.84) from Barceloneta to Montjuïc, and the Telefèric de Montjuïc (p.89), which then takes you up to the castle at the top of Montjuïc. Neither is for the faint-hearted child or sickly infant.

Las Golondrinas Sightseeing boat rides around the port and local coast. See p.34.

Mirador de Colón See the city from the top of the Columbus statue at the bottom of the Ramblas. See p.79.

Torre de Collserola Stunning views from the telecommunications tower near Tibidabo. Under-3s go free. See p.130.

Tren Turístic de Montjuïc The little trolley-train rumbles around the Montjuïc hillside, connecting all the attractions. See p.89.

Theme parks

Catalunya en Miniatura Torrelles de Llobregat, 17km southwest of Barcelona (A2 highway, exit 5) ☎936 890 960, ⓦwww.catalunyaenminiatura.com. A theme park with 170 Catalan monuments in miniature, plus mini-train rides, children's shows and playground. Daily 10am–6pm, later opening April–Sept, closed Mon Nov–March.

Illa Fantasia Vilassar de Dalt, 25km north of Barcelona, just short of Mataró (exit 9 on the main highway) ☎937 514 553, ⓦwww.illafantasia.com. Supposedly the largest water park in Europe, with slides, splash pools, swimming pools, water games and picnic areas. Buy a combined ticket (*billete combinado*) at Barcelona Sants station and you can travel free on the train to Premià de Mar, and then take the free connect-

ing bus to the park. Mid-May to mid-Sept daily 10am–7pm.

Port Aventura 1hr south of Barcelona, near Salou and La Pineda (exit 35 on A7) ☎977 779 090, ⓦwww.portaventura.es. Universal Studios' massive theme park based on five different cultures – Mexico, the Wild West, Polynesia, China and the Mediterranean – plus the Costa Caribe water adventure park. On-site hotels, shops, restaurants and shows, as well as fairground rides (including the biggest roller-coaster in Europe). Two-day and two-park combination tickets offer the best value. Trains from Passeig de Gràcia/Barcelona Sants run directly to Port Aventura's own station (1hr 15min; info from RENFE ☎902 240 202). Daily March–Oct 10am–8pm; July & Aug 10am–midnight; Nov–Dec Sat & Sun only; daily Christmas & New Year.

Tibidabo Dubbed "La Muntanya Magica", the rides and shows in the mountain-top amusement park (see p.129) are unbeatable as far as location goes, though tame compared to those at Port Aventura.

⑮

Directory

Airlines Air Berlin ☏901 116 402, ⓦwww
.airberlin.com; Air Europa ☏902 401 501,
ⓦwww.aireuropa.com; British Airways
☏902 111 333, ⓦwww.britishairways.com;
Delta ☏901 116 946, ⓦwww.delta.com;
EasyJet ☏902 299 992, ⓦwww.easyjet.
com; Iberia ☏902 400 550, ⓦwww.iberia.
es; Ryanair ☏807 220 022, ⓦwww.ryanair.
com; Spanair ☏902 131 415, ⓦwww.spa-
nair.com; Transvia ☏902 114 478, ⓦwww
.transvia.com; Virgin Express ☏902 888
459, ⓦwww.virgin-express.com; Vueling
☏902 333 933, ⓦwww.vueling.com.

Airport El Prat de Llobregat ☏932 983 838
for general information, see the website for
up-to-the-minute flight information, ⓦwww
.aena.es. Trains to the airport depart every
20min (roughly 6am–midnight) from Barcelona Sants; otherwise Aérobus (☏934 156
020) runs every 11min from Pl. de Catalunya,
Pg. de Gràcia and Pl. d'Espanya (Mon–Fri
5.30am–11.15pm, Sat & Sun 6am–11.15pm;
€3.60). Barcelona Bus (☏902 361 550) service from the Estació del Nord bus station to
Girona airport (€11) connects with all Ryanair
departures; and there's a bus service (☏807
220 220) from Barcelona Sants station (rear
exit) to Reus airport (€11), also to connect
with Ryanair and other departures.

American Express Office at Ramblas 74,
Barri Gòtic, Ⓜ Liceu ☏933 427 311; open
Mon–Sat 9am–9pm. Card services, cur-
rency exchange and money transfers.

Banks and exchange Main bank branches
are in Pl. de Catalunya and along Pg. de

Gràcia, and there are ATMs all over the city,
including at airport arrivals, Barcelona Sants
train station, Estació del Nord bus station
and Pl. de Catalunya tourist office. For
out-of-hours exchange offices look down
the Ramblas, or go to Barcelona Sants
(daily 8am–8pm); El Corte Inglés, Pl. de
Catalunya (Mon–Sat 10am–9.30pm); Postal
Transfer, Pl. Urquinaona at c/Roger de Lluria
(Mon–Fri 10am–11pm, Sat 11am–midnight,
Sun noon–11pm); or Turisme de Catalunya
tourist office, Pl. de Catalunya 17 (Mon–Sat
9am–9pm, Sun 9am–2pm).

Bike rental Half-day rental costs around
€10–15, full-day €25, with the following
companies: Biciclot, c/de la Verneda 16–18,
Eixample, Ⓜ Clot ☏933 077 475, and Pg.
Marítim 33–35, Port Olímpic, Ⓜ Ciutadella-Vila
Olímpica ☏932 219 778, ⓦwww.biciclot.net;
Bicitram, Avgda. Marquès de l'Argentera 15,
La Ribera, Ⓜ Barceloneta ☏607 226 069 (Sat
& Sun & hols only); Fat Tire Bikes, c/Escudel-
lers 48, Barri Gòtic Ⓜ Liceu/Drassanes ☏933
013 612, ⓦwww.fattirebiketoursbarcelona.
com; Un Coxte Menys/Bicicleta Barcelona, c/
Esparteria 3, La Ribera Ⓜ Barceloneta ☏932
682 105, ⓦwww.bicicletabarcelona.com. For
bike tours of the city, see p.33.

British Council The British Council, c/Amigó
83, Sant Gervasi, FGC Muntaner ☏932
419 700, ⓦwww.britishcouncil.es, has an
English-language library, an arts and events
programme, lists of language schools and
noticeboard advertising lessons and accommodation.

Absolutely anything about the city – addresses and telephone numbers, festivals
dates or council office locations – can be gleaned from the Ajuntament's enormously
useful website, ⓦwww.bcn.es, which has an English-language version. Or you can
call ☏010 (some English-speaking operators available), again with virtually any
request for information.

Buses The main bus station is Barcelona Nord, c/de Ali-Bei, Ⓜ Arc de Triomf ☎ 902 260 606, ⓦ www.barcelonanord.com, three blocks north of Parc de la Ciutadella – an information office here is open daily 7am–9pm. Companies (all listed on the bus station website) operate services across Catalunya, Spain and Europe – it's a good idea to reserve a ticket in advance on long-distance routes (a day before at the station is usually fine, or buy online).

Car and motorbike rental The major chains have outlets at the airport and at, or near, Barcelona Sants station. For local outfits and city locations, call the companies direct or check their websites. EasyCar no phone, internet reservations only ⓦ www.easycar.com; Europcar ☎ 902 105 030, ⓦ www.europcar.com; Laser ☎ 933 229 012, ⓦ www.laserrentacar.com; Motissimo (for bikes) ☎ 934 908 401, ⓦ www.motissimo.es; Pepecar ☎ 902 360 535, ⓦ www.pepecar.com; Vanguard (cars and bikes) ☎ 934 393 880, ⓦ www.vanguardrent.com.

Consulates Most foreign consulates in Barcelona are open to the public for enquiries Mon–Fri, usually 9am–1pm & 3–5pm, though the morning shift is the most reliable. Australia, Pl. Gala Placidia 1–3, Gràcia Ⓜ Diagonal/FGC Gràcia ☎ 934 909 013, ⓦ www.embaustralia.es; Britain, Avgda. Diagonal 477, Eixample, Ⓜ Hospital Clinic ☎ 933 666 200, ⓦ www.ukinspain.com; Canada, c/Elisenda de Pinós 10, Sàrria, FGC Reina Elisenda ☎ 932 042 700, ⓦ www.canadaes.org; Republic of Ireland, Gran Via Carles III 94, Les Corts, Ⓜ Maria Cristina/Les Corts ☎ 934 915 021; New Zealand, Trav. de Gràcia 64, Gràcia, FGC Gràcia ☎ 932 090 399; USA, Pg. de la Reina Elisenda 23, Sàrria, FGC Reina Elisenda ☎ 932 802 227, ⓦ www.embusa.es.

Dentists Dentists are all private, so it's wise to have travel insurance. For an English-speaking dentist, call ☎ 010 or contact the Pl. de Catalunya tourist office, or look in the local Yellow Pages (*Paginas Amarillas*) under "Clinicas dentales" or "Dentistes".

Doctors Any local health-care centre (Centre d'Atenció Primària, CAP) can provide non-emergency assistance. In the old town, there's one at c/del Rec Comtal 24, Sant Pere, Ⓜ Arc de Triomf ☎ 933 101 421 (Mon–Fri 9am–7pm, Sat 9am–5pm). Or call ☎ 010 or consult ⓦ www.bcn.es for a full list. For minor complaints a local pharmacy

can often give good advice (see below), though in an emergency call ☎ 061 or go to one of the hospitals listed below.

Electricity supply The electricity supply is 220v and plugs come with two round pins – bring an adaptor (and transformer) to use UK and US cellphone chargers, etc.

Emergency services ☎ 112 for ambulance, police and fire services; ☎ 061 for ambulance; ☎ 080 for fire service; ☎ 091 for police.

Ferries Departures to the Balearics are from the Estació Marítima, Moll de Barcelona, Port Vell, Ⓜ Drassanes ☎ 900 760 760. Services are on regular ferries or the quicker, and more expensive high-speed ferries or catamarans. Buy tickets inside the terminal from Trasmediterranea (☎ 902 454 645, ⓦ www.trasmediterranea.es) to Palma de Mallorca, Mahón and Ibiza; Iscomar Ferry (☎ 902 119 128, ⓦ www.iscomarferrys.com) to Palma de Mallorca; or Balearia (☎ 902 160 180, ⓦ www.balearia.net) to Palma de Mallorca. Navi Grandi Veloci (☎ 934 439 898, ⓦ www1.gnv.it) has a year-round service to Genoa, Italy.

Hospitals For emergency hospital treatment go to one of the following central hospitals, which have 24hr accident and emergency services: Centre Perecamps, Avgda. Drassanes 13–15, El Raval, Ⓜ Drassanes ☎ 934 410 600; Hospital Clinic i Provincial, c/Villaroel 170, Eixample, Ⓜ Hospital Clinic ☎ 932 275 400; Hospital del Mar, Pg. Marítim 25–29, Vila Olímpica, Ⓜ Ciutadella-Vila Olímpica ☎ 932 483 000; Hospital de la Santa Creu i Sant Pau, c/Sant Antoni Maria Claret, Eixample, Ⓜ Hospital de Sant Pau ☎ 932 919 000.

Internet access There are Internet shops and cybercafés all over Barcelona, and competition has driven prices down to around €1 an hour. A stroll down the Ramblas, or through the Barri Gòtic, La Ribera, El Raval and Grácia will reveal a host of possibilities. There's also wireless access in an increasing number of bars, hotels and public places.

Language schools The cheapest Spanish or Catalan classes in Barcelona are at the Escola Oficial d'Idiomes, Avgda. Drassanes s/n, El Raval, Ⓜ Drassanes ☎ 933 249 330, ⓦ www.eoibd.es – expect queues when you sign on. Or try International House, c/Trafalgar 14, Eixample, Ⓜ Urquinaona ☎ 932 684 511, ⓦ www.ihes.com/bcn. The Generalitat offers low-cost Catalan classes

⑯

DIRECTORY

for non-Spanish speakers through the Centre per a la Normalització Linguística; call ☎010 for information. Language courses for beginners are also offered at most Spanish universities; contact Barcelona University at Gran Via de les Corts Catalanes 585, Eixample, Ⓜ Universitat ☎934 035 519, Ⓦ www.ub.es.

Laundries Lavomatic, a self-service laundry, has two old-town branches, both open Mon–Sat 9am–9pm; at Pl. Joaquim Xirau 1, Barri Gòtic, Ⓜ Drassanes ☎933 425 119; and at c/Consolat del Mar 43–45, Pl. del Palau, La Ribera, Ⓜ Barceloneta ☎932 684 768. There's also LavaExpress, at c/Ferlandina 34, El Raval, Ⓜ Universitat, no phone (daily 8am–11pm), and at c/Nou de Sant Francesc 5, Barri Gòtic Ⓜ Drassanes, no phone (daily 8am–11pm). At Roca, c/Joaquín Costa 16, El Raval, Ⓜ Universitat ☎934 425 982 (Mon–Fri 8.30am–5.30pm, Sat 8am–2pm) you can leave your laundry for a standard wash-and-dry (around €7–8). There are inexpensive laundry services in most of the youth hostels and some pensions; hotels will charge considerably more.

Left-luggage At Barcelona Sants the *consigna* is open daily 7am–11pm and costs €3–4.50 a day. There are lockers at Estació de França, Passeig de Gràcia station and Barcelona Nord bus station (all 6am–11.30pm; €3–4.50).

Libraries Biblioteca de Catalunya, c/de l'Hospital 56, El Raval, Ⓜ Liceu ☎932 702 300, Ⓦ www.gencat.net/bc (Mon–Fri 9am–8pm, Sat 9am–2pm) – a letter of academic reference is required, though there is the Biblioteca Popular Sant Pau (public library) in the same building (Tues, Thurs & Sat 10am–2pm, Mon–Fri 3.30pm–8pm). The Biblioteca de l'Universitat de Barcelona, Gran Via de Corts Catalanes 585, Eixample, Ⓜ Universitat ☎934 035 315, Ⓦ www.bib. ub.es (Mon–Fri 8am–8.30pm; Oct–June also Sat 9am–2pm) is open to the public. The British Council (see p.242) has the only English-language lending library in Barcelona (free access, €55 a year to use the loan and Internet services). At the Caixa Forum arts centre, Avgda. Marquès de Comillas 6–8, Montjuïc Ⓜ Espanya, the Mediateca library (☎934 768 651, Ⓦ www.mediatecaonline. net) is an open-access library for arts and culture books, music, magazines and reference material.

Lost property The best bet is the main lost property office (*objectes perduts*), around the corner from the Ajuntament at c/de la Ciutat 9, Barri Gòtic, Ⓜ Jaume I (Mon–Fri 9.30am–1.30pm; ☎010). You could also try the TMB customer service centre at Universitat metro station, or call the Institut Metropolità del Taxi (lost property line ☎902 101 464, Ⓦ www.barcelonataxi.com) which hangs on to anything left in a taxi.

Newspapers and magazines You can buy foreign newspapers at the stalls down the Ramblas, and around Pl. de Catalunya, on Pg. de Gràcia, on Rambla de Catalunya and at Barcelona Sants. The same stalls also sell an impressive array of international magazines and trade papers. If you can't find what you're looking for there, try FNAC at El Triangle on Pl. de Catalunya, which has an excellent ground-floor magazine section, or Llibreria Mallorca, Rambla de Catalunya 86, Eixample, Ⓜ Passeig de Gràcia, which stocks a large selection of British and American newspapers and magazines.

Office services Workcenter, Pl. Urquinaona at c/Ausias Marc, Eixample, Ⓜ Urquinaona ☎933 908 350 or 902 115 011, Ⓦ www .workcenter.es; 24hr photocopying, scanning, printing, 1hr photo development, internet, fax and DHL courier service.

Pharmacies For minor health complaints look for the green cross of a *farmàcia*, where highly trained staff can give advice (often in English), and are able to dispense many drugs (including some antibiotics) available only on prescription in other countries. Usual hours are weekdays 9am–1pm & 4–8pm. At least one in each neighbourhood is open daily 24hr (and marked as such), or phone ☎010 for information on those open out of hours – Farmacia Clapies, Ramblas 98, Ⓜ Liceu (☎933 012 843) is a convenient 24hr pharmacy. A list of out-of-hours pharmacies can also be found in the window of each pharmacy store.

Police The easiest place to report a crime is at the Guàrdia Urbana (municipal police) station at Ramblas 43, opposite Pl. Reial, Ⓜ Liceu ☎933 441 300 (24hr; English spoken). If you've had something stolen, you need to go to the Policía Nacional office at c/Nou de la Rambla 80, El Raval, Ⓜ Paral. lel ☎932 902 849 (you must go in person to get the report for your insurance claim; take your passport, provided that wasn't stolen, of course). Otherwise, contact the police on the following numbers: Mossos d'Esquadra

☎088, Policía Nacional ☎091, Guàrdia Urbana ☎092.

Post offices The main post office (*Correus*) in Barcelona is on Pl. d'Antoni López, at the eastern end of Pg. de Colom, Barri Gòtic, Ⓜ Barceloneta/Jaume I ☎02 197 197, ⓦ www.correos.es (Mon–Sat 8.30am–10pm, Sun noon–10pm). There's a poste restante/general delivery service here (*llista de correus*), plus express post, fax service, mobile phone top-ups, phonecard sales and bill payments. Other central post office branches are at Ronda Universitat 23 and c/ Aragó 282, both in Eixample (both Mon–Fri 8.30am–8.30pm, Sat 9.30am–1am). Each city neighbourhood also has a post office, though these have far less comprehensive opening hours and services. For stamps it's easier to visit a tobacconist (look for the brown-and-yellow *tabac* signs). Postal Transfer, Pl. Urquinaona at c/Roger de Lluria, Eixample, Ⓜ Urquinaonoa (Mon–Fri 10am–11pm, Sat 11am–midnight, Sun noon–11pm), offers after-hours postal services plus money exchange, fax, photocopying and phonecard sales.

Residence permits In Barcelona, residence permits where required – for EU and non-EU nationals – are issued by the Oficina d'Estrangers at Avgda. Marqués de l'Argentera 4, La Ribera, Ⓜ Barceloneta ☎934 820 544 or 934 820 530 (Mon–Fri 9am–2pm). NIE (foreigner's ID number) applications are dealt with at Pg. de Joan Borbó 32, Barceloneta, Ⓜ Barceloneta ☎932 440 610, ⓦ www.mir.es.

Smoking laws Since January 1, 2006, smoking in public places has been regulated by law. Bars, clubs and cafés smaller than 100 square metres can choose to be entirely smoking or non-smoking – signs on the door tell you which it is. Premises bigger than 100 square metres can have separate smoking areas.

Taxis Barna Taxis ☎933 577 755; Fono-Taxi ☎933 001 100; Radio Taxi 033 ☎933 033 033; Servi-Taxi ☎933 300 300; Taxi Amic ☎934 208 088.

Ticket agencies You can buy concert, sporting and exhibition tickets with a credit card using the ServiCaixa (☎902 332 211, ⓦ www.servicaixa.com) automatic dispensing machines in branches of La Caixa savings bank. It's also possible to order tickets by phone or online through ServiCaixa or Tel-Entrada (☎902 101 212, ⓦ www.

telentrada.com). For advance tickets for all Ajuntament-sponsored concerts and events visit the Palau de la Vireina, Ramblas 99.

Time Barcelona is 1hr ahead of the UK. 6hr ahead of New York and Toronto, 9hr ahead of Los Angeles, 9hr behind Sydney and 11hr behind Auckland. This applies except for brief periods during the changeovers to and from daylight saving (in Spain the clocks go forward in the last week of March, back again in the last week of Oct).

Toilets Public ones are few and far between, and averagely clean, but sometimes don't have any paper (best to carry your own). Bars and restaurants are more likely to have proper (and cleaner) toilets, though you can't guarantee it – even in the poshest of places. Ask for *toaleta* or *serveis* (*lavabo* or *servicios* in Spanish). Dones or Damas (Ladies) and Home or Caballeros (Gentlemen) are the usual signs.

Trains For national rail enquiries, sales and reservations, contact RENFE (☎902 240 202, ⓦ www.renfe.es). Barcelona Sants (Pl. dels Paisos Catalans, Sants; Ⓜ Sants Estació is the main terminal for domestic and international trains – there's a train information office (daily 6.30am–10.30pm), advance ticket booking counters and other services. Regional and local commuter services are operated by FGC (☎932 051 515, ⓦ www.fgc.es), with services from Pl. de Catalunya or Pl. de Espanya.

▽ Barcelona metro system

Travel agencies General travel agencies are found on the Gran Vía de les Corts Catalanes, Pg. de Gràcia, Vía Laietana and the

Ramblas. For city tours, Catalunya holidays and local trips, contact Julia Tours, Ronda Universitat 5, Eixample, Ⓜ Universitat ☎ 933 176 454 or 933 176 209. For youth and student travel try Asatej, Ramblas 140, 5° ☎ 934 126 338, Ⓦ www.asatej.com. The American Express office, Pg. de Gràcia 101, Eixample, Ⓜ Diagonal ☎ 932 550 000, also has a travel agency.

Water Water from the tap is safe to drink, but it doesn't taste very nice. You'll always be given bottled mineral water in a bar or restaurant.

Women's Barcelona Ca la Dona, c/de Casp 38, Eixample, Ⓜ Urquinaona ☎ 934 127 161, Ⓦ www.caladona.org, is a women's centre hosting meetings for women's groups, and with a library and bar. The Ajuntament's official women's resource centre, the Centre Municipal d'Informació i Recursos per a les Dones (CIRD), Avgda. Diagonal 233, 5°, Eixample, Ⓜ Monumental/Glòries ☎ 934 132 722, Ⓦ www.cird.bcn. es (Mon–Fri noon–2pm, plus Wed & Thurs 4–7pm), publishes a monthly calendar of events and news (see the website). Llibreria Pròleg, c/Dagueria 13, Barri Gòtic, Ⓜ Jaume I ☎ 933 192 425, Ⓦ www.llibreriaproleg. com, is a bookshop specializing in women's issues. The Barcelona Women's Network (Ⓦ www.bcnwomensnetwork.com) is a social, business and networking club for English-speaking women living and working in the city.

Contexts

Contexts

A history of Barcelona and Catalunya

Catalunya is more than a part of Spain: the Catalan people have a deeply felt individual identity, rooted in a rich and – at times – glorious past. Perhaps its most conspicuous manifestation these days is in the resurgence of the language, which takes precedence over Castilian Spanish on street names and signs, and has staged a dramatic comeback after being banned from public use during the Franco dictatorship. However, linguistics is only one element in Catalan regionalism.

Catalan cultural identity can be traced back as far as the ninth century. From the quilt of independent counties of the eastern Pyrenees, a powerful dynastic entity, dominated by Barcelona, and commonly known as the Crown of Aragón, developed over the next six hundred years. Its merger with Castile-Leon in the late 1400s led to eventual inclusion in the new Spanish Empire of the sixteenth century – and marked the decline of Catalan independence and its eventual subjugation to Madrid. It has rarely been a willing subject, which goes some way to explaining how ingrained are the Catalan notions of social and cultural divorce from the rest of the country.

Early civilizations and invasions

In the very earliest times, the area which is now Catalunya saw much the same population movements and invasions as the rest of the Iberian peninsula. During the **Upper Paleolithic** period (35,000–10,000 BC) cave-dwelling hunter-gatherers lived in parts of the Pyrenees, and **dolmens**, or stone burial chambers, from around 5000 BC still survive. No habitations from this period have been discovered but it can be conjectured that huts of some sort were erected, and farming had certainly begun. By the start of the **Bronze Age** (around 2000 BC), the Pyrenean people had begun to move into fortified villages in the coastal lowlands.

The first of a succession of **invasions** of the region began sometime after 1000 BC, when the Celtic "urnfield people" crossed the Pyrenees into the region, settling in the river valleys. These people lived side by side with indigenous Iberians, and the two groups are commonly, if erroneously, referred to as **Celtiberians**.

Meanwhile, on the coast, the **Greeks** had established trading posts at Roses and Empúries by around 550 BC. Two centuries later, though, the coast (and the rest of the peninsula) had been conquered by the North African **Carthaginians**, who founded Barcino (later Barcelona) in around 230 BC, on a low hill where the cathedral now stands. The Carthaginians' famous commander, Hannibal, went on to cross the Pyrenees in 214 BC and attempted to invade Italy. But the result of the Second Punic War (218–201 BC) – much of which was fought in Catalunya – was to expel the Carthaginians from the Iberian peninsula in favour of the Romans, who made their new base at the former Carthaginian stronghold of Tarragona.

Roman Catalunya

The **Roman colonization** of the Iberian peninsula was far more intense than anything previously experienced and met with great resistance from the

Celtic and Iberian tribes. It was almost two centuries before the conquest was complete, by which time Spain had become the most important centre of the Roman Empire after Italy. Tarragona (known as Tarraco) was made a provincial capital; fine monuments were built, the remains of which can still be seen in and around the city, and an infrastructure of roads, bridges and aqueducts came into being – much of which was used well into recent times. Barcelona was of less importance, although in 15 BC the emperor Augustus granted it the lengthy name of Colonia Julia Augusta Faventia Pia.

In the first two centuries AD, the Spanish mines and the granaries of Andalucia brought unprecedented wealth, and **Roman Spain** enjoyed a period of stable prosperity in which the region of Catalunya played an influential part. In Tarraco and the other Roman towns, the inhabitants were granted full Roman citizenship; the former Greek settlements on the Costa Brava had accepted Roman rule without difficulty and consequently experienced little interference in their day-to-day life.

Towards the third century AD, however, the Roman political framework began to show signs of decadence and corruption. Although at a municipal level the structure did not disappear completely until the Muslim invasions of the eighth century, it became increasingly vulnerable to **barbarian invasions** from northern Europe. The Franks and the Suevi swept across the Pyrenees, sacking Tarraco in 262 and destroying Barcelona. It was subsequently retaken by the Romans and rather belatedly defended by a circuit of walls and towers, part of which can still be seen. Within two centuries, however, Roman rule had ended, forced on the defensive by new waves of Suevi, Alans and Vandals and finally superseded by the **Visigoths** from Gaul, former allies of Rome and already Romanized to some degree.

The Visigoths established their first Spanish capital at Barcelona in 531 (before eventually basing themselves further south at Toledo), and built a kingdom encompassing most of modern Spain and the southwest of modern France. Their triumph, however, was relatively short-lived. Ruling initially as a caste apart from the local people, with a distinct status and laws, the Visigoths lived largely as a warrior elite, and were further separated from the local people by their adherence to Arian Christianity, which was considered heretical by the Catholic Church. Under their domination, the economy and the quality of life in the Roman towns declined, while within their ranks a series of plots and rivalries – exacerbated by their system of elective monarchy – pitted members of the ruling elite against each other. In 589 King Reccared converted to Catholicism, but religious strife only multiplied – resistance on the part of Arian Christians lead to reaction, one of the casualties of which was the sizeable Jewish population of the peninsula, who were enslaved en masse in the seventh century.

The Moors and the Spanish Marches

Divisions within the Visigothic kingdom coincided with the Islamic expansion in North Africa, which reached the shores of the Atlantic in the late seventh century. In 711 (or 714, no one is sure) Tariq ibn Ziyad, governor of Tangier, led a force of several thousand largely Berber troops across the Straits of Gibraltar (the name of which is a corruption of the Arabic, *jebl at-Tariq*, "Tariq's mountain") and routed the Visigothic nobility near Jerez de la Frontera. With no one to resist, the stage for the **Moorish conquest of Spain** was set. Within ten years, the Muslim Moors had advanced to control most of modern Catalunya – they destroyed Tarragona and forced Barcelona to surrender – although the more inaccessible parts of the Pyrenees retained their independence. It was not simply a military conquest. The Moors had little manpower, and so granted a limited autonomy to the local population in exchange for payment of tribute. They did not force the indigenous people to convert to Islam, and Jews and Christians lived securely as second-class citizens. In areas of the peninsula that remained under Muslim power through the ninth century, a new ethnic group emerged: the "Mozarabs", Christians who lived under Muslim rule, and adopted Arabic language, dress and social customs.

In the power vacuum of southern France, Moorish raiding parties continued beyond the Pyrenees and reached as far north as Poitiers in 732, where Charles Martel, the de facto ruler of Merovingian France, dealt them a minor defeat which convinced them to withdraw. Martel's son Pepin, and his famous grandson **Charlemagne** (768–814), both strove to restore order in the south and push back the invaders, with Charlemagne's empire including the southern slopes of the Pyrenees and much of Catalunya. After being ambushed and defeated by the Basques at Roncesvalles in 778, Charlemagne switched his attention to the Mediterranean side of the Pyrenees, attempting to defend his empire against the Muslims. He took Girona in 785 and his son Louis directed the successful siege of Barcelona in 801. Continued Frankish military success meant that Muslim influence in Catalunya had waned long before the Battle of Las Navas de Tolosa in 1212 (see overleaf) – the turning point for the reconquest of the peninsula as a whole.

With the capture of Barcelona, the **Frankish counties** of Catalunya became a sort of buffer zone, known as the **Spanish Marches**. Separate territories, each ruled by a count and theoretically owing allegiance to the Frankish king (or emperor), were primitive proto-feudal entities, almost exclusively agrarian, and ruled by a small hereditary military elite. It was the building of local fortifications to protect and control the population, reaching its greatest pitch between 1000 and 1200, which led to the term *catlá* ("lord of the castle") being used to refer to the people of the area – the root of today's "**Catalan**" (Castilian has an analogous root). Also, and as happened across much of the former Roman Empire, spoken Latin had taken on geographical particularities, and the "Romance" languages, including Catalan, had begun to develop. A document from 839 recording the consecration of the cathedral at La Seu d'Urgell is seen as the first Catalan-language historical document.

From Wilfred the Hairy to Ramon Berenguer IV

As the Frankish empire of Charlemagne disintegrated in the decades following his death, the counties of the Marches began to enjoy greater independence, which was formalized in 878 by Guifré el Pelós – known in English as **Wilfred the Hairy**. Wilfred was count of Urgell and the Cerdagne and, after adding Barcelona to his holdings, named himself its first count, founding a dynastic line that was to rule until the 1400s. He also made important territorial gains, inheriting Girona and Besalù, and regaining control of Montserrat. In the wake of the Muslim withdrawal from the area, **Christian outposts** had been established throughout Catalunya, and Wilfred continued the process, founding Benedictine monasteries at Ripoll (about 880) and Sant Joan de les Abadesses (888), where his daughter was the first abbess.

Wilfred died in 898 on an expedition against Muslim enemies and was followed by a succession of rulers who attempted to consolidate his gains. Early counts, like **Ramon Berenguer I** (1035–76), concentrated on establishing their superiority over the other local counts, which was bitterly resisted. **Ramon Berenguer III** (1144–66) added considerable territory to his realms with his marriage in 1113 to a Provençal heiress, and made alliances and commercial treaties with Muslim and Christian powers around the western Mediterranean.

The most important stage in Catalunya's development as a significant power, however, came in 1137 with the marriage of **Ramon Berenguer IV** to Petronella, the two-year-old daughter of King Ramiro II of Aragón. This led to the **dynastic union of Catalunya and Aragón**. Although this remained a loose and tenuous federation – the regions retained their own parliaments and customs – it provided the platform for rapid expansion over the next three centuries. As importantly, Ramon managed to tame almost all of the other counts, forcing them to recognize his superior status and in the course of this he promulgated the **Usatges de Barcelona**, a code of laws and customs defining feudal duties, rights and authorities – sneakily putting Ramon I's name on them to make them appear older than they were. He also captured Muslim Tortosa and Lleida in 1148–49, which mark the limits of the modern region of Catalunya, but now the region began to look east for its future, across the Mediterranean.

The Kingdom of Catalunya and Aragón

Ramon Berenguer IV was no more than a count, but his son **Alfons I** (who succeeded to the throne in 1162) also inherited the title of King of Aragón (where he was Alfonso II), and became the first count-king of what historians later came to call the **Crown of Aragón**. To his territories he added Roussillon and much of southern France, becoming known as "Emperor of the Pyrenees"; he also made some small gains against the Berber Almohads who now dominated Muslim Iberia, and allied with and intrigued against neighbouring Christian kingdoms of Navarre and Castile.

Under the rule of Alfons's son, Pere (Peter) the Catholic, the kingdom suffered both successes and reverses. Pere gained glory as one of the military leaders in the decisive defeat of Muslim forces at the **Battle of Las Navas de Tolosa** in 1212, but, swept up into the Albigensian Wars through his ties of lordship to the Counts of Toulouse, he was killed by Catholic forces at Muret a year later. In the years of uncertainty that followed the succession of his five-year-old son, **Jaume I** (1213–76), later known as "the Conqueror", his rivals took advantage of the power vacuum and stripped the count-kings of Provence. Although they would retain Roussillon and acquire Montpellier, for all intents and purposes this signalled the **end of Catalan aspirations north of the Pyrenees**.

The golden age

In spite of these setbacks, Catalunya's age of glory was about to begin in earnest, with the 63-year reign of the extraordinary Jaume. Shrugging off the tutelage of his Templar masters at the age of thirteen, he then personally took to the field to tame his rebellious nobility. This accomplished, he embarked on a series of campaigns of conquest, which brought him Muslim Mallorca in 1229, Menorca in 1231 and Ibiza in 1235 (which explains why the Balearics share a common language with the region). Next he turned south and conquered the city of Valencia in 1238, establishing a new kingdom of which he was also ruler. Valencia, however, was no easy territory to govern, and the region's Muslim inhabitants rose up in a series of revolts which outlasted the king's reign.

Recognizing that **Mediterranean expansion** was where Catalunya's future lay, Jaume signed the **Treaty of Corbeil** in 1258, renouncing his rights in France (except for Montpellier, the Cerdagne and Roussillon), in return for the

French King Louis's renunciation of claims in Catalunya. In this period Catalunya's **economic development** was rapid, fuelled by the exploits of Barcelona's mercantile class, who were quick to see the possibilities of Mediterranean commerce. Maritime customs were codified in the so-called *Llibre del Consolat de Mar*, trade relations were established with North Africa and the Middle East, and consulates opened in foreign ports to protect Catalan interests.

Equally important during Jaume's reign was the establishment of the **Corts**, Catalunya's first parliament – one of the earliest such bodies in Europe, and demonstrative of the confidence developing within the region. In 1249, the first governors of Barcelona were elected, nominating councillors to help them who became known as the Consell de Cent.

On Jaume's death, his kingdom was divided between his sons, one of whom, **Pere II** ("the Great"), took Catalunya, Aragón and Valencia. Connected through marriage to the Sicilian Crown, Pere used the 1282 "Sicilian Vespers" rising against Charles of Anjou to press his claim to the island. In August that year, Pere was crowned at Palermo, and Sicily became the base for Catalan exploits throughout the Mediterranean. Athens and Neopatras were taken between 1302 and 11 by Catalan mercenaries, the *almogávares*, and famous sea-leaders-cum-pirates such as Roger de Flor and Roger de Llúria fought in the name of the Catalan-Aragonese crown. Malta (1283), Corsica (1323), Sardinia (1324) and Naples (1423) all fell under the influence of successive count-kings.

With the territorial gains came new developments with a wider significance. Catalan became used as a trading language throughout the Mediterranean, and 1289 saw the first recorded meeting of a body which became known as the **Generalitat**, a sort of committee of the Corts. Within it were represented each of the three traditional estates – commons, nobility and clergy – and it gradually became responsible for administering public order and justice, and maintaining an arsenal and fleet for the defence of the kingdom.

Social and economic developments

By the mid-fourteenth century Catalunya was at its economic peak. Barcelona had become an important city with impressive new buildings, both religious and secular, to match its status as a regional superpower – the cathedral, church of Santa Maria del Mar, the Generalitat building, the Ajuntament (with its Consell de Cent meeting room) and the Drassanes shipyards all testify to Barcelona's wealth in this period. Catalan became established as a **literary language**, and Catalan works are recognized as the precursor of much of the great medieval European literature: the Mallorcan Ramon Llull's *Book of Contemplation* appeared in 1272, and his romance *Blanquerna* was written a century before Chaucer's *Canterbury Tales*. **Architecture** progressed from Romanesque to Gothic styles, with churches displaying features which have become known as Catalan-Gothic – such as spacious naves, hexagonal belfries and a lack of flying buttresses.

Even while this great maritime wealth and power were being celebrated in such fashion, the seeds of decline were being sown. The **Black Death** made its first appearance in the Balearics in 1348 and visited Catalunya several times over the next forty years, and by the end of the century half the population had succumbed to the disease. As a result, there was increasing pressure on the peasantry by the landowners, who were determined not to let their profits fall.

The rise of Castile

The last of Wilfred the Hairy's dynasty of Catalan count-kings, Martin the Humane (Martí el Humà), died in 1410 without an heir. After nearly five hundred years of continuity, there were six claimants to the throne, and in 1412 nine specially appointed counsellors elevated Ferdinand (Ferran) de Antequera, son of a Catalan princess, to the vacant throne.

Ferran ruled for only four years, but his reign and that of his son, Alfons, and grandson, John (Joan) II, spelled the end for Catalunya's influence in the Mediterranean. The Castilian rulers were soon in dispute with the Consell de Cent; illegal taxes were imposed, funds belonging to the Generalitat were appropriated, and most damagingly non-Catalans started to be appointed to key positions in the Church, state offices and the armed forces. In 1469 John's son, Prince Ferdinand (Ferran), who was born in Aragón, married Isabel of Castile, a union that would eventually finish off Catalan independence.

Both came into their inheritances quickly, Isabel taking Castile in 1474 and the Catalan-Aragónese crown coming to Ferdinand in 1479. The two largest kingdoms in Spain were thus united, the ruling pair becoming known as "**Los Reyes Católicos**" ("Els Reis Catòlics" in Catalan), the Catholic monarchs. Their energies were devoted to the reconquest and unification of Spain: they finally took back Granada from the Moors in 1492, and initiated a wave of Christian fervour at whose heart was the **Inquisition**. Ferdinand and Isabel shared in the religious bigotry of their contemporaries, although Isabel, under the influence of her personal confessor and advisors, was the more reactionary of the two. In Catalunya, the Inquisition was established in 1487, and aimed to purify the Catholic faith by rooting out heresy. It was directed mainly at the secret **Jews**, most of whom had been converted by force (after the pogrom of 1391) to Christianity. It was suspected that their descendants, known as **New Christians**, continued to practise their old faith in secrecy, and in 1492, an edict forced some seventy thousand Jews to flee the country. The Jewish population in Barcelona was completely eradicated in this way, while communities elsewhere – principally in Girona, Tarragona and Lleida – were massively reduced, and those who remained were forced to convert to Christianity.

Also in 1492, the final shift in Catalunya's outlook occurred with the triumphal return of **Christopher Columbus** from the New World, to be received in Barcelona by Ferdinand and Isabel. As trade routes shifted away from the Mediterranean, this was no longer such a profitable market. Castile, like Portugal, looked to the Americas for trade and conquest, and the exploration and exploitation of the New World was spearheaded by the Andalucían city of Seville. Meanwhile, Ferdinand gave the Supreme Council of Aragón control over Catalan affairs in 1494. The Aragónese nobility, who had always resented the success of the Catalan maritime adventures, now saw the chance to complete their control of Catalunya by taking over its ecclesiastical institutions – with Catalan monks being thrown out of the great monasteries of Poblet and Montserrat.

Habsburg and Bourbon rule

Charles I, a **Habsburg**, came to the throne in 1516 as a beneficiary of the marriage alliances made by the Catholic monarchs. Five years later he was elected emperor of the **Holy Roman Empire** (as Charles V), inheriting not only Castile, Aragón and Catalunya, but also Flanders, the Netherlands, Artois, the Franche-Comté and all the American colonies. With such responsibilities, it became inevitable that attention would be diverted from Spain, whose chief function became to sustain the Holy Roman Empire with gold and silver from the Americas. It was in this era that Madrid was established as capital city of the Spanish Empire, and the long rivalry began between Madrid and Barcelona.

Throughout the **sixteenth century**, Catalunya continued to suffer under the Inquisition, and – deprived of trading opportunities in the Americas – became an impoverished region. Habsburg wars wasted the lives of Catalan soldiers, banditry in the region increased as the economic situation worsened, and emigration from certain areas followed. By the middle of the **seventeenth century**, Spain's rulers were losing credibility as the disparity between the wealth surrounding Crown and Court and the poverty of the mass of the population produced a source of perpetual tension.

With Spain and France at war in 1635, the Catalans took advantage of the situation and revolted, declaring themselves an **independent republic** under the protection of the French King Louis XIII. This, the "War of the Reapers" – after the marching song *Els Segadors* (The Reapers), later the Catalan national anthem – ended in 1652 with the surrender of Barcelona to the Spanish army. The **Treaty of the Pyrenees** in 1659 finally split the historical lands of Catalunya as the Spanish lost control of Roussillon and part of the Cerdagne to France.

In 1700, when the Habsburg king Charles II died heirless, France's Louis XIV saw an opportunity to fulfil his longtime ambition of putting a Bourbon on the Spanish throne. He managed to secure the succession of his grandson, Philippe d'Anjou, under condition that the latter renounced his rights to the throne of France. This deal put a Bourbon on the throne of Spain, but led to war with the other claimant, Archduke Charles of Austria: the resulting **War of the Spanish Succession** lasted thirteen years from 1701, with Catalunya (along with England) lining up on the Austrian side in an attempt to regain its ancient rights and in the hope that victory would give it a share of the American trade dominated by the Castilians since the late fifteenth century.

However, the **Treaty of Utrecht** in 1714 gave the throne to the **Bourbon** (*Borbón* in Castilian, *Borbó* in Catalan) Philippe, now Philip V of Spain, and initiated a fresh period of repression from which the Catalans took a century to recover. Barcelona lay under siege for over a year, and with its eventual capitulation a fortress was built at Ciutadella to subdue the city's inhabitants – the final defeat, on September 11, is still commemorated every year as a Catalan holiday, La Diada. The universities at Barcelona and Lleida were closed, the Catalan language was banned, the Consell de Cent and Generalitat were abolished – in short, Catalunya was finished as even a partially autonomous region.

Throughout the **eighteenth century**, Catalunya's interests were subsumed within those of Bourbon Spain, and successive monarchs were determined to Castilianize the region. When neighbouring France became aggressively expansionist following the Revolution of 1789, Spain was a natural target, first for the Revolutionary armies and later for the machinations of Napoleon. In 1805, during the **Napoleonic Wars**, the French fleet (along with the Spanish who had been forced into an alliance) was defeated at Trafalgar. Shortly after, Charles IV was forced to abdicate; Napoleon installed his brother Joseph on the throne three years later. Attempting to broaden his appeal among Spain's subjects, the French emperor proclaimed a separate government of Catalunya – independent of Joseph's rule – with Catalan as its official language. The region's response was an indication of how far Catalunya had become integrated into Spain during the Bourbon period – despite their history the Catalans supported the Bourbon cause solidly during the ensuing **Peninsular War** (1808–14), ignoring Napoleon's blandishments. Girona was defended heroically from the French in a seven-month siege, while Napoleon did his cause no good at all by attacking and sacking the holy shrine and monastery at Montserrat. Fierce local resistance was eventually backed by the muscle of a British army, and the French were at last driven out.

The slow Catalan revival

Despite the political emasculation of Catalunya, there were signs of **economic revival** from the end of the seventeenth century onwards. During the 1700s there was a gradual growth in agricultural output, partly caused by a doubling of the population: more land was put under cultivation, and productivity improved with the introduction of easy-to-cultivate maize from the Indies. Barcelona also saw a steady increase in trade, since from 1778 Catalunya was allowed to trade with the Americas for the first time; in this way, the shipping industry received a boost and Catalunya was able to export its textiles to a wider market. The other great export was wine, whose widespread production in the region also dates from this period. A chamber of commerce was founded in Barcelona in 1758, and other economic societies followed as commercial interests increased.

After the Napoleonic Wars, industry in Catalunya developed apace – it was an **industrialization** that appeared nowhere else in Spain. In the mid-nineteenth century, the country's first **railway** was built from Barcelona to Mataró, and later extended south to Tarragona, and north to Girona and the French border. **Manufacturing** industries appeared as the financial surpluses from the land were invested, encouraging a shift in population from the land to the towns; olive oil production in Lleida and Tarragona helped supply the whole country; and previously local industries flourished on a wider scale – in the wine-growing districts, for example, *cava* (champagne-like wine) production was introduced in the late nineteenth century, supported closely by the age-old cork industry of the Catalan forests. From 1890, hydroelectric power was harnessed from the Pyrenees, and by the end of the century **Barcelona** was the fastest-growing city in Spain – it was one of only six with more than 100,000 inhabitants.

Equally important was the first stirring of what became known as the **Renaixença** (Renaissance), in the mid-nineteenth century. Despite being banned in official use and public life, the Catalan **language** had never died out. Books began to appear again in Catalan – a dictionary in 1803 and a grammar in 1814 – and the language was revived among the bourgeoisie and intellectuals in the cities as a means of making subtle nationalist and political points. Catalan **poetry** became popular, and the late medieval **Jocs Florals** (Floral Games), a sort of literary competition, were revived in 1859 in Barcelona: one winner was the great Catalan poet, Jacint Verdaguer (1845–1902). Catalan **drama** developed (although even in the late nineteenth century there were still restrictions on performing wholly Catalan plays), led mainly by the dramatist Pitarra. The only discipline that didn't show any great advance was prose literature – partly because the Catalan language had been so debased with Castilian over the centuries that writers found it difficult to express themselves in a way that would appeal to the population.

Prosperity led to the rapid **expansion of Barcelona**, particularly the mid-nineteenth century addition to the city of the planned Eixample district. Encouraged by wealthy patrons and merchants, architects like Puig i Cadafalch, Domènech i Montaner and Antoni Gaudí were in the vanguard of the **modernista** movement which changed the face of the city. Culture and business came together with the **Universal Exhibition** of 1888, based around the *modernista* buildings of the Parc de la Ciutadella, and the **International Exhibition** on Montjuïc in 1929, which boasted creations in the style of *modernisme*'s successor, *noucentisme*.

The seeds of civil war

In 1814, the repressive Ferdinand VII had been restored to the Spanish throne, and, despite the Catalan contribution to the defeat of the French, he stamped out the least hint of liberalism in the region, abolishing virtually all Catalunya's remaining privileges. On his death, the Crown was claimed both by his daughter Isabel II (with liberal support) and by his brother Charles (backed by the Church and the conservatives). The ensuing **First Carlist War** (1833–39) ended in victory for Isabel, who came of age in 1843. Her reign was a long record of scandal, political crisis and constitutional compromise, until liberal army generals under the leadership of General Prim eventually effected a coup in 1868, forcing Isabel to abdicate. However, the experimental **First Republic** (1873–75) failed, and following the **Second Carlist War** the throne went to Isabel's son, Alfonso XII.

Against this unstable background, local dissatisfaction increased and the years preceding World War I saw a growth in working-class **political movements**. Barcelona's textile workers organized a branch affiliated to the communist First International, founded by Karl Marx, and the region's wine growers also banded together to seek greater security. Tension was further heightened by the **loss of Cuba** in 1898, which only added to local economic problems, with the return of soldiers seeking employment in the cities where there was none.

A call-up for army reserves to fight in Morocco in 1909 provoked a general strike and the so-called **Tragic Week** (Setmana Trágica) of rioting in Barcelona, and then throughout Catalunya, in which over one hundred people died. Catalans objected violently to the suggestion that they should go to fight abroad for a state that did little for them at home, and the city's streets saw burning churches, barricades and popular committees, though there was little direction to the protest. What the Tragic Week did prove to Catalan workers was the need to be better organized for the future. A direct result was the establishment of the Confederación Nacional del Trabajo – the **CNT** – in 1911, which included many of the Catalan working-class organizations.

During **World War I** Spain was neutral, though inwardly turbulent since soaring inflation and the cessation of exports following the German blockade of the North Atlantic hit the country hard. As rumblings grew among the workers and political organizations, the army moved decisively, crushing a general strike of 1917. The Russian Revolution had scared the conservative businessmen of the region, who offered cooperation with the army in return for political representation in the country's government. However, the situation did not improve. Violent strikes and assassinations plagued Barcelona, while the CNT and the union of the socialists, the CGT, both saw huge increases in their membership. In 1923, **General Primo de Rivera**, the captain-general of Catalunya, overthrew the national government in a military coup that had the full backing of the Catalan middle class, establishing a dictatorship which enjoyed initial economic success. There was no real stability in the dictatorship, however, and new political factions were taking shape throughout the country. The general resigned in 1930, dying a few months later, but the hopes of some for the restoration of the monarchy's political powers were short-lived. The success of the anti-monarchist parties in the municipal elections of 1931 led to the abdication of the king and the foundation of the **Second Republic**.

The Second Republic

In 1931, Catalunya, under Francesc Macià, leader of the Republican Left, declared itself to be an **independent republic**, and the Republican flag was raised over the Ajuntament in Barcelona. Madrid refused to accept the declaration, though a statute of limited autonomy was granted in 1932. Despite the initial hope that things would improve, the government was soon failing to satisfy even the least of expectations which it had raised. In addition, all the various strands of political ideology that had been fermenting in Spain over the previous century were ready to explode. **Anarchism** in particular was gaining strength among the frustrated middle classes as well as among workers and peasantry. The **Communist Party** and the left-wing **socialists**, driven into alliance by their mutual distrust of the "moderate" socialists in government, were also forming a growing bloc. There was little real unity of purpose on either Left or Right, but their fear of each other and their own exaggerated boasts made each seem an imminent threat. On the right, the **Falangists** (founded in 1923 by José Antonio Primo de Rivera, son of the dictator) made uneasy bedfellows with conservative traditionalists and dissident elements in the army upset by modernizing reforms.

In an atmosphere of growing confusion, the left-wing **Popular Front** alliance, including the Catalan Republican Left, won the general election of January 1936 by a narrow margin, and an all-Republican government was formed. In Catalunya, Lluís Companys became president of the Generalitat. Normal life, though, became increasingly impossible: the economy was crippled by strikes, peasants took agrarian reform into their own hands, and the government singularly failed to exert its authority over anyone. Finally, on July 17, 1936, the military garrison in Morocco rebelled under **General Francisco Franco**'s leadership, to be followed by uprisings at military garrisons throughout the country. It was the culmination of years of scheming in the army, but the event was far from the overnight success its leaders almost certainly expected. Much of the south and west quickly fell into the hands of the Nationalists, but Madrid and the industrialized northeast remained loyal to the Republican government. In Barcelona, although the military garrison supported Franco, it was soon subdued by local Civil Guards and the workers, while local leaders set up militias in preparation for the coming fight.

In October 1936 Franco was declared military commander and head of state; fascist Germany and Italy recognized his regime as the legitimate government of Spain in November. The Civil War was on.

Civil War

The **Spanish Civil War** (1936–39) was one of the most bitter and bloody the world has seen. Violent reprisals were visited on their enemies by both sides – the Republicans shooting priests and local landowners wholesale, and burning churches and cathedrals; the Nationalists carrying out mass slaughter of the population of almost every town they took. It was also to be the first modern war – Franco's German allies demonstrated their ability to inflict terror on civilian populations with their bombing raids on Gernika and Durango, while radio became an important propaganda weapon, with Nationalists offering starving Republicans the "white bread of Franco".

Catalunya was devoutly Republican from the outset with many of the rural areas particularly attracted by anarchism, an ideology that embodied their traditional values of equality and personal liberty. However, despite sporadic help from Russia and the 35,000 volunteers of the **International Brigades**, the Republic could never compete with the professional armies and the massive assistance from fascist Italy and Nazi Germany that the Nationalists enjoyed. Foreign volunteers arriving in Barcelona were sent to the front with companies that were ill-equipped, lines of communication were poor, and, furthermore, the Left was torn by internal divisions which at times led almost to civil war within its own ranks. George Orwell's account of this period in his *Homage to Catalonia* is instructive: fighting in an anarchist militia, he was eventually forced to flee the country when the infighting became intolerable, though many others like him were not so fortunate and ended up in prison or executed.

Eventually, the nonintervention of the other European governments effectively handed victory to the Nationalists. The Republican government fled Madrid first for Valencia, and then moved on to base itself at Barcelona in 1937. The **Battle of the Ebro** around Tortosa saw massive casualties on both sides; Nationalist troops advanced on Valencia in 1938, and from the west were also approaching Catalunya from their bases in Navarre. When Bilbao was taken by the Nationalists, the Republicans' fight on the **Aragón front** was lost. The final Republican hope – that war in Europe over Czechoslovakia would draw the Allies into a war against fascism and deprive Franco of his foreign aid – evaporated in September 1938, with the British Prime Minister Chamberlain's capitulation to Hitler at Munich, and Franco was able to call on new arms and other supplies from Germany for a final offensive against Catalunya. The **fall of Barcelona** came on January 25, 1939 – the Republican parliament held its last meeting at Figueres a few days later. Republican soldiers, cut off in the valleys of the Pyrenees, made their way across the high passes into France, joined by women and children fearful of a fascist victory. Among the refugees and escapees was **Lluís Companys**, president of the Generalitat, who was later captured in France by the Germans, returned to Spain and ordered by Franco to be shot at the castle prison on Montjuïc in 1940.

Catalunya in Franco's Spain

Although the Civil War left more than half a million dead, destroyed a quarter of a million homes and sent a third of a million people (including 100,000 Catalans) into exile, Franco was in no mood for reconciliation. With his government recognized by Allied powers, including Britain and France, he set up **war tribunals** which ordered executions and provided concentration camps in which upwards of two million people were held until "order" had been established by authoritarian means. Until as late as the mid-1960s, isolated partisans in Catalunya (and elsewhere in Spain) continued to resist fascist rule.

The **Catalan language** was banned again, in schools, churches, the press and in public life; only one party was permitted and censorship was rigorously enforced. The economy was in ruins, and Franco did everything possible to further the cause of Madrid against Catalunya, starving the region of investment and new industry. Pyrenean villagers began to drift down into the towns and cities in a fruitless search for work, accelerating the depopulation of the mountains.

After **World War II** (during which the country was too weak to be anything but neutral), Spain was economically and politically isolated. There were serious strikes in 1951 in Barcelona and in 1956 across the whole of Catalunya.

What saved Franco was the acceptance of **American aid**, offered by General Eisenhower in 1953 on the condition that Franco provide land for US air bases – a condition he was more than willing to accept. Prosperity did increase after this, fuelled in the 1960s and 1970s by a growing tourist industry, but Catalunya (along with the Basque country, another thorn in Franco's side) was still economically backward, with investment per head lower than anywhere else in the country. Absentee landlords took much of the local revenue, a situation exacerbated by Franco's policy of encouraging emigration to Catalunya from other parts of Spain (and granting the immigrants land) in an attempt to dilute regional differences.

Despite the **cultural and political repression**, the distinct Catalan identity was never really obliterated: the Catalan Church retained a feisty independence, while Barcelona emerged as the most important publishing centre in Spain. Clandestine language and history classes were conducted, and artists and writers continued to produce work in defiance of the authorities. Nationalism in Catalunya, however, did not take the same course as the Basque **separatist movement**, which engendered the terrorist organization ETA (Euzkadi ta Azkatasuna; "Basque Homeland and Freedom"). There was little violence against the state in Catalunya and no serious counterpart to ETA. The Catalan approach was subtler: an audience at the Palau de la Música sang the unofficial Catalan anthem when Franco visited in 1960; a massive petition against language restrictions was raised in 1963; and a sit-in by Catalan intellectuals at Montserrat was organized in protest against repression in the Basque country.

As Spain became comparatively more wealthy, so the political bankruptcy of Franco's regime and its inability to cope with popular demands became clearer. Higher incomes, the need for better education and a creeping invasion of Western culture made the anachronism of Franco ever more apparent. His only reaction was to attempt to withdraw what few signs of increased liberalism had crept through, and his last years mirrored the repression of the postwar period.

Franco's death and the new democracy

When Franco died in 1975, **King Juan Carlos** was officially designated to succeed as head of state – groomed for the succession by Franco himself. The king's initial moves were cautious in the extreme, appointing a government dominated by loyal Franquistas, who had little sympathy for the growing opposition demands for "democracy without adjectives". In the summer of 1976 demonstrations, particularly in Madrid, ended in violence, with the police upholding the old authoritarian ways.

To his credit, Juan Carlos recognized that some real break with the past was urgent and inevitable, and, accepting the resignation of his prime minister, set in motion the process of **democratization**. His newly appointed prime minister, Adolfo Suárez, steered through a Political Reform Act, which allowed for a two-chamber parliament and a referendum in favour of democracy; he also legitimized the Socialist Party (the PSOE) and the Communists, and called elections for the following year, the first since 1936.

In the elections of 1977, the **Pacte Democratico per Catalunya** – an alliance of pro-Catalan parties – gained ten seats in the lower house of the Spanish parliament (Basque nationalists won a similar number) dominated by Suárez's own centre-right UCD party but also with a strong Socialist presence. In a spirit of consensus and amnesty, it was announced that Catalunya was to be granted a degree of autonomy, and a million people turned out on the streets of Barcelona to witness the re-establishment of the Generalitat and to welcome home its president-in-exile, **Josep Tarradellas**. A new Spanish constitution of 1978 allowed for a sort of devolution within a unitary state, and the **Statute of Autonomy** for Catalunya was approved on December 18, 1979, with the first regional elections taking place in March 1980. Although the Socialists had won the mayoral election of 1978, it was the conservative **Jordi Pujol i Soley** and his coalition party **Convergència i Unió** (CiU) who gained regional power – and who proceeded to dominate the Catalan parliament for the next quarter of a century. In a way, the pro-conservative vote made it easy for the central government to deal with Catalunya, since the demands for autonomy here did not have the extreme political dimension they had in the Basque country.

After the failure of an attempted **military coup** in February 1981, led by Civil Guard Colonel Tejero, the **elections of 1982** saw Felipe González's PSOE elected with a massive swing to the Left in a country that had been firmly in the hands of the Right for forty-three years. The **1986** general election gave González a renewed mandate, during which time Spain entered the **European Community**, decided by referendum to stay in NATO, and boasted one of the fastest-growing economies in Western Europe. However, high unemployment, wage controls and a lack of social security measures led to diminishing support and the PSOE began losing much of its credibility. Narrow victories in two more elections kept the Socialists in power but after the 1993 results were counted it was clear that they had failed to win an overall majority and were forced to rely on the support of the Catalan nationalist coalition, CiU, to retain power. This state of affairs well suited Jordi Pujol, who was now in a position to pursue some of the Catalan nationalists' more long-cherished aims, in particular the right to retain part of the region's own income-tax revenue.

Contemporary politics

Following allegations of sleaze and the disclosure of the existence of a secret "dirty war". It is against the Basque terrorists, the calling of a **general election in 1996** came as no surprise and neither did the overall result. In power for almost fourteen years, the PSOE finally succumbed to the greater appeal of the conservative Partido Popular (PP), under **José Maria Aznar** – the first conservative government in Spain since the return of democracy. However, the PP came in well short of an outright majority and Aznar was left with the same problem as González before him – relying on the Catalan nationalists and other smaller regionalist parties to maintain his party in power.

In the **general election of 2000**, a resounding victory in the national parliament, whilst Catalunya was left under CiU control. For the first time, the PP was no longer dependent on other parties to pass legislation and was high on confidence, though within two years Aznar's government had begun to lose its way. In particular, Aznar's fervent support of US and British **military action in Iraq** in 2003 led to huge discontent. Polls showed that ninety percent of Spaniards opposed the conflict – manifested in Barcelona by a cacophonous nightly anti-war banging of pots and pans from the city's balconies.

However, in the local elections of 2003, Aznar and the PP defied the polls, holding off the PSOE in many major cities (Barcelona excepted). With the PSOE beset by corruption scandals and affected by the strong separatist showing in regional elections, it seemed that the best the PSOE could hope for was to deny the PP an absolute majority in the **2004 general election**. That was before the dramatic events of March 11, 2004, when terrorists struck at the heart of **Madrid**, killing 200 people in coordinated train bombings. Spain went to the polls in shock a few days later, and voted in the PSOE against all expectations. With millions on the streets in the days after the attacks, it seemed the PP had been punished both for supporting the war in Iraq, and – prematurely to many – for blaming the bombings on the Basque separatists, ETA.

The Socialists took power in a minority administration led by PSOE prime minister **José Luis Rodriguez Zapatero**, forced to rely on parliamentary support from Catalan separatists and other regional parties. A leftish coalition in Catalunya itself (see p.000) soon raised the whole question of Catalunya's status within the Spanish nation, since Zapatero had previously promised to accept whatever demands for greater autonomy emanated from the new Catalan parliament. The consequent **statute of autonomy bill,** approved by the Catalan government in September 2005 and sent to Madrid, opened up all sorts of national faultlines, as the bill sought to go well beyond Spanish constitutional limits, defining Catalunya as a "nation" within Spain and claiming full tax-raising powers and a parallel judicial system. This is a popular call in Catalunya – supported by ninety percent of the Catalan parliament's deputies – but causes huge distrust elsewhere in Spain, on all sides of the political spectrum. Zapatero was immediately put under pressure from his own PSOE party – many of whose members have no truck with Catalan separatism – while there was predictable opposition from the PP and from much of the Madrid-based media. More worrying was the rumble from a Spanish general that the army might be forced to intercede if the Spanish constitution and national unity were threatened – he was quickly sacked, but it's a reminder that military intervention in democratic Spain (as recently as 1981) is still considered an option by some of the more extreme conservative forces in the country.

At the time of writing, the future of the autonomy bill was unclear. Some agreement was reached in early 2006 on a watered-down version that increased Catalunya's tax-raising powers and redefined in general (though not legal) terms the region as a "nation". But the ERC has rejected any compromise – and brought over 100,000 people on to the streets in February 2006 in support of their stance, while for very different reasons the conservative PP sees any statute reform as a step towards the breaking up of Spain. With the statute bill due before Spain's constitutional court, and any finally agreed statute to be put to a regional referendum, there's still plenty of room for argument and horse-trading. Meanwhile, the calling in early 2006 of a permanent cease-fire by armed Basque separatist organization ETA has further put regionalism high on the Spanish national agenda. Faced with a general election due in 2008, Zapatero has to balance successfully the conflicting demands of party, coalition, region and state if he's to engineer another victory.

City and state – Barcelona and Catalunya today

The province's official title is the **Comunitat Autonoma de Catalunya**. It's one of seventeen "autonomous communities" recognized by the Spanish constitution of 1978, with Catalunya defined as a "nationality" (rather than, crucially, a "nation") by the 1979 statute of autonomy.

The Catalan government, based in Barcelona – the **Generalitat** – enjoys a very high profile, employing eighty thousand people in sixteen departments or ministries, controlling social services, urban planning, culture, regional transport, industry, trade, tourism, fisheries and agriculture. However, as long as the budget is based on **tax** collected by central government and then returned proportionately, the scope for real independence is limited, as the Generalitat has no tangible resources of its own and is forced to **share jurisdiction** on strategic matters like health, education and justice with the Spanish state. In addition, although an autonomous part of Spain, Catalunya is not officially recognized at international level.

However, over the years steps have been taken to create at least the illusion of independence. Catalan tourism, trade and industry (as opposed to Spanish) are increasingly promoted abroad, while two of the most visible symbols of the Spanish state, the Guardia Civil and the Policía Nacional, are gradually being scaled down, with urban **policing** and rural and highway duties being taken over by the Mossos d'Esquadra, Catalunya's autonomous police force. Culturally, emphasis has been on the promotion of the **Catalan language** – currently one of the fastest-growing languages in the world. The Generalitat has succeeded in having all of Catalunya's children taught in Catalan, while the entire machinery of regional government is conducted in Catalan.

Parliament and local politics

The **Parlament de Catalunya** (Parliament of Catalunya) comprises a single chamber of 135 members, with elections held every four years. It sits in the old Ciutadella arsenal building in Parc de la Ciutadella, in parliamentary sessions that run from September to December and February to June, though extraordinary sessions can be called outside these months. As well as legislating for Catalunya within the strictures of the Statute of Autonomy, parliament also appoints the senators who represent the Generalitat in the Spanish Senate and has the right to initiate legislation in the Spanish Congress.

From 1980 (when autonomy was granted) until 2003, **Catalunya** consistently elected right-wing governments, led by the conservative Convergència i Unió (CiU) president of the Generalitat, **Jordi Pujol i Soley**. The Catalan predilection for the Right may come as a surprise in view of the past, but Catalunya is nothing if not pragmatic, and such administrations are seen as better able to protect Catalan business interests. The main opposition was provided by the **Partit Socialista de Catalunya** (PSC), sister party of the national PSOE, while other Catalan parties, like the pro-independence **Esquerra Republicana de Catalana** (ERC) and the **Catalunya Verds** (Greens), have usually attracted minority support.

However, by way of contrast to conservative Catalunya, **Barcelona** itself remains by and large a socialist stronghold. Part of this is due to the city's industrial heritage, but it's also in good measure the result of the large immigrant population from elsewhere in Spain, who are little attracted to the CiU's brand of Catalan nationalism. Between 1982 and 1997, the **Ajuntament** (city council) was led by an incredibly popular and charismatic socialist mayor, **Pasqual Maragall i Mira**, who took much of the credit for the hosting of the 1992 Olympic Games and consequent reshaping of the city. However, much to the consternation of locals, he stepped down from his post as mayor in 1997, leaving his deputy, the little-known **Joan Clos**, to fill his shoes. Despite initial worries, Clos has done enough to convince the city that he can take Barcelona in the same pioneering direction as his predecessor – Clos was elected to a full four-year term in 1999 (with an increased majority) and re-elected in 2003.

Maragall, meanwhile, moved on to take charge of the PSC in Catalunya, and with Pujol's announcement that he wouldn't stand again for the presidency, the **2003 parliamentary elections** were ostensibly a straight fight between the CiU, under Pujol's former deputy Artur Mas, and Maragall's PSC. On one level, that was indeed the case, as the two parties finished neck and neck, the PSC polling slightly more votes but winning slightly fewer seats than the CiU. However, the surprise was the performance of the pro-independence ERC, under the leadership of **Josep-Lluís Carod-Rovira**, which effectively doubled its vote from 1999 to hold the balance of power. After a short period of haggling, a coalition of the Left, led by the PSC and under the presidency of Pasqual Maragall, replaced the nationalists in power.

It was not the easy alliance that it appeared on paper, since the separatist ERC favours full Catalan independence, not something the PSC (or the national PSOE) supports. Nonetheless, prompted by the manoeuvring of the ERC, the first left-wing Catalan government since 1980 has pushed the

CONTEXTS | A history of Barcelona and Catalunya

prospect of greater Catalan autonomy to centre stage with the overwhelming approval by parliament in September 2005 of the **Estatut** – the proposed reform of the Catalan Statute of Autonomy – currently before the Spanish parliament. It's an explosive issue outside Catalunya, but the underlying tenets are longstanding aims of Catalan separatists – nationhood, tax-raising powers, judicial authority and language primacy.

Despite their differences, most political strands within Catalunya are convinced of the merits of some kind of **devolution**. Yet the proposed reformed statute means different things to different parties: to the PP and conservatives, granting more regional autonomy puts at risk the Spanish nation; to the Socialists, declaring Catalunya a "nation" is a welcome step towards a strong federal state; while for the separatists, it's nothing less than a call to independence.

Perhaps the most telling development for Catalunya in the end will turn out to be the onward march of **European integration**. Spain's regional governments already have representatives at the European Union, working on committees alongside the Spanish delegates. In addition, the Spanish government is committed to consulting the regions on any European issues that affect them directly, and there are ongoing discussions about making Catalan an official EU language.

Taxes, development and the economy

Catalans of all persuasions have long demanded the right to raise more of their own **taxes** and spend them on self-regulation – arguing that under the present system of autonomy Catalunya pays more to the Spanish state than it receives. In response to the Estatut proposals the Spanish government agreed in 2006 that Catalunya can now collect and administer half of the income tax and VAT raised locally.

Catalunya's solid **economy** makes it, along with the Basque country and Madrid, one of the most prosperous regions of the country. Around half of all new firms starting business in Spain do so in Catalunya, and Barcelona is the third-richest city in the country, and Europe's most popular convention site; it boasts nearly a fifth of Spain's GDP, relatively low unemployment, and Europe's largest savings bank, La Caixa. Tourism is an important factor, accounting for fourteen percent of Catalunya's GDP, with over twelve million visitors a year now coming to the region. Other major employers are telecommunications, metal products and chemical and pharmaceutical industries.

The **1992 Olympics** are still regarded as a turning point in the city's recent history. They were an important boost, involving radical restoration of the old-town and port areas and prompting massive new developments – at a pace which the city has endeavoured to maintain ever since. In recent years, among countless other ambitious projects, this has meant the complete renovation of the **Port Vell** neighbourhood, a cleanup of **El Raval** and the current regeneration of **Poble Nou** as part of the so-called **Project 22@**. Other **current development schemes** include the remodelling of the Glòries district, the further expansion of the city's airport and metro system, the completion of a high-velocity train (AVE) link with Madrid and France and concomitant building of a new transport interchange at La Sagrera, the transformation of the Arenes bullring into a leisure centre, and even the mooted completion of the Sagrada Família – all evidence that Barcelona's economic development is far from finished.

Social matters

Economic success has led to familiar urban social problems. More than half of Catalunya's seven million inhabitants now live in the city and its metropolitan region, with many complaining that the high-profile regeneration projects do little for their needs. **Hotel building** has reached epidemic proportions and rents and property prices in general have boomed, depriving the young, the old and the poor of affordable **housing** and other amenities. That said, both the Olympic and Project 22@ schemes have incorporated social housing, leisure facilities and green spaces, while the public transport system in particular is something of a European model of excellence.

Nonetheless, there are tensions in an increasingly crowded, developed city. Noise in residential areas is a perennial problem, and the Ajuntament has been getting tough in enforcing **noise restrictions** and closing down transgressing bars and clubs. The city council has also been getting more serious about dealing with squatters, known as **okupas**, whose banner- and graffiti-clad buildings have long been a familiar sight, especially in and around Gràcia. In the past, Barcelona has been tolerant of the *okupas* but concern from some residents about drugs and noise has persuaded the city council to close down many squats in recent years. In the same vein, the police have come down hard on **botellóns** – the mass, impromptu outdoor drinking parties that sprout up in Barcelona and other Spanish cities from time to time.

As elsewhere in Europe, **immigration** is another point of contemporary debate. While immigrants from elsewhere in Spain have long settled in Barcelona (indeed, were encouraged to do so by Franco to dilute Catalan nationalism), those bearing the brunt of racism are the newcomers from North Africa, the Indian subcontinent and South America. Popular wisdom has come to equate North Africans with petty crime, whereas Romanies are treated largely as pariahs. It's dangerous nonsense with at least some of its roots in a Catalan nationalism that prides itself on a certain cultural superiority, but such bigoted views aren't simply confined to the Right – senior figures on the Left, too, have warned of the "dangers" of allowing too many "foreigners" into Catalunya. The facts, of course, tell a different story. Just seven percent of the Catalan population at large has its origin outside Spain, though as most of these people live or work in the capital it's easy to construct a prejudice from their higher profile in the city. In contrast, almost a third of the Catalan population comes from other parts of Spain, while the fastest-growing immigrant population is actually that of other Europeans, free to settle in Catalunya with the relaxation of EU residency rules.

Catalan cookery

M any people judge the food of Catalunya to be the best in Spain. The region certainly has one of the oldest culinary traditions: its inns were celebrated by travellers in medieval times, while the first Spanish cookery book was published in Barcelona in 1477. Historically, Catalunya shares some of its dishes and methods with the region of Valencia to the south and parts of France (such as Roussillon) to the north, but nonetheless it's possible to identify within its borders a distinct cuisine. Fish and rice have always played a major part in Catalan cookery, but there's also an emphasis on mixed flavours which you won't find anywhere else in Spain – some common traditional examples are rabbit cooked with snails, chicken with shellfish, meat or poultry with fruit, and vegetables with raisins and nuts. Meanwhile, contemporary Catalan chefs (see p.190) have rewritten the rule book regarding taste and texture, and their deconstructivist menus – featuring intensely flavoured foams, reductions and concentrates – are currently at the forefront of cutting-edge European cuisine.

We've stuck to traditional **recipes** below, the sort of dishes you're likely to eat on a day-to-day basis in Barcelona and Catalunya. You don't need much in the way of special **equipment**, though a *paella* (the dish is named after the wide, flat metal pan it's cooked in) and a *cassola* (earthenware casserole dish) are both useful. They're widely available these days from specialist cookery stores. Other than that, you only need to be insistent on the best and freshest **ingredients** – the finest tomatoes you can buy, proper salted Catalan anchovies, authentic rice and, above all, good olive oil. All the recipes below are for four people, unless otherwise stated.

Pa amb tomàquet

The "bread with tomato" combination is a classic taste of Catalunya, eaten for breakfast, or as a snack or appetizer. In traditional grill-restaurants and taverns you'll often be brought the wherewithal to do-it-yourself before your meal arrives – a basket of toasted bread, a handful of garlic cloves and an over-ripe tomato or two. The basic method is given below, but, for more of a meal, pile on shavings of ham or cheese, grilled vegetables or anchovy fillets.

Ingredients
Good continental bread
Vine-ripened tomatoes
Peeled garlic cloves
Olive oil
Salt

Method
Cut large slices from a loaf of good continental bread, preferably the dense, heavy variety, and grill them (a ribbed cast-iron grill-pan is ideal for this). Cut the garlic cloves in two and drag the cut sides over the toast. Cut the tomatoes in two and squeeze and rub well over the garlic-impregnated toast. Dribble generous amounts of olive oil over the slices and add salt to taste.

Amanida Catalana

Salad (*amanida*) is usually served as a first course in Catalunya and can be very filling.

Ingredients

3 large tomatoes, thickly sliced
2 hard-boiled eggs, quartered
24 green olives
1 large Spanish onion, very thinly sliced
1 large roasted red pepper (see Escalivada, below), cut into strips
Crunchy lettuce, as much as you require
200g tinned tuna
8 plump anchovy fillets

Method

This is one of the most common of restaurant salads, and with it you can improvise to your heart's content, but don't toss the ingredients all together – it's a composed salad, laid out on a plate, rather a bowl of mixed salad. For a more elaborate dish you can add shredded carrot or pickled vegetables, sliced cheese or thinly cut dry-cured ham or pork, salami or spiced sausage. Dress salad with salt and olive oil.

Escalivada

This fantastic mix of grilled peppers, onions and aubergine is a restaurant and domestic staple. It's usually available as a starter or an accompaniment to grills and roasts, or you can buy it ready-made on deli counters in Catalan markets. It's also very easy to make.

Ingredients

2 large aubergines
4 red peppers
4 small onions
Olive oil
1 clove garlic, chopped very finely (optional)
Salt

Method

Grill the vegetables whole on a barbecue, or under a grill, turning them until the skins are blackened all over. Or simply place them on separate trays and roast them in the oven on a high heat for the same effect – you'll still need to turn them periodically. When they are done, put the blackened vegetables in a shallow casserole dish or on a tray and cover them with a cloth or lid for ten minutes (some people place them in a paper bag). This process allows them to steam while they cool down, making it easier to remove the blackened skins. When they are cool enough to handle, peel the skins. Slice the soft internal pulp of the aubergine into strips; seed the peppers and cut into thin strips; remove the tough outer skin of the onions and separate out the soft inner leaves. Spread out the vegetables on a serving dish, dribble with oil, scatter with minced garlic if you like, and season with salt.

Espinacs a la Catalana

"Catalan spinach" can either be served as a starter or as an accompaniment to a main dish. You can use greens instead of fresh spinach, but you should remove the hard stems before cooking.

Ingredients

500g fresh spinach
3 tablespoons raisins, soaked in hot water, then drained
3 tablespoons pine nuts
2 tablespoons olive oil
2 cloves garlic, finely chopped
1 small onion, finely chopped

Method

Put the spinach in boiling water, cook for three minutes until tender and then drain, squeezing out excess water. Put to one side. Heat the oil in the pan, add the garlic and onion and cook gently until soft, taking care not to burn the garlic. Add the spinach, drained raisins and pine nuts, and toss together while heating through. Add salt and pepper to taste.

Sarsuela

This wonderful fish casserole is served in most coastal towns, using whatever fish and shellfish is available. You'll have to buy what you can, though you should be aiming for large prawns in their shells, different kinds of white fish (such as cod or hake), squid, mussels or clams. In Catalunya, crayfish or lobster are often added, too. The point is to go for a variety of fish: the word *sarsuela* refers to a comic musical variety show.

Ingredients

3–4 tablespoons olive oil
2 cloves garlic, finely chopped
2 large tomatoes, skinned, seeded and finely chopped
2 onions, sliced
1 tablespoon Spanish brandy
1 teaspoon paprika
1 bay leaf
1 cup/quarter-pint dry white wine
2 tablespoons chopped parsley
2 lemons, cut into wedges
Assorted white fish, enough for a couple of fair-sized chunks each
8 large prawns in their shells
4 small squid
16 mussels/32 clams
Ground black pepper
Salt

Method

Clean the fish and cut into chunks; slice the squid into rings; leave the large prawns as they are. Scrub and clean the mussels or clams. Boil the fishy leftovers (skin and heads; if you've bought fillets, use a couple of chunks and a few small prawns) in a pot of water, adding salt and pepper, some fresh herbs and a sliced onion, to give a fish stock – which, when reduced a little, should be strained and put aside.

Heat the oil in a large pot or casserole, add the garlic, onion and chopped tomatoes and cook slowly for ten minutes – this is the *sofregit* (see box above). Turn up the heat, add the brandy and flame, then turn it back down and add the paprika, fish stock, white wine and bay leaf. Stir the mixture, put in the chunks of white fish and simmer for five minutes. Stir, add the squid and prawns and simmer for another five minutes; then add the mussels or clams, cover and cook for a further five minutes or so, until the fish is ready and the mussels or clams have opened. Take care not to break up the fish by stirring too often. Add salt and pepper to taste, and garnish with fresh parsley and lemon wedges before serving.

Grilled fish with romesco sauce

There are many different varieties of *romesco* sauce, which originates from the Tarragona province, and you can experiment with the quantities of the ingredients below until you find the taste that suits you. Made with small chilli peppers, fresh or dried, it can be a very hot sauce, though you can substitute cayenne pepper or even paprika for these, if you want to control the heat.

Ingredients

4 fish steaks, marinaded in olive oil, chopped garlic and lemon juice
2 lemons, quartered
2 tablespoons olive oil
1 small onion, finely chopped
3 tomatoes, skinned, seeded and chopped
3 cloves garlic, finely chopped
10–15 almonds (toasted under the grill)
2 tablespoons dry white wine
Chilli peppers/cayenne pepper/ paprika to taste
1 tablespoon red wine vinegar
Salt

Method

Fry the onion and the garlic in the olive oil until soft, add the tomatoes, white wine and chilli peppers and cook over a low heat for twenty minutes. Crush or grind the almonds and add to the mixture, adding enough extra olive oil to achieve the consistency of a purée. Add the vinegar and a pinch of salt. Either put the whole lot through a blender or food processor, or pass through a sieve – you're aiming for a smooth, rather thick sauce. Leave to cool at room temperature. Take the fish out of the marinade, grill, and serve with lemon wedges. Serve the sauce separately, to be dipped in or spooned over.

Pollastre amb gambes

The combination of chicken (*pollastre*) and prawns (*gambes*) is typically Catalan, otherwise known as *mar i muntanya* (sea and mountain).

Ingredients
8 chicken pieces
12–16 medium prawns in their shells, washed
3 tablespoons olive oil
1 onion, finely chopped
2 cloves garlic, finely chopped
2 tomatoes, skinned, seeded and chopped
1 carrot, peeled and finely chopped
Quarter-cup Spanish brandy
Half-cup dry white wine
Quarter-cup beef stock (you can use a stock cube)
2 tablespoons chopped parsley
Ground pepper
Salt

Method
Salt and pepper the chicken pieces, heat the oil in a large pan, and then add the chicken pieces and prawns. Take the prawns out after a minute or so, put to one side, and cook the chicken until golden-brown on all sides. Add the onion, garlic, tomatoes and carrot, and cook until soft (about 15min). Turn up the heat, add the brandy and flame (stand well back), then – when the flames have died down – turn the heat back down and add the wine, stock, half of the parsley, salt and pepper. Cover and cook for another twenty minutes, then add the prawns and cook for another ten minutes. Take out the chicken and prawns, put them on a warm serving dish and strain the sauce over them, sprinkling with the rest of the parsley.

Crema Catalana

The one dessert you'll be offered everywhere in Catalunya is *Crema Catalana*. It rounds off a meal impressively if you make it at home; the only tricky part is caramelizing the sugar topping.

Ingredients
2 cups milk
Peel of half a lemon
1 cinnamon stick
4 egg yolks
7 tablespoons sugar
1 tablespoon cornflour

Method
Simmer the milk with the lemon peel and cinnamon stick for a few minutes, then take out the lemon and cinnamon from the pan. Beat the egg yolks and

half of the sugar together, beat in the cornflour, too, then add the beaten egg mixture slowly into the milk and continue to simmer. Stir constantly until thick and smooth, taking care not to let the mixture boil, and then pour into a wide, shallow serving dish. Let the mixture cool and then put in the fridge.

When you want to serve it, sprinkle the rest of the sugar evenly over the custard so that it forms a thick layer on the top. To caramelize the sugar topping, you can use a kitchen blowtorch – or simply heat a wide knife or metal spatula and press down on the sugar until it goes brown and crunchy. Repeat this over the whole top of the dessert, wiping the knife or spatula clean and reheating it every time.

Books

The selection of books reviewed below provides useful background on the city's history, people and institutions. Despite a long pedigree, Catalan literature is hard to find in translation, though novels set in Barcelona by (mostly foreign) authors provide a feel of the city past and present. A good first stop for all books is the online bookseller **Amazon** (⊛www.amazon.co.uk, www.amazon. com), which has all of the books listed below as well as other hard-to-find and specialist titles. In Barcelona, most of the major **bookshops** (see p.232) carry English-language guides and titles about the city, or look in the **museum bookshops** (particularly in MNAC, MACBA, Caixa Forum, Museu Picasso and Fundació Joan Miró) for books on art, design and architecture. The online literary magazine ⊛**www.barcelonareview.com** has plenty in the archive on Spanish and Catalan writers, art, culture and life.

History

Barcelona

Jimmy Burns *Barça: A People's Passion*. On one level it's simply an informative history of the city's famous football team, alma mater of Cruyff, Lineker, Maradona, Ronaldinho et al. However, like the club itself, the book is so much more than that, as Burns examines Catalan pride and nationalism through the prism of sport.

Felipe Fernandez-Armesto *Barcelona: A Thousand Years of the City's Past*. An expertly written appraisal of what the author sees as the formative years of the city's history, from the tenth to the early twentieth century.

Robert Hughes *Barcelona*. The renowned art critic casts his accomplished eye over two thousand years of Barcelona's history and culture, with special emphasis on the nineteenth and early twentieth centuries – explaining, in his own words, "the zeitgeist of the place and the connective tissue between the cultural icons".

Matthew Stewart *Monturiol's Dream*. Witty and engaging account of the life and work of Narcís Monturiol, the nineteenth-century Catalan utopian visionary, revolutionary and inventor of the world's first true submarine. Stewart places Monturiol firmly at the centre of Barcelona's contemporary social and political turmoil – printing seditious magazines, manning the barricades in the 1850s, fleeing into exile and returning to pursue his pioneering invention.

Colm Tóibín *Homage to Barcelona*. Echoing Orwell, the Irish writer pays his own homage to the city, tracing Barcelona's history through its artists, architects, personalities, organizations and rulers.

Spain

Raymond Carr *Modern Spain 1875–1980* and *The Spanish Tragedy: the Civil War in Perspective*. Two of the best books available on twentieth-century Spanish history – both are well-written narratives.

John Hooper *The New Spaniards*. Excellent portrait of post-Franco Spain and the new generation. It's a bit dated now (last revised in 1995), but even so, if you buy just one book for general background on the rest of the country, this should be it.

Hugh Thomas *Rivers of Gold: The Rise of the Spanish Empire*. Thomas' scholarly but eminently accessible history provides a fascinating snapshot of Spain's most glorious period – the meteoric imperial rise in the late fifteenth and early sixteenth centuries, when characters like Ferdinand and Isabella, and Columbus and Magellan, shaped the country's outlook for the next three hundred years.

Civil War

Gerald Brenan *The Spanish Labyrinth*. First published in 1943, Brenan's record of the background to the Civil War is tinged by personal experience, yet still impressively rounded.

🏃 **George Orwell** *Homage to Catalonia*. Stirring account of the Civil War fight on the Aragón front and Orwell's participation in the early exhilaration of revolution in Barcelona. A forthright, honest and entertaining tale, covering Orwell's injury and subsequent flight from the factional infighting in Republican Spain.

Paul Preston *A Concise History of the Spanish Civil War* and *Franco*. The leading historian of twentieth-century Spain offers *Civil War*, an easily accessible introduction to the subject, and *Franco*, a penetrating and monumental biography of Franco and his regime.

Hugh Thomas *The Spanish Civil War*. Exhaustive political study of the period that's still the best single telling of the convoluted story of the Civil War.

Art, architecture and style

🏃 **Gijs van Hensbergen** *Gaudí: The Biography*. A worthy biography of "arguably the world's most famous architect". Van Hensbergen puts substantial flesh on the man while placing his work firmly in context, as Spain lost her empire and Catalunya slowly flexed her nationalist muscles.

John Richardson *A Life of Picasso*. The definitive multi-volume biography - Volume 1, covering the period 1881–1906, is an extremely readable account of the artist's early years, covering the whole of his time in Barcelona.

Phyllis Richardson *Style City: Barcelona*. Part guide, part celebration of everything that's considered cool about contemporary Barcelona. The book covers the sharpest restaurant interiors to the latest galleries, artisans' studios to Art Nouveau bars, accompanied by 350 colour photographs that show Barcelona in its most flattering light.

Philippe Thiébaut *Gaudí: Builder of Visions*. Read van Hensbergen for the life, but pick up this pocket-sized volume for its excellent photographic coverage – not just Gaudí buildings and interiors, but sketches, historical photographs and architectural insights that add up to a useful gateway to his work in the city and surroundings.

Christopher Woodward *The Buildings of Europe: Barcelona*. This little guide was written in 1992, so stops well short of the latest round of city reconstruction, but its thumbnail sketches and short essays about buildings, streets, squares and parks are handy reference points. Particularly good on the period 1800–1910 (industrialization to *modernisme*), and the often neglected Franco era of architecture.

Food and wine

Colman Andrews *Catalan Cuisine*. The best available – possibly the *only* available – English-language book dealing with Spain's most adventurous regional cuisine. Full of historical and anecdotal detail, it's a pleasure to read, let alone cook from (no pictures, though).

Penelope Casas *The Foods and Wines of Spain*. Casas roams across every region of Spain in this classic Spanish cookery book, including the best

Catalan literature and writers

Catalan was established as a literary language as early as the thirteenth century, and a **golden age** of medieval Catalan literature followed, lasting until the mid-sixteenth century, with another cultural and literary flowering in the nineteenth century known as the **Renaixença** (Renaissance). However, this long pedigree has suffered two major interruptions: first, the rise of Castile and later Bourbon rule, which saw the Catalan language eclipsed and then suppressed; and a similar suppression under Franco, when there was a ban on Catalan books and publications. In the post-Civil War period there was some relaxation of the ban, but it's only been since the return of democracy to Spain that Catalan literature has once again been allowed to flourish. Catalan and Spanish speakers and readers are best served by the literature, since there's little still in translation – the Amazon websites are a good first stop for the translated authors mentioned below. The vernacular works of mystic and philosopher **Ramon Llull** (1233–1316) mark the onset of a true Catalan literature – his *Blanquerna* was one of the first books to be written in any Romance language, while the later chivalric epic *The White Tyrant* (*Tirant lo Blanc*) by **Joanot Martorell** (1413–68) represents a high point of the golden age. None of the works of the leading lights of the nineteenth-century *Renaixença* are readily available in translation, and it's to *Solitude* (*Solitud*) by **Victor Català** (1869–1966) that you have to look for the most important pre-Civil War Catalan novel. This tragic tale of a woman's life and sexual passions in a Catalan mountain village was first published in 1905, pseudonymously by Caterina Albert i Paradís, who lived most of her life in rural northern Catalunya.

During and after the Civil War, many authors found themselves under forcible or self-imposed exile, including **Pere Calders i Rossinyol** (1912–94), best known for his short stories, and **Mercè Rodoreda i Gurgui** (1909–83), whose *Camellia Street* (*El carrer de les Camèlies*) and *My Cristina and Other Tales* (*La meva Cristina i altres contes*) are relatively easily found in translation. For something lighter, there are the works of **Maria Antònia Oliver i Cabrer** (born 1946), novelist, children's author and short-story writer born in Mallorca, whose early novels were influenced by her birthplace, but whose *Study in Lilac* (*Estudi en Lila*) and *Antipodes* introduce fictional Barcelona private eye Lonia Guiu.

Not all Catalan writers write in Catalan, but rather in Spanish, including perhaps the best-known of all – **Manuel Vasquez Montalban** (1939–2003), crime writer *par excellence*, and novelist, poet, journalist, political commentator and committed communist to boot. His Pepe Carvalho books do nothing less than expose the shortcomings of the new Spanish democracy in fast-changing Barcelona. Montalban's contemporary **Juan Marse** (born 1933) uses the post-Civil War dictatorship as the background for many of his Barcelona-set novels, and it's the same period that spawned the Barcelona blockbuster *The Shadow of the Wind* by **Carlos Ruiz Záfon** (born Barcelona, 1964). For other new Catalan writers, such as **Albert Sánchez Piñol** (born Barcelona, 1965), nationality seems incidental at best – his well-regarded first novel *Cold Skin*, is a creepy sci-fi, pyschological tale of solitude on an Antarctic island where something stirs as soon as the sun goes down. His 2006 novel, *Pandora al Congo*, is yet to be translated into English, but mixes fantasy, horror and adventure in a colonial setting.

C

CONTEXTS | Books

dishes that Catalunya has to offer. Her *Paella* and *Tapas: The Little Dishes of Spain* cover the rest of the bases. **Jan Read** *Wines of Spain*. All you need to know to sort out your Penedès from your Priorat – an explanation of regions and producers, plus tasting notes and tips for wine tourists.

Novels set in Barcelona

Bernado Atxaga *The Lone Man*. The noted Basque novelist set his well-received psychological thriller during the 1982 World Cup, when two ETA gunmen hole up in a Barcelona hotel.

John Bryson *To the Death, Amic*. Barcelona, under siege during the Civil War, is the backdrop for a coming-of-age novel recounting the adventures of ten-year-old twins Enric and Josep.

Miguel Cervantes *Don Quixote*. Barcelona is the only city that Cervantes gives its real name in his picaresque classic – in the Barcelona chapters, Don Quixote and Sancho Panza see the ocean for the first time, while Quixote fights a duel on Barceloneta beach against the Knight of the White Moon.

Juan Marse *Lizard Tails*, *Shanghai Nights*. Marse (born 1933) spent his formative years in a Barcelona scarred by Civil War, and ruptured childhood and family hardship are themes that emerge in much of his work. Only a couple of works have thus far been translated into English: *Lizard Tails* is an evocation of post-Civil War childhood, while *Shanghai Nights* – again, Barcelona and war to the fore – is billed as "a tale of the human spirit".

Eduardo Mendoza *City of Marvels*, *The Truth About the Savolta Case*, *The Year of the Flood*. Mendoza's first and best novel, *City of Marvels* is set in the expanding Barcelona of 1880–1920, full of rich underworld characters and riddled with anarchic and comic turns. The milieu is reused with flair in *The Truth About the Savolta Case*, while *The Year of the Flood* adds a light touch to an unusual amorous entanglement in 1950s Barcelona.

Manuel Vasquez Montalban *Murder in the Central Committee, Southern Seas, The Angst-Ridden Executive, An Olympic Death, Offside*. Montalban's greatest creation, the fast-living gourmand-detective Pepe Carvalho, ex-communist and CIA agent, first appeared in print in 1972, investigating foul deeds in the city in a series of wry and racy Chandleresque thrillers. Only a handful have been translated into English, with *Murder in the Central Committee* a good place to start, as Carvalho confronts his communist past. *Southern Seas* won the Planeta, Spain's biggest literary prize, while the city's institutions and events come under typical scrutiny in *An Olympic Death* and *Offside*. Also look for Montalban's *Barcelonas* – part guidebook, part discursive analysis of everything from sex to soccer in Barcelona.

Raul Nuñez *The Lonely Hearts Club*. A parade of grotesque and hard-bitten characters haunt the city in this oddball but likeable romantic comedy.

Colm Tóibín *The South*. Barcelona provides the background for Tóibín's first novel about an Irish woman looking for a new life.

Barbara Ellen Wilson *Gaudí Afternoon*. Pacy feminist thriller making good use of Gaudí's architecture as a backdrop for deception and skulduggery.

Carlos Ruiz Záfon *The Shadow of the Wind*. The international bestseller by the Barcelona-born, one-time LA screenwriter Záfon. It's a literary, Eco-like thriller set in the aftermath of the Civil War, and has generated rave reviews.

Language

Language

Language

In Barcelona, **Catalan** (Català) has more or less taken over from Castilian (Castellano) **Spanish** as the language on street signs, maps, official buildings and notices etc. On paper it looks like a cross between French and Spanish and is generally easy to read if you know those two. Spoken Catalan is harder to come to grips with, as the language itself is not phonetic, and accents vary from region to region. Few visitors realize how important Catalan is to those who speak it: never commit the error of calling it a dialect. However, despite the preponderance of the Catalan language, you'll get by perfectly well in Spanish, as long as you're aware of the use of Catalan in timetables, on menus, and so on. You'll find some basic pronunciation rules below, for both Spanish and Catalan, and a selection of words and phrases in both languages. Spanish is certainly easier to pronounce, but don't be afraid to try Catalan, especially in the more out-of-the-way places – you'll generally get a good reception if you at least try communicating in the local language.

Numerous **Spanish phrasebooks** are available, not least the *Spanish Rough Guide Phrasebook*, laid out dictionary-style for instant access. Note that many of the phrasebooks available in North America are geared to New World, Latin American usage rather than "European" Spanish. In Barcelona, *Parla Català* (Pia) is the only readily available English–Catalan phrasebook, though there are more extensive (and expensive) Catalan–English dictionaries and teach-yourself Catalan guides available (consult ⊛www.amazon.co.uk, www.amazon.com). The University of Barcelona has an excellent **online English–Catalan phrasebook**, with an audio option, ⊛www.intercat.gencat.es/guia.

Pronunciation

Castilian (Spanish)

Unless there's an accent, words ending in d, l, r or z are **stressed** on the last syllable, all others on the second last. All **vowels** are pure and short; combinations have predictable results.

A somewhere between the "A" sound of back and that of father.

E as in get.

I as in police.

O as in hot.

U as in rule.

C is lisped before E and I, hard otherwise: cerca is pronounced "thairka".

G works the same way, a guttural "H" sound (like the ch in loch) before E or I, a hard G elsewhere – gigante becomes "higante".

H is always silent.

J the same sound as a guttural G: jamón is pronounced "hamon".

LL sounds like an English Y: tortilla is pronounced "torteeya".

N is as in English unless it has a tilde (accent) over it, when it becomes NY: mañana sounds like "man-yarna".

QU is pronounced like an English K.

R is rolled, RR doubly so.

V sounds more like B, vino becoming "beano".

X has an S sound before consonants, normal X before vowels.

Z is the same as a soft C, so cerveza becomes "thairbaitha".

Catalan

With Catalan, don't be tempted to use the few rules of Spanish pronunciation you may know – in particular the soft Spanish Z and C don't apply, so unlike in the rest of Spain the city is not "Barthelona" but "Barcelona", as in English.

A as in hat if stressed, as in alone when unstressed.

E varies, but usually as in get.

I as in police.

IG sounds like the "tch" in the English scratch; lleig (ugly) is pronounced "yeah-tch".

O a round full sound, when stressed, otherwise like a soft U sound.

U somewhere between the U of put and rule.

Ç sounds like an English S; plaça is pronounced "plassa".

C followed by an E or I is soft; otherwise hard.

G followed by E or I is like the "zh" in Zhivago; otherwise hard.

H is always silent.

J as in the French "Jean".

L.L is best pronounced (for foreigners) as a single L sound; but for Catalan speakers it has two distinct L sounds.

LL sounds like an English Y or LY, like the "yuh" sound in million.

N as in English, though before F or V it sometimes sounds like an M.

NY corresponds to the Castilian Ñ.

QU before E or I sounds like K, unless the U has an umlaut (Ü), in which case, and before A or O, as in "quit".

R is rolled, but only at the start of a word; at the end it's often silent.

T is pronounced as in English, though sometimes it sounds like a D; as in viatge or dotze.

V at the start of a word sounds like B; in all other positions it's a soft "F" sound.

W is pronounced like a B/V.

X is like SH or CH in most words, though in some, like exit, it sounds like an X.

Z is like the English Z in zoo.

Useful words and phrases

Words and phrases below are given in the following order: **English** – Spanish – *Catalan*.

Basics

Yes, No, OK	Sí, No, Vale	*Sí, No, Val*
Please, Thank you	Por favor, Gracias	*Si us plau, Gràcies*
Where? When?	Dónde? Cuando?	*On? Quan?*

What? How much?	Qué? Cuánto?	*Què? Quant?*
Here, There	Aquí, Allí/Allá	*Aquí, Allí/Allá*
This, That	Esto, Eso	*Això, Allò*
Now, Later	Ahora, Más tarde	*Ara, Mès tard*
Open, Closed	Abierto/a, Cerrado/a	*Obert, Tancat*
With, Without	Con, Sin	*Amb, Sense*
Good, Bad	Bueno/a, Malo/a	*Bo(na), Dolent(a)*
Big, Small	Gran(de), Pequeño/a	*Gran, Petit(a)*
Cheap, Expensive	Barato, Caro	*Barat(a), Car(a)*
Hot, Cold	Caliente, Frío	*Calent(a), Fred(a)*
More, Less	Más, Menos	*Mes, Menys*
I want	Quiero	*Vull (pronounced "vwee")*
I'd like	Quisiera	*Voldria*
Do you know?	¿Sabe?	*Vostès saben?*
I don't know	No sé	*No sé*
There is (is there?)	(¿)Hay(?)	*Hi ha(?)*
What's that?	¿Qué es eso?	*Què és això?*
Give me (one like that)	Deme (uno así)	*Doneu-me (a bit brusque)*
Do you have?	¿Tiene?	*Té…?*
The time	La hora	*L'hora*
Today, Tomorrow	Hoy, Mañana	*Avui, Demà*
Yesterday	Ayer	*Ahir*
Day before yesterday	Ante ayer	*Abans-d'ahir*
Next week	La semana que viene	*La setmana que ve*
Next month	El mes que viene	*El mes que ve*

Greetings and responses

Hello, Goodbye	Hola, Adiós	*Hola, Adéu*
Good morning	Buenos días	*Bon dia*
Good afternoon/night	Buenas tardes/noches	*Bona tarde/nit*
See you later	Hasta luego	*Fins després*
Sorry	Lo siento/Disculpéme	*Ho sento*
Excuse me	Con permiso/Perdón	*Perdoni*
How are you?	¿Cómo está (usted)?	*Com va?*
I (don't) understand	(No) Entiendo	*(No) Ho entenc*
Not at all/You're welcome	De nada	*De res*
Do you speak English?	¿Habla (usted) inglés?	*Parleu anglès?*
I (don't) speak Spanish/Catalan	(No) Hablo español	*(No) Parlo Català*
My name is…	Me llamo…	*Em dic…*
What's your name?	¿Como se llama usted?	*Com es diu?*
I am English/	Soy inglés(a)/	*Sóc anglès(a)/*
Scottish/	escocés(a)/	*escocès(a)/*
Australian/	australiano(a)/	*australian(a)/*
Canadian/	canadiense(a)/	*canadenc(a)/*
American/	americano(a)/	*americà (a)/*
Irish	irlandes(a)	*irlandès (a)*

Finding accommodation

Do you have a room?	¿Tiene una habitación?	Té alguna habitació?
…with two beds/double bed	…con dos camas/cama matrimonial	…amb dos llits/llit per dues persones
…with shower/bath	…con ducha/baño	…amb dutxa/bany
It's for one person (two people)	Es para una persona (dos personas)	Per a una persona (dues persones)
For one night (one week)	Para una noche (una semana)	Per una nit (una setmana)
It's fine, how much is it?	¿Está bien, cuánto es?	Esta bé, quant és?
It's too expensive	Es demasiado caro	És massa car
Don't you have anything cheaper?	No tiene algo más barato?	En té de mé sbon preu?
Can one…?	¿Se puede…?	Es pot…?
…camp (near) here	…acampar aqui (cerca)	…acampar a la vora
Is there a hostel nearby?	¿Hay un hostal aquí cerca?	Hi ha un hostal a la vora?

Directions and transport

How do I get to…?	¿Por donde se va a…?	Per anar a…?
Left, Right, Straight on	Izquierda, Derecha, Todo recto	A la dreta, A l'esquerra, Tot recte
Where is…?	¿Dónde está…?	On és…?
…the bus station	…la estación de autobuses	…l'estació de autobuses
…the train station	…la estación de ferrocarril	…l'estació
…the nearest bank	…el banco más cercano	…el banc més a prop
…the post office	…el correos/la oficina de correos	…l'oficina de correus
…the toilet	…el baño/aseo/servicio	…la toaleta
It's not very far	No es muy lejos	No és gaire lluny
Where does the bus to …leave from?	¿De dónde sale el autobús para…?	De on surt el autobús a…?
Is this the train for Barcelona?	¿Es este el tren para Barcelona?	Aquest tren va a Barcelona?
I'd like a (return) ticket to…	Quisiera un billete (de iday vuelta) para…	Voldria un bitlet (d'anar i tornar) a…
What time does it leave (arrive in)?	¿A qué hora sale (llega a)?	A quina hora surt (arriba a)?

Numbers

one	un/uno/una	un(a)
two	dos	dos (dues)
three	tres	tres
four	cuatro	quatre
five	cinco	cinc

six	seis	*sis*
seven	siete	*set*
eight	ocho	*vuit*
nine	nueve	*nou*
ten	diez	*deu*
eleven	once	*onze*
twelve	doce	*dotze*
thirteen	trece	*tretze*
fourteen	catorce	*catorze*
fifteen	quince	*quinze*
sixteen	dieciseis	*setze*
seventeen	diecisiete	*disset*
eighteen	dieciocho	*divuit*
nineteen	diecinueve	*dinou*
twenty	veinte	*vint*
twenty-one	veintiuno	*vint-i-un*
thirty	treinta	*trenta*
forty	cuarenta	*quaranta*
fifty	cincuenta	*cinquanta*
sixty	sesenta	*seixanta*
seventy	setenta	*setanta*
eighty	ochenta	*vuitanta*
ninety	noventa	*novanta*
one hundred	cien(to)	*cent*
one hundred and one	ciento uno	*cent un*
one hundred and two	ciento dos	*cent dos (dues)*
two hundred	doscientos	*dos-cents (dues-centes)*
five hundred	quinientos	*cinc-cents*
one thousand	mil	*mil*
two thousand	dos mil	*dos mil*

Days and months

Monday	lunes	*dilluns*
Tuesday	martes	*dimarts*
Wednesday	miércoles	*dimecres*
Thursday	jueves	*dijous*
Friday	viernes	*divendres*
Saturday	sábado	*dissabte*
Sunday	domingo	*diumenge*
January	enero	*gener*
February	febrero	*febrer*
March	marzo	*març*
April	abril	*abril*
May	mayo	*maig*
June	junio	*juny*
July	julio	*juliol*

August	agosto	*agost*
September	septiembre	*setembre*
October	octubre	*octobre*
November	noviembre	*novembre*
December	diciembre	*desembre*

Food and drink

Words and phrases below are given in the following order: **English** – Spanish – *Catalan*.

Some basic words

To have breakfast	Desayunar	*Esmorzar*
To have lunch	Comer	*Dinar*
To have dinner	Cenar	*Sopar*
Knife	Cuchillo	*Ganivet*
Fork	Tenedor	*Forquilla*
Spoon	Cuchara	*Cullera*
Table	Mesa	*Taula*
Bottle	Botella	*Ampolla*
Glass	Vaso	*Got*
Menu	Carta	*Carta*
Soup	Sopa	*Sopa*
Salad	Ensalada	*Amanida*
Hors d'oeuvres	Entremeses	*Entremesos*
Omelette	Tortilla	*Truita*
Sandwich	Bocadillo	*Entrepà*
Toast	Tostadas	*Torrades*
Tapas	Tapes	*Tapes*
Butter	Mantequilla	*Mantega*
Eggs	Huevos	*Ous*
Bread	Pan	*Pa*
Olives	Aceitunas	*Olives*
Oil	Aceite	*Oli*
Vinegar	Vinagre	*Vinagre*
Salt	Sal	*Sal*
Pepper	Pimienta	*Pebre*
Sugar	Azucar	*Sucre*
The bill	La cuenta	*El compte*
I'm a vegetarian	Soy vegetariano/a	*Sóc vegetarià/vegetariana*

Cooking terms

Assorted	surtido/variado	*assortit*
Baked	al horno	*al forn*
Char-grilled	a la brasa	*a la brasa*

Fresh	fresco	*fresc*
Fried	frito	*fregit*
Fried in batter	a la romana	*a la romana*
Garlic mayonnaise	alioli	*all i oli*
Grilled	a la plancha	*a la plantxa*
Pickled	en escabeche	*en escabetx*
Roast	asado	*rostit*
Sauce	salsa	*salsa*
Sautéed	salteado	*saltat*
Scrambled	revuelto	*remenat*
Seasonal	del tiempo	*del temps*
Smoked	ahumado	*fumat*
Spit-roasted	al ast	*a l'ast*
Stewed	guisado	*guisat*
Steamed	al vapor	*al vapor*
Stuffed	relleno	*farcit*

Fish and seafood/Pescado y mariscos/peix i marisc

Anchovies	Anchoas/Boquerones	*Anxoves/Seitons*
Baby squid	Chipirones	*Calamarsets*
Bream	Dorada	*Orada*
Clams	Almejas	*Cloïses*
Crab	Cangrejo	*Cranc*
Cuttlefish	Sepia	*Sipia*
Eels	Anguilas	*Anguiles*
Hake	Merluza	*Lluç*
Langoustines	Langostinos	*Llagostins*
Lobster	Langosta	*Llagosta*
Monkfish	Rape	*Rap*
Mussels	Mejillones	*Musclos*
Octopus	Pulpo	*Pop*
Oysters	Ostras	*Ostres*
Perch	Mero	*Mero*
Prawns	Gambas	*Gambes*
Razor clams	Navajas	*Navalles*
Red mullet	Salmonete	*Moll*
Salmon	Salmón	*Salmó*
Salt cod	Bacalao	*Bacallà*
Sardines	Sardinas	*Sardines*
Scallops	Vieiras	*Vieires*
Sea bass	Lubina	*Llobarro*
Sole	Lenguado	*Llenguado*
Squid	Calamares	*Calamars*
Swordfish	Pez espada	*Peix espasa*
Trout	Trucha	*Truita (de riu)*

| Tuna | Atún | *Tonyina* |
| Whitebait | Chanquete | *Xanguet* |

Meat and poultry/Carne y aves/Carn i aviram

Beef	Buey	*Bou*
Boar	Jabalí	*Senglar*
Charcuterie	Embutidos	*Embotits*
Chicken	Pollo	*Pollastre*
Chorizo sausage	Chorizo	*Xoriço*
Cured ham	Jamón serrano	*Pernil serrà*
Cured pork sausage	Longaniza	*Llonganissa*
Cutlets/Chops	Chuletas	*Costelles*
Duck	Pato	*Ànec*
Ham	Jamón York	*Pernil dolç*
Hare	Liebre	*Llebre*
Kid/goat	Cabrito	*Cabrit*
Kidneys	Riñones	*Ronyons*
Lamb	Cordero	*Xai/Be*
Liver	Hígado	*Fetge*
Loin of pork	Lomo	*Llom*
Meatballs	Albóndigas	*Mandonguilles*
Partridge	Perdiz	*Perdiu*
Pigs' trotters	Pies de cerdo	*Peus de porc*
Pork	Cerdo	*Porc*
Rabbit	Conejo	*Conill*
Sausages	Salchichas	*Salsitxes*
Snails	Caracoles	*Cargols*
Steak	Bistec	*Bistec*
Tongue	Lengua	*Llengua*
Veal	Ternera	*Vedella*

Vegetables/Verduras y legumbres/Verdures i llegums

Artichokes	Alcachofas	*Carxofes*
Asparagus	Esparragos	*Esparrecs*
Aubergine	Berenjena	*Albergínia*
Avocado	Aguacate	*Alvocat*
Broad/lima beans	Habes	*Faves*
Cabbage	Col	*Col*
Carrots	Zanahorias	*Pastanagues*
Cauliflower	Coliflor	*Col-i-flor*
Chickpeas	Garbanzos	*Cigrons*
Courgette	Calabacín	*Carbassó*
Cucumber	Pepino	*Concombre*
Garlic	Ajo	*All*
Haricot beans	Judías blancas	*Mongetes*

Herbs	Hierbas	*Herbes*
Lentils	Lentejas	*Llenties*
Leeks	Puerros	*Porros*
Mushrooms	Champiñones	*Xampinyons*
Onion	Cebolla	*Ceba*
Peas	Guisantes	*Pèsols*
Peppers	Pimientos	*Pebrots*
Potatoes	Patatas	*Patates*
Spinach	Espinacas	*Espinacs*
Tomatoes	Tomates	*Tomàquets*
Turnips	Nabos	*Naps*
Wild mushrooms	Setas	*Bolets*

Fruit/Fruta/Fruita

Apple	Manzana	*Poma*
Apricot	Albaricoque	*Albercoc*
Banana	Plátano	*Plàtan*
Cherries	Cerezas	*Cireres*
Figs	Higos	*Figues*
Grapes	Uvas	*Raïm*
Melon	Melón	*Meló*
Orange	Naranja	*Taronja*
Peach	Melocotón	*Pressec*
Pear	Pera	*Pera*
Pineapple	Piña	*Pinya*
Strawberries	Fresas	*Maduixes*

Desserts/Postres/Postres

Cake	Pastel	*Pastís*
Cheese	Queso	*Formatge*
Fruit salad	Macedonia	*Macedonia*
Crème caramel	Flan	*Flam*
Ice cream	Helado	*Gelat*
Rice pudding	Arroz con leche	*Arròs amb llet*
Tart	Tarta	*Tarta*
Yoghurt	Yogur	*Yogur*

Catalan specialities

Amanida Catalana Salad served with sliced meats (sometimes cheese)

Ànec amb peres Duck with pears

Arròs a banda Rice with seafood, the rice served separately

Arròs a la Cubana Rice with fried egg and home-made tomato sauce

Arròs a la marinera Paella: rice with seafood and saffron

Arròs negre "Black rice", cooked in squid ink

Bacallà a la llauna Salt cod baked with garlic, tomato and paprika

Bacallà amb mongetes Salt cod with stewed haricot beans

Botifarra (amb mongetes) Grilled Catalan pork sausage (with stewed haricot beans)

Bunyols Fritters, which can be sweet (like little doughnuts, with sugar) or savoury (salt-cod or wild mushroom)

Calçots Large char-grilled spring onions, eaten with *romesco* sauce, available February–March

Canelons Cannelloni, baked pasta with ground meat and bechemal sauce

Conill all i oli Rabbit with garlic mayonnaise

Conill amb cargols Rabbit with snails

Crema Catalana Crème caramel, with caramelized sugar topping

Entremesos Hors d'oeuvres of mixed meat and cheese

Escalivada Grilled aubergine, pepper and onion

Escudella i carn d'olla A winter dish of stewed mixed meat and vegetables, served broth first, meat and veg second

Espinacs a la Catalana Spinach cooked with raisins and pine nuts

Esqueixada Salad of salt cod with peppers, tomatoes, onions and olives, a summer dish

Estofat de vedella Veal stew

Faves a la Catalana Stewed broad beans, with bacon and *botifarra, a regional classic*

Fideuà Short, thin noodles (the width of vermicelli) served with seafood, accompanied by *all i olli*

Fideus a la cassola Short, thin noodles baked with meat

Fricandó (amb bolets) Braised veal (with wild mushrooms)

Fuet Catalan salami

Llagosta amb pollastre Lobster with chicken in a rich sauce

Llenties guisades Stewed lentils

Mel i mató Curd cheese and honey, a typical dessert

Oca amb naps Goose with turnips

Pa amb tomàquet Bread (often grilled), rubbed with tomato, garlic and olive oil

Panellets Marzipan cakes, served for All Saints' Day

Perdiu a la vinagreta Partridge in vinegar gravy

Perdiu amb col Partridge with cabbage dumplings

Pollastre al cava Chicken with *cava* (champagne) sauce

Pollastre amb gambes Chicken with prawns

Postres de músic Cake of dried fruit and nuts

Rap amb all cremat Monkfish with creamed garlic sauce

Salsa romesco Spicy sauce (with chillis, ground almonds, hazelnuts, garlic, tomato and wine), often served with grilled fish

Samfaina Ratatouille-like stew (onions, peppers, aubergine, tomato), served with salt cod or chicken

Sarsuela Fish and shellfish stew

Sípia amb mandonguilles Cuttlefish with meatballs

Sopa d'all Garlic soup, often with egg and bread

Suquet de peix Fish and potato casserole

Xató Mixed salad of olives, salt cod, preserved tuna, anchovies and onions

Drinks

Beer	Cerveza	*Cervesa*
Wine	Vino	*Vi*
Champagne	Champan	*Xampan/Cava*
Sherry	Jerez	*Xerès*
Coffee	Café	*Cafè*
Espresso	Café solo	*Cafè sol*
Large black coffee	Café Americano	*Cafè Americà*
Large white coffee	Café con leche	*Cafè amb llet*
Small white coffee	Café cortado	*Cafè tallat*
Decaff	Descafeinado	*Descafeinat*
Tea	Té	*Te*

Drinking chocolate	Chocolate	*Xocolata*
Juice	Zumo	*Suc*
Crushed ice drink	Granizado	*Granissat*
Milk	Leche	*Llet*
Tiger nut drink	Horchata	*Orxata*
Water	Agua	*Aigua*
Mineral water	Agua mineral	*Aigua mineral*
...(sparkling)	...(con gas)	*...(amb gas)*
...(still)	...(sin gas)	*...(sense gas)*

A glossary of Catalan words

Ajuntament Town hall (city council)
Avinguda Avenue
Barcino Roman name for Barcelona
Barri Suburb or quarter
Bodega Cellar, wine bar or warehouse
Caixa Savings bank
Call Jewish quarter
Camí Path
Capella Chapel
Carrer Street
Casa House
Cava Catalan "champagne"
Castell Castle
Comarca County
Correus Post office
Església Church
Estació Station
Estany Lake
Festa Festival
Font Waterfall
Forn Bakery
Generalitat Catalan government
Gòtic Gothic (eg Barri Gòtic, Gothic quarter)
Granja Milk bar/café

Guiri Foreigner
Llotja Stock exchange building
Mercat Market
Modernisme Catalan Art Nouveau
Monestir Monastery or convent
Museu Museum
Palau Aristocratic mansion/palace
Passatge Passage
Passeig Promenade/boulevard; also the evening stroll thereon
Pati Inner courtyard
Pastisseria Cake/pastry shop
Plaça Square
Platja Beach
Pont Bridge
Porta Gateway
Rambla Boulevard
Renaixença Renaissance
Ríu River
Sant/a Saint
Sardana Catalunya's national folk dance
Serra Mountain range
Seu Cathedral
Terrassa Outdoor terrace

Small print and

Index

A Rough Guide to Rough Guides

Published in 1982, the first Rough Guide – to Greece – was a student scheme that became a publishing phenomenon. Mark Ellingham, a recent graduate in English from Bristol University, had been travelling in Greece the previous summer and couldn't find the right guidebook. With a small group of friends he wrote his own guide, combining a highly contemporary, journalistic style with a thoroughly practical approach to travellers' needs.

The immediate success of the book spawned a series that rapidly covered dozens of destinations. And, in addition to impecunious backpackers, Rough Guides soon acquired a much broader and older readership that relished the guides' wit and inquisitiveness as much as their enthusiastic, critical approach and value-for-money ethos.

These days, Rough Guides include recommendations from shoestring to luxury and cover more than 200 destinations around the globe, including almost every country in the Americas and Europe, more than half of Africa and most of Asia and Australasia. Our ever-growing team of authors and photographers is spread all over the world, particularly in Europe, the USA and Australia.

In the early 1990s, Rough Guides branched out of travel, with the publication of Rough Guides to World Music, Classical Music and the Internet. All three have become benchmark titles in their fields, spearheading the publication of a wide range of books under the Rough Guide name.

Including the travel series, Rough Guides now number more than 350 titles, covering: phrasebooks, waterproof maps, music guides from Opera to Heavy Metal, reference works as diverse as Conspiracy Theories and Shakespeare, and popular culture books from iPods to Poker. Rough Guides also produce a series of more than 120 World Music CDs in partnership with World Music Network.

Visit www.roughguides.com to see our latest publications.

Rough Guide travel images are available for commercial licensing at www.roughguidespictures.com

Rough Guide credits

Text editor: Lucy White
Layout: Dan May
Cartography: Katie Lloyd-Jones
Picture editor: Harriet Mills
Production: Aimee Hampson
Proofreader: David Price
Cover design: Chloë Roberts
Photographer: Tim Kavanagh

....

Editorial: **London** Kate Berens, Claire Saunders, Geoff Howard, Ruth Blackmore, Polly Thomas, Richard Lim, Alison Murchie, Karoline Densley, Andy Turner, Keith Drew, Edward Aves, Nikki Birrell, Helen Marsden, Alice Park, Sarah Eno, Joe Staines, Duncan Clark, Peter Buckley, Matthew Milton, Tracy Hopkins, David Paul, Ruth Tidball; **New York** Andrew Rosenberg, Steven Horak, AnneLise Sorensen, Amy Hegarty, April Isaacs, Sean Mahoney, Ella Steim
Design & Pictures: **London** Simon Bracken, Dan May, Diana Jarvis, Mark Thomas, Jj Luck, Harriet Mills, Chloë Roberts; **Delhi** Madhulita Mohapatra, Umesh Aggarwal, Ajay Verma, Jessica Subramanian, Amit Verma, Ankur Guha, Pradeep Thapliyal, Sachin Tanwar

Production: Sophie Hewat, Katherine Owers, Aimee Hampson
Cartography: **London** Maxine Repath, Ed Wright, Katie Lloyd-Jones; **Delhi** Jai Prakash Mishra, Rajesh Chhibber, Ashutosh Bharti, Rajesh Mishra, Animesh Pathak, Jasbir Sandhu, Karobi Gogoi, Amod Singh, Alakananda Bhattacharya
Online: **New York** Jennifer Gold, Suzanne Welles, Kristin Mingrone; **Delhi** Manik Chauhan, Narender Kumar, Shekhar Jha, Rakesh Kumar, Chhandita Chakravarty
Marketing & Publicity: **London** Richard Trillo, Niki Hanmer, David Wearn, Louise Maher, Jess Carter; **New York** Geoff Colquitt, Megan Kennedy, Katy Ball; **Delhi** Reem Khokhar
Custom publishing and foreign rights: Philippa Hopkins
Manager India: Punita Singh
Series editor: Mark Ellingham
Reference Director: Andrew Lockett
PA to Publishing Director: Megan McIntyre
Publishing Director: Martin Dunford

Publishing information

This 7th edition published November 2006 by
Rough Guides Ltd,
80 Strand, London WC2R 0RL
345 Hudson St, 4th Floor,
New York, NY 10014, USA
14 Local Shopping Centre, Panchsheel Park,
New Delhi 110017, India
Distributed by the Penguin Group
Penguin Books Ltd,
80 Strand, London WC2R 0RL
Penguin Putnam, Inc.
375 Hudson Street, NY 10014, USA
Penguin Group (Australia)
250 Camberwell Road, Camberwell,
Victoria 3124, Australia
Penguin Books Canada Ltd,
10 Alcorn Avenue, Toronto, Ontario,
Canada M4V 1E4
Penguin Group (NZ)
67 Apollo Drive, Mairangi Bay, Auckland 1310,
New Zealand
Cover concept by Peter Dyer.

Typeset in Bembo and Helvetica to an original design by Henry Iles.

Printed and bound in China

© Jules Brown

324pp includes index

A catalogue record for this book is available from the British Library

ISBN 1-84353-681-1

ISBN 13: 9781843536819

The publishers and authors have done their best to ensure the accuracy and currency of all the information in **The Rough Guide to Barcelona**, however, they can accept no responsibility for any loss, injury, or inconvenience sustained by any traveller as a result of information or advice contained in the guide.

1   3   5   7   9   8   6   4   2

Help us update

We've gone to a lot of effort to ensure that the 7th edition of **The Rough Guide to Barcelona** is accurate and up to date. However, things change – places get "discovered", opening hours are notoriously fickle, restaurants and rooms raise prices or lower standards. If you feel we've got it wrong or left something out, we'd like to know, and if you can remember the address, the price, the time, the phone number, so much the better. We'll credit all contributions, and send a copy of the next edition (or any other Rough Guide if you prefer) for the best letters. Everyone who writes

to us and isn't already a subscriber will receive a copy of our full-colour thrice-yearly newsletter. Please mark letters: "**Rough Guide Barcelona Update**" and send to: Rough Guides, 80 Strand, London WC2R 0RL, or Rough Guides, 4th Floor, 345 Hudson St, New York, NY 10014. Or send an email to **mail@roughguides.com**
Have your questions answered and tell others about your trip at
www.roughguides.atinfopop.com

SMALL PRINT

Acknowledgements

Jules would like to thank María Luisa Albacar at Turisme de Barcelona and Lluís Bosch of the Ajuntament de Barcelona, as well as Katrien Claus, Craig Grimes, Isabel Gonzalez, Soledad Godoy Ribero, Bibiana Serra and Daniel Guillén Hidalgo, all of whom provided valuable help and assistance. At Rough Guides, thanks to Geoff Howard and Lucy White for seeing the project through. And, at home, the usual profuse thanks to Katie, and to Foxton and Ripley for re-arranging my notes and brochures whenever they got a chance.

Readers' letters

Thanks to all the readers who have taken the time to write in with comments and suggestions (and apologies if we've inadvertently omitted or misspelt anyone's name):

Phil, Hilary and Pippa André, Maria Bali, Richard and Anne Baldwin, Paul Battigan, Kristina Blagojevitch, Ian Bolton, Andrew J.F. Bruce, M.R. Bryant, Daniel Burdsey, Paul Connell, Brian Cotterill, Traci Curl & Gareth Walker, Judy Daniels, Nik Devlin, Lynne Dickens, Nick Dines, Trudy Douglas, Kate Driver, Jill and James Durie, Jonathan Fisk, Shirsten Fry, Paul Gallagher, Thomas Graham, Roger Hunter, Roger Kennington, Lizzie and Dick Mayes, Hilda McCavanagh, Amanda McGee, Emma Metcalfe, Marilyn Mowbray, Ann Pattison, Maxine Prince, Mark Hodges & Melisande Prince-Hodges, Geraldine Pugh, Mary-Elizabeth Raw, Hugh Rayment-Pickard, Derek Ricketts, Ruth Rudd, Molly Sendall, Monica Shelley, Julia Speht, Helen Storey de Espinoza, Emma-Louise Tinniswood, Claire Veares, Louis Victor, Geoff and Tracy Walker, Pip Wright, Andrew Young.

Photo credits

All photos © Rough Guides except the following:

Cover
Front picture: La Sagrada Familia © Getty
Back picture: Street entertainers, La Ramblas
   © Alamy

Things not to miss
02 *Waiting* (Margot) 1901 (oil on canvas), Pablo
   Picasso (1881-1973) Museu Picasso, Barcelona
   © The Bridgeman Art Library/Giraudon/DACS
03 Gran Teatre del Liceu © DK Images
04 Sagrada Família © DK Images
08 Monestir de Pedralbes © Rough Guides,
   photo by Ian Aitken
09 FC Barcelona vs Real Zaragoza at Camp Nou
   stadium © Khaled Kassem/Alamy
13 Monserrat, Monastery of the Black Virgin ©
   Linny Cunningham/Stone/Getty
14 Parc del Collserola © Rough Guides, photo
   by Ian Aitken
15 Barri Gòtic © Rough Guides, photo by Ian
   Aitken
16 Barceloneta restaurants © DK Images
18 The Cascada in Parc de la Ciutadella ©
   Richard Klune/Corbis
19 Sitges © Rough Guides, photo by Ian Aitken
21 Els Encants flea market © Rough Guides,
   photo by Ian Aitken
23 Fish stall at Boqueria market © Joe Beynon/
   Axiom
24 Paseo de Colon beach, Barcelona © Impact
   Photos

Colour insert: Festive Barcelona
Font Magica Mercé © Gabriel de Freitas /Alamy
Festes de La Mercé © Andrew Watson/Alamy
Wizard at La Mercé © Dominic Harrison /Alamy
St Jordis day © Pat Behnke/Alamy
Castellers in Barcelona © Andrew Watson/Alamy
Teatre Grec © Rough Guides photo by Ian Aitken

Colour insert: Gaudí and modernisme
Coloured chimney at Palau Guell © B J Gadie/
   Elvele Images/Alamy
Batlló © Rough Guides, photo by Ian Aitken

Black and whites
p.80 Sunbathing at Port Vell © Rough Guides,
   photo by Ian Aitken
p.96 Estadi Olimpic © Rough Guides, photo by
   Ian Aitken
p.136 Sitges © DK Images
p.201 Bosc de les Fades bar © Rough Guides,
   photo by Ian Aitken
p.213 Harlem Jazz Club © Rough Guides, photo
   by Ian Aitken
p.218 Dietrich Club © Rough Guides, photo by
   Ian Aitken
p.228 Windsurfing, Barcelona © Rough Guides,
   photo by Ian Aitken

Index

Map entries are in colour.

INDEX

I

W

Y

Z

INDEX

Map symbols

maps are listed in the full index using coloured text

▬▬▪	International boundary	⊙	Statue
▬ ▬ ▬	Chapter boundary	⬙	Viewpoint
▬▬▬	Motorway	★	Bus stop
═══	Major road	⊜	RENFE
══	Minor road	⬤M	Metro station
▬▬▬	Pedestrianised road	⌇	FF.CC. station
▦▦▦	Steps	ⓘ	Tourist office
▬▪▬	Railway	⊠	Post office
··········	Funicular railway	⊞	Hospital
●----●	Cable car	▬	Building
▬▬	Wall	⊞	Church
──	Waterway	◯	Stadium
✈	Airport		Park
⛪	Abbey		Forest
♙	Monastery		Beach
⛨	Church (regional)	⊞	Cemetery

MAP SYMBOLS

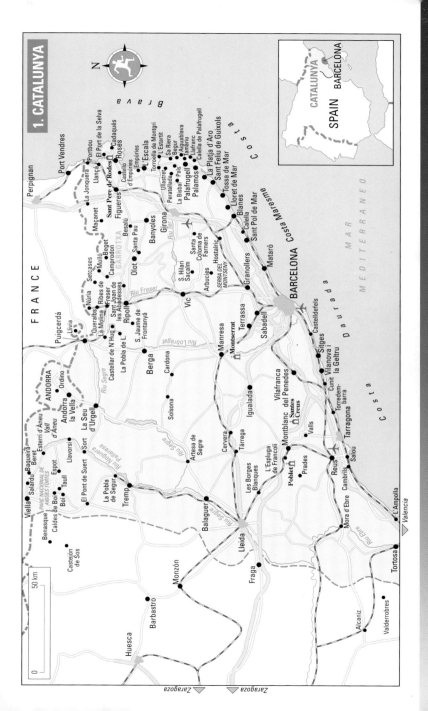

1. CATALUNYA

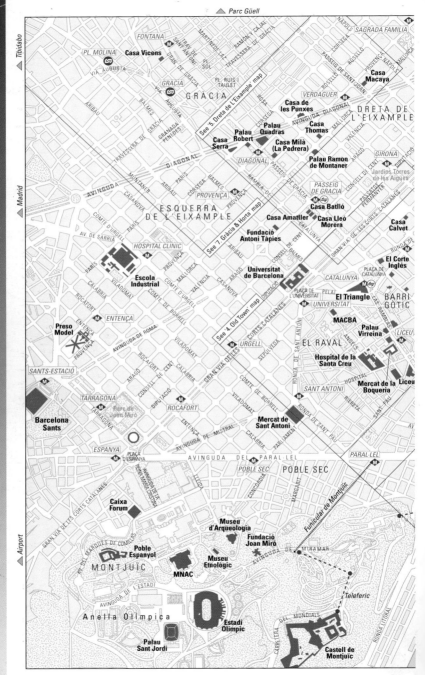

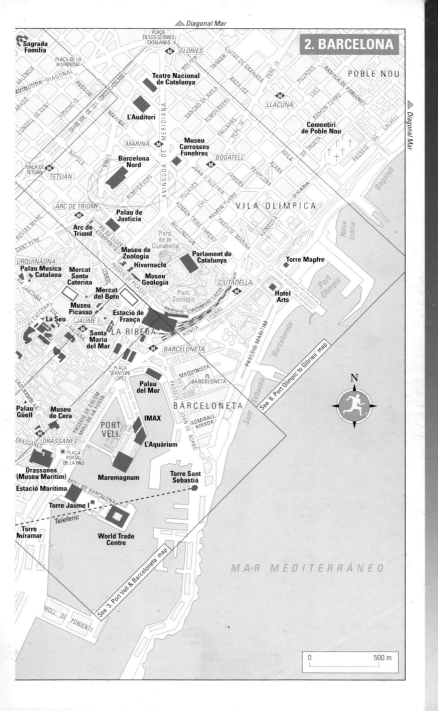

Sagrada Familia

PLAÇA DE LES GLORIES CATALANES

GLORIES

POBLE NOU

PLAÇA DE LA HISPANITAT

VALÈNCIA

AVINGUDA DIAGONAL

PASSEIG DE SANT JOAN

ARAGÓ

CONSELL DE CENT

DIPUTACIÓ

GRAN VIA DE LES CORTS CATALANES

MARINA

SARDENYA

SICÍLIA

Teatre Nacional de Catalunya

SANCHO DE AVILA

ALMOGAVERS

PALLARS

PERE IV

TANGER

CIUTAT DE GRANADA

BADAJOZ

PUJADES

RAMBLA DE POBLENOU

LLULL

LLACUNA

RAMON TURRO

Cementiri de Poble Nou

L'Auditori

NÁPOLS

PLAÇA DE TETUAN

TETUAN

MARINA

AVINGUDA DE MERIDIANA

Barcelona Nord

AVINGUDA DE MERIDIANA

Museu Carrosses Funebres

BOGATELL

ZAMORA

ÁVILA

PAMPLONA

DR TRUETA

D'ICARIA

PASSEIG DE CALVELL

Bogatell

ARC DE TRIOMF

Arc de Triomf

Palau de Justicia

PG DE LLUIS COMPANYS

PUJADES

LLULL

ROMAN TRIAS TARGAS

JOAN D'AUSTRIA

RAMON TURRÓ

VILA OLÍMPICA

Nova Icaria

AUSIAS MARC

SANT PERE

URQUINAONA

Palau Musica Catalana

Mercat Santa Caterina

VIA LAIETANA

Museu de Zoologia

Hivernacle

Museu Geologia

Parc de la Ciutadella

WELLINGTON

Parlament de Catalunya

PASSEIG DE MARINA

AVINGUDA

Torre Mapfre

Port Olimpic

Mercat del Born

PASSEIG DE PICASSO

Parc Zoológic

CIUTADELLA

Hotel Arts

Museu Picasso

La Seu

JAUME I

Santa Maria del Mar

Estació de França

LA RIBERA

PASSEIG CIRCUNVAL·LACIO

RONDA LITORAL

Barceloneta

PASSEIG MARITIM

Barceloneta

See 6. Port Olimpic to Glòries map

N

PLAÇA D'ANTONI LOPEZ

Palau del Mar

MAQUINISTA

PL BARCELONETA

Sant Sebastià

Palau Güell

Museu de Cera

PORT VELL

IMAX

L'Aquàrium

ADMIRALL AIXADA

JOAN DE BORBO

BARCELONETA

PASSEIG DE COLOM

RAMBLA DE LA MAR

DRASSANES

DRASSANES

PLAÇA PORTAL DE LA PAU

Drassanes (Museu Maritim)

Estació Marítima

Maremagnum

MOLL DE BARCELONA

Torre Sant Sebastià

Torre Jaume I

Teleferic

Torre Miramar

World Trade Centre

See 3. Port Vell & Barceloneta map

MAR MEDITERRÁNEO

MOLL DE PONIENTE

△ Diagonal Mar

0 _____ 500 m

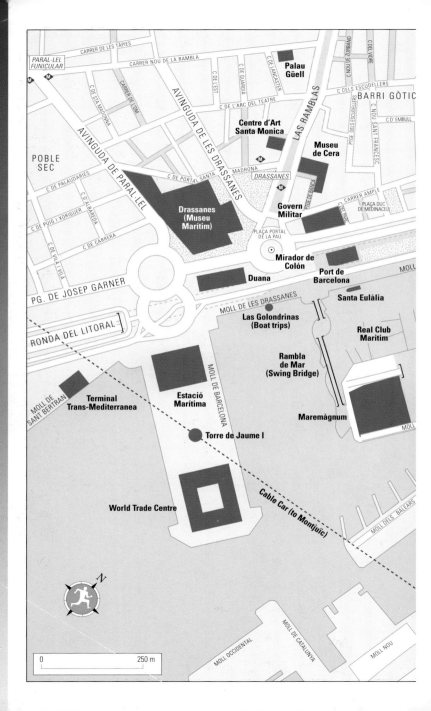

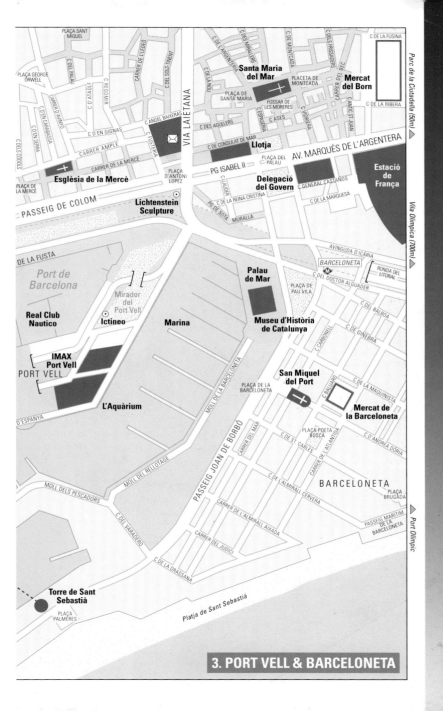

PLAÇA SANT MIQUEL

PLAÇA GEORGE ORWELL

C DEL PALAU

C D'EN CARABASSA

C D'EN GIGNAS

C D'EN SERRA

C DELS CODOLS

C DE L'ESPARTERIA

C REGOMIR

C AVINYO

C DE LA LLEDÓ

C DE LES MOLLERES

C DE MONTCADA

C DELS FRISSADORES

C DE LA FUSINA

C DE LA NAU

CARRER DE LA SEU

Santa Maria del Mar

PLACETA DE MONTCADA

Mercat del Born

PLAÇA DE SANTA MARIA

CARRER DE L'ARGENTERIA

C ANGEL BAIXERAS

C DES AGULLERS

FOSSAR DE LES MORERES

C ASES

CARRER DE LA VIDRIERIA

C ANTIC ST JUAN

C DE LA RIBERA

C DEL SOLS TRIENT

C FUSTERIA

VIA LAIETANA

Llotja

CARRER AMPLE

C DE CONSULAT DE MAR

CARRER DE LA MERCÈ

PLAÇA D'ANTONI LOPEZ

AV. MARQUÉS DE L'ARGENTERA

Església de la Mercè

PLAÇA DE LA MERCÈ

PG ISABEL II

PLAÇA DEL PALAU

Delegació del Govern

C GENERAL CASTAÑOS

C CLAUDER

Estació de França

PASSEIG DE COLOM

Lichtenstein Sculpture

PG DE LA REINA CRISTINA

PG DE SOTA MURALLA

C DE LA MARQUESA

AVINGUDA D'ICARIA

DE LA FUSTA

BARCELONETA

RONDA DEL LITORAL

Port de Barcelona

Mirador del Port Vell

Ictineo

Palau de Mar

C DEL DOCTOR AGUADER

PLAÇA DE PAU VILA

C DEL BALBOA

Real Club Nautico

Marina

Museu d'Història de Catalunya

C DE GINEBRA

C CARBONELL

IMAX Port Vell

PORT VELL

San Miquel del Port

C DE LA MAQUINISTA

PLAÇA DE LA BARCELONETA

C BALUARD

L'Aquàrium

D'ESPANYA

Mercat de la Barceloneta

C D'ANDREA DÒRIA

MOLL DE LA BARCELONETA

CARRER DEL MAR

C DE ST CARLES

PLAÇA POETA BOSCÀ

CARRER DE L'ATLANTIDA

MOLL DEL RELLOTGE

PASSEIG JOAN DE BORBÓ

C DE L'ALMIRALL CERVERA

BARCELONETA

PLAÇA BRUGADA

MOLL DELS PESCADORS

C DEL VARADERO

CARRER DE L'ALMIRALL AIXADA

PASSEIG MARÍTIM DE LA BARCELONETA

Port Olímpic

CARRER DEL JUDICI

C DE LA DRASSANA

Torre de Sant Sebastià

PLAÇA PALMÉRES

Platja de Sant Sebastià

3. PORT VELL & BARCELONETA

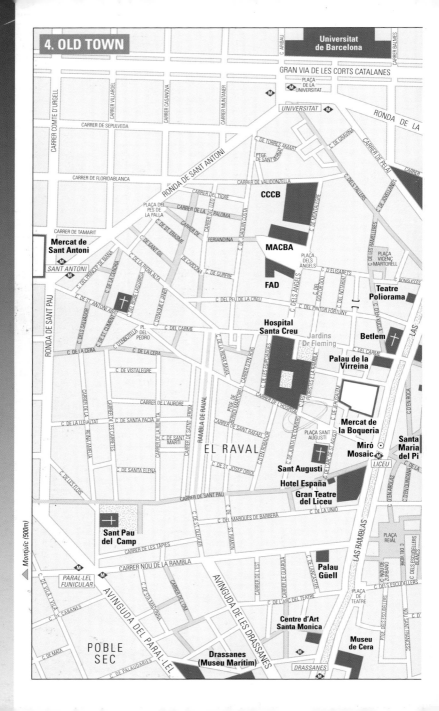

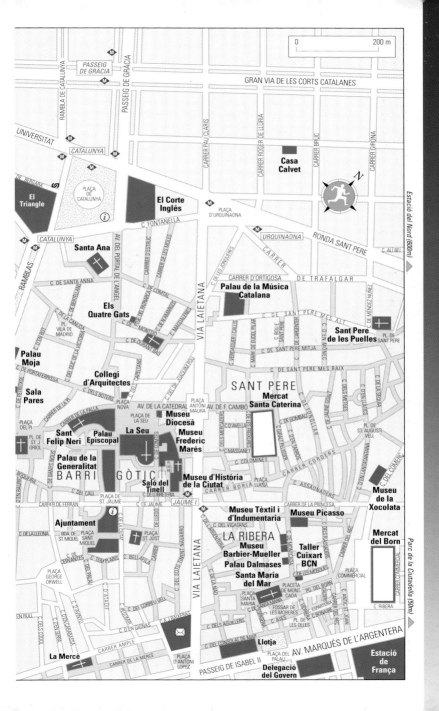

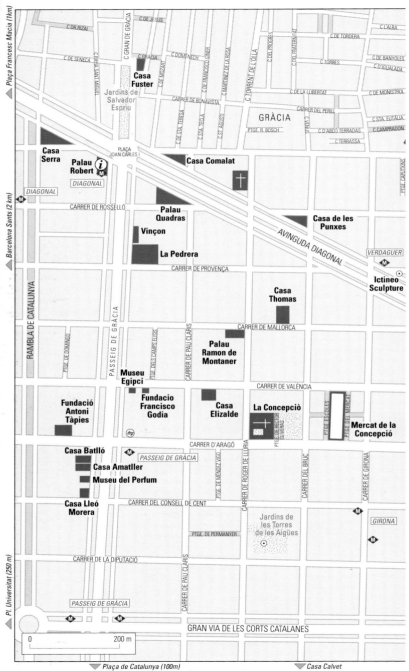

Plaça Francesc Macià (1km)

Barcelona Sants (2 km)

Pl. Universitat (250 m)

C. DR. RIZAL
C GRAN DE GRACIA
C DE JESUS
C. L'ALBA
C DE SENECA
C RERA SANT MIQUEL
C GRACIA
C DOMENECH
C DE TORDERA
C DE MIZRAT
C FRANCISCO GINER
C MARTINEZ DE LA ROSA
C TORRES
C DE BANYOLES
C D'IGUALADA

Casa
Fuster

Jardins de
Salvador
Espriu

CARRER DE BONAVISTA
C DE LA LIBERTAT
C DE MONISTROL

C DE STA. TERESA
C STA. TECLA
C ST. AGUSTI
C TORRENT DE L'OLLA
C DEL PROGRES
C DEL FRATERNITAT
CARRER DEL PERILL
GRÀCIA
C STA. EULÀLIA
C CAMPRADON

PTGE. R. BOSCH
SIRENA C.
C D'ABDÓ TERRADAS
C TERRASSA

Casa
Serra

PLAÇA
JOAN CARLES I

Palau
Robert (i)

Casa Comalat

DIAGONAL

DIAGONAL

CARRER DE ROSSELLÓ

Palau
Quadras

Casa de les
Punxes

Vinçon

AVINGUDA DIAGONAL

VERDAGUER

La Pedrera

CARRER DE PROVENÇA

Ictineo
Sculpture

RAMBLA DE CATALUNYA

PASSEIG DE GRÀCIA

PTGE. DE DOMINGO

PTGE. DELS CAMPS ELISIS

CARRER DE PAU CLARIS

Casa
Thomas

CARRER DE MALLORCA

Palau
Ramon de
Montaner

Museu
Egipci

CARRER DE VALÈNCIA

Fundació
Antoni
Tàpies

Fundacio
Francisco
Godia

Casa
Elizalde

La Concepció

PTGE. DE RECTOR OLIVERAS

PTGE. DEL MERCAT

PTGE. ESCOLES

Mercat de la
Concepció

Casa Batlló

PASSEIG DE GRÀCIA

CARRER D'ARAGÓ

Casa Amatller

PTGE. DE MÉNDEZ VIGIL

CARRER DE ROGER DE LLÚRIA

CARRER DEL BRUC

CARRER DE GIRONA

Museu del Perfum

Casa Lleó
Morera

CARRER DEL CONSELL DE CENT

GIRONA

Jardins de
les Torres
de les Aigües

PTGE. DE PERMANYER

CARRER DE LA DIPUTACIÓ

CARRER DE PAU CLARIS

PASSEIG DE GRÀCIA

GRAN VIA DE LES CORTS CATALANES

0   200 m

Plaça de Catalunya (100m)

Casa Calvet

CARRER DE SANT ANTONI MARIA CLARET

PTGE. LLAVALLOT

CARRER DE LA INDUSTRIA

PTGE. D'ALIÓ

CARRER D'EN GRASSO

CISCLE SOLER

PTGE. DE LES TORRES

PASSEIG DE SANT JOAN

CARRER DE CÒRSEGA

PTGE. MARINER

CARRER DE SARDENYA

CARRER DE LA MARINA

PTGE. CONRADI

CARRER DE ROSSELLÓ

CARRER DE NÀPOLS

CARRER DE SICÍLIA

PTGE. DE SIMÓ

SAGRADA FAMÍLIA

Ⓜ   Ⓜ

CARRER DE ROGER DE FLOR

CARRER DE PROVENÇA

Ⓜ

Ⓜ VERDAGUER

Casa Macaya

PLAÇA DE LA SAGRADA FAMÍLIA

Sagrada Família

PLAÇA MOSSÈN JACINT VERDAGUER

CARRER DE MALLORCA

PTGE. GAIOLÀ

PTGE. MAIOL

PTGE. FONT

CARRER DE VALÈNCIA

Casa Planells

AVINGUDA DIAGONAL

CARRER DE NÀPOLS

CARRER DE BAILÈN

PASSEIG DE SANT JOAN

CARRER D'ARAGÓ

CARRER DE ROGER DE FLOR

CARRER DEL CONSELL DE CENT

CARRER DE SICÍLIA

CARRER DE SARDENYA

MONUMENTAL Ⓜ

CARRER MARINA

PTGE. DE TASSO

CARRER DE LA DIPUTACIÓ

TETUAN Ⓜ

PTGE. DE BOCABELLA

PTGE. DE PAGÈS

PLAÇA DE TETUAN

Ⓜ

GRAN VIA DE LES CORTS CATALANES

▽ Parc de la Ciutadella (900m)   ▽ Estació del Nord (500m)

Hospital Santa Creu i Sant Pau ▷

Teatre Nacional de Catalunya ▷

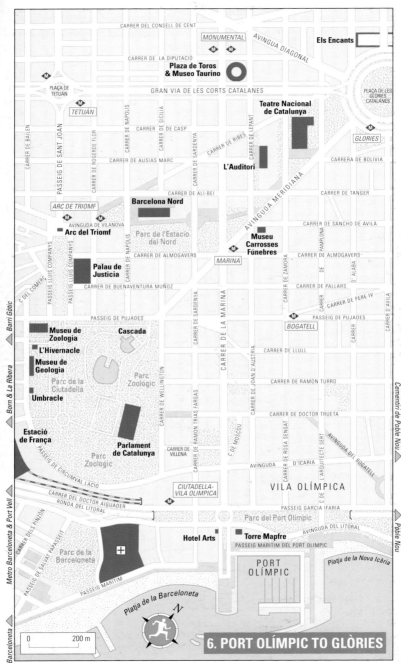

CARRER DEL CONSELL DE CENT

MONUMENTAL

AVINGUA DIAGONAL

Els Encants

CARRER DE LA DIPUTACIÓ

Plaza de Toros & Museo Taurino

PLAÇA DE TETUÁN

TETUÁN

GRAN VIA DE LES CORTS CATALANES

PLAÇA DE LES GLÒRIES CATALANES

Teatre Nacional de Catalunya

CARRER DE NAPOLS

CARRER DE SICILIA

CARRER DE DE CASP

CARRER DE SARDENYA

CARRER DE RIBES

CARRER DE LEPANT

GLÒRIES

CARRER DE BALEN

PASSEIG DE SANT JOAN

CARRER DE ROGER DE FLOR

CARRERA DE BOLIVIA

CARRER DE AUSIAS MARC

L'Auditori

CARRER DE ALI-BEI

CARRER DE TANGER

ARC DE TRIOMF

Barcelona Nord

AVINGUDA DE VILANOVA

Arc del Triomf

Parc de l'Estacio del Nord

AVINGUDA MERIDIANA

CARRER DE SANCHO DE AVILA

PASSEIG LLUIS COMPANYS

CARRER DE NAPOLS

CARRER DE ALMOGAVERS

Museu Carrosses Fúnebres

CARRER DE PAMPLONA

CARRER DE ALMOGAVERS

C DEL COMERÇ

PASSEIG LLUIS COMPANYS

Palau de Justicia

MARINA

DE

D'ALABA

CARRER DE BUENAVENTURA MUÑOZ

CARRER DE ZAMORA

CARRER DE PALLARS

CARRER DE PERE IV

CARRER D'AVILA

PASSEIG DE PUJADES

CARRER DE SARDENYA

CARRER DE LA MARINA

PASSEIG DE PUJADES

BOGATELL

Museu de Zoologia

Cascada

L'Hivernacle

Museu de Geologia

Parc de la Ciutadella

Parc Zoològic

Umbracle

CARRER DE LLULL

CARRER DE RAMON TURRO

CARRER DE DOCTOR TRUETA

Estació de França

CARRER DE WELLINGTON

CARRER DE RAMON TRIAS FARGAS

CARRER DE JOAN D'AUSTRIA

CARRER DE ROSA SENSAT

C DE MOSCOU

L'ARQUITECTE SERT

AVINGUDA DEL BOGATELL

Parlament de Catalunya

CARRER DE VILLENA

Parc Zoològic

PASSEIG DE CIRCUMVAL LACIO

CIUTADELLA-VILA OLIMPICA

AVINGUDA D'ICARIA

VILA OLÍMPICA

C DE

CARRER DEL DOCTOR AIGUADER

RONDA DEL LITORAL

PASSEIG GARCIA IFARIA

Parc del Port Olimpic

CARRER DELS PINZON

CARRER DE SALVAT PAPASSEIT

Parc de la Barceloneta

Hotel Arts

Torre Mapfre

PASSEIG MARITIM DEL PORT OLIMPIC

AVINGUDA DEL LITORAL

Platja de la Nova Icària

PASSEIG MARITIM

PORT OLÍMPIC

Platja de la Barceloneta

N

6. PORT OLÍMPIC TO GLÒRIES

Barceloneta

Metro Barceloneta & Port Vell

Born & La Ribera

Barri Gòtic

Cementiri de Poble Nou

Poble Nou

| 0 | 200 m |

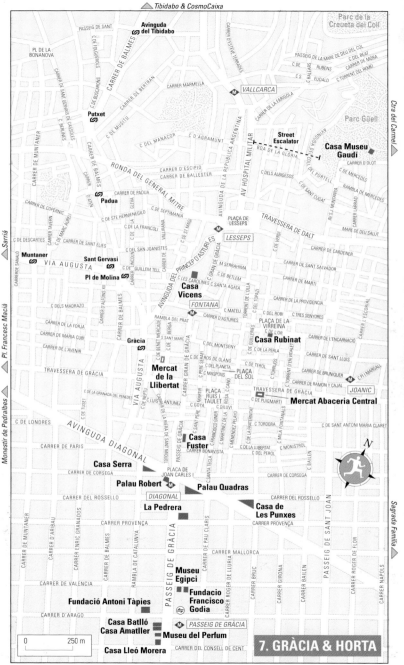

Tibidabo & CosmoCaixa

Parc de la Creueta del Coll

Cra del Carmel

PASSEIG DE SANT
Avinguda del Tibidabo

PL DE LA BONANOVA

CARRER DE BALMES

CARRER DE FIGUEROLES

CARRER DE BERTRAN

CARRER MARMELLA

PASSEIG DE LA MARE DE DEU DEL COL

C DE
RUBENS
C DEL BEAT
C DE MORA
C S BALEARS
C EUDALD
C TORRENT DEL REMEI

VALLCARCA

CARRER DE LA FARIGOLA

Parc Güell

Casa Museu Gaudí

CARRER DE MUSITU

Putxet

C DE BUSCAROSS

C DE SANT GERVASI DE CASSOLES

C BERLINES

CARRER DE BALMES

C DEL MANACOR

C D'AGRAMUNT

Street Escalator

BDA DE LA GLORIA

C DE VOLONTAIA

C DEL PORTELL

C DE SANT CUGAT

CARRER D'OLOT

C DE MERCEDES

RAMBLA DE MERCEDES

AV J.J. MUNTANIA

CARRER LARRAD

MARE DE DEU SALUT

RONDA DEL GENERAL MITRE

CARRER D'ESCIPIO
CARRER DE BALLESTER

AV HOSPITAL MILITAR

AVINGUDA DE LA REPUBLICA ARGENTINA

C DELS ALBIGESOS

C DE SANT CUGAT

CARRER DE MUNTANER

CARRER DE COPERNIC

CARRER DE BALMES

CARRER TAVERN

C MARC AURELI

Padua

CARRER DE PADUA

C DE SEPTIMANIA

C DE STE HERMENEGILD

C DE LA FRANCOLI

C DE ST MAGI

PLAÇA DE LESSEPS

LESSEPS

TRAVESSERA DE DALT

CARRER DE CARDENER

C DESCARTES

C DE CARRER DE SANT ELIES

CARRER SANALO

C DEL SAN JOANISTES

CARRER DE SANT SALVADOR

Muntaner

Sant Gervasi

VIA AUGUSTA

Pl de Molina

C DE GUILLEM TELL

AVINGUDA DEL PRINCEP D'ASTURIES

C GRAN DE GRACIA

M SERRAHIMA

C DE BETLEM

C VERDI

CARRER DE MARTI

C DELS MADRAZO

C D'ALFONS XII

CARRER DE BALMES

C LES CAROLINES

C SANTA AGATA

Casa Vicens

CARRER DE SANT SALVADOR

CARRER DE LA FORJA

CARRER DE MARIA CUBI

CARRER DE L'AVENIR

RAMBLA DEL PRAT

FONTANA

CARRER D'ASTURIES

C DE MATEU

TORRENT DE L'OLLA

C DEL ROBI

C TRES SENYORES

CARRER DE LA PROVIDENCIA

Gràcia

C DE BENET MERCADE

S SANT MARC

C SANT MARC

PLAÇA DE LA VIRREINA

C DE L'OR

Casa Rubinat

CARRER DE L'ENCARNACIO

C DE BERGA

C DEL MONTSENY

C GUILLERIES

TRAVESSERA DE GRÀCIA

VIA AUGUSTA

Mercat de la Llibertat

C DE GRACIA

C DE PERE SERAFI DE OLANO

C DEL PLANETA

C DE LA PERLA

C DE TEROL

CARRER DE SANT LLUIS

C DE TEROL

C D'EN VIDALL

CARRER DE BRUNIQUER

C P.I. MARGALL

C DE LA GRANADA DEL PENEDES

C DE MASPONS

PLAÇA DEL SOL

C TORRIJOS

CARRER DE RAMON Y CAJAL

JOANIC

C DE NEPLU

C LUISTE ANTUNEZ

PLAÇA MARTI

C GOYA

PLAÇA RIUS I TAULET

C DE PUIGMARTI

TRAVESSERA DE GRÀCIA

Mercat Abaceria Central

AVINGUDA DIAGONAL

CARRER DE PARIS

PASSEIG DE GRACIA

C DE LA RIERA DE SANT MIQUEL

C SANT PERE

C DE LUDIVU

C MARTINEZ DE LA ROSA

C DILUVI

C TORDERA

C DE SANT ANTONI MARIA CLARET

C DE LONDRES

CARRER DE TUSET

C FRANCISCO GINER

C MENENDEZ PELAYO

C DE LA FRATERNITAT

MILA I FONTANALS

C MONISTROL

Casa Fuster

CARRER BONAVISTA

C SANTA TECLA

C DE LA LLIBERTAT

C DEL PEROL

C BAILEN

N

Casa Serra

CARRER DE CORSEGA

PLAÇA DE JOAN CARLES I

Palau Quadras

CARRER DE CORSEGA

Palau Robert

DIAGONAL

La Pedrera

Casa de Les Punxes

CARRER DEL ROSSELLO

CARRER DEL ROSSELLO

PASSEIG DE SANT JOAN

CARRER DE MUNTANER

CARRER D'ARIBAU

CARRER ENRIC GRANADOS

CARRER DE BALMES

RAMBLA DE CATALUNYA

PASSEIG DE GRÀCIA

CARRER DE PAU CLARIS

CARRER DE LLURIA

CARRER ROGER DE LLURIA

CARRER BRUC

CARRER GIRONA

CARRER BAILEN

CARRER ROGER DE FLOR

CARRER NAPOLS

CARRER PROVENÇA

CARRER PROVENÇA

CARRER MALLORCA

Sagrada Família

Museu Egipci

Fundació Antoni Tàpies

CARRER DE VALENCIA

Fundacio Francisco Godia

CARRER D'ARAGO

Casa Batlló
Casa Amatller

PASSEIG DE GRÀCIA

Museu del Perfum

Casa Lleó Morera

CARRER DEL CONSELL DE CENT

0   250 m

7. GRÀCIA & HORTA

Sarrià

Pl. Francesc Macià

Monestir de Pedralbes

Plaça de Catalunya

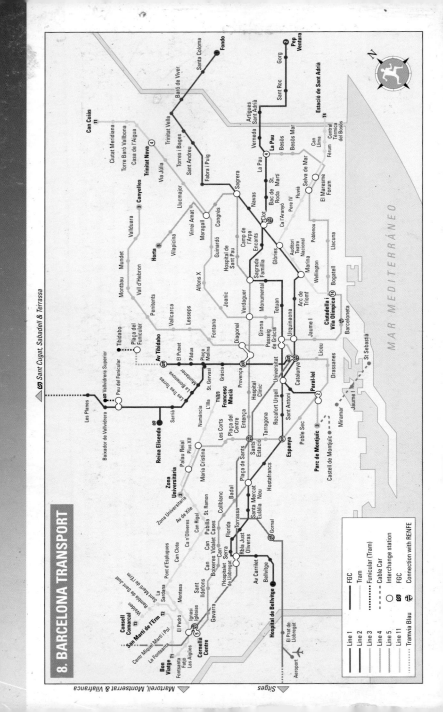

8. BARCELONA TRANSPORT